# THE DOWN RIVER PEOPLE™

S0-BOD-359

Published by
**ARCHAIA**™

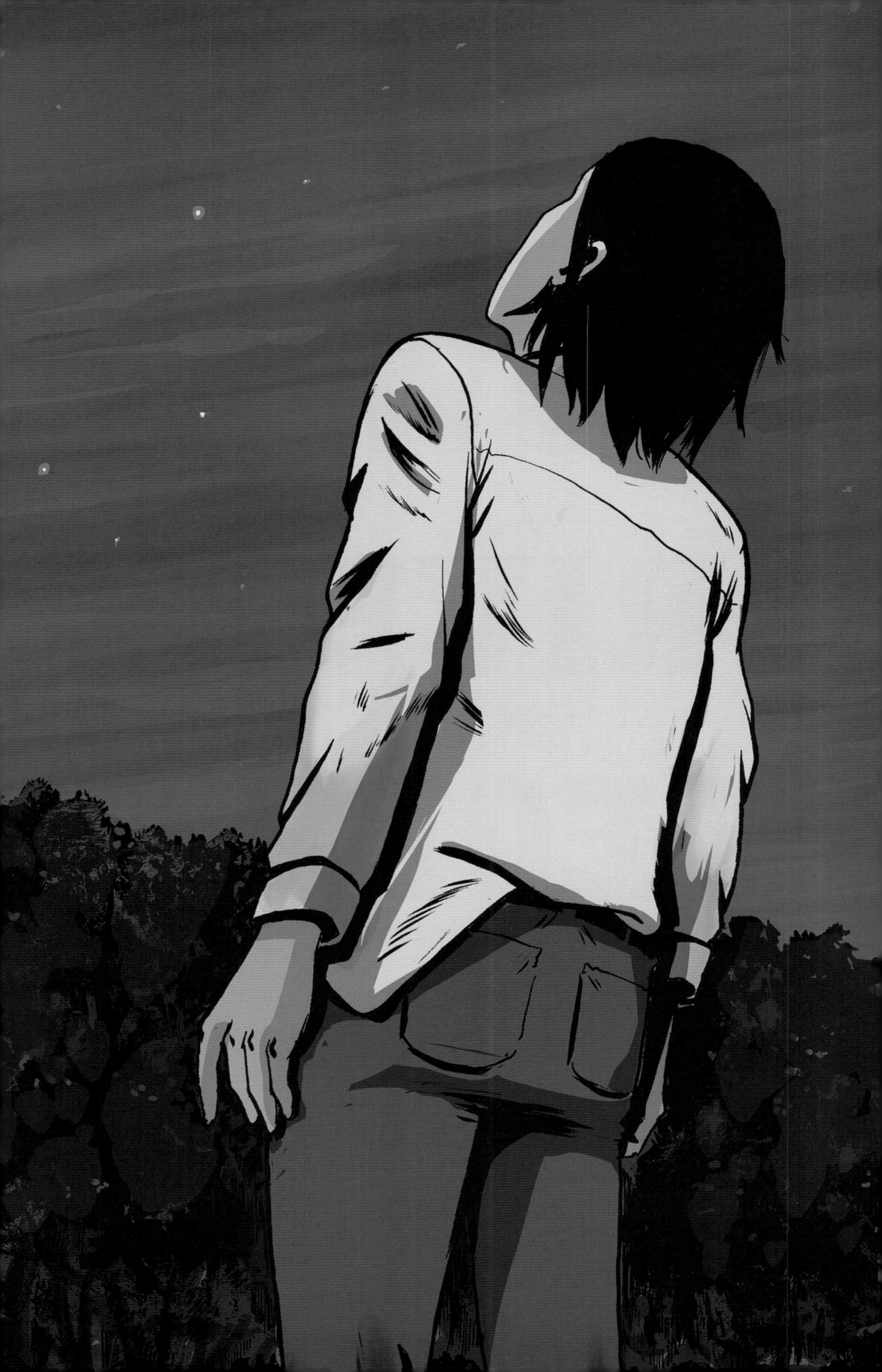

Written by
**Adam Smith**

Illustrated by
**Matthew Fox**

Lettered by
**Mike Fiorentino**

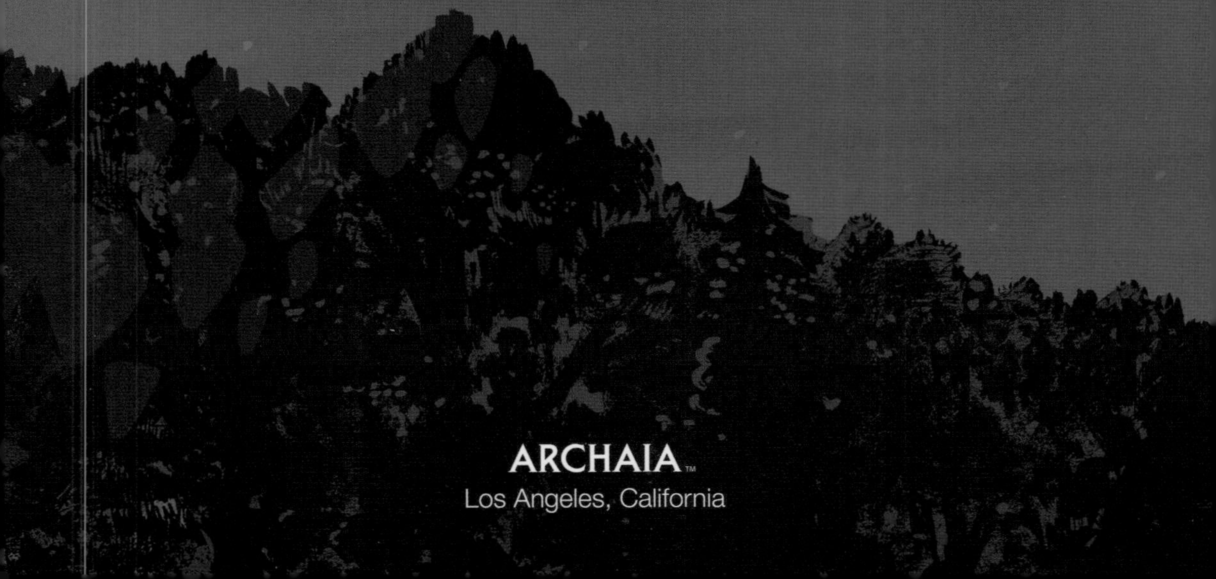

ARCHAIA™
Los Angeles, California

Cover by
**Scott Newman** with art by **Matthew Fox**

Designer
**Scott Newman**

Assistant Editor
**Allyson Gronowitz**

Editor
**Cameron Chittock**

Executive Editor
**Sierra Hahn**

**Ross Richie** CEO & Founder
**Joy Huffman** CFO
**Matt Gagnon** Editor-in-Chief
**Filip Sablik** President, Publishing & Marketing
**Stephen Christy** President, Development
**Lance Kreiter** Vice President, Licensing & Merchandising
**Bryce Carlson** Vice President, Editorial & Creative Strategy
**Kate Henning** Director, Operations
**Spencer Simpson** Director, Sales
**Scott Newman** Manager, Production Design
**Elyse Strandberg** Manager, Finance
**Sierra Hahn** Executive Editor
**Jeanine Schaefer** Executive Editor
**Dafna Pleban** Senior Editor
**Shannon Watters** Senior Editor
**Eric Harburn** Senior Editor
**Sophie Philips-Roberts** Associate Editor
**Amanda LaFranco** Associate Editor
**Jonathan Manning** Associate Editor
**Gavin Gronenthal** Assistant Editor
**Gwen Waller** Assistant Editor
**Allyson Gronowitz** Assistant Editor

**Ramiro Portnoy** Assistant Editor
**Kenzie Rzonca** Assistant Editor
**Shelby Netschke** Editorial Assistant
**Michelle Ankley** Design Lead
**Marie Krupina** Production Designer
**Grace Park** Production Designer
**Chelsea Roberts** Production Designer
**Samantha Knapp** Production Design Assistant
**José Meza** Live Events Lead
**Stephanie Hocutt** Digital Marketing Lead
**Esther Kim** Marketing Lead
**Breanna Sarpy** Live Events Coordinator
**Amanda Lawson** Marketing Assistant
**Morgan Perry** Retail Sales Lead
**Holly Aitchison** Digital Sales Coordinator
**Megan Christopher** Operations Coordinator
**Rodrigo Hernandez** Operations Coordinator
**Zipporah Smith** Operations Coordinator
**Jason Lee** Senior Accountant
**Sabrina Lesin** Accounting Assistant
**Lauren Alexander** Administrative Assistant

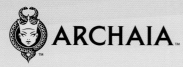

**THE DOWN RIVER PEOPLE, May 2021.** Published by Archaia, a division of Boom Entertainment, Inc. The Down River People ™ & © 2021 Adam Christopher Smith & George Matthew Fox. All rights reserved. Archaia™ and the Archaia logo are trademarks of Boom Entertainment, Inc., registered in various countries and categories. All characters, events, and institutions depicted herein are fictional. Any similarity between any of the names, characters, persons, events, and/or institutions in this publication to actual names, characters, and persons, whether living or dead, events, and/or institutions is unintended and purely coincidental.

BOOM! Studios, 5670 Wilshire Boulevard, Suite 400, Los Angeles, CA 90036-5679. Printed in China. First Printing.

ISBN: 978-1-68415-563-7, eISBN: 978-1-64144-729-4

This story is for everyone who's afraid of what they might become. I found a sense of solace in its writing, and I guess the hope is that you will, too. Thank you to Angela, Matt, and the rest of my family for shaping the book and my life.
—**Adam Smith**


This book is for you, but I couldn't have done it without the love and support of Ilyane, my wife. Thank you to Adam, for sharing this story with me. And thank you to Cameron Chittock and Sierra Hahn for their endless patience and support.
—**Matthew Fox**

# CHAPTER ONE

# DIFFERENT WAYS TO BURY OUR DEAD

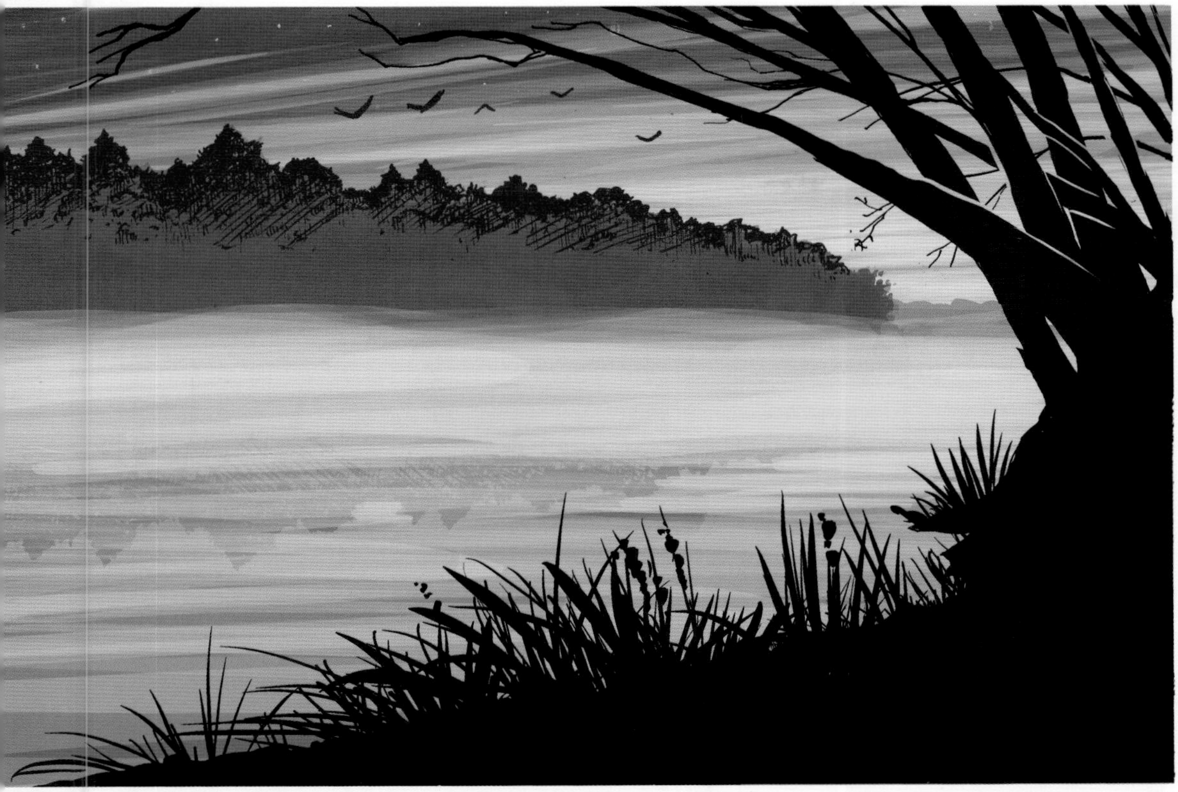
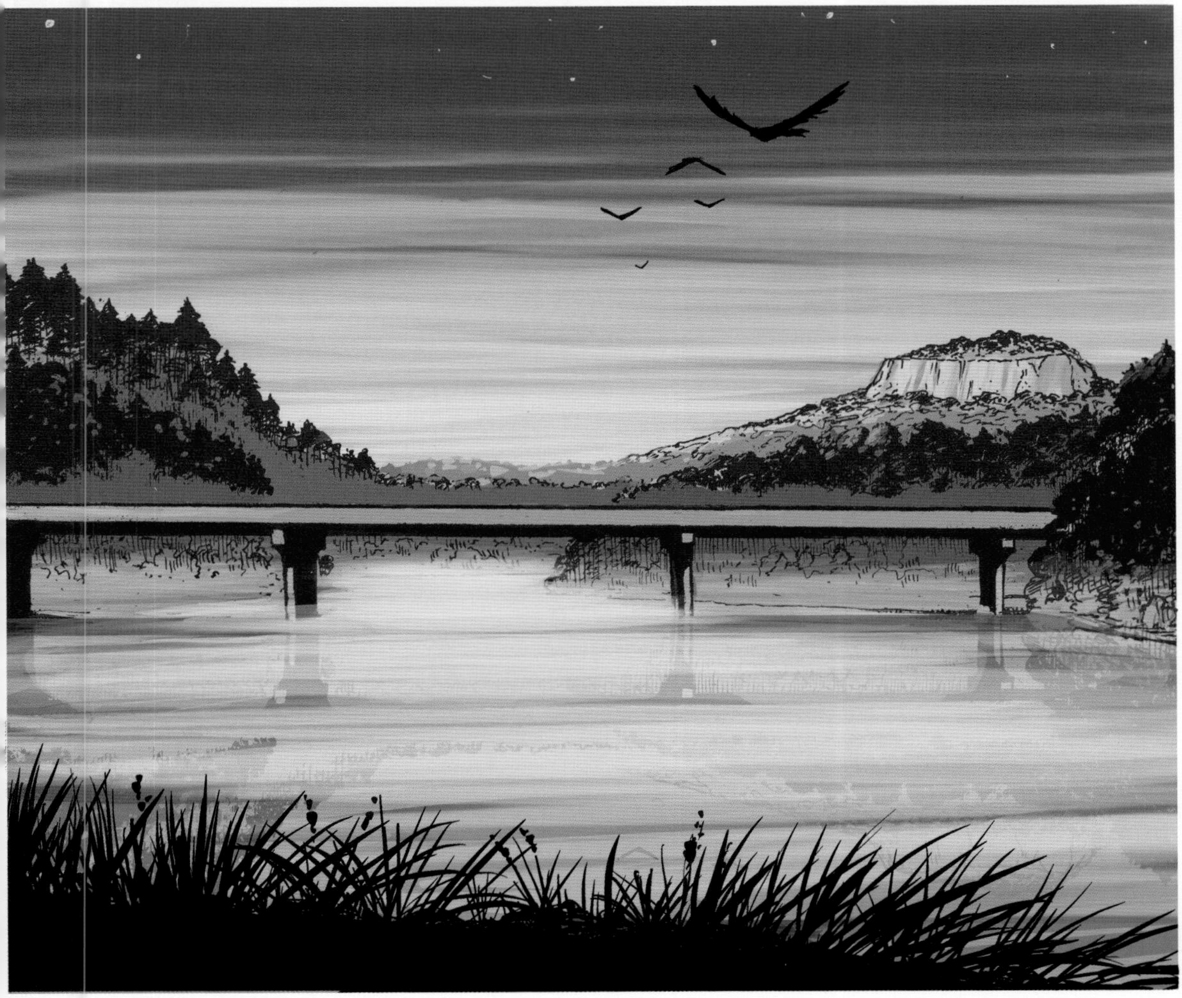

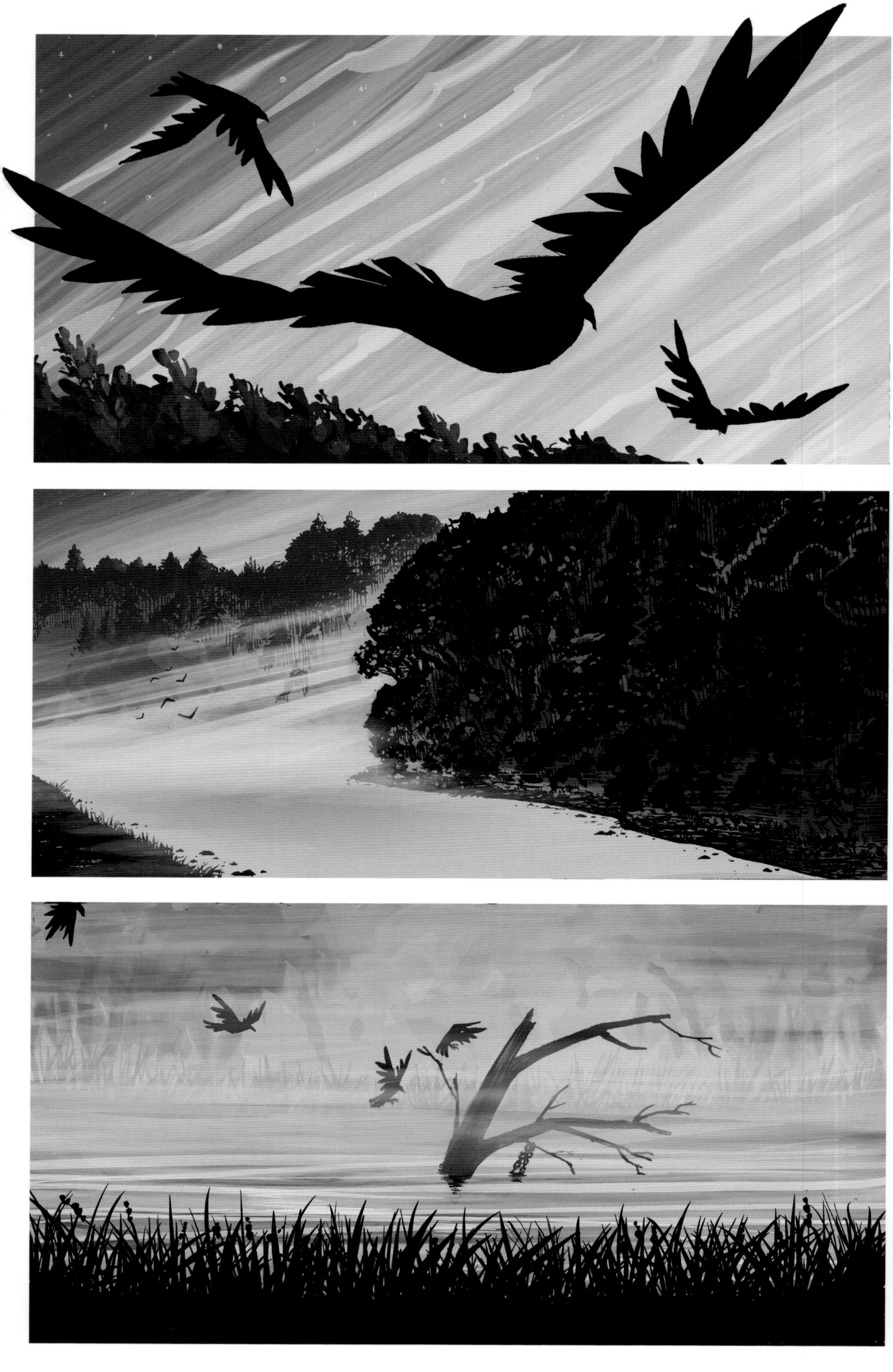

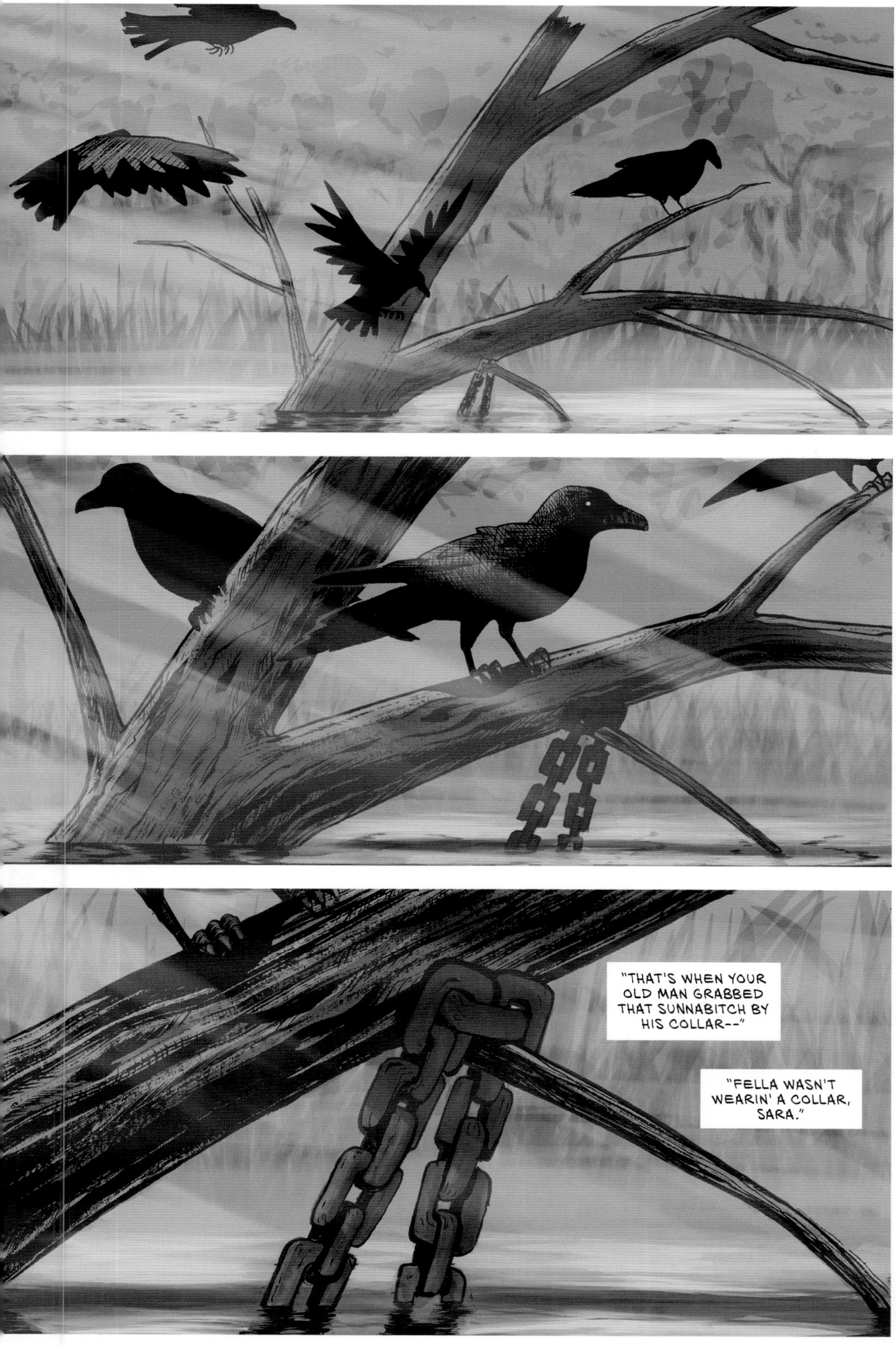
"THAT'S WHEN YOUR OLD MAN GRABBED THAT SUNNABITCH BY HIS COLLAR--"
"FELLA WASN'T WEARIN' A COLLAR, SARA."

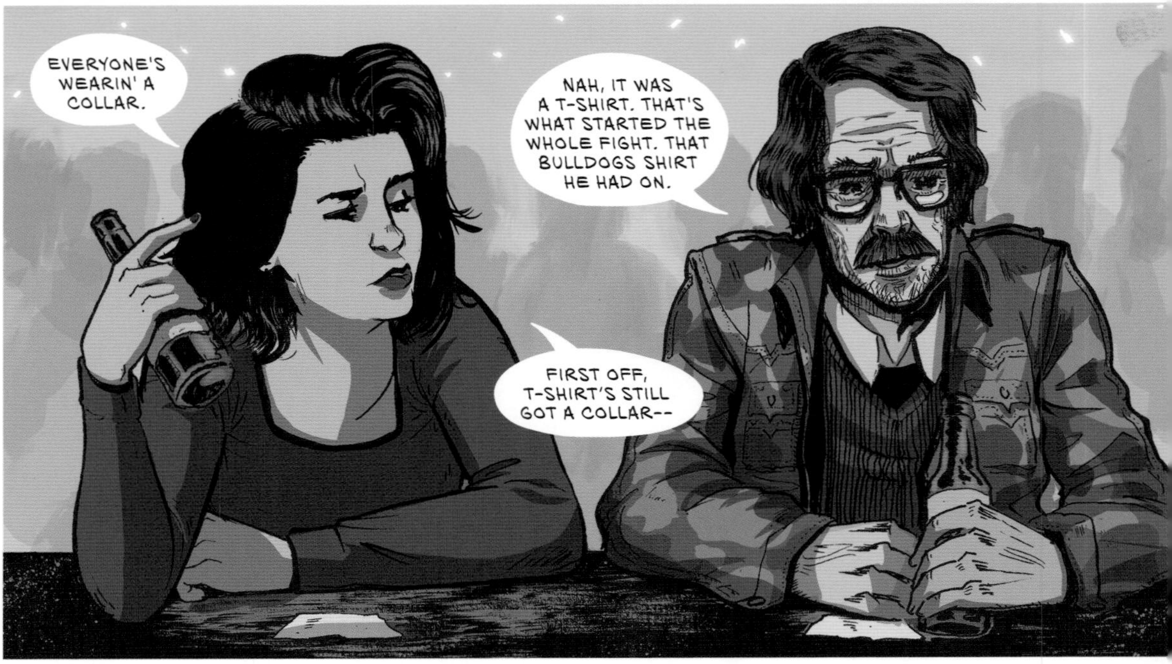
EVERYONE'S WEARIN' A COLLAR.
NAH, IT WAS A T-SHIRT. THAT'S WHAT STARTED THE WHOLE FIGHT. THAT BULLDOGS SHIRT HE HAD ON.
FIRST OFF, T-SHIRT'S STILL GOT A COLLAR--

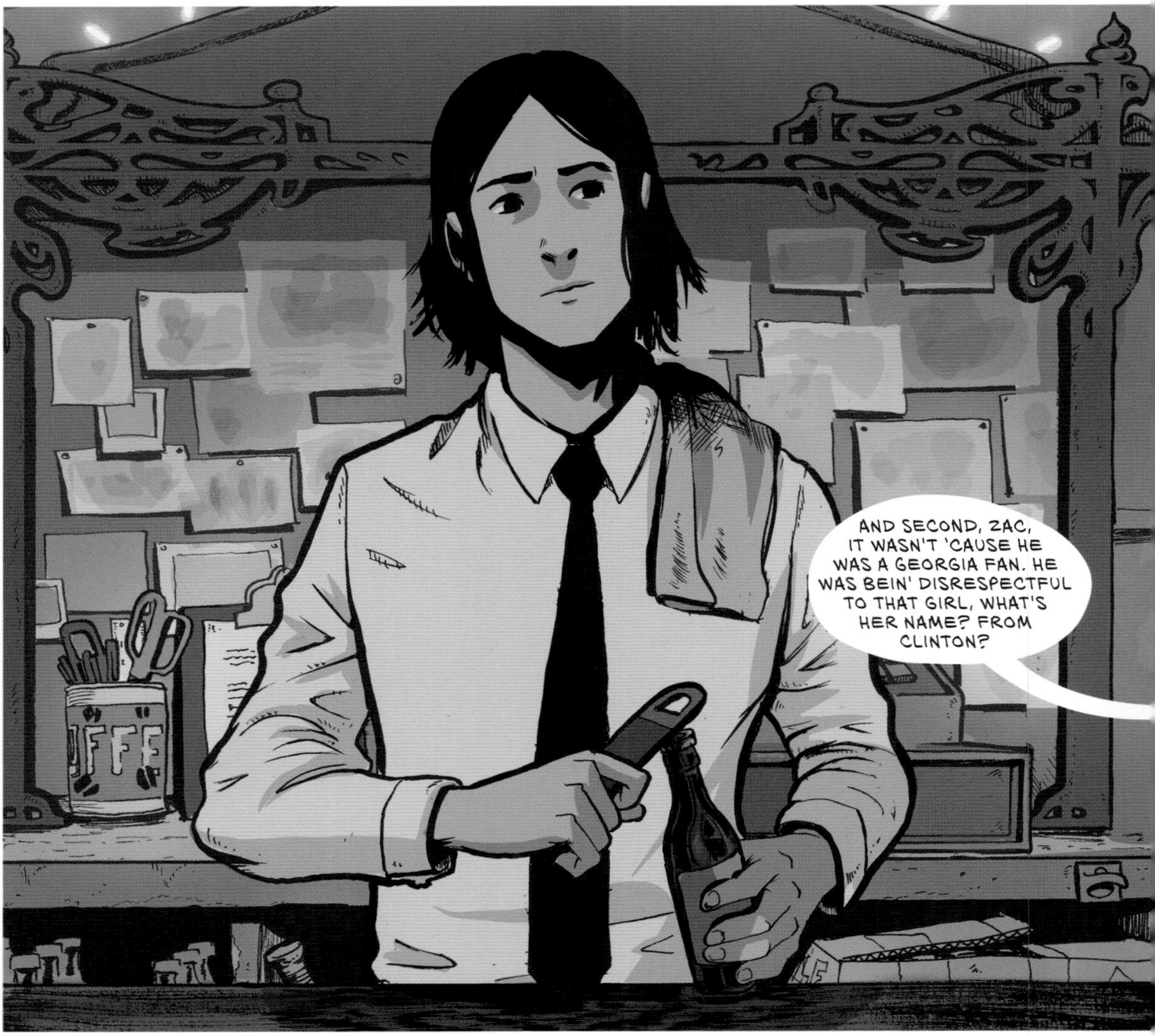
AND SECOND, ZAC, IT WASN'T 'CAUSE HE WAS A GEORGIA FAN. HE WAS BEIN' DISRESPECTFUL TO THAT GIRL, WHAT'S HER NAME? FROM CLINTON?

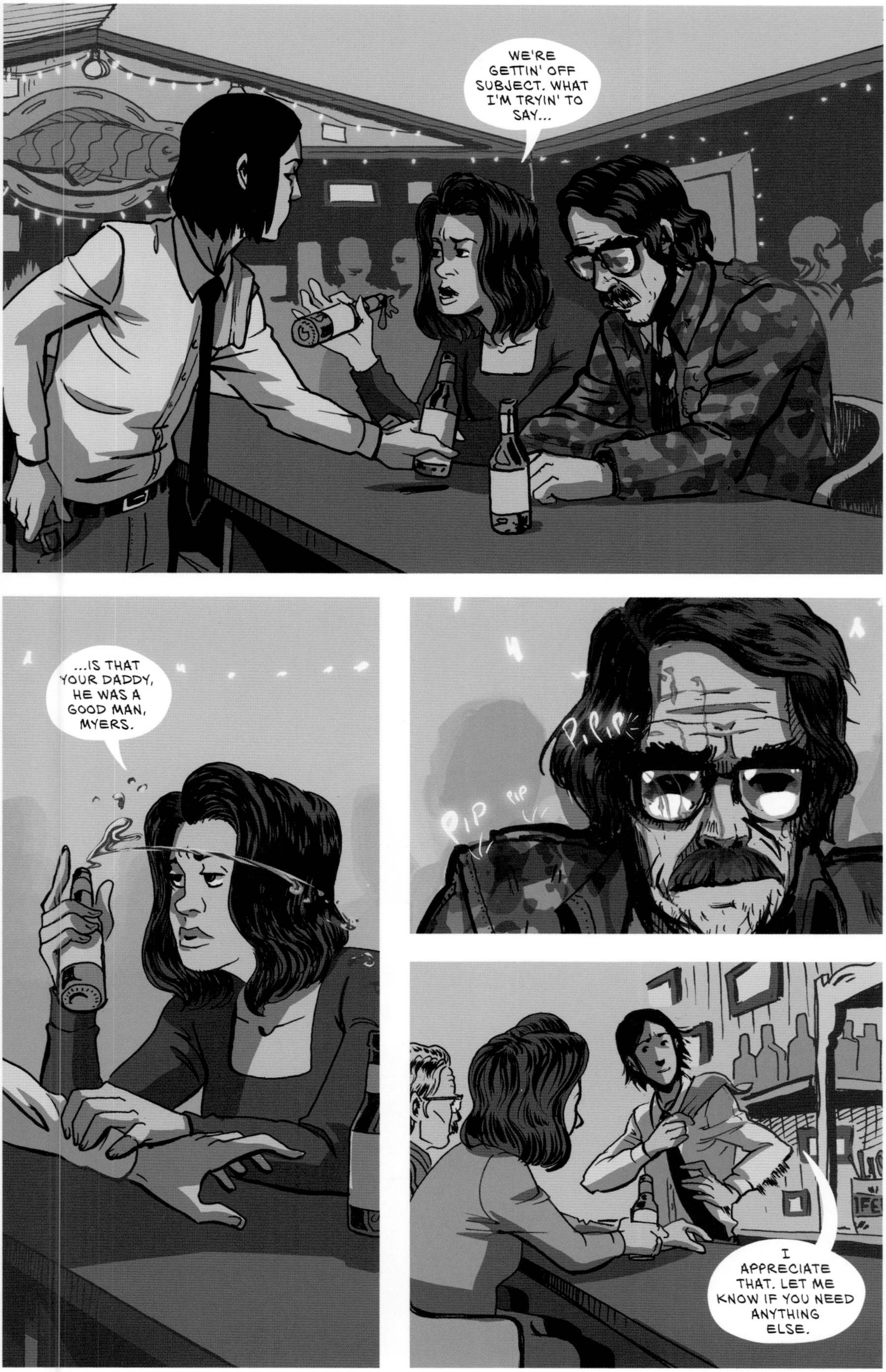
WE'RE GETTIN' OFF SUBJECT. WHAT I'M TRYIN' TO SAY...
...IS THAT YOUR DADDY, HE WAS A GOOD MAN, MYERS.
PIP PIP
PIP PIP
I APPRECIATE THAT. LET ME KNOW IF YOU NEED ANYTHING ELSE.

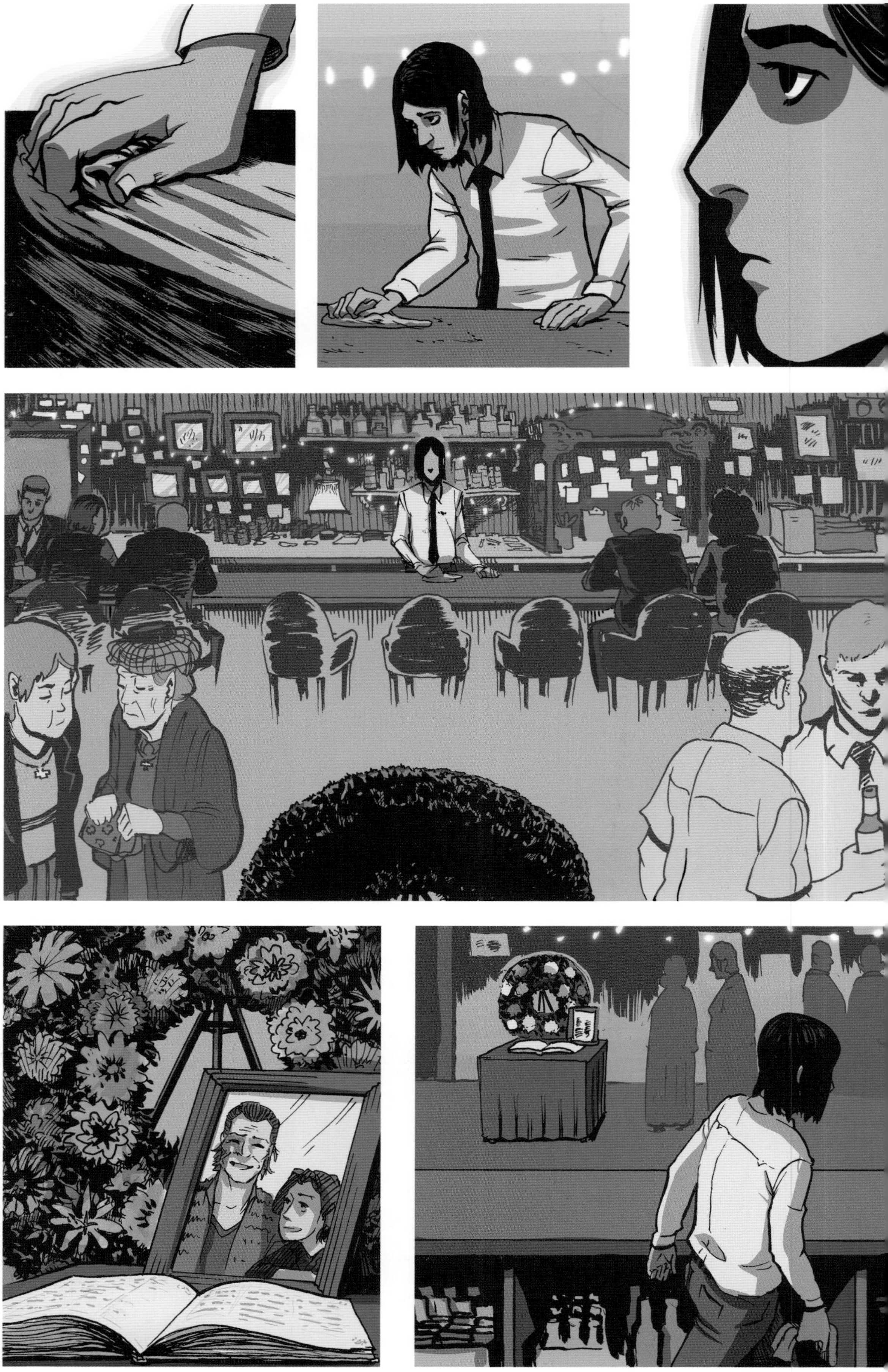

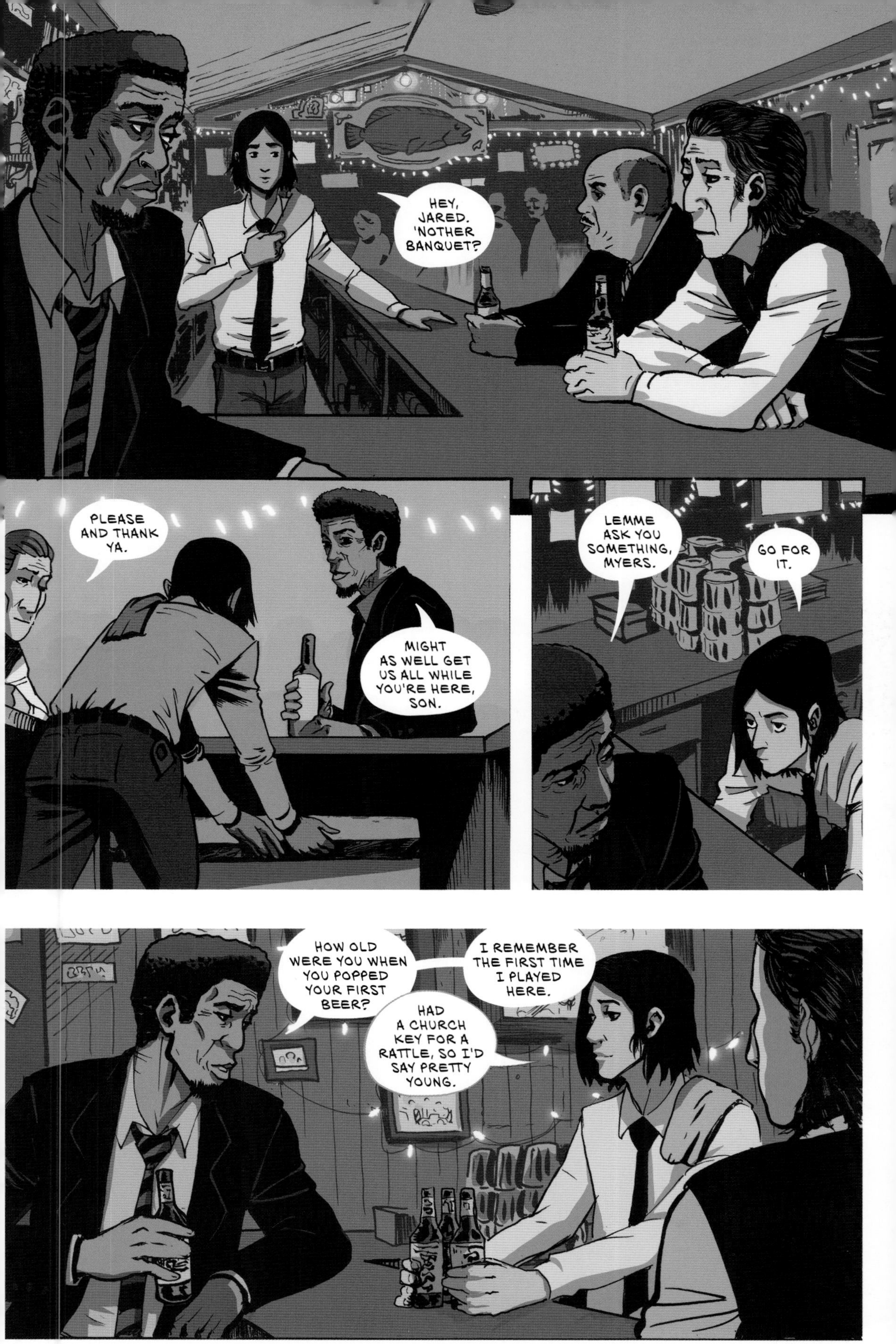
HEY, JARED. 'NOTHER BANQUET?
PLEASE AND THANK YA.
MIGHT AS WELL GET US ALL WHILE YOU'RE HERE, SON.
LEMME ASK YOU SOMETHING, MYERS.
GO FOR IT.
HOW OLD WERE YOU WHEN YOU POPPED YOUR FIRST BEER?
HAD A CHURCH KEY FOR A RATTLE, SO I'D SAY PRETTY YOUNG.
I REMEMBER THE FIRST TIME I PLAYED HERE.

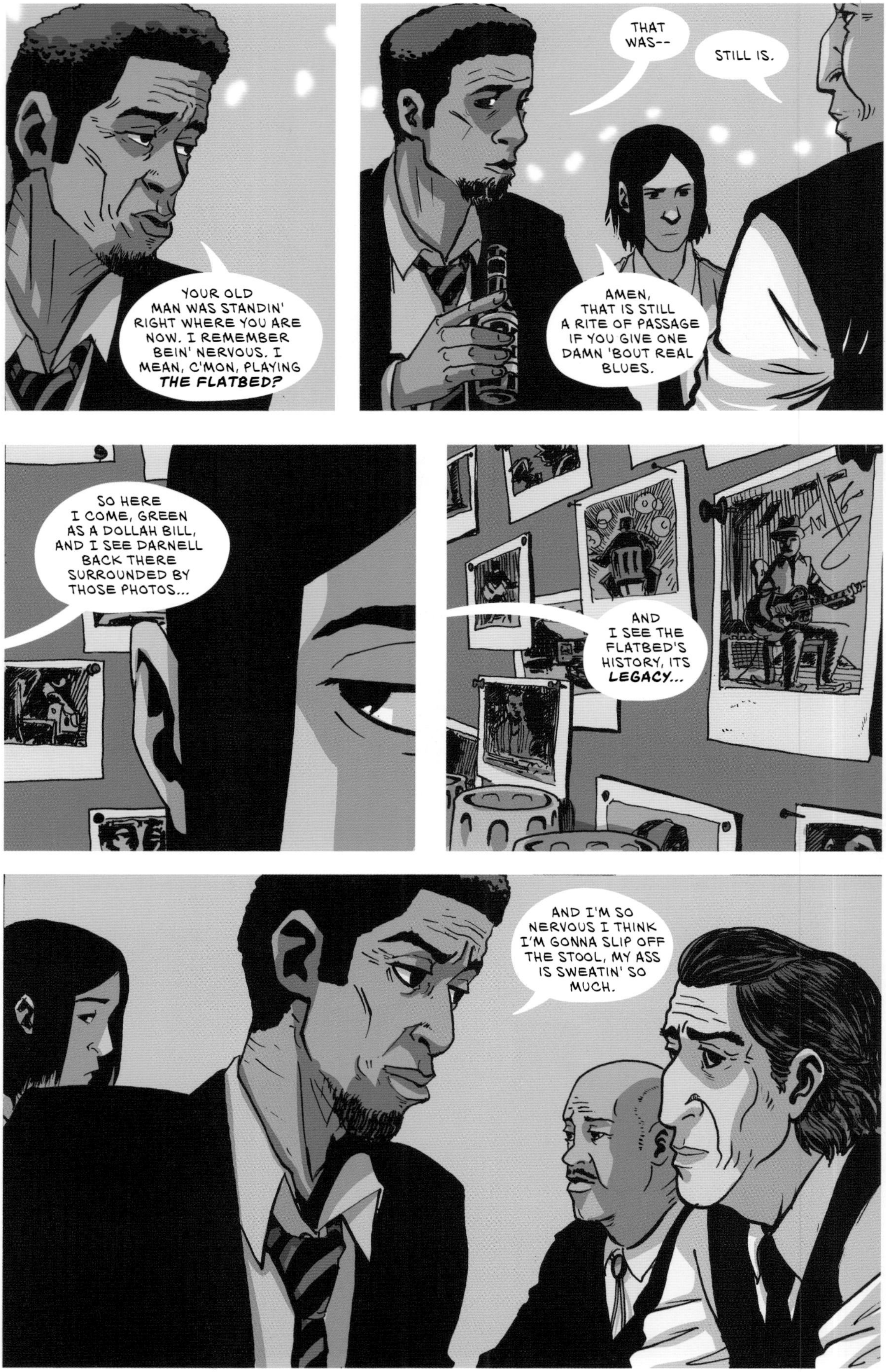
YOUR OLD MAN WAS STANDIN' RIGHT WHERE YOU ARE NOW. I REMEMBER BEIN' NERVOUS. I MEAN, C'MON, PLAYING **THE FLATBED?**
THAT WAS--
STILL IS.
AMEN, THAT IS STILL A RITE OF PASSAGE IF YOU GIVE ONE DAMN 'BOUT REAL BLUES.
SO HERE I COME, GREEN AS A DOLLAH BILL, AND I SEE DARNELL BACK THERE SURROUNDED BY THOSE PHOTOS...
AND I SEE THE FLATBED'S HISTORY, ITS **LEGACY...**
AND I'M SO NERVOUS I THINK I'M GONNA SLIP OFF THE STOOL, MY ASS IS SWEATIN' SO MUCH.

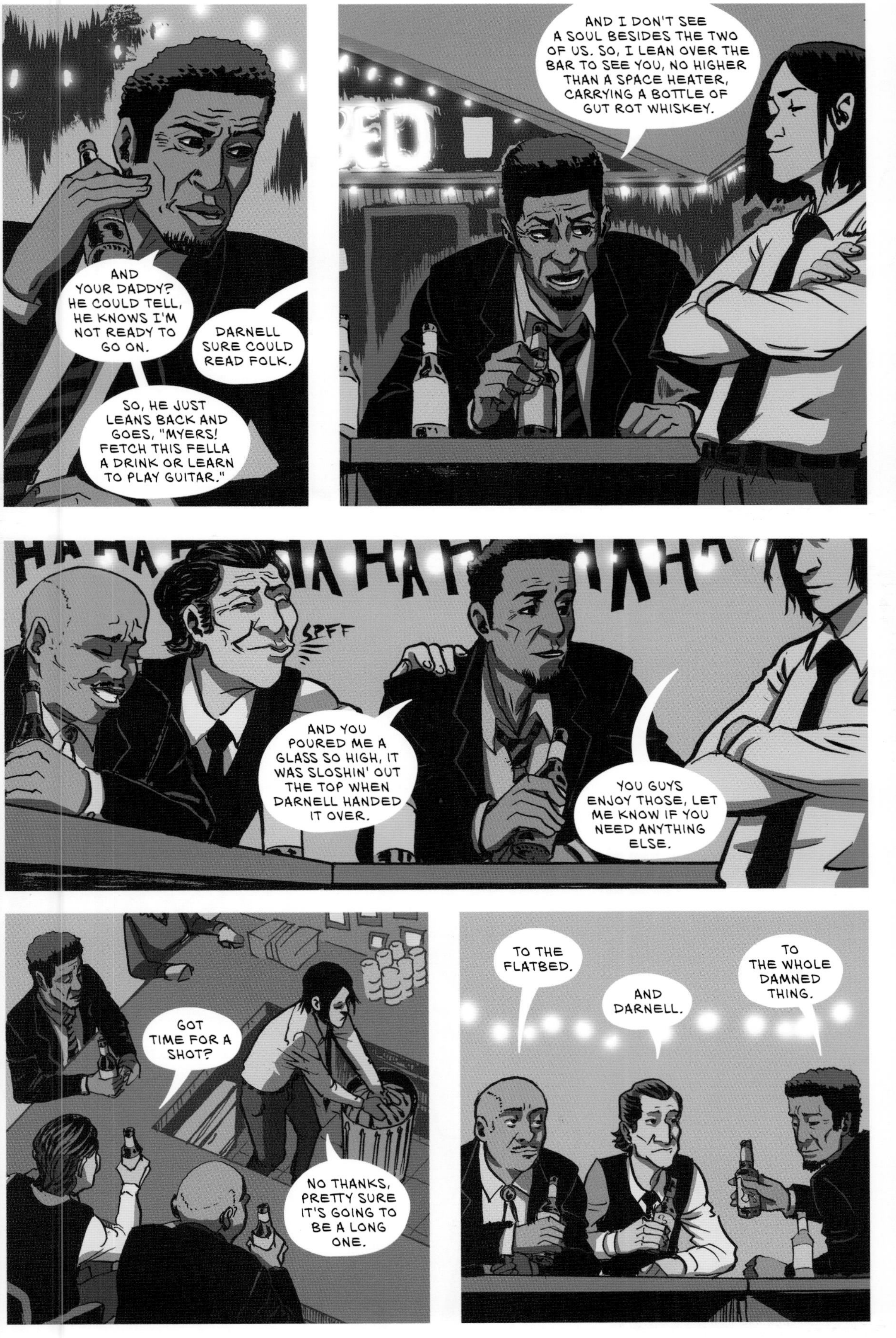
AND YOUR DADDY? HE COULD TELL, HE KNOWS I'M NOT READY TO GO ON.
DARNELL SURE COULD READ FOLK.
SO, HE JUST LEANS BACK AND GOES, "MYERS! FETCH THIS FELLA A DRINK OR LEARN TO PLAY GUITAR."
AND I DON'T SEE A SOUL BESIDES THE TWO OF US. SO, I LEAN OVER THE BAR TO SEE YOU, NO HIGHER THAN A SPACE HEATER, CARRYING A BOTTLE OF GUT ROT WHISKEY.
BED
SPFF
AND YOU POURED ME A GLASS SO HIGH, IT WAS SLOSHIN' OUT THE TOP WHEN DARNELL HANDED IT OVER.
YOU GUYS ENJOY THOSE, LET ME KNOW IF YOU NEED ANYTHING ELSE.
GOT TIME FOR A SHOT?
NO THANKS, PRETTY SURE IT'S GOING TO BE A LONG ONE.
TO THE FLATBED.
AND DARNELL.
TO THE WHOLE DAMNED THING.

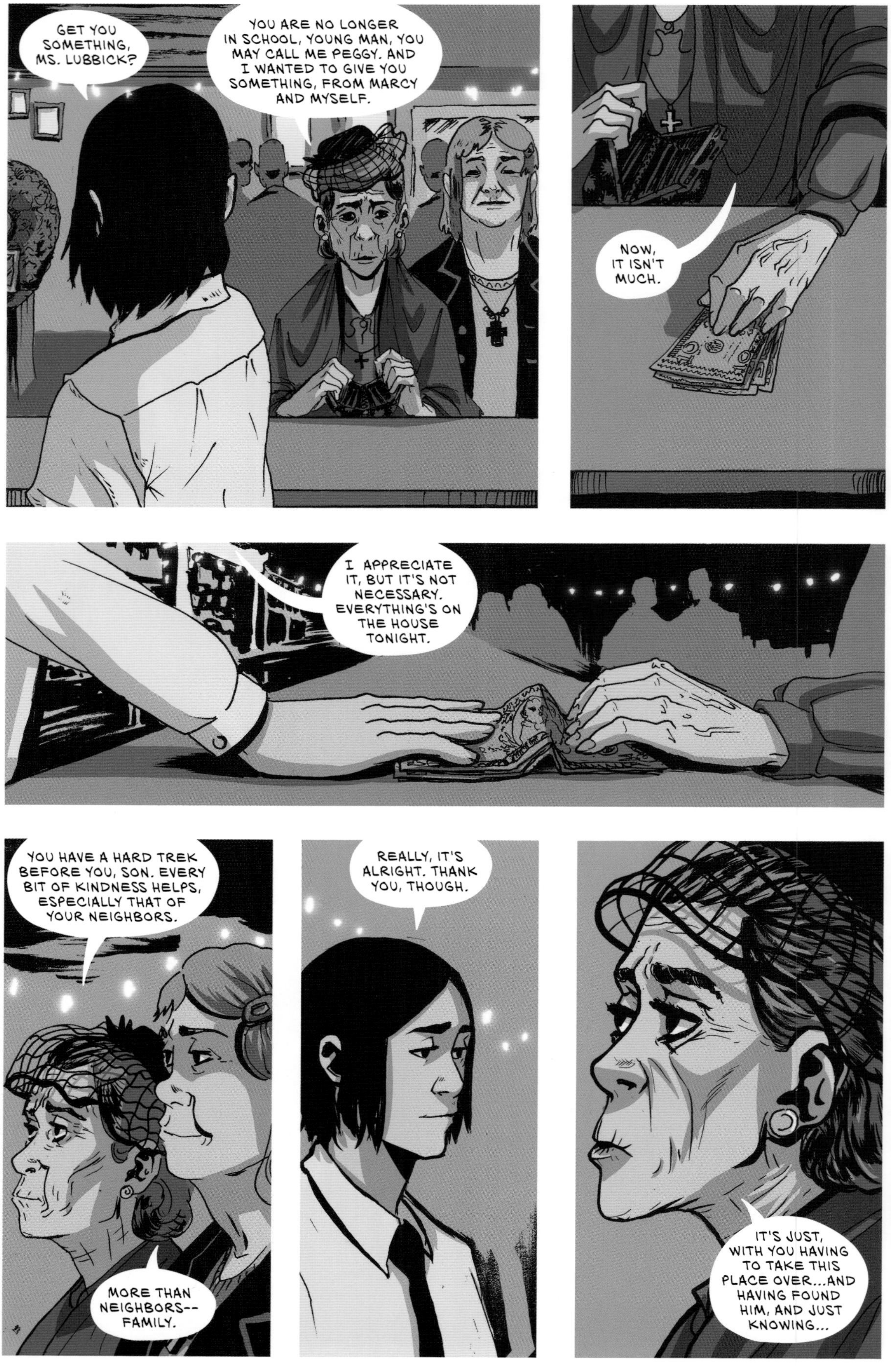
GET YOU SOMETHING, MS. LUBBICK?
YOU ARE NO LONGER IN SCHOOL, YOUNG MAN, YOU MAY CALL ME PEGGY. AND I WANTED TO GIVE YOU SOMETHING, FROM MARCY AND MYSELF.
NOW, IT ISN'T MUCH.
I APPRECIATE IT, BUT IT'S NOT NECESSARY. EVERYTHING'S ON THE HOUSE TONIGHT.
YOU HAVE A HARD TREK BEFORE YOU, SON. EVERY BIT OF KINDNESS HELPS, ESPECIALLY THAT OF YOUR NEIGHBORS.
MORE THAN NEIGHBORS-- FAMILY.
REALLY, IT'S ALRIGHT. THANK YOU, THOUGH.
IT'S JUST, WITH YOU HAVING TO TAKE THIS PLACE OVER...AND HAVING FOUND HIM, AND JUST KNOWING...

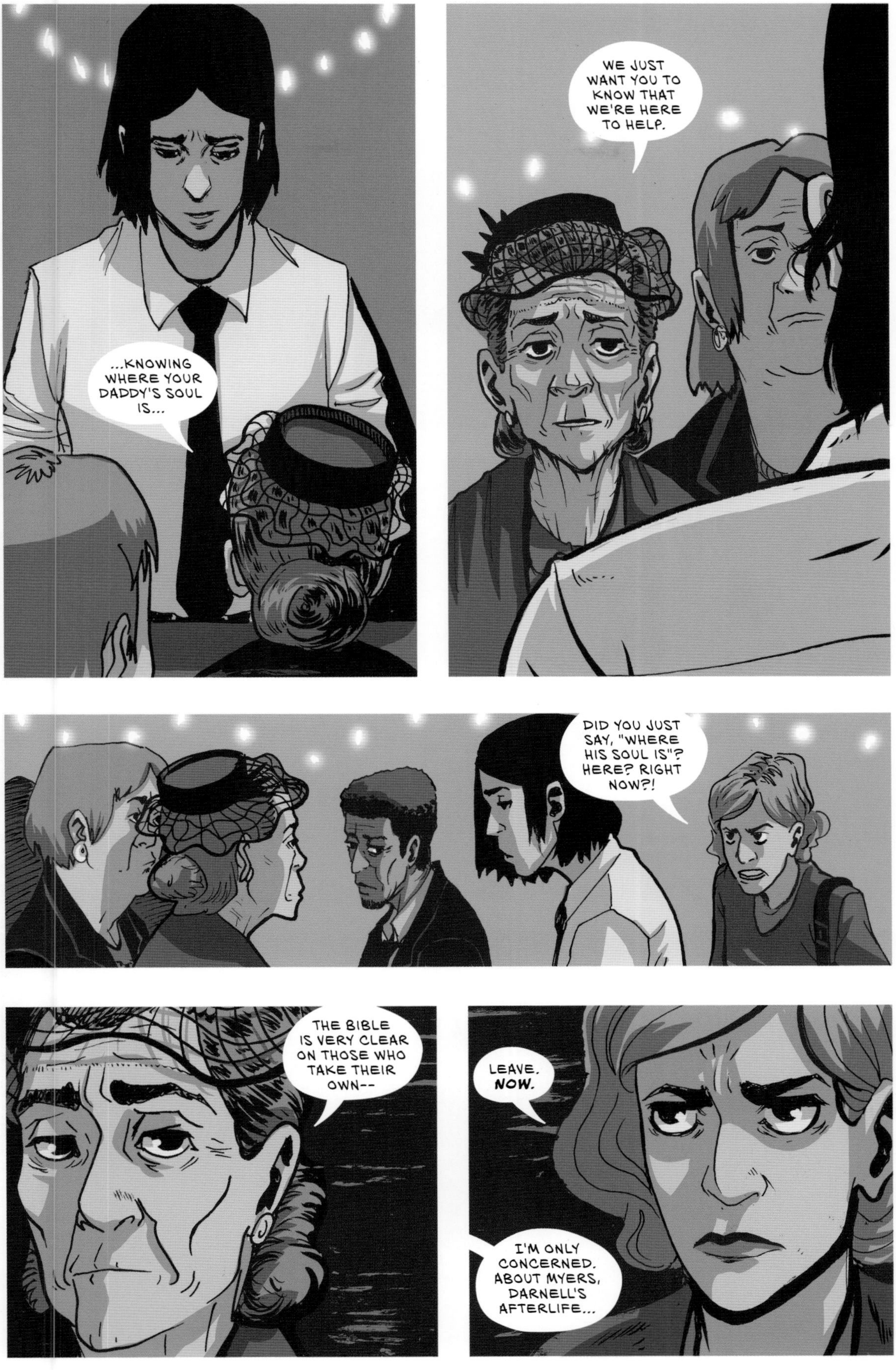
...KNOWING WHERE YOUR DADDY'S SOUL IS...
WE JUST WANT YOU TO KNOW THAT WE'RE HERE TO HELP.
DID YOU JUST SAY, "WHERE HIS SOUL IS"? HERE? RIGHT NOW?!
THE BIBLE IS VERY CLEAR ON THOSE WHO TAKE THEIR OWN--
LEAVE. **NOW.**
I'M ONLY CONCERNED. ABOUT MYERS, DARNELL'S AFTERLIFE...

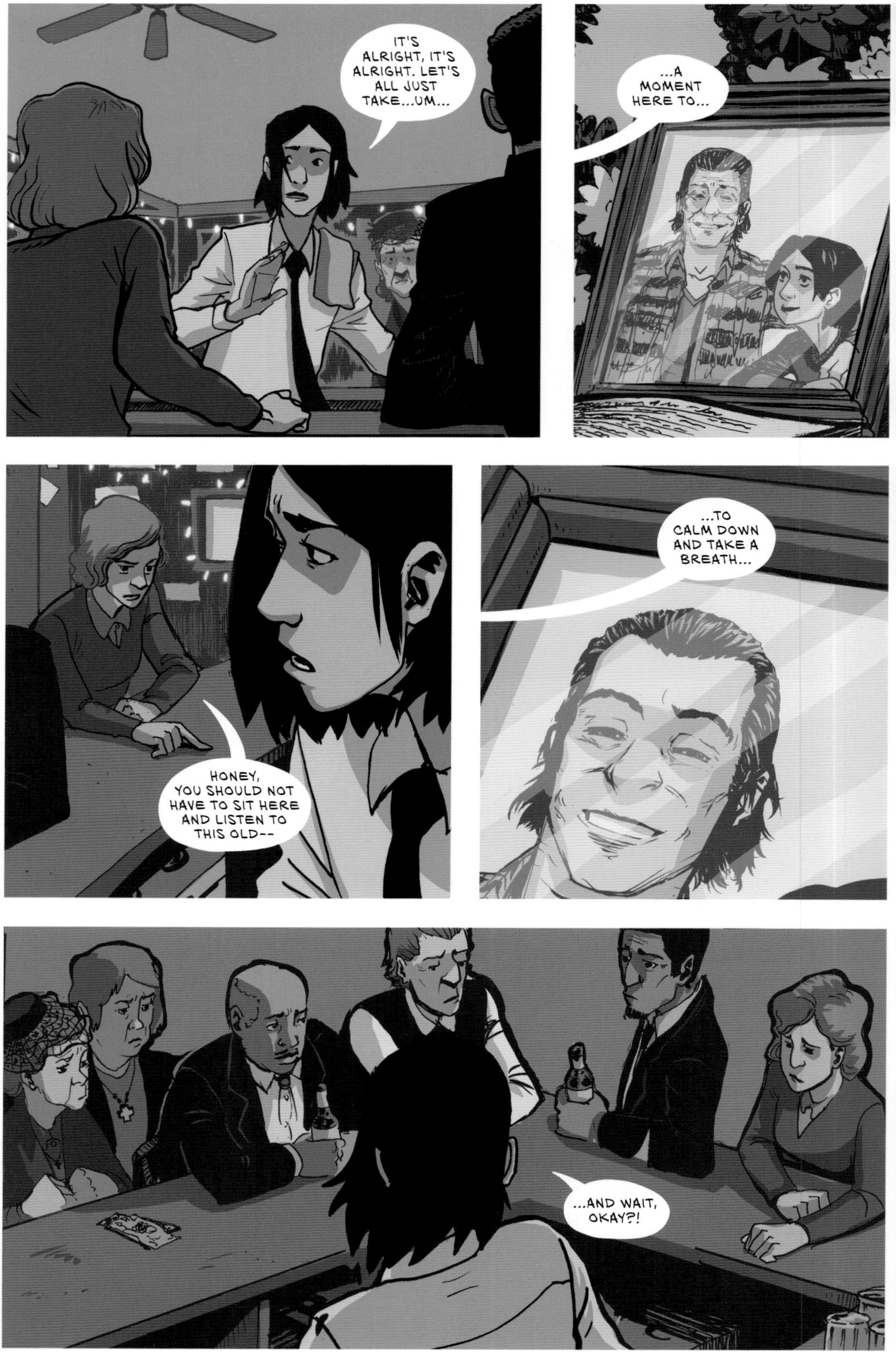
IT'S ALRIGHT, IT'S ALRIGHT. LET'S ALL JUST TAKE...UM...
...A MOMENT HERE TO...
HONEY, YOU SHOULD NOT HAVE TO SIT HERE AND LISTEN TO THIS OLD--
...TO CALM DOWN AND TAKE A BREATH...
...AND WAIT, OKAY?!

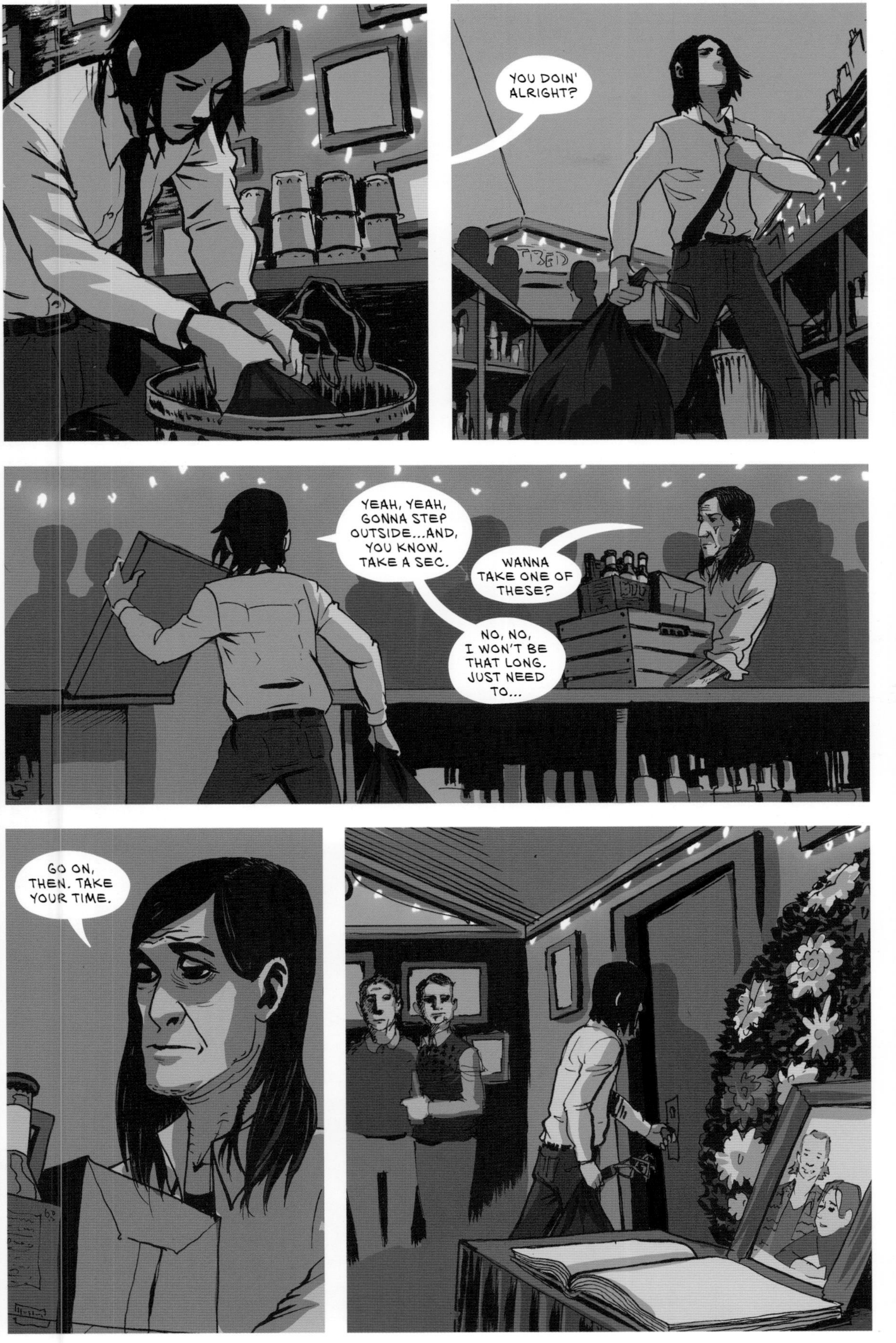
YOU DOIN' ALRIGHT?
YEAH, YEAH, GONNA STEP OUTSIDE...AND, YOU KNOW. TAKE A SEC.
WANNA TAKE ONE OF THESE?
NO, NO, I WON'T BE THAT LONG. JUST NEED TO...
GO ON, THEN. TAKE YOUR TIME.

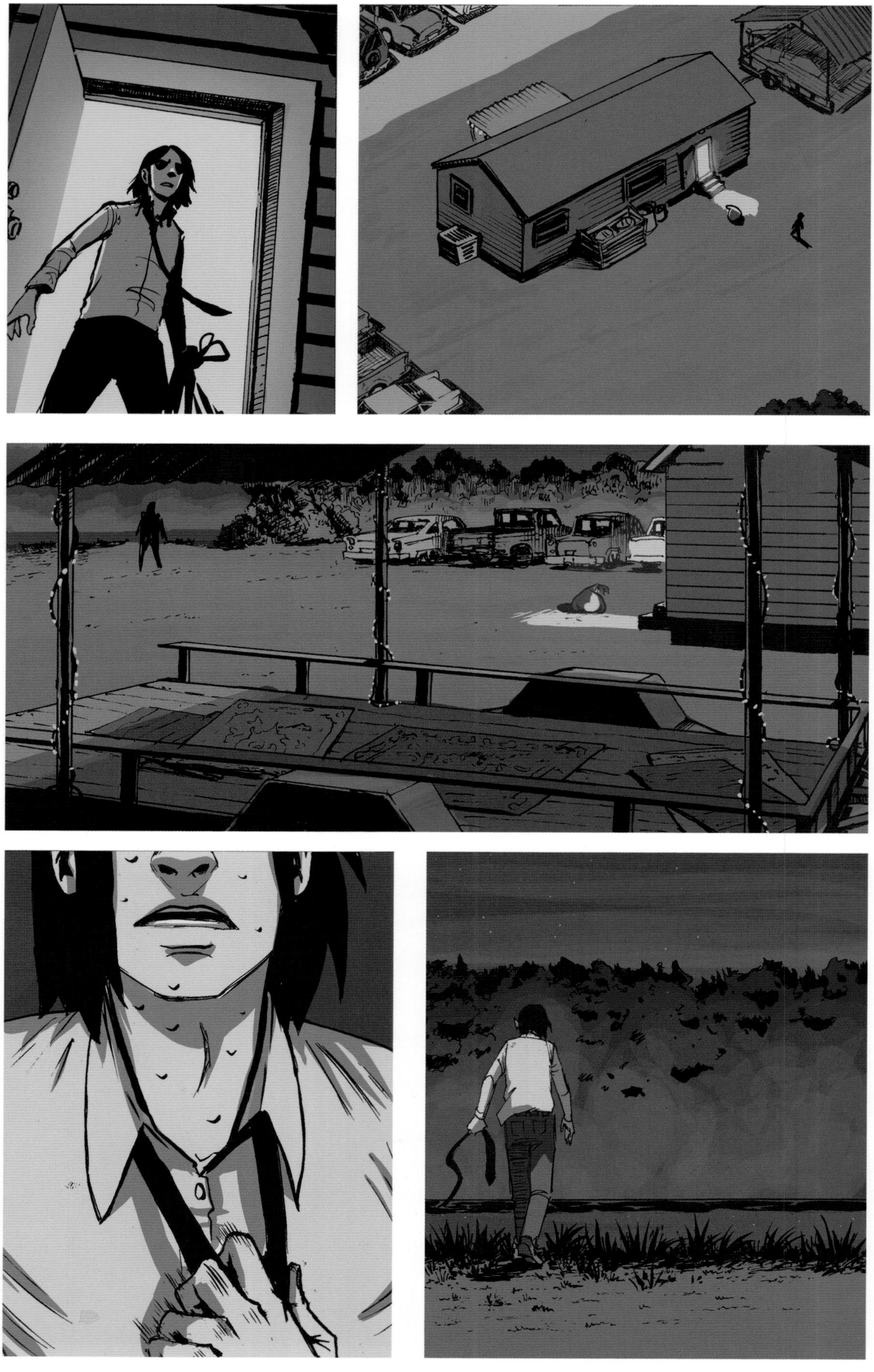

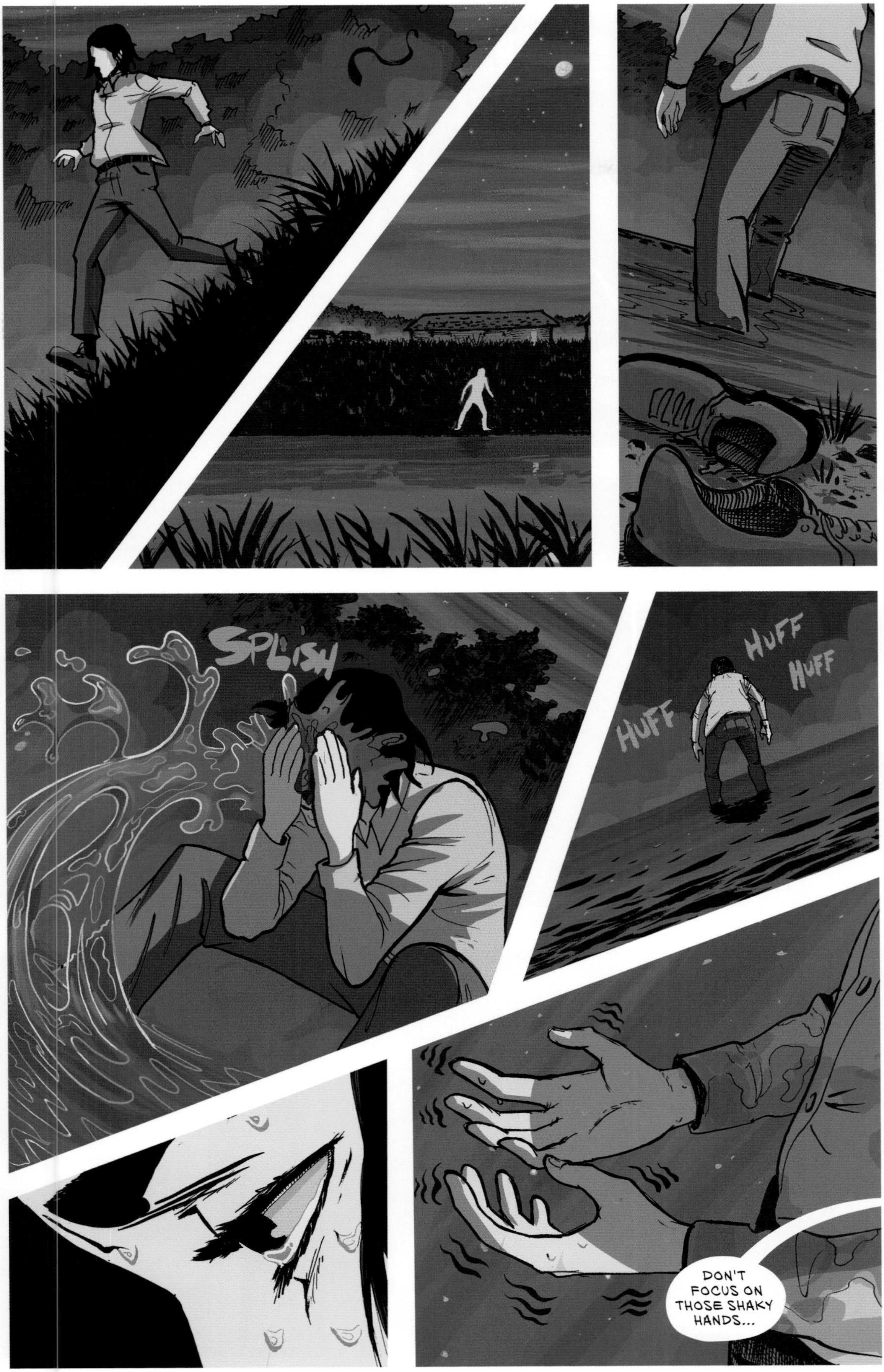
SPLISH
HUFF
HUFF
HUFF
DON'T FOCUS ON THOSE SHAKY HANDS...

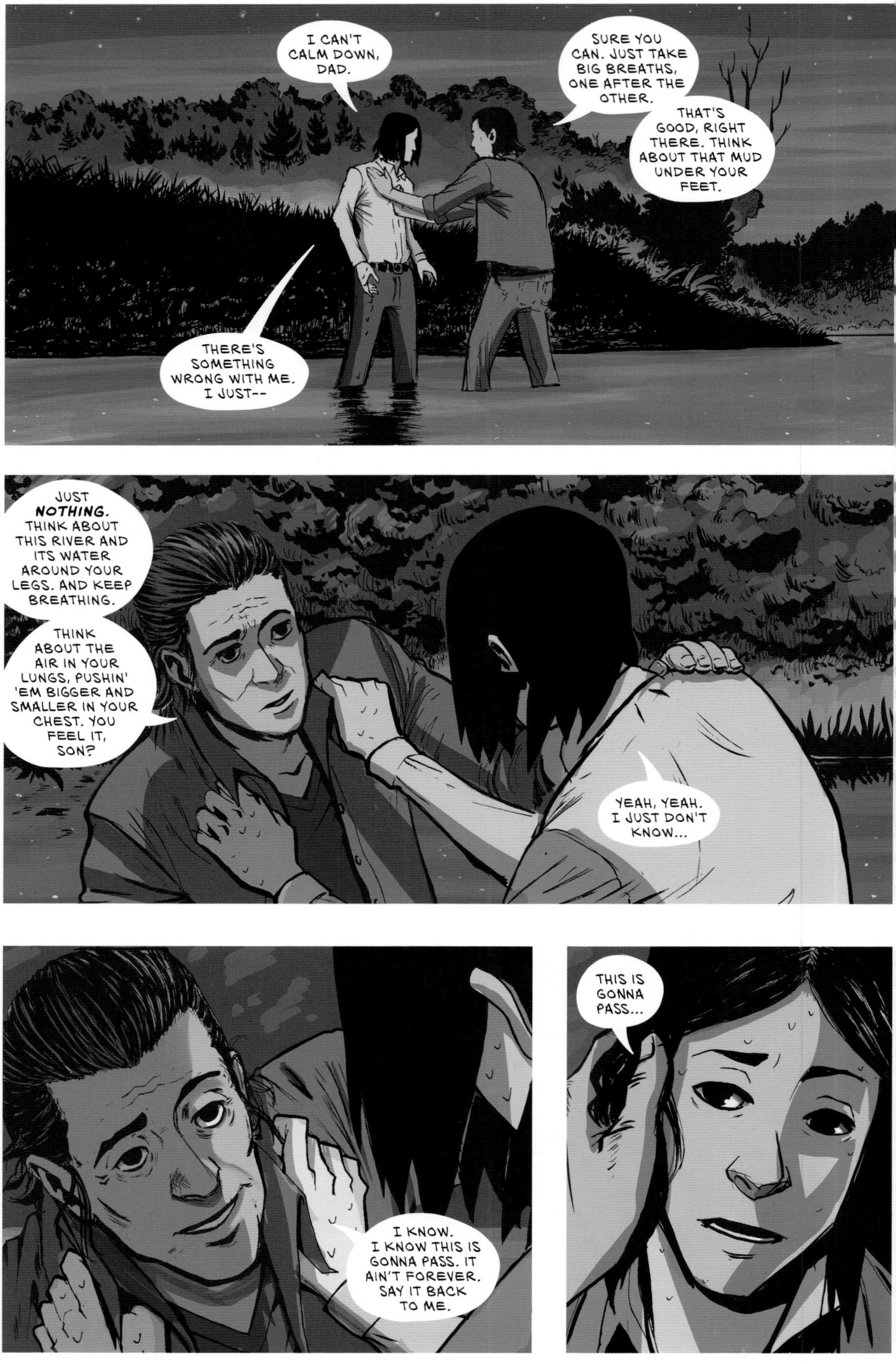
I CAN'T CALM DOWN, DAD.
SURE YOU CAN. JUST TAKE BIG BREATHS, ONE AFTER THE OTHER.
THAT'S GOOD, RIGHT THERE. THINK ABOUT THAT MUD UNDER YOUR FEET.
THERE'S SOMETHING WRONG WITH ME. I JUST--
JUST **NOTHING.** THINK ABOUT THIS RIVER AND ITS WATER AROUND YOUR LEGS. AND KEEP BREATHING.
THINK ABOUT THE AIR IN YOUR LUNGS, PUSHIN' 'EM BIGGER AND SMALLER IN YOUR CHEST. YOU FEEL IT, SON?
YEAH, YEAH. I JUST DON'T KNOW...
I KNOW. I KNOW THIS IS GONNA PASS. IT AIN'T FOREVER. SAY IT BACK TO ME.
THIS IS GONNA PASS...

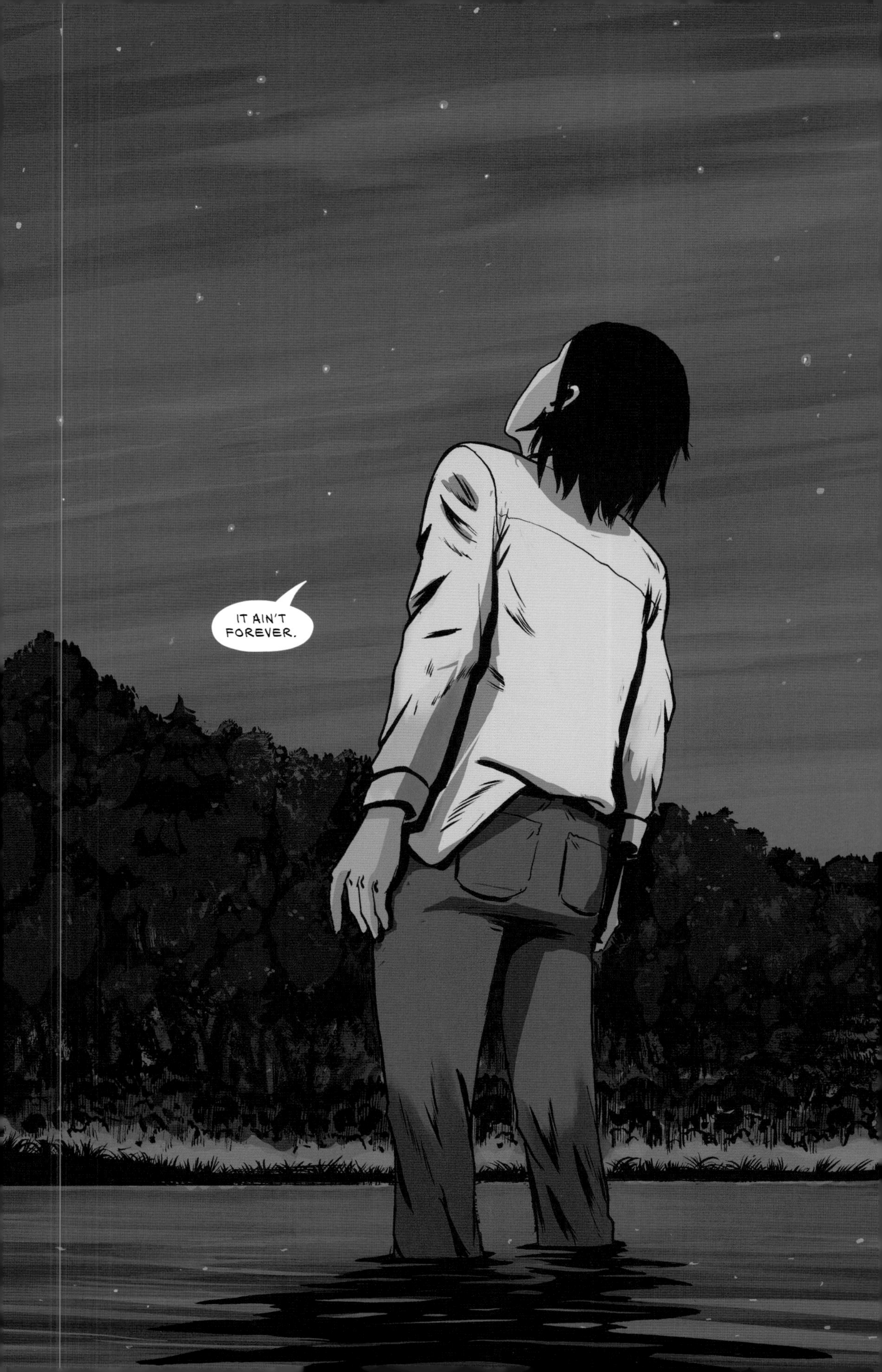
IT AIN'T FOREVER.

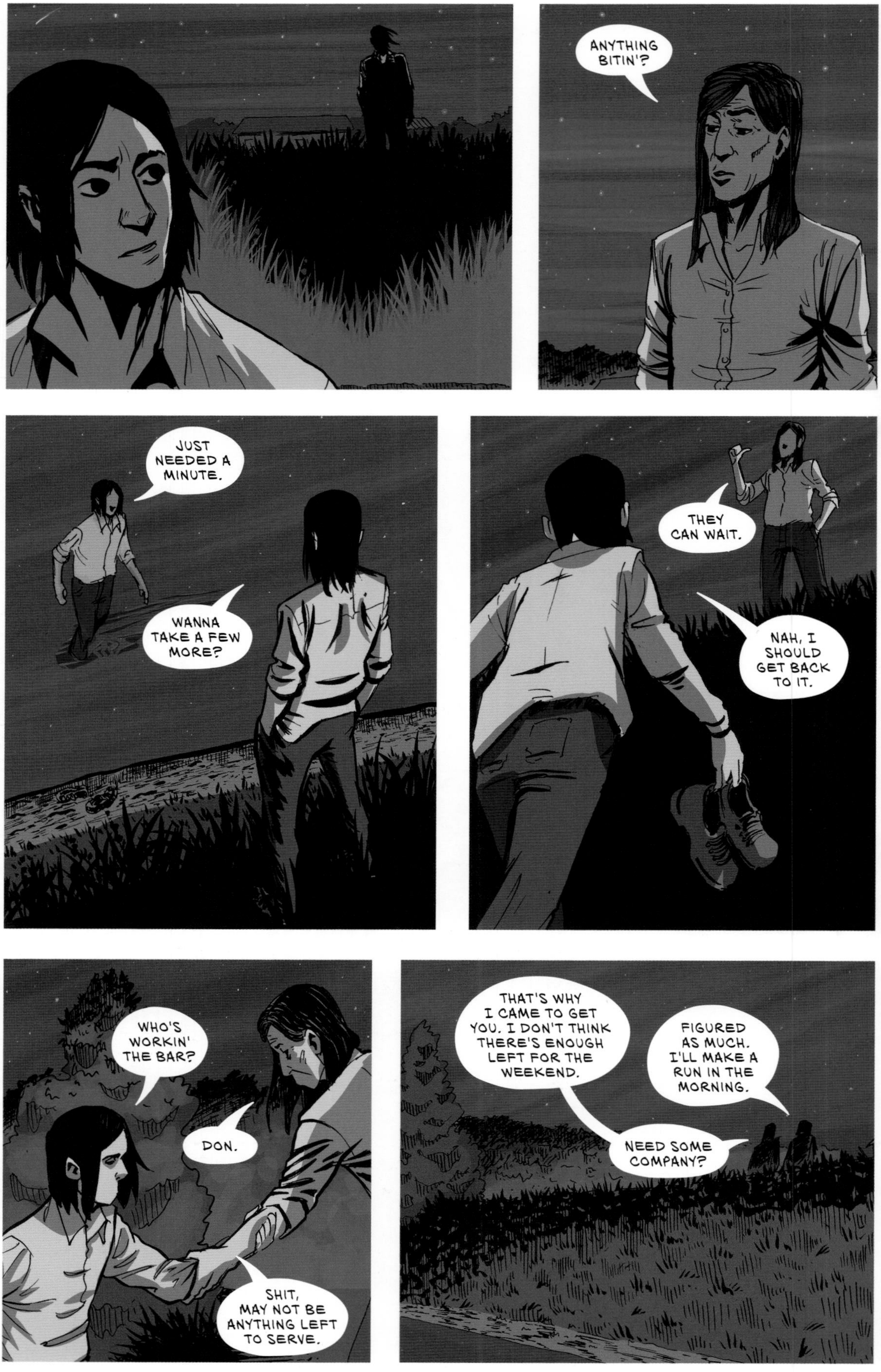
ANYTHING BITIN'?
JUST NEEDED A MINUTE.
WANNA TAKE A FEW MORE?
THEY CAN WAIT.
NAH, I SHOULD GET BACK TO IT.
WHO'S WORKIN' THE BAR?
DON.
SHIT, MAY NOT BE ANYTHING LEFT TO SERVE.
THAT'S WHY I CAME TO GET YOU. I DON'T THINK THERE'S ENOUGH LEFT FOR THE WEEKEND.
FIGURED AS MUCH. I'LL MAKE A RUN IN THE MORNING.
NEED SOME COMPANY?

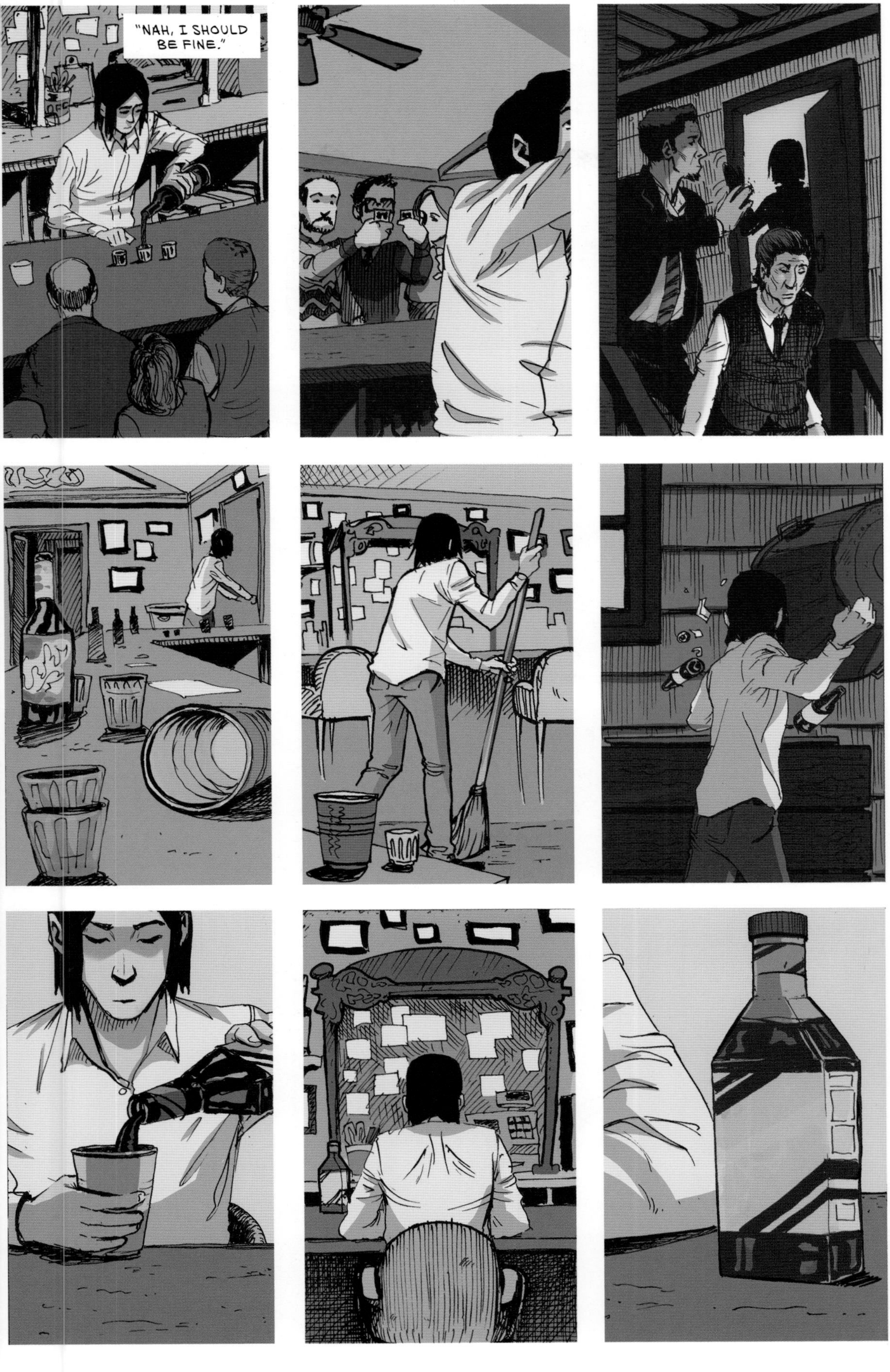
"NAH, I SHOULD BE FINE."

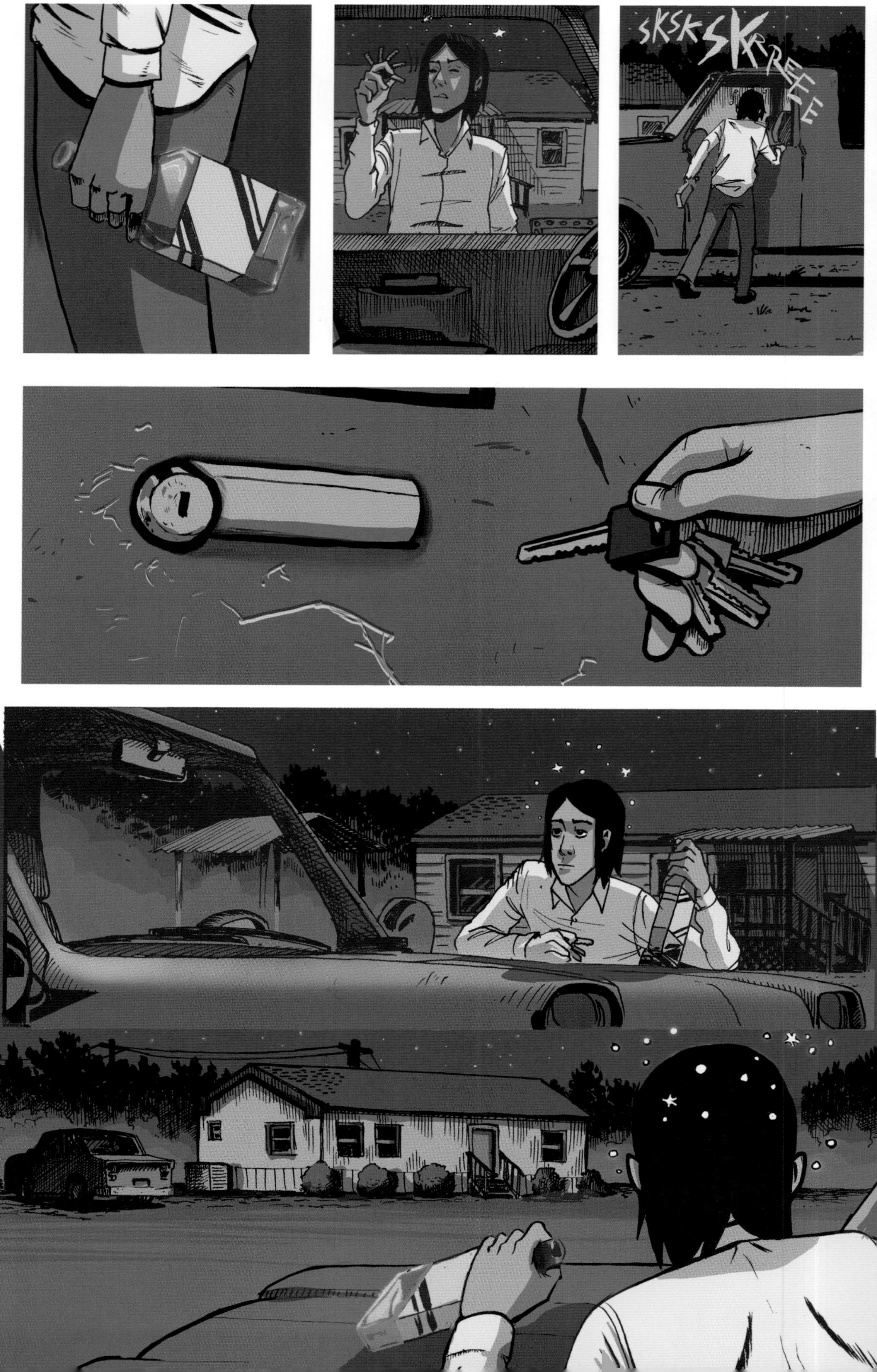
SKSKSKRREEEE

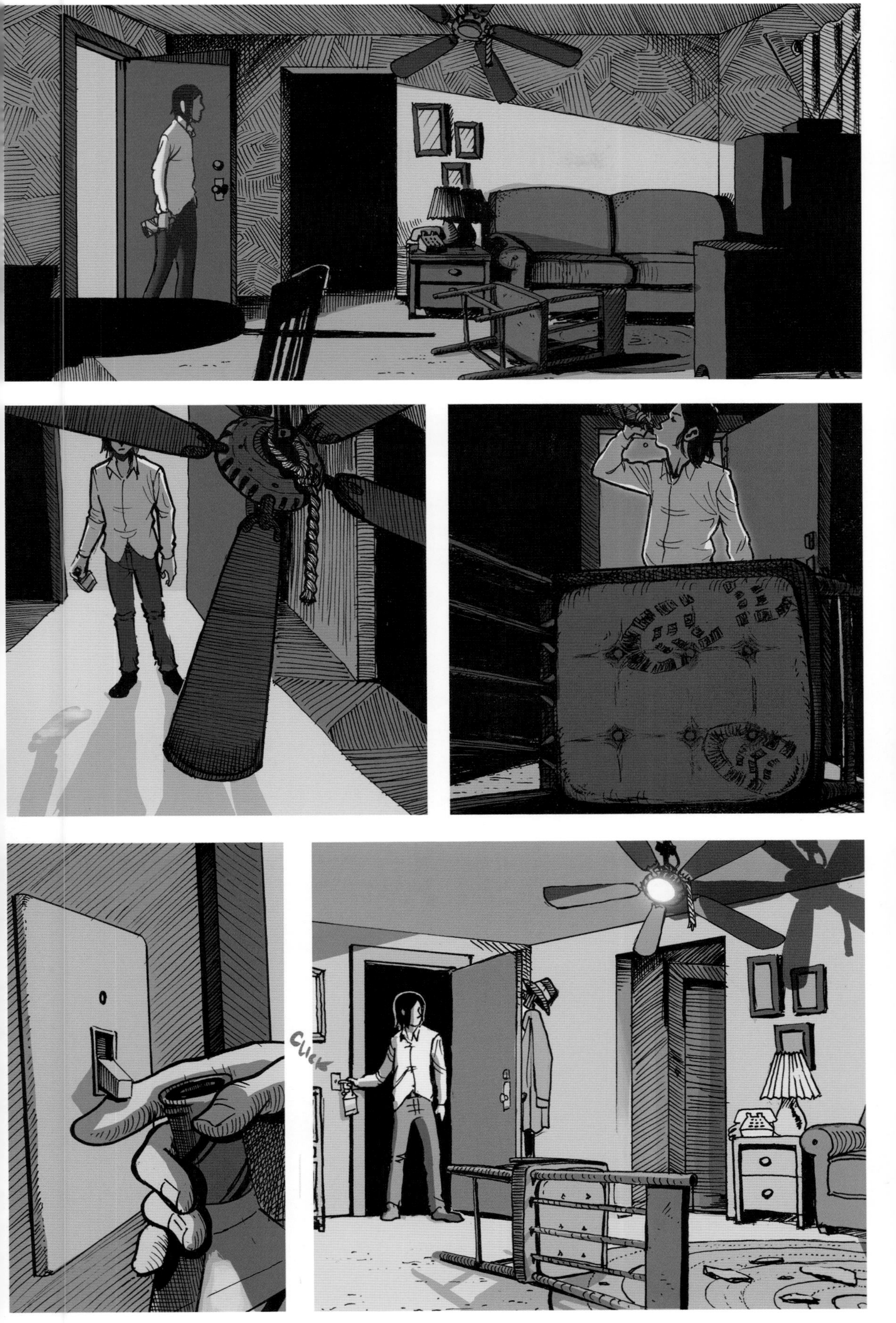
CLICK

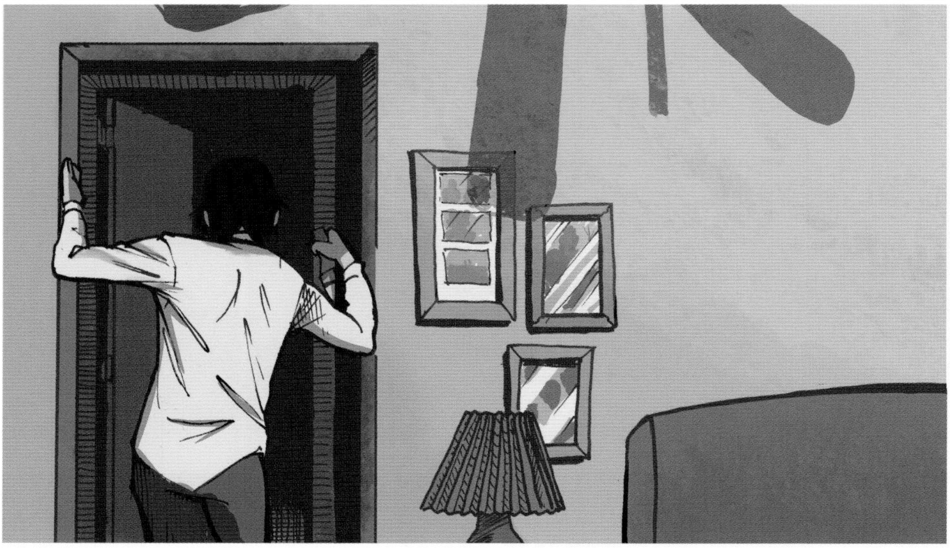

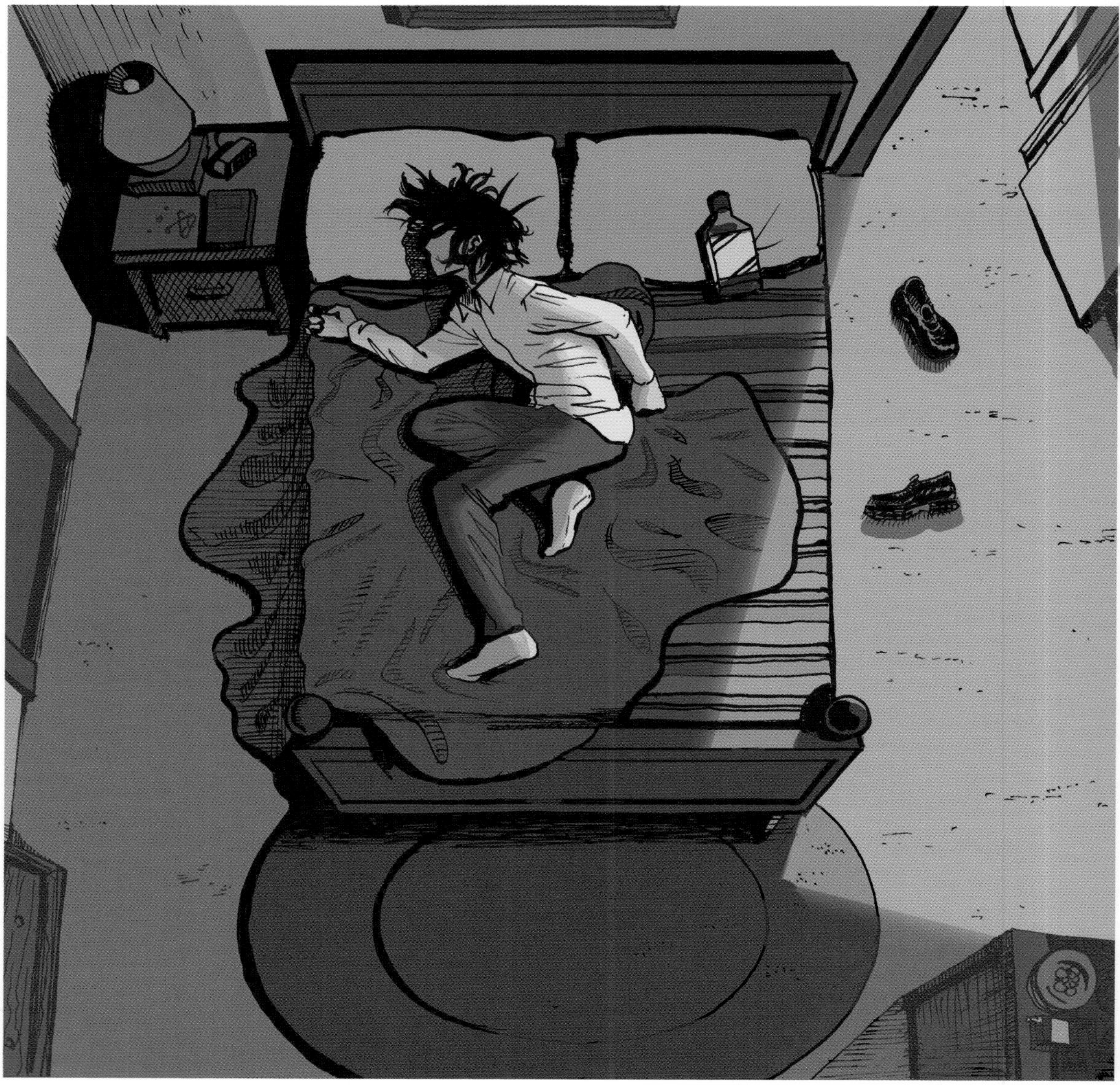

# CHAPTER TWO

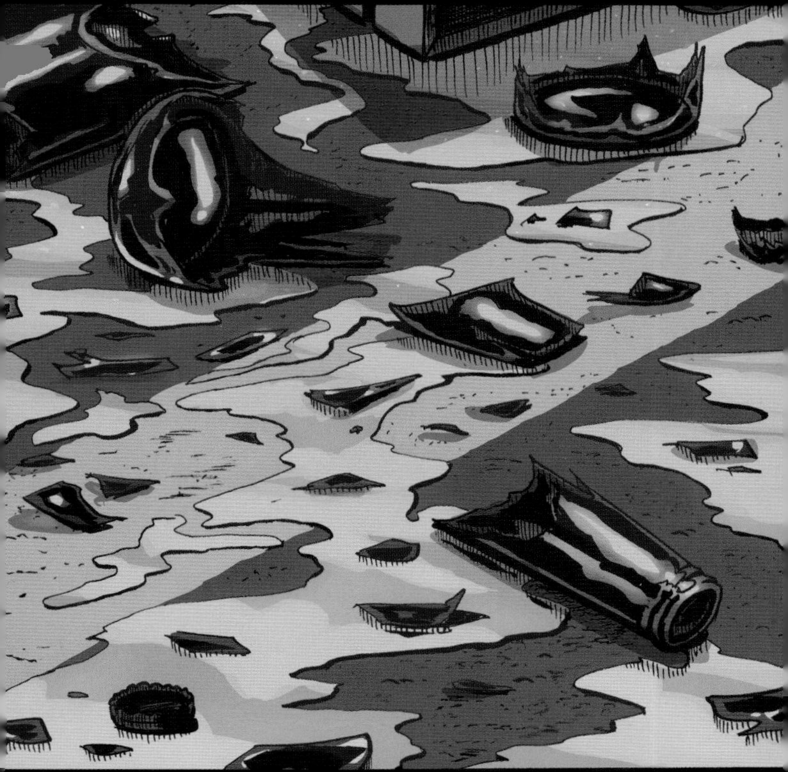

# STATE SIGNS

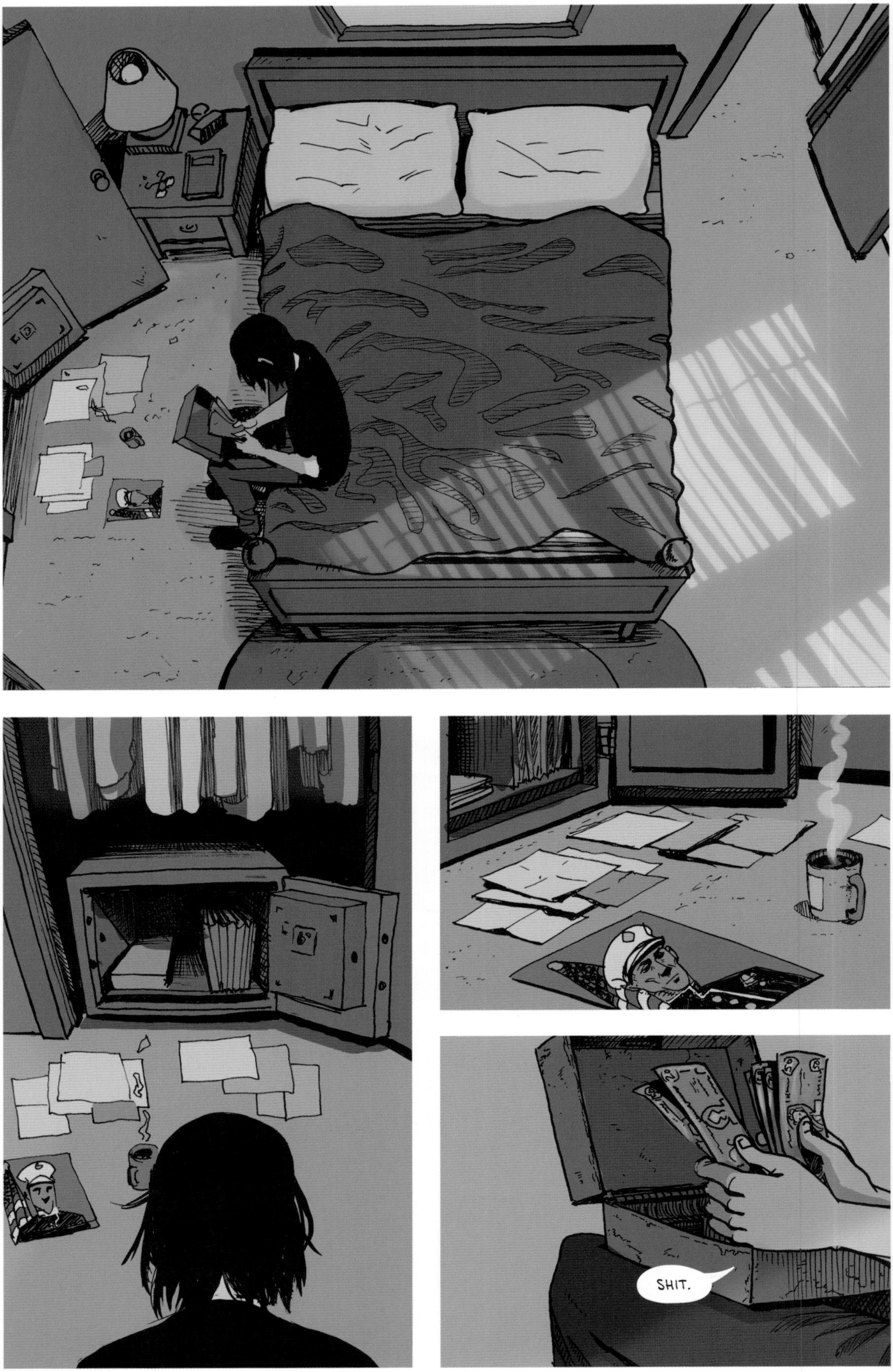
SHIT.

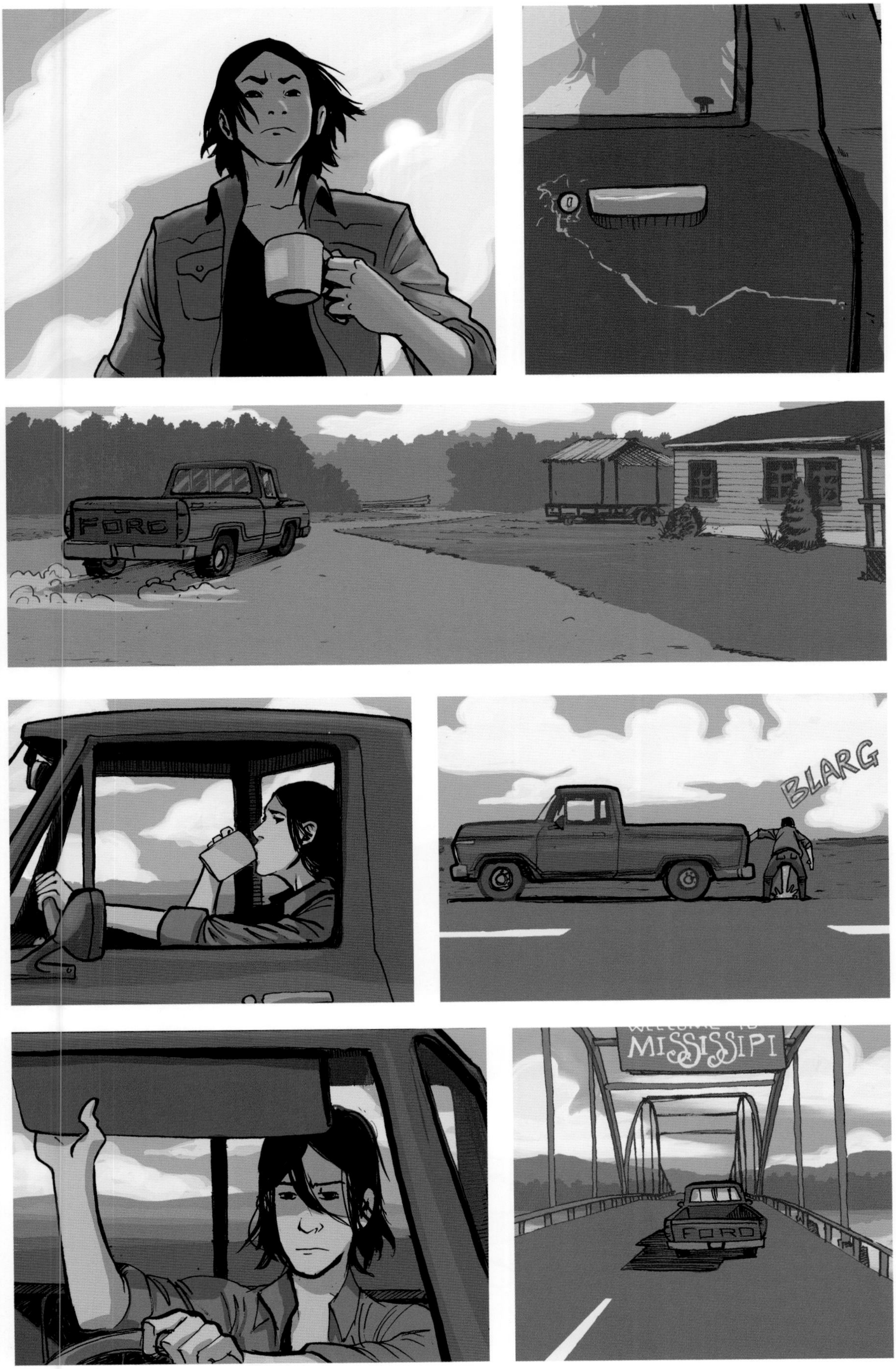
FORD
BLARG
MISSISSIPI
FORD

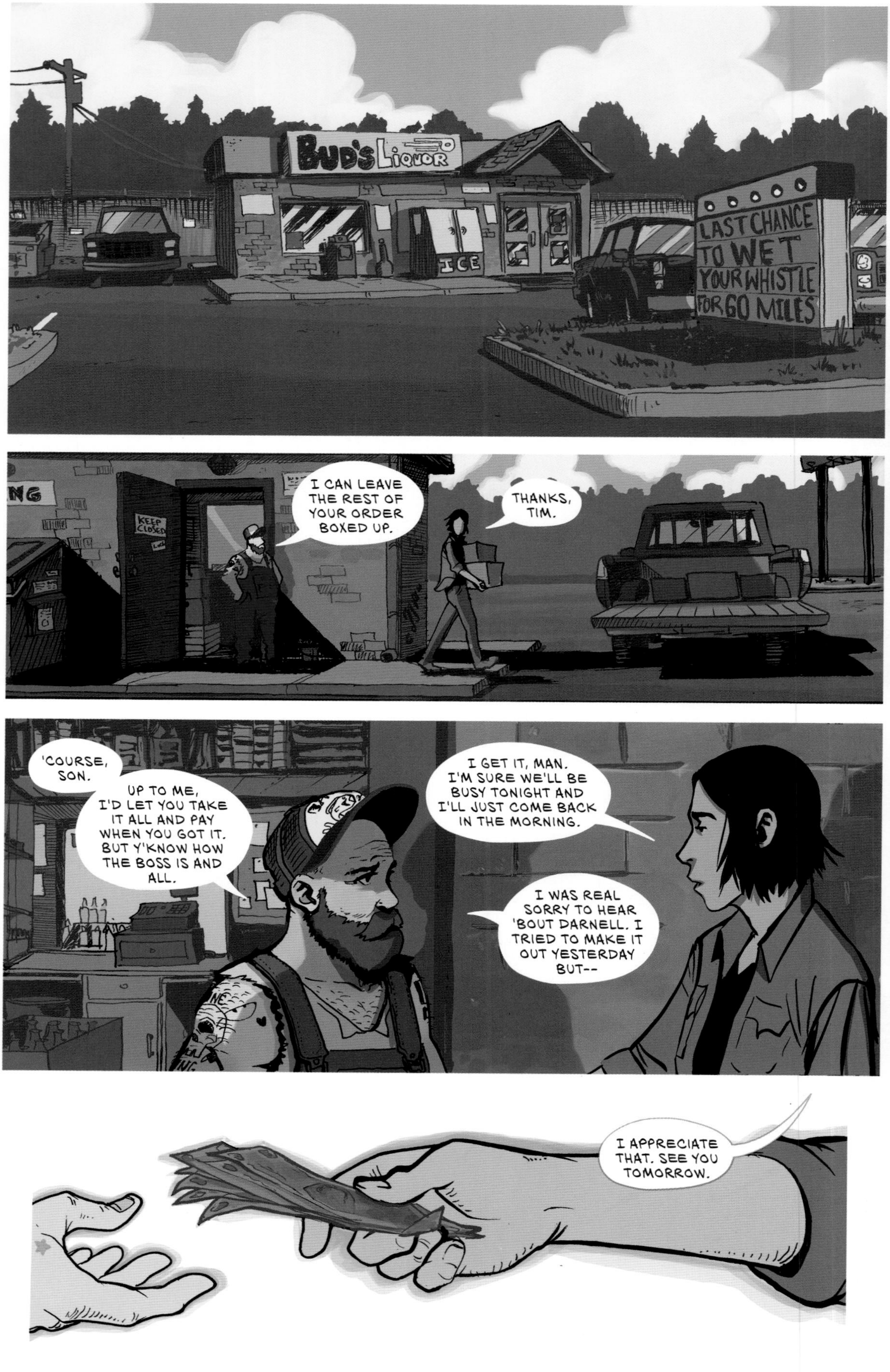
BUD'S LIQUOR
LAST CHANCE TO WET YOUR WHISTLE FOR 60 MILES
ICE
KEEP CLOSED
I CAN LEAVE THE REST OF YOUR ORDER BOXED UP.
THANKS, TIM.
'COURSE, SON.
UP TO ME, I'D LET YOU TAKE IT ALL AND PAY WHEN YOU GOT IT. BUT Y'KNOW HOW THE BOSS IS AND ALL.
I GET IT, MAN. I'M SURE WE'LL BE BUSY TONIGHT AND I'LL JUST COME BACK IN THE MORNING.
I WAS REAL SORRY TO HEAR 'BOUT DARNELL. I TRIED TO MAKE IT OUT YESTERDAY BUT--
I APPRECIATE THAT. SEE YOU TOMORROW.

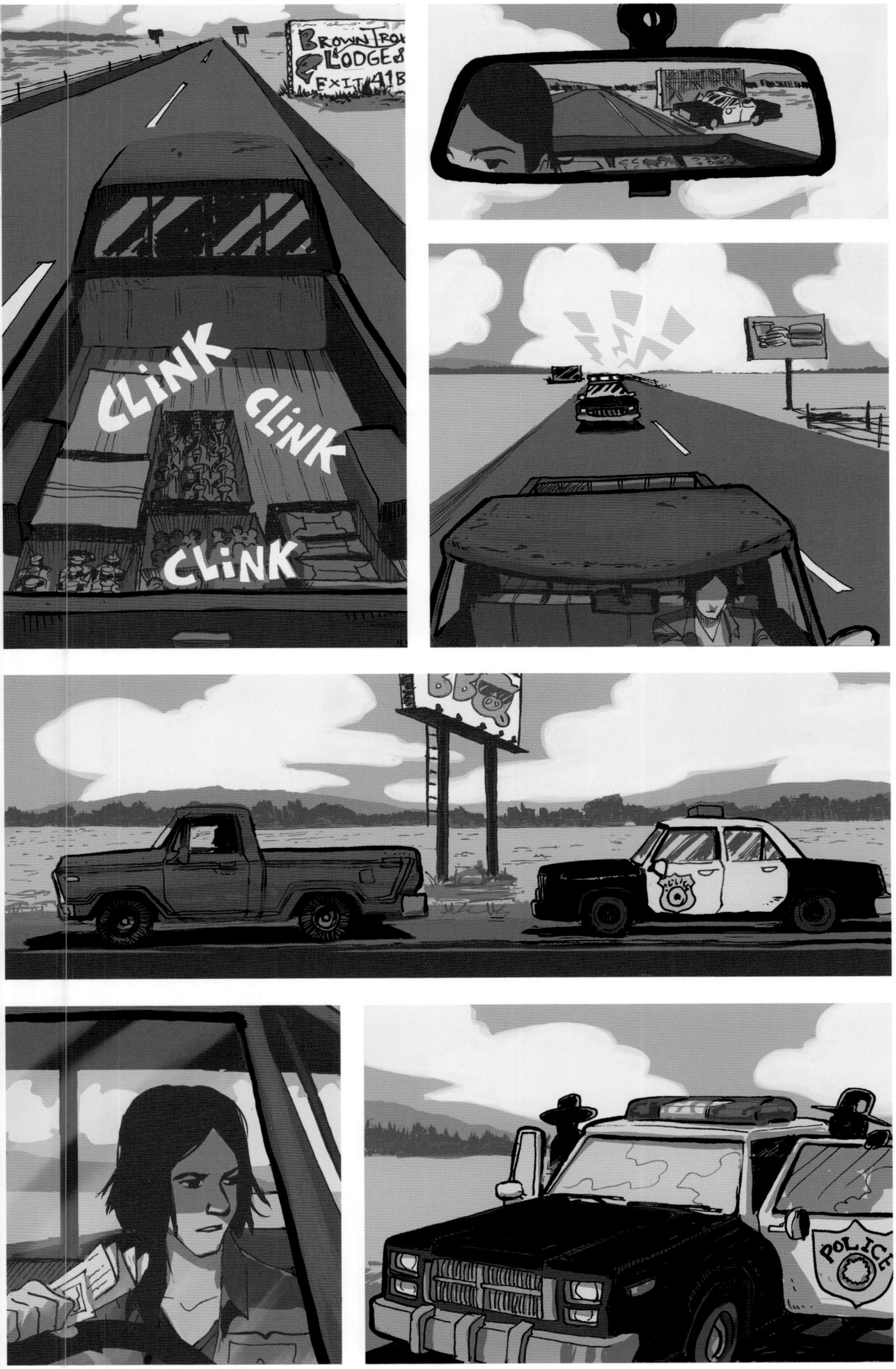

BROWN TRO
LODGES
EXIT 41B
CLINK
CLINK
CLINK
POLICE

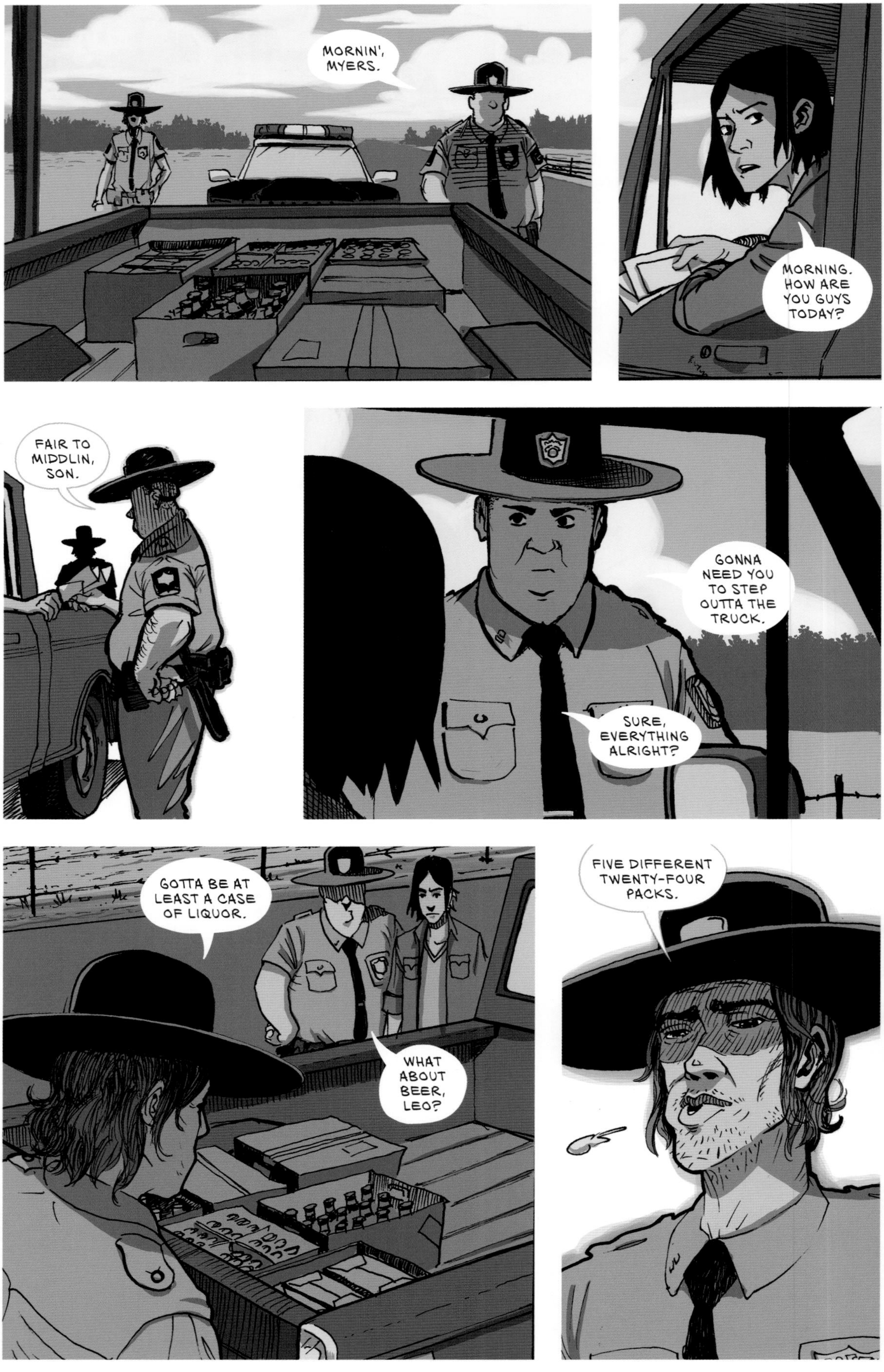
MORNIN', MYERS.
MORNING. HOW ARE YOU GUYS TODAY?
FAIR TO MIDDLIN, SON.
GONNA NEED YOU TO STEP OUTTA THE TRUCK.
SURE, EVERYTHING ALRIGHT?
GOTTA BE AT LEAST A CASE OF LIQUOR.
WHAT ABOUT BEER, LEO?
FIVE DIFFERENT TWENTY-FOUR PACKS.

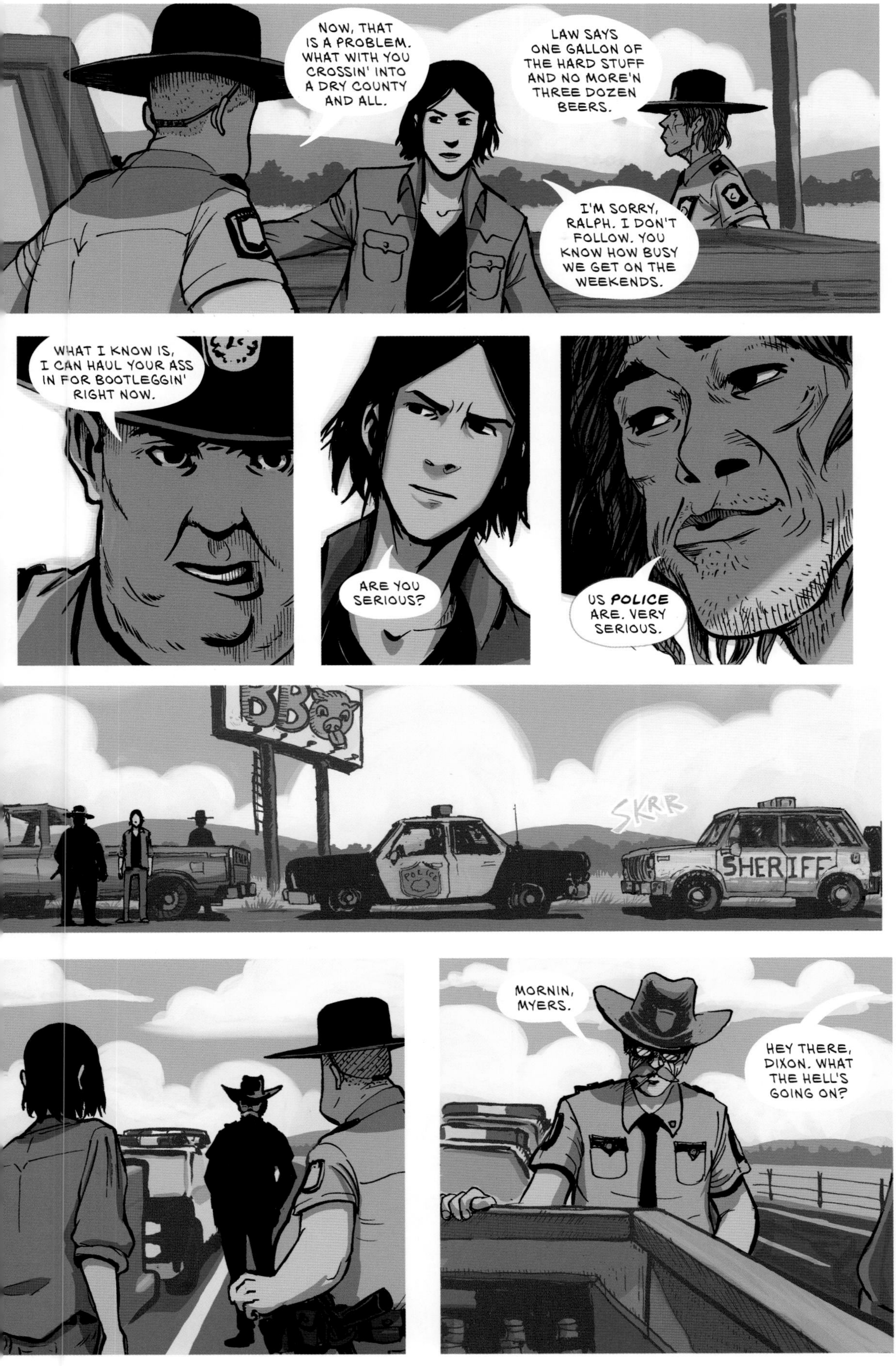
NOW, THAT IS A PROBLEM. WHAT WITH YOU CROSSIN' INTO A DRY COUNTY AND ALL.
LAW SAYS ONE GALLON OF THE HARD STUFF AND NO MORE'N THREE DOZEN BEERS.
I'M SORRY, RALPH. I DON'T FOLLOW. YOU KNOW HOW BUSY WE GET ON THE WEEKENDS.
WHAT I KNOW IS, I CAN HAUL YOUR ASS IN FOR BOOTLEGGIN' RIGHT NOW.
ARE YOU SERIOUS?
US **POLICE** ARE. VERY SERIOUS.
BBQ
SKRR
POLICE
SHERIFF
MORNIN, MYERS.
HEY THERE, DIXON. WHAT THE HELL'S GOING ON?

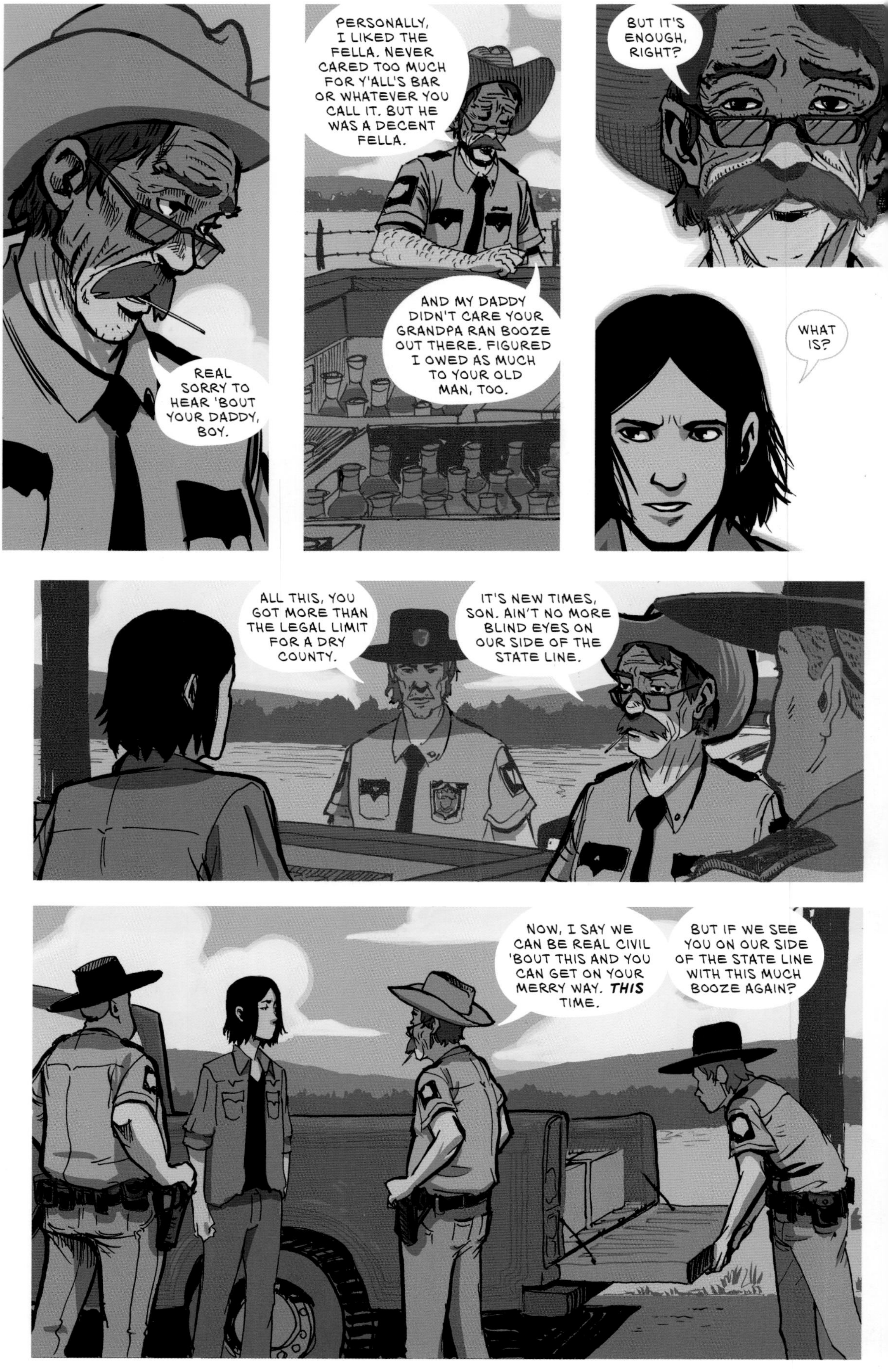
REAL SORRY TO HEAR 'BOUT YOUR DADDY, BOY.
PERSONALLY, I LIKED THE FELLA. NEVER CARED TOO MUCH FOR Y'ALL'S BAR OR WHATEVER YOU CALL IT. BUT HE WAS A DECENT FELLA.
AND MY DADDY DIDN'T CARE YOUR GRANDPA RAN BOOZE OUT THERE. FIGURED I OWED AS MUCH TO YOUR OLD MAN, TOO.
BUT IT'S ENOUGH, RIGHT?
WHAT IS?
ALL THIS, YOU GOT MORE THAN THE LEGAL LIMIT FOR A DRY COUNTY.
IT'S NEW TIMES, SON. AIN'T NO MORE BLIND EYES ON OUR SIDE OF THE STATE LINE.
NOW, I SAY WE CAN BE REAL CIVIL 'BOUT THIS AND YOU CAN GET ON YOUR MERRY WAY. *THIS* TIME.
BUT IF WE SEE YOU ON OUR SIDE OF THE STATE LINE WITH THIS MUCH BOOZE AGAIN?

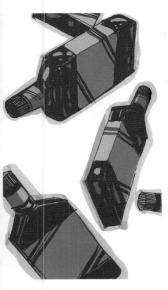

THIS IS THE WARNIN'.

NEXT TIME ENDS WITH YOU IN LOCK UP.

CRASH

HEY!!

THAT'S ALL WE GOT!

HOLD IT, MYERS!

GET YOUR DAMN HANDS OFF ME, MAN! HOW MANY TIMES HAVE YOU DRANK AT OUR BAR?!

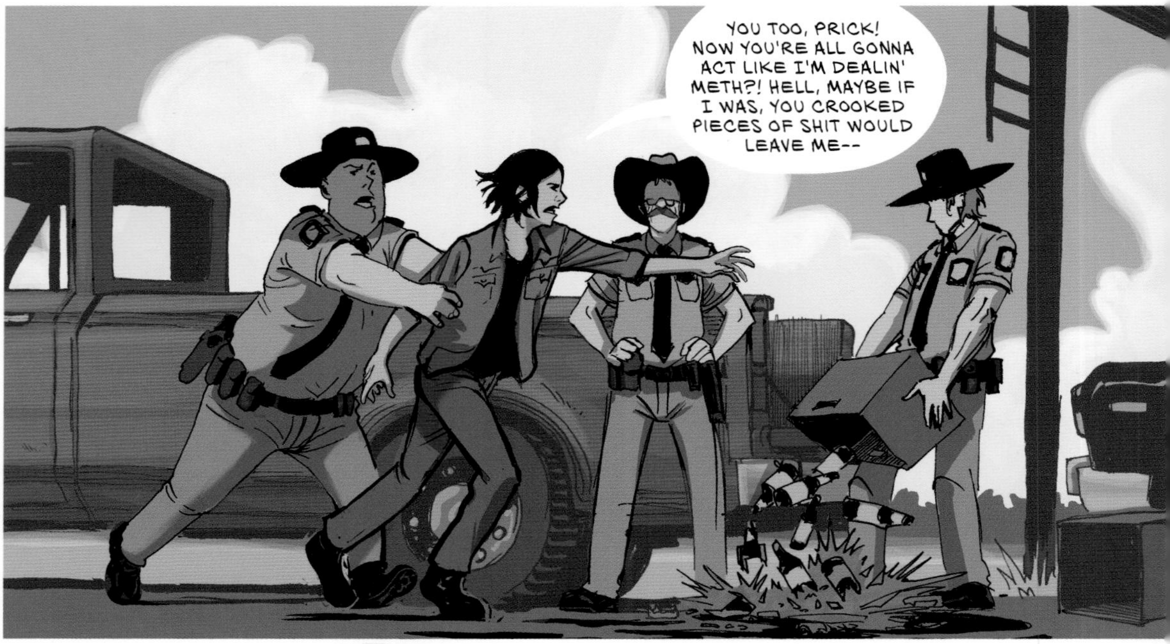
YOU TOO, PRICK! NOW YOU'RE ALL GONNA ACT LIKE I'M DEALIN' METH?! HELL, MAYBE IF I WAS, YOU CROOKED PIECES OF SHIT WOULD LEAVE ME--
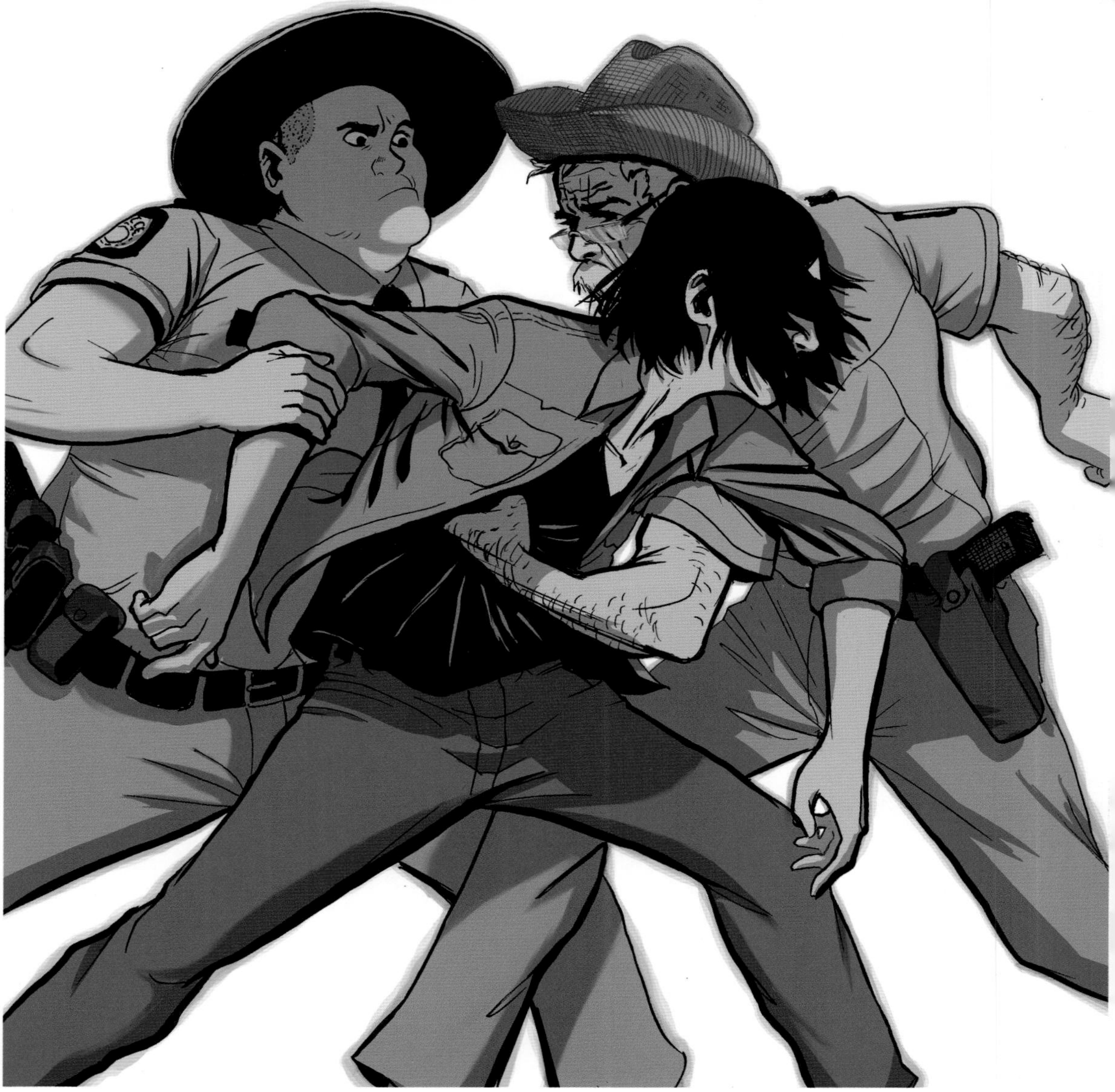

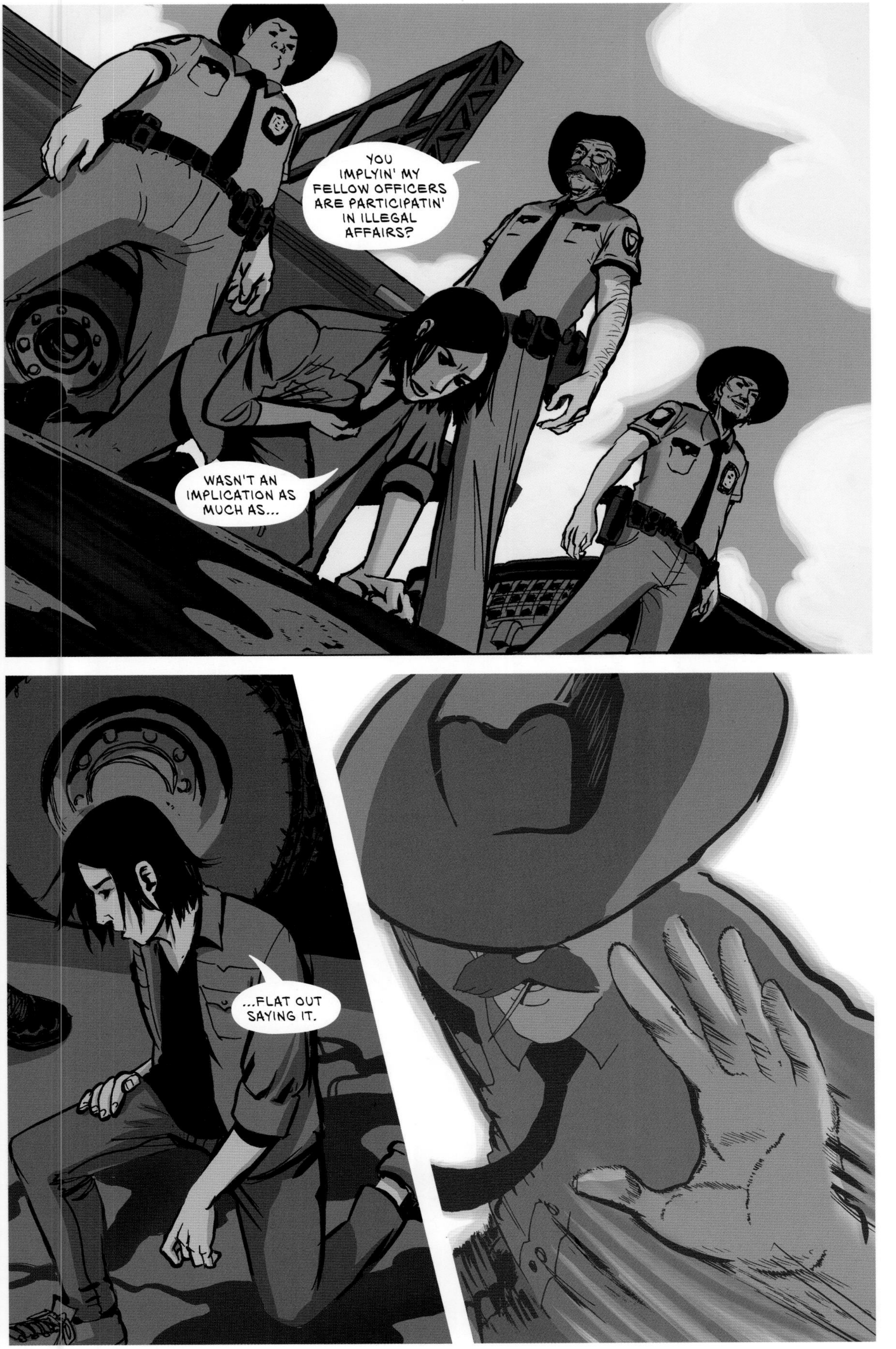
YOU IMPLYIN' MY FELLOW OFFICERS ARE PARTICIPATIN' IN ILLEGAL AFFAIRS?
WASN'T AN IMPLICATION AS MUCH AS...
...FLAT OUT SAYING IT.

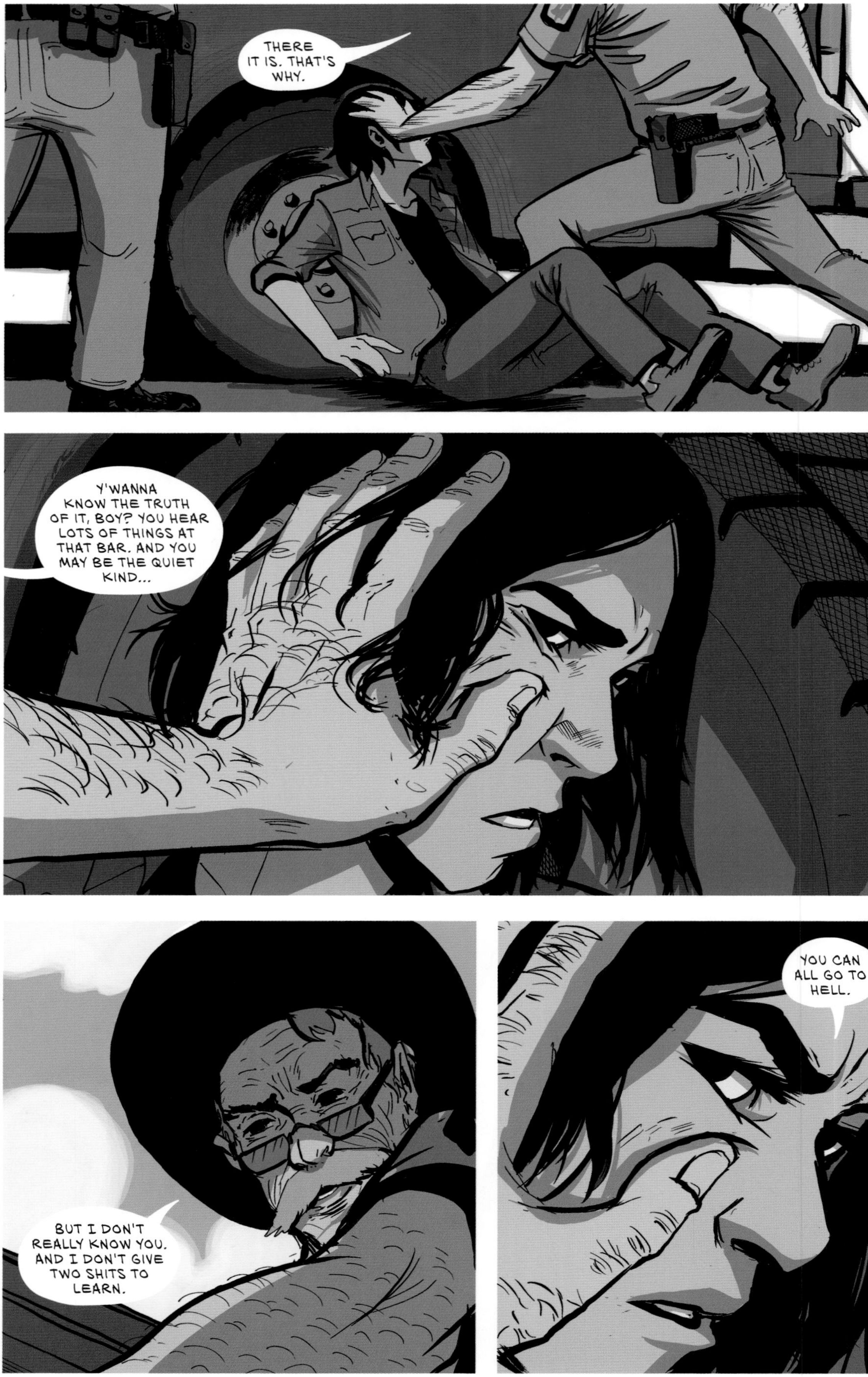
THERE IT IS. THAT'S WHY.
Y'WANNA KNOW THE TRUTH OF IT, BOY? YOU HEAR LOTS OF THINGS AT THAT BAR. AND YOU MAY BE THE QUIET KIND...
BUT I DON'T REALLY KNOW YOU. AND I DON'T GIVE TWO SHITS TO LEARN.
YOU CAN ALL GO TO HELL.

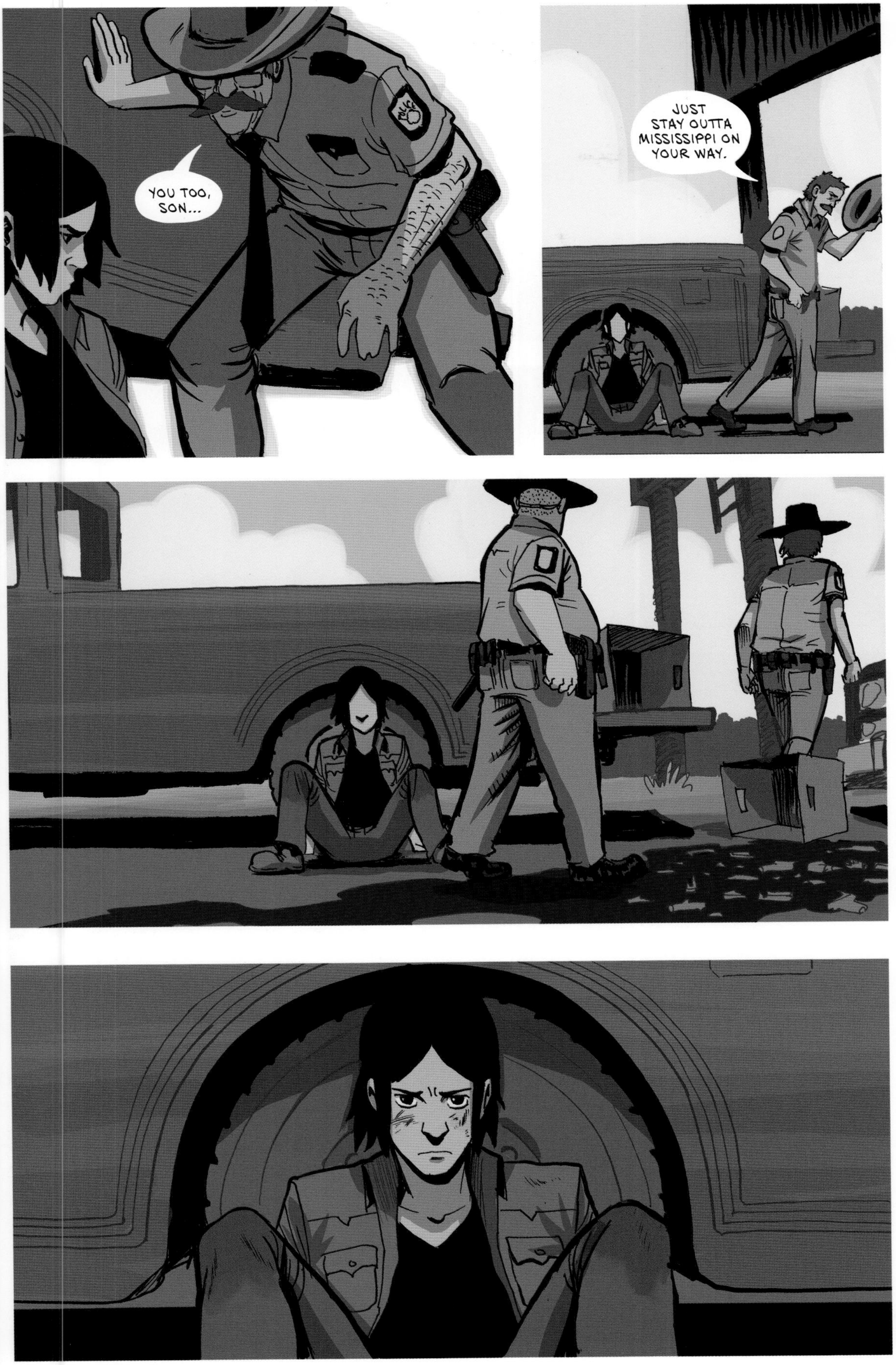
YOU TOO, SON...
JUST STAY OUTTA MISSISSIPPI ON YOUR WAY.

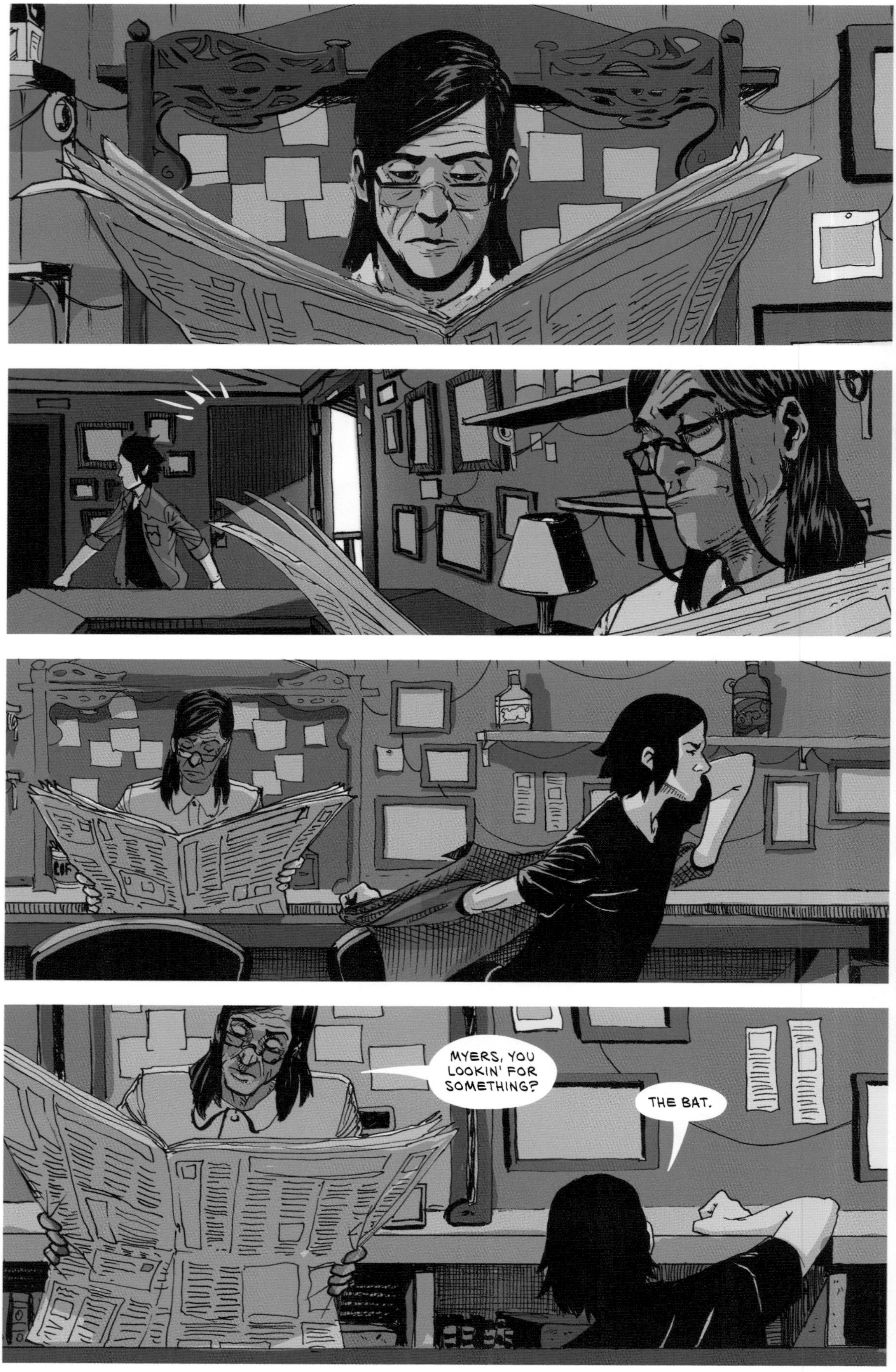
MYERS, YOU LOOKIN' FOR SOMETHING?
THE BAT.

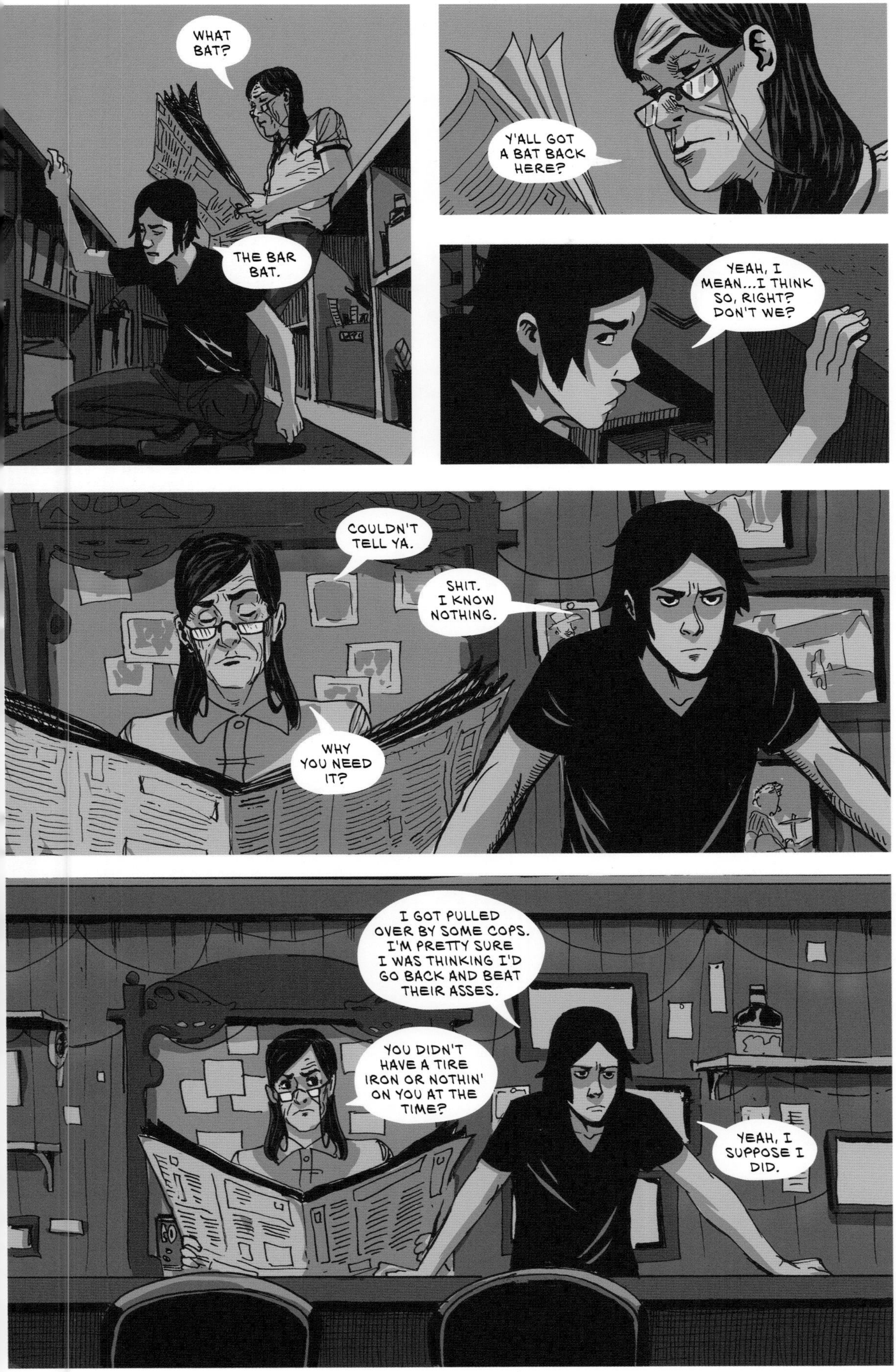
WHAT BAT?
THE BAR BAT.
Y'ALL GOT A BAT BACK HERE?
YEAH, I MEAN...I THINK SO, RIGHT? DON'T WE?
COULDN'T TELL YA.
SHIT. I KNOW NOTHING.
WHY YOU NEED IT?
I GOT PULLED OVER BY SOME COPS. I'M PRETTY SURE I WAS THINKING I'D GO BACK AND BEAT THEIR ASSES.
YOU DIDN'T HAVE A TIRE IRON OR NOTHIN' ON YOU AT THE TIME?
YEAH, I SUPPOSE I DID.

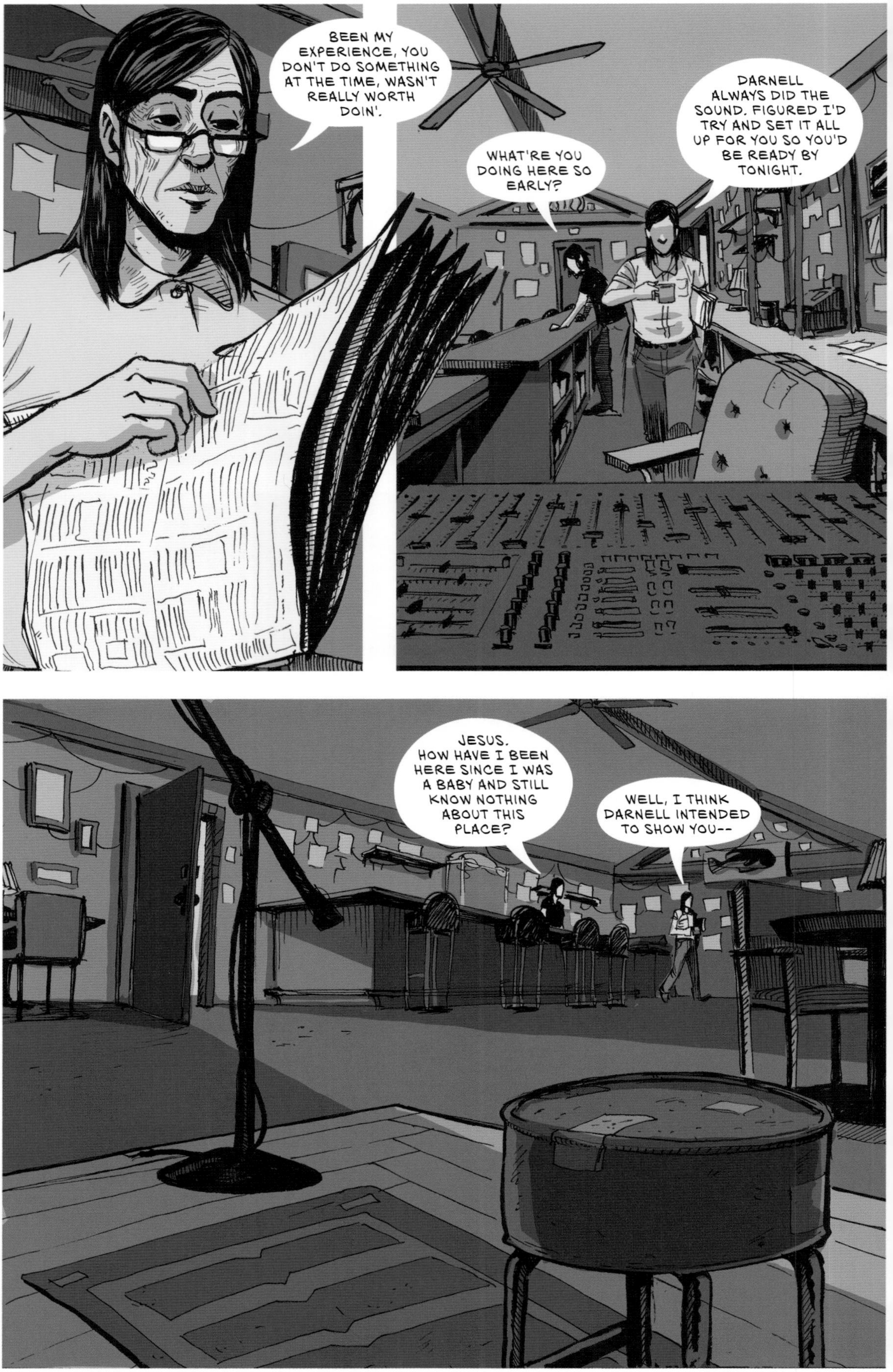
BEEN MY EXPERIENCE, YOU DON'T DO SOMETHING AT THE TIME, WASN'T REALLY WORTH DOIN'.
WHAT'RE YOU DOING HERE SO EARLY?
DARNELL ALWAYS DID THE SOUND. FIGURED I'D TRY AND SET IT ALL UP FOR YOU SO YOU'D BE READY BY TONIGHT.
JESUS. HOW HAVE I BEEN HERE SINCE I WAS A BABY AND STILL KNOW NOTHING ABOUT THIS PLACE?
WELL, I THINK DARNELL INTENDED TO SHOW YOU--

HE DIDN'T.

THE BAND SHOULD BE GOOD FOR TONIGHT. JUST LET 'EM KNOW ABOUT THAT FADER. IT STICKS.

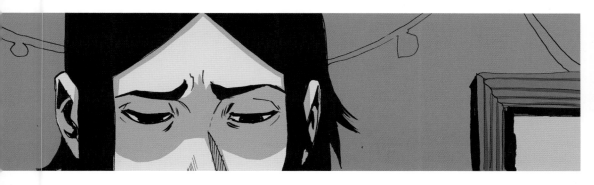

# CHAPTER THREE

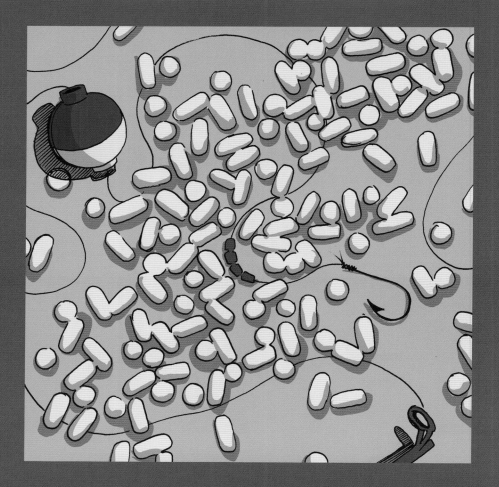

# RODS AND LURES

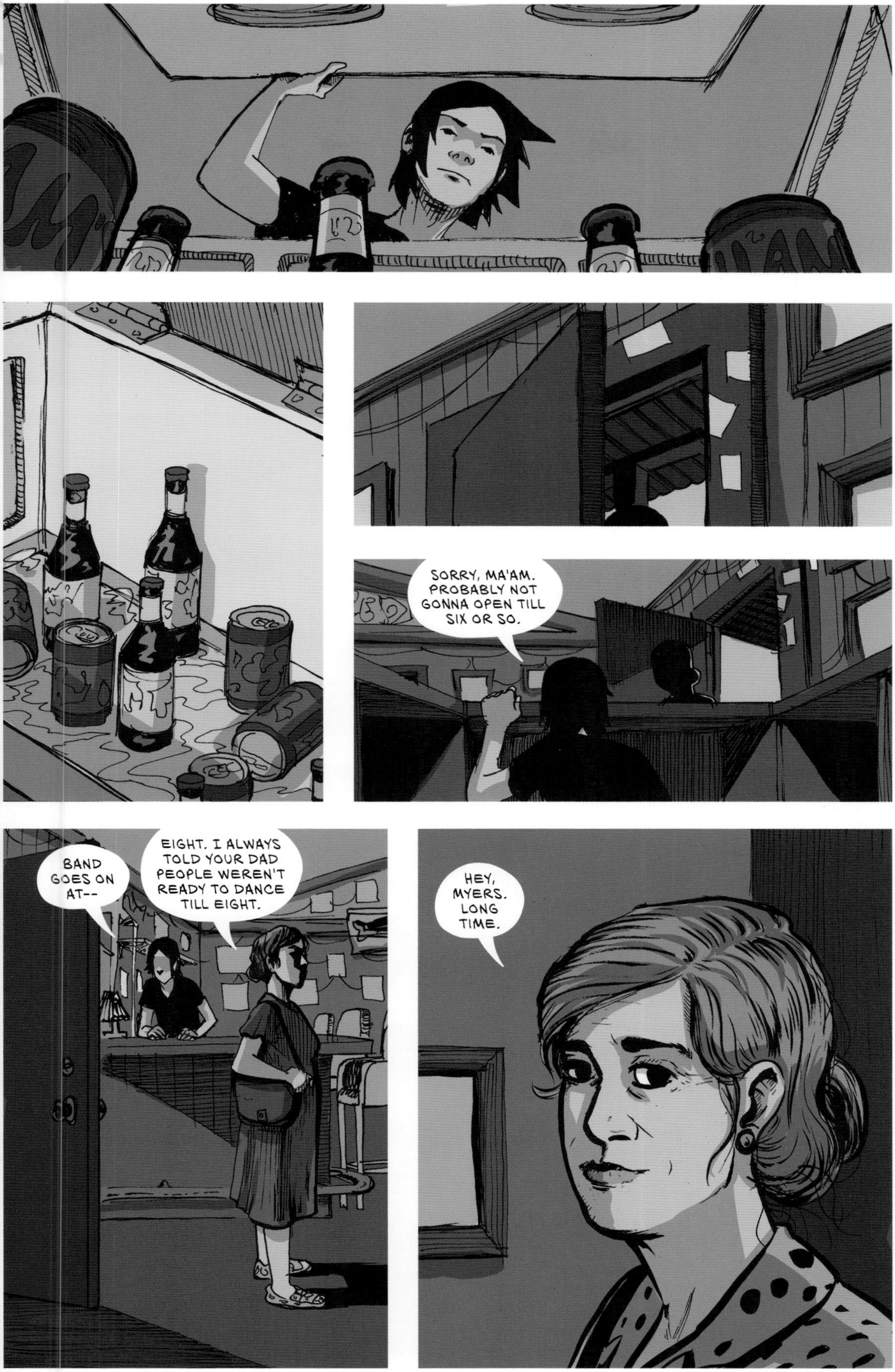
SORRY, MA'AM. PROBABLY NOT GONNA OPEN TILL SIX OR SO.
BAND GOES ON AT--
EIGHT. I ALWAYS TOLD YOUR DAD PEOPLE WEREN'T READY TO DANCE TILL EIGHT.
HEY, MYERS. LONG TIME.

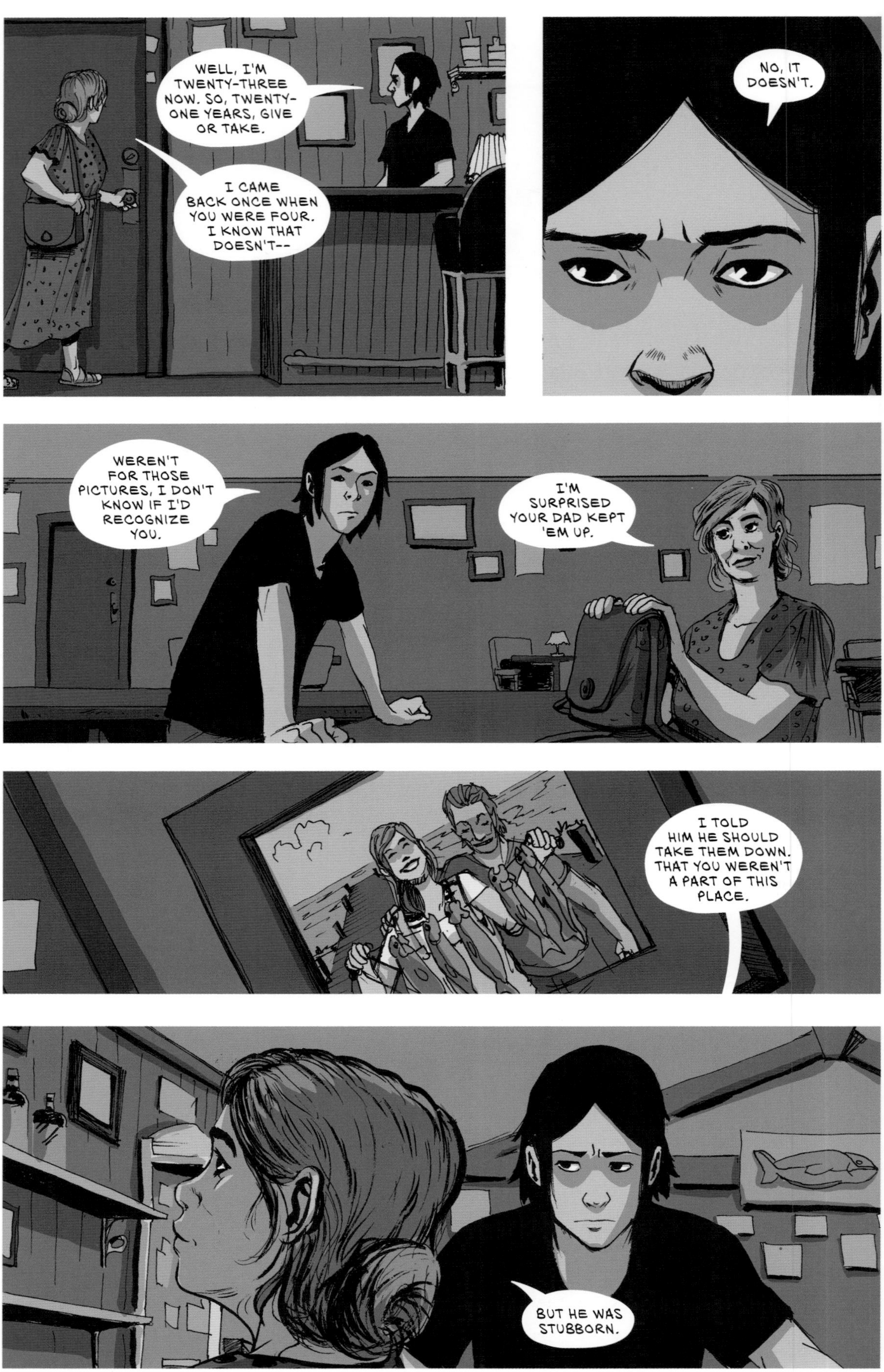
WELL, I'M TWENTY-THREE NOW. SO, TWENTY-ONE YEARS, GIVE OR TAKE.
I CAME BACK ONCE WHEN YOU WERE FOUR. I KNOW THAT DOESN'T--
NO, IT DOESN'T.
WEREN'T FOR THOSE PICTURES, I DON'T KNOW IF I'D RECOGNIZE YOU.
I'M SURPRISED YOUR DAD KEPT 'EM UP.
I TOLD HIM HE SHOULD TAKE THEM DOWN. THAT YOU WEREN'T A PART OF THIS PLACE.
BUT HE WAS STUBBORN.

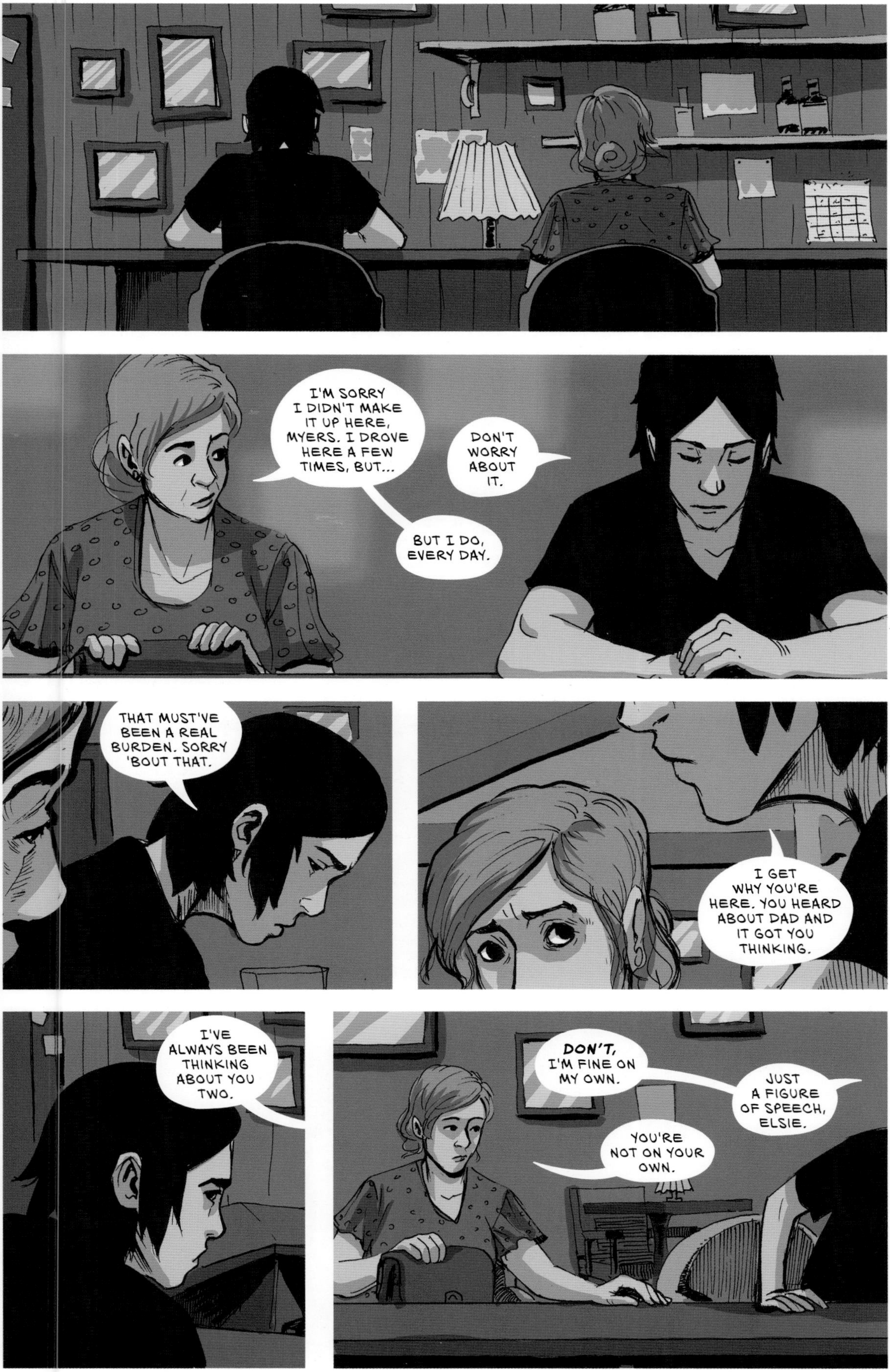
I'M SORRY I DIDN'T MAKE IT UP HERE, MYERS. I DROVE HERE A FEW TIMES, BUT...
DON'T WORRY ABOUT IT.
BUT I DO, EVERY DAY.
THAT MUST'VE BEEN A REAL BURDEN. SORRY 'BOUT THAT.
I GET WHY YOU'RE HERE. YOU HEARD ABOUT DAD AND IT GOT YOU THINKING.
I'VE ALWAYS BEEN THINKING ABOUT YOU TWO.
DON'T, I'M FINE ON MY OWN.
JUST A FIGURE OF SPEECH, ELSIE.
YOU'RE NOT ON YOUR OWN.

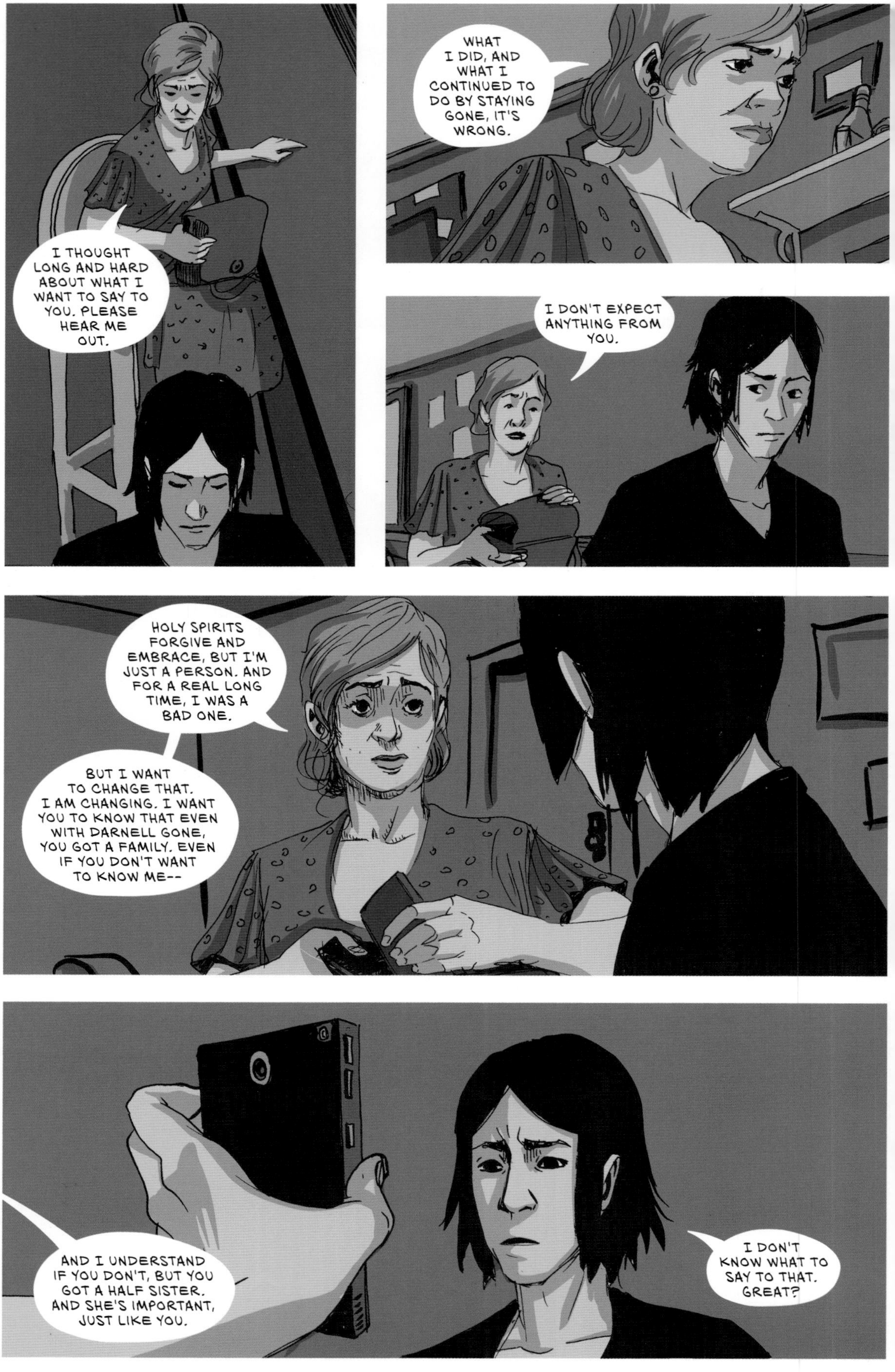
I THOUGHT LONG AND HARD ABOUT WHAT I WANT TO SAY TO YOU. PLEASE HEAR ME OUT.
WHAT I DID, AND WHAT I CONTINUED TO DO BY STAYING GONE, IT'S WRONG.
I DON'T EXPECT ANYTHING FROM YOU.
HOLY SPIRITS FORGIVE AND EMBRACE, BUT I'M JUST A PERSON. AND FOR A REAL LONG TIME, I WAS A BAD ONE.
BUT I WANT TO CHANGE THAT. I AM CHANGING. I WANT YOU TO KNOW THAT EVEN WITH DARNELL GONE, YOU GOT A FAMILY. EVEN IF YOU DON'T WANT TO KNOW ME--
AND I UNDERSTAND IF YOU DON'T, BUT YOU GOT A HALF SISTER. AND SHE'S IMPORTANT, JUST LIKE YOU.
I DON'T KNOW WHAT TO SAY TO THAT. GREAT?

THIS IS A LOT, AND I KNOW IT'S UNFAIR TO JUST LET YOU KNOW OUT OF NOWHERE.

I JUST NEED YOU TO KNOW WE'RE NOT FAR. SHE'S NOT FAR.

AND WE WANT TO HELP. ALL OF US.

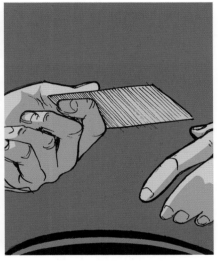

YOU **OWN** THE FATHER OF WATERS NOW?

ME AND MY HUSBAND, 'BOUT TWELVE YEARS NOW.

WOW, THAT'S **WHAT?** TWO, THREE HOURS AWAY?

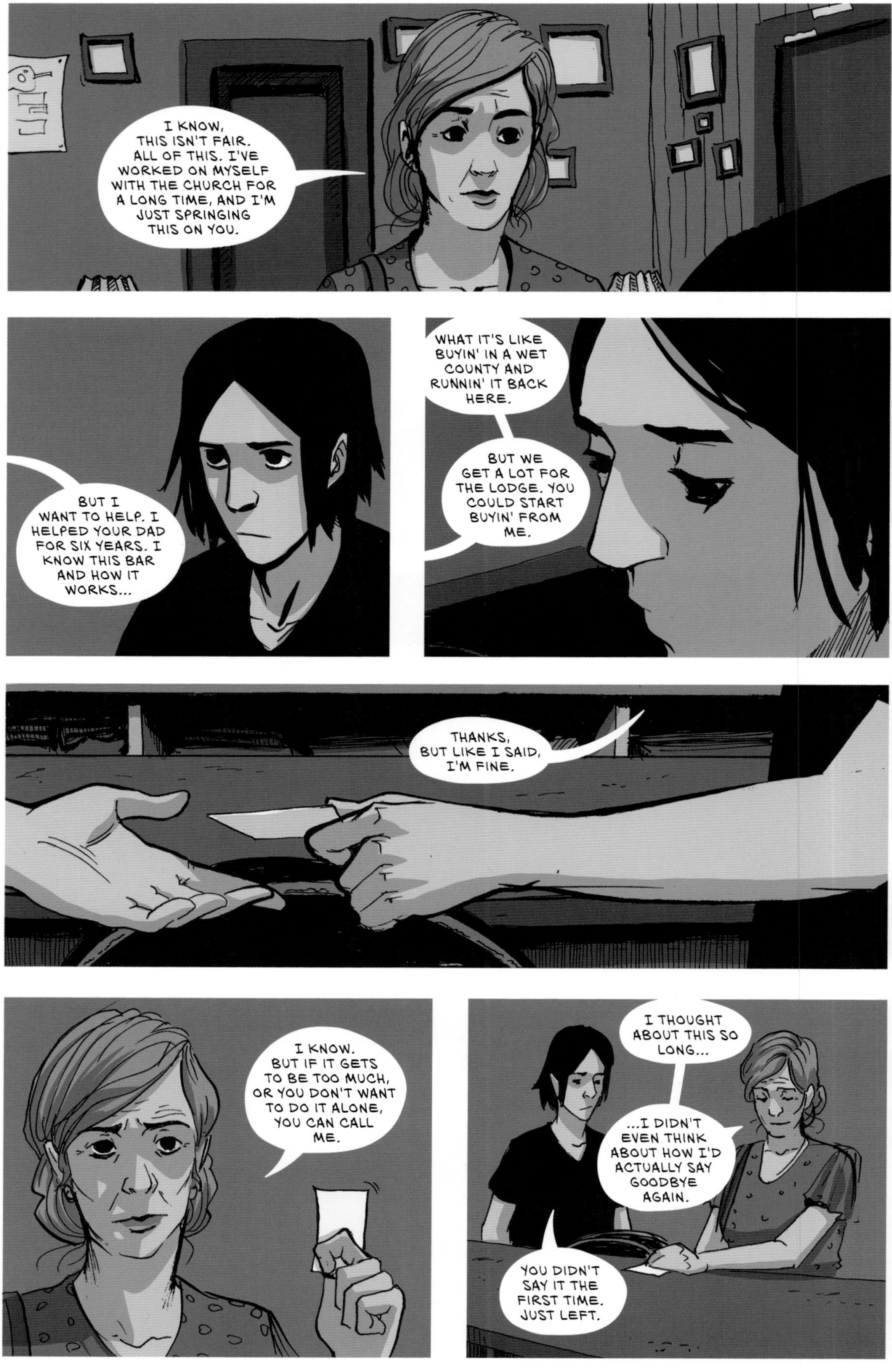
I KNOW, THIS ISN'T FAIR. ALL OF THIS. I'VE WORKED ON MYSELF WITH THE CHURCH FOR A LONG TIME, AND I'M JUST SPRINGING THIS ON YOU.
BUT I WANT TO HELP. I HELPED YOUR DAD FOR SIX YEARS. I KNOW THIS BAR AND HOW IT WORKS...
WHAT IT'S LIKE BUYIN' IN A WET COUNTY AND RUNNIN' IT BACK HERE.
BUT WE GET A LOT FOR THE LODGE. YOU COULD START BUYIN' FROM ME.
THANKS, BUT LIKE I SAID, I'M FINE.
I KNOW. BUT IF IT GETS TO BE TOO MUCH, OR YOU DON'T WANT TO DO IT ALONE, YOU CAN CALL ME.
I THOUGHT ABOUT THIS SO LONG...
...I DIDN'T EVEN THINK ABOUT HOW I'D ACTUALLY SAY GOODBYE AGAIN.
YOU DIDN'T SAY IT THE FIRST TIME. JUST LEFT.

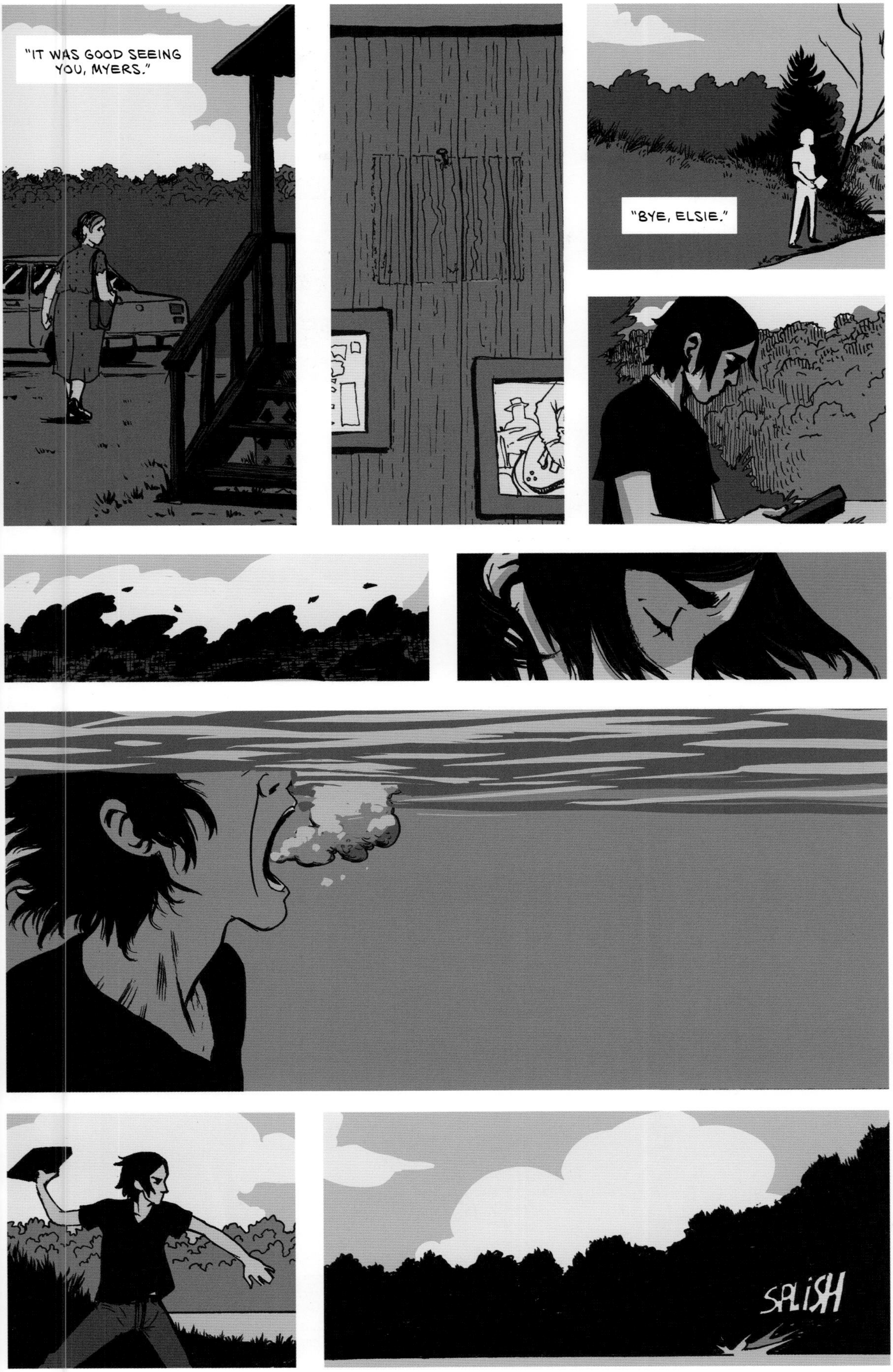
"IT WAS GOOD SEEING YOU, MYERS."
"BYE, ELSIE."
SPLISH

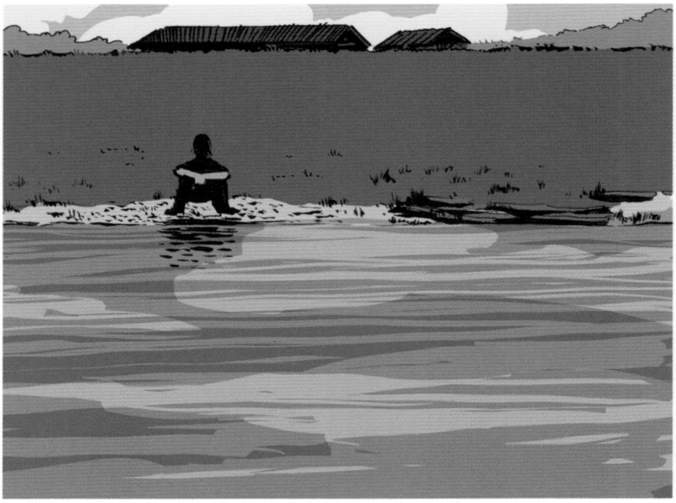

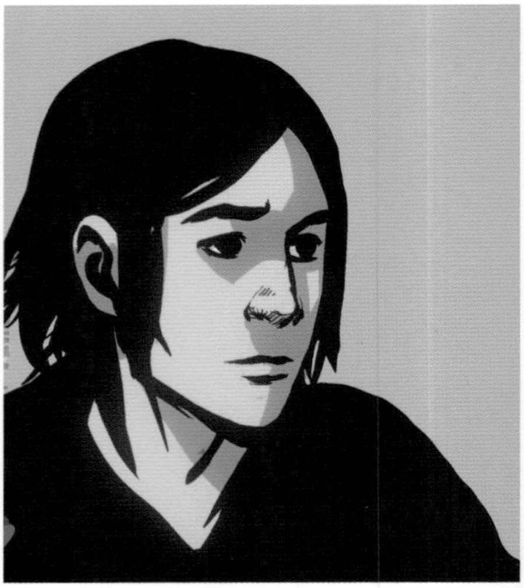

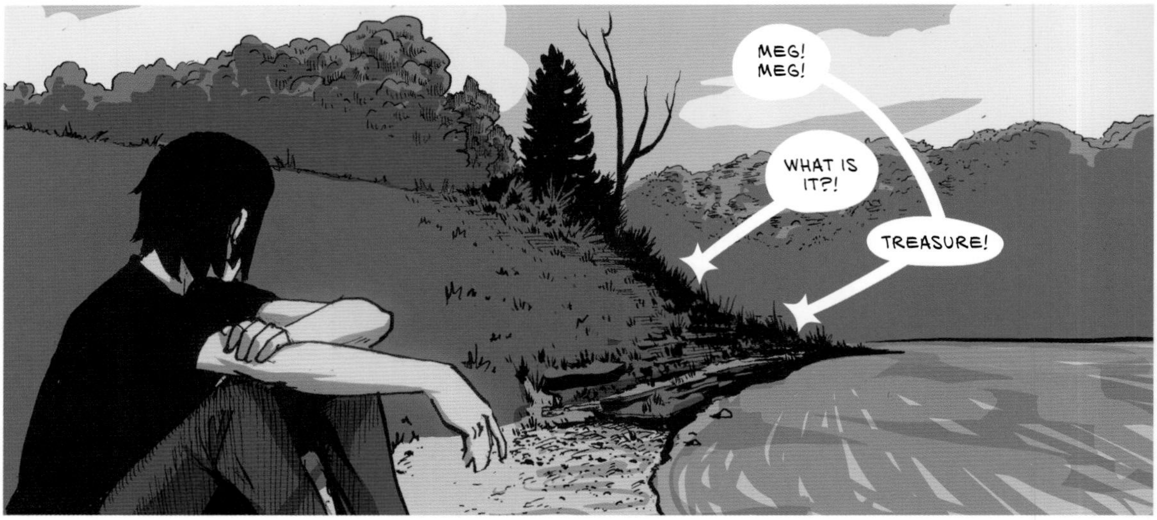
MEG! MEG!
WHAT IS IT?!
TREASURE!

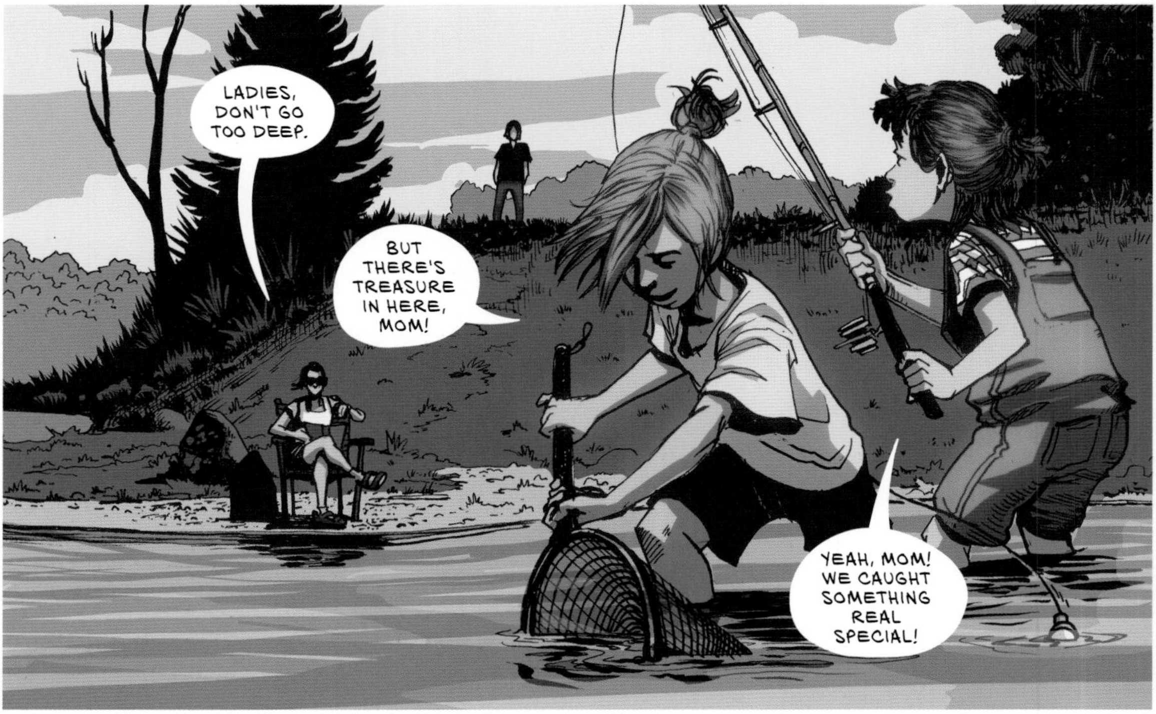
LADIES, DON'T GO TOO DEEP.
BUT THERE'S TREASURE IN HERE, MOM!
YEAH, MOM! WE CAUGHT SOMETHING REAL SPECIAL!

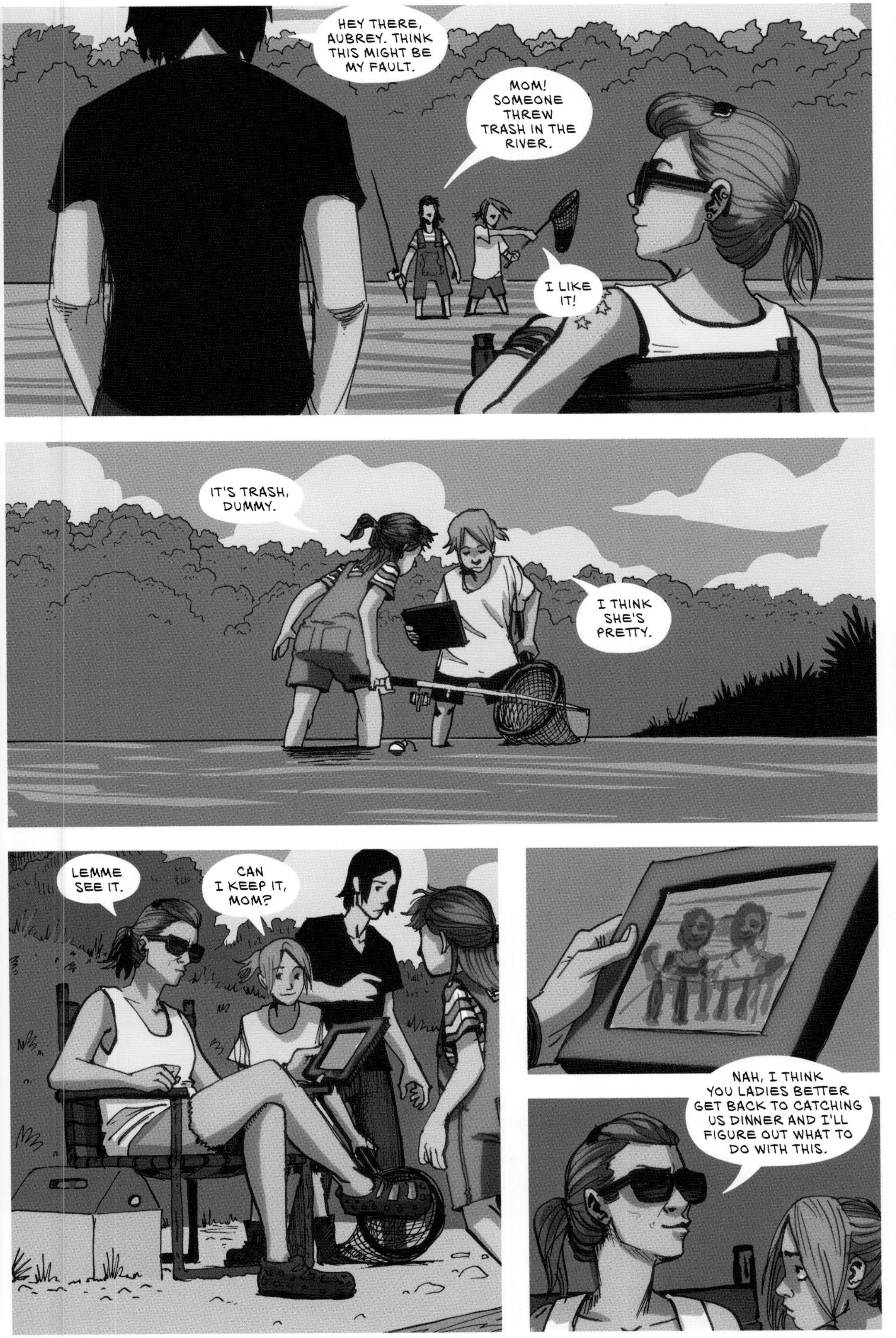
HEY THERE, AUBREY. THINK THIS MIGHT BE MY FAULT.
MOM! SOMEONE THREW TRASH IN THE RIVER.
I LIKE IT!
IT'S TRASH, DUMMY.
I THINK SHE'S PRETTY.
LEMME SEE IT.
CAN I KEEP IT, MOM?
NAH, I THINK YOU LADIES BETTER GET BACK TO CATCHING US DINNER AND I'LL FIGURE OUT WHAT TO DO WITH THIS.

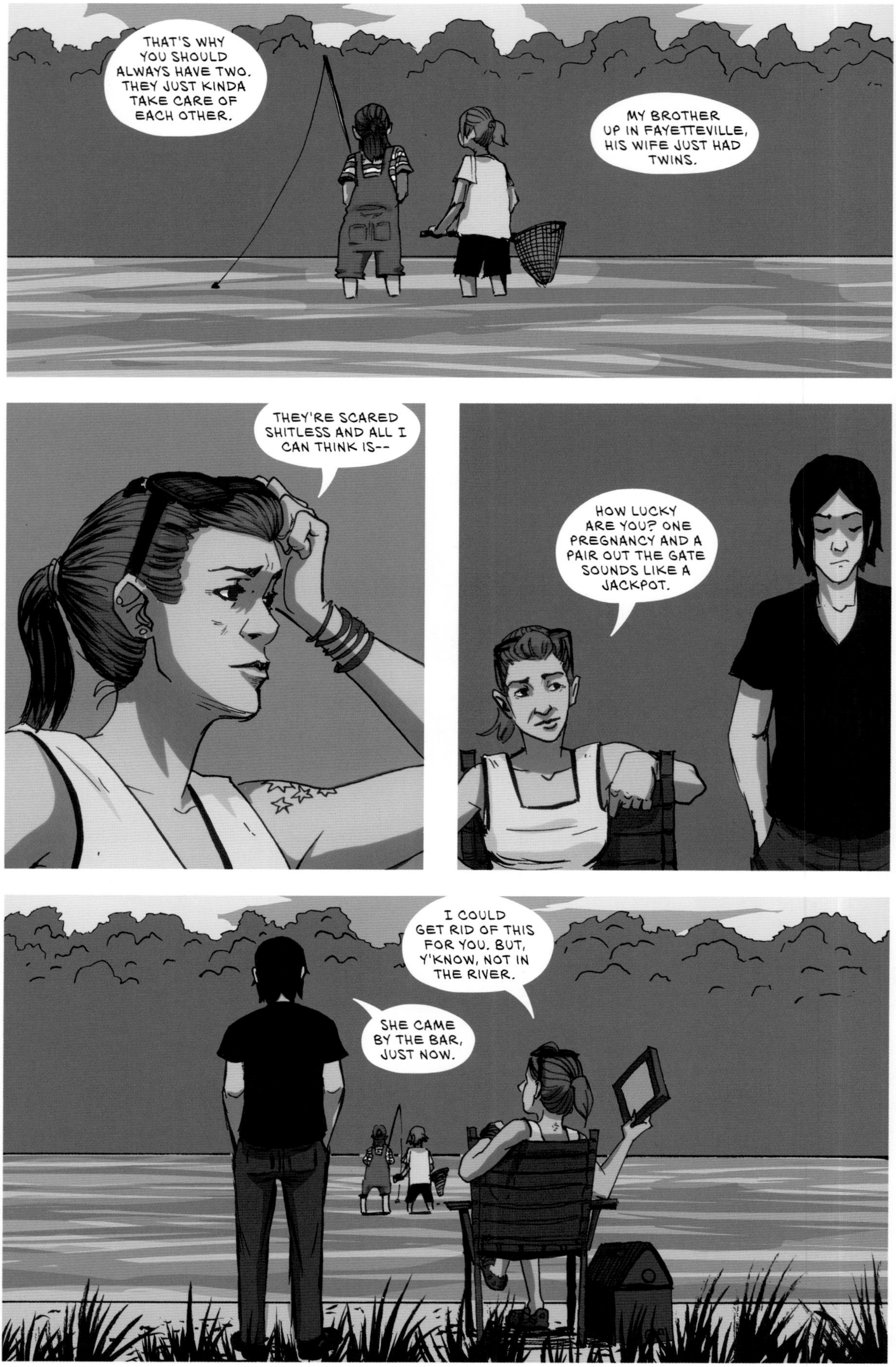
THAT'S WHY YOU SHOULD ALWAYS HAVE TWO. THEY JUST KINDA TAKE CARE OF EACH OTHER.
MY BROTHER UP IN FAYETTEVILLE, HIS WIFE JUST HAD TWINS.
THEY'RE SCARED SHITLESS AND ALL I CAN THINK IS--
HOW LUCKY ARE YOU? ONE PREGNANCY AND A PAIR OUT THE GATE SOUNDS LIKE A JACKPOT.
I COULD GET RID OF THIS FOR YOU. BUT, Y'KNOW, NOT IN THE RIVER.
SHE CAME BY THE BAR, JUST NOW.

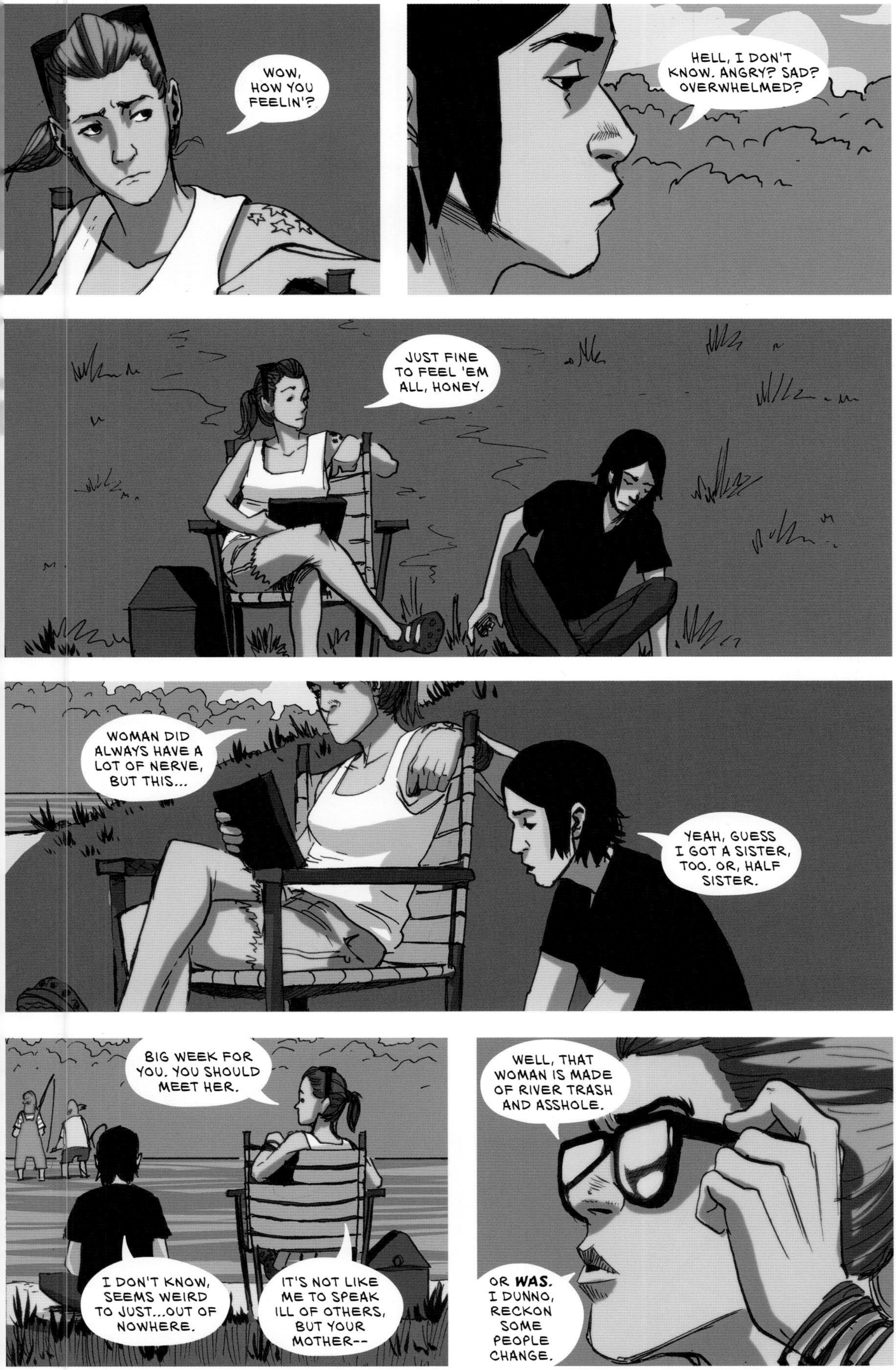
WOW, HOW YOU FEELIN'?
HELL, I DON'T KNOW. ANGRY? SAD? OVERWHELMED?
JUST FINE TO FEEL 'EM ALL, HONEY.
WOMAN DID ALWAYS HAVE A LOT OF NERVE, BUT THIS...
YEAH, GUESS I GOT A SISTER, TOO. OR, HALF SISTER.
BIG WEEK FOR YOU. YOU SHOULD MEET HER.
I DON'T KNOW, SEEMS WEIRD TO JUST...OUT OF NOWHERE.
IT'S NOT LIKE ME TO SPEAK ILL OF OTHERS, BUT YOUR MOTHER--
WELL, THAT WOMAN IS MADE OF RIVER TRASH AND ASSHOLE.
OR **WAS.** I DUNNO, RECKON SOME PEOPLE CHANGE.

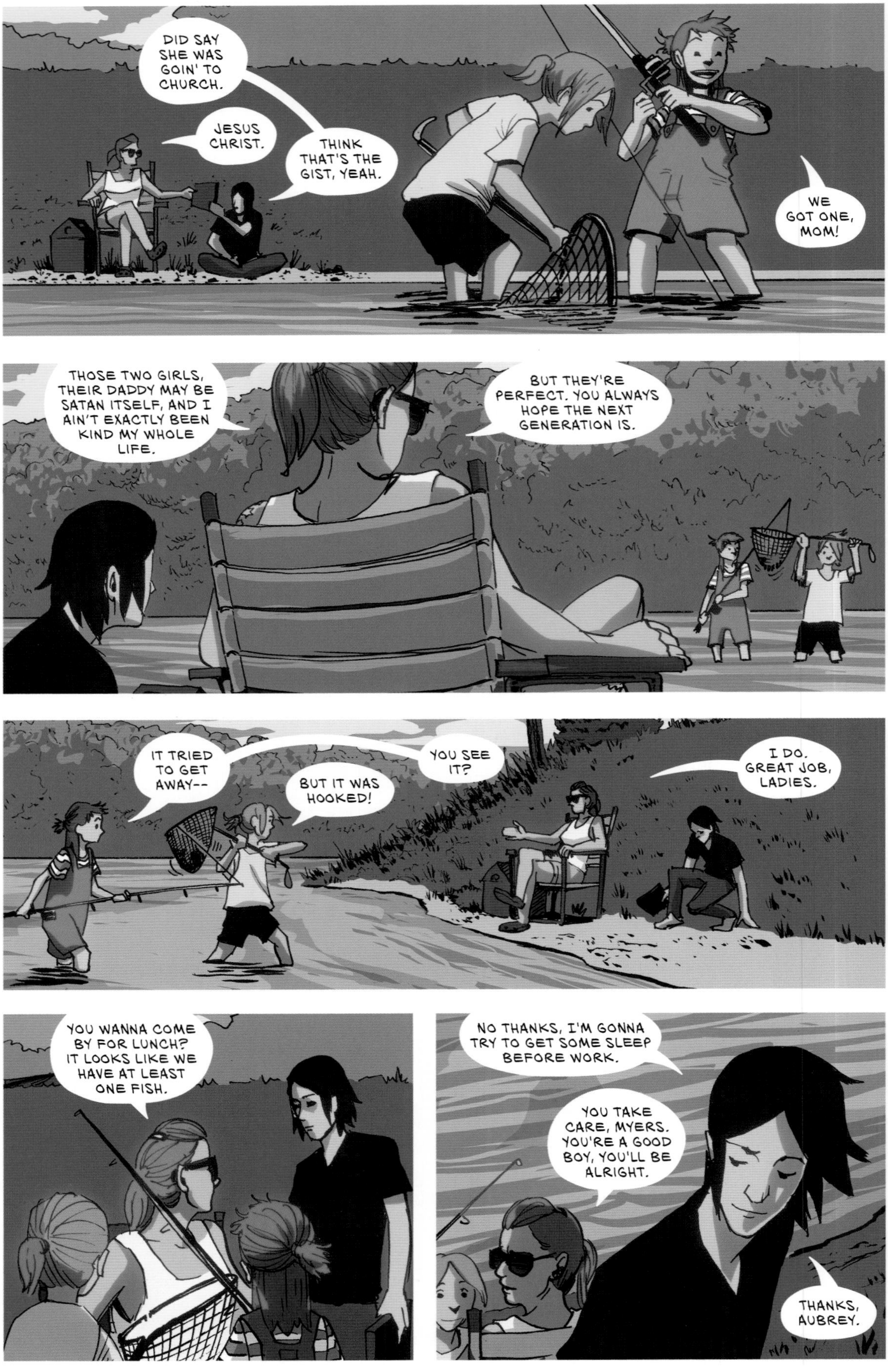
DID SAY SHE WAS GOIN' TO CHURCH.
JESUS CHRIST.
THINK THAT'S THE GIST, YEAH.
WE GOT ONE, MOM!
THOSE TWO GIRLS, THEIR DADDY MAY BE SATAN ITSELF, AND I AIN'T EXACTLY BEEN KIND MY WHOLE LIFE.
BUT THEY'RE PERFECT. YOU ALWAYS HOPE THE NEXT GENERATION IS.
IT TRIED TO GET AWAY--
BUT IT WAS HOOKED!
YOU SEE IT?
I DO. GREAT JOB, LADIES.
YOU WANNA COME BY FOR LUNCH? IT LOOKS LIKE WE HAVE AT LEAST ONE FISH.
NO THANKS, I'M GONNA TRY TO GET SOME SLEEP BEFORE WORK.
YOU TAKE CARE, MYERS. YOU'RE A GOOD BOY, YOU'LL BE ALRIGHT.
THANKS, AUBREY.

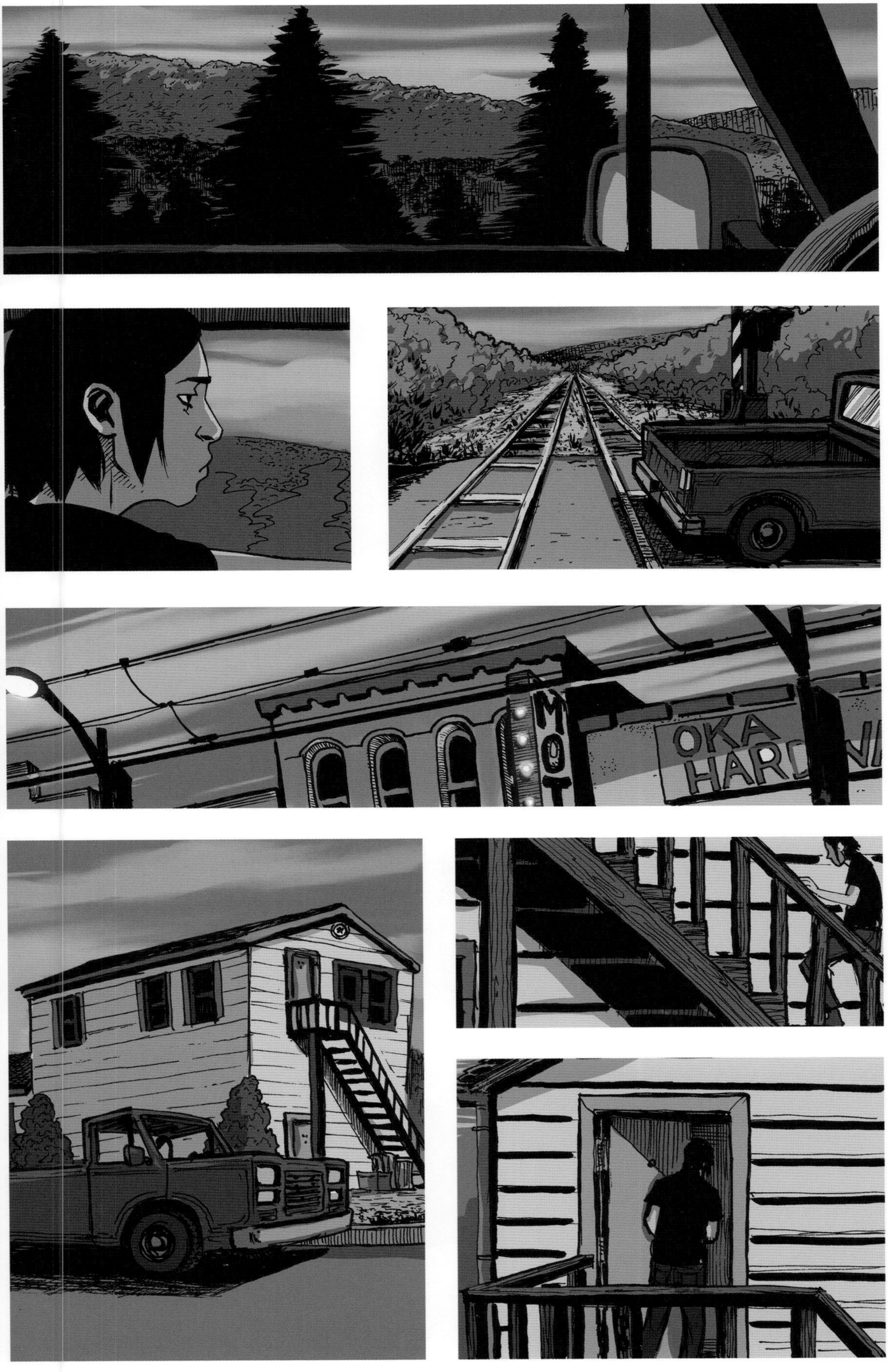
MOT
OKA
HARD

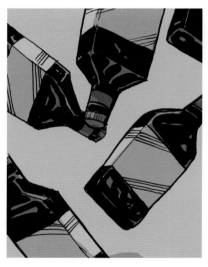

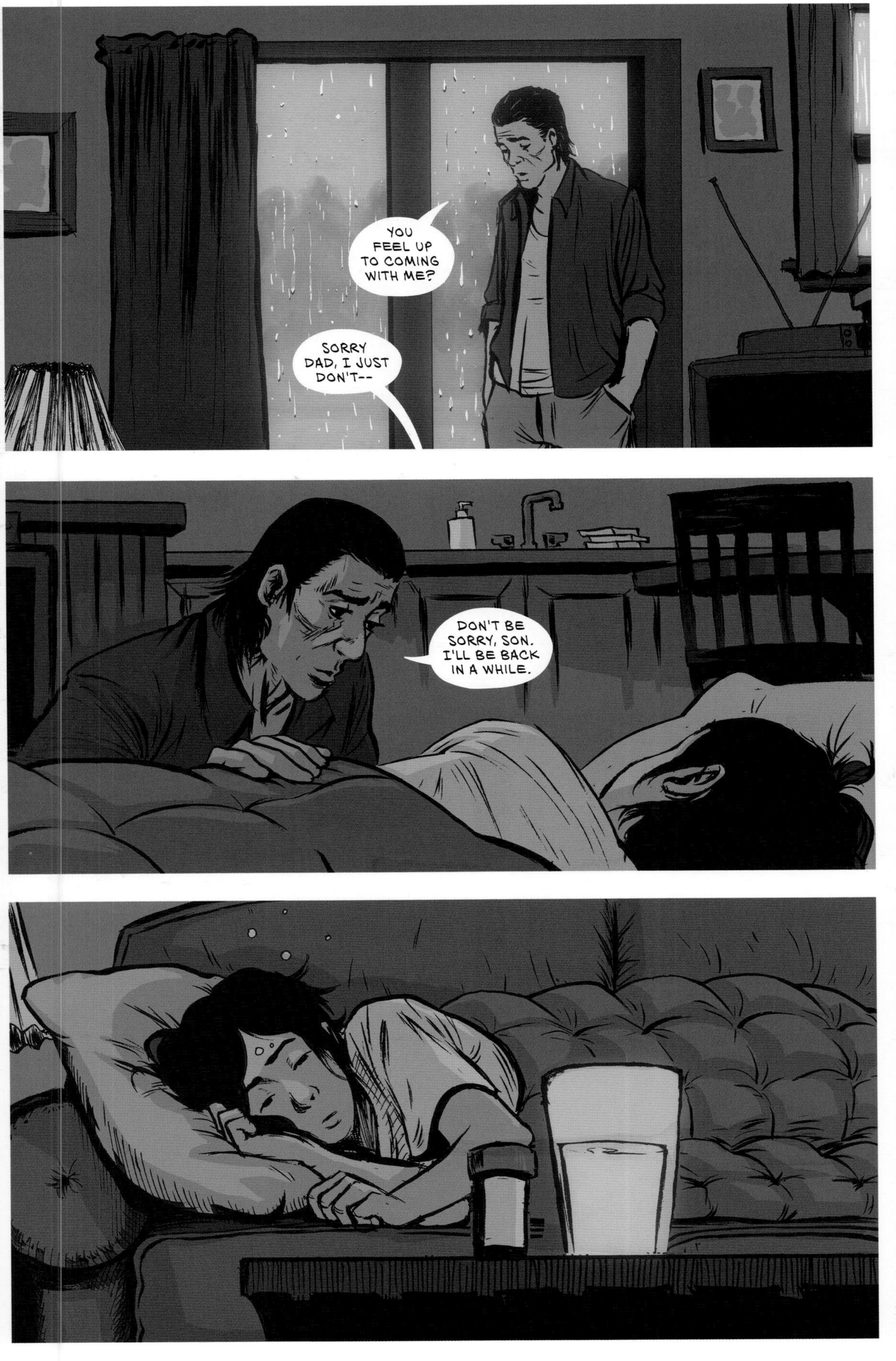
YOU FEEL UP TO COMING WITH ME?
SORRY DAD, I JUST DON'T--
DON'T BE SORRY, SON. I'LL BE BACK IN A WHILE.

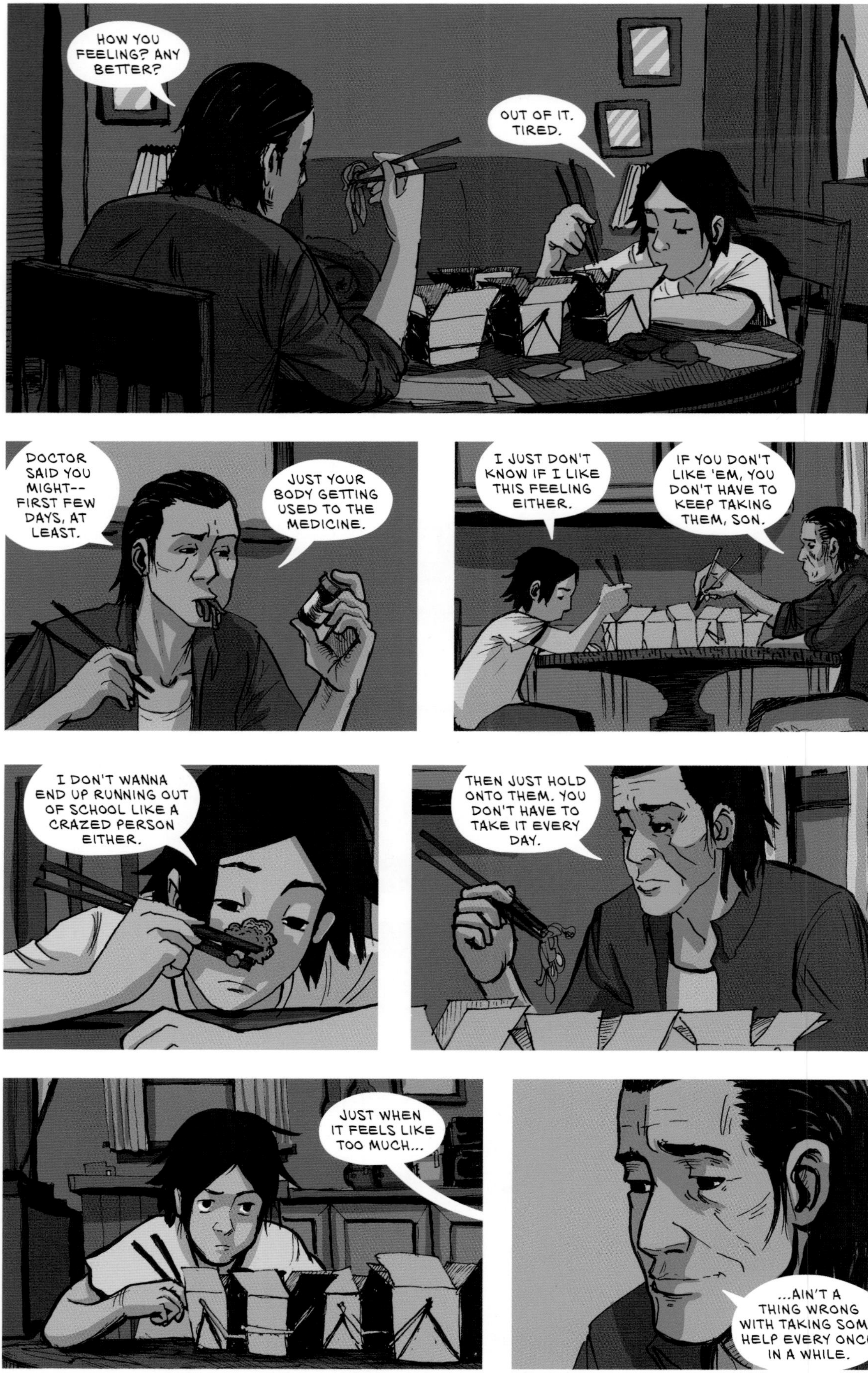
HOW YOU FEELING? ANY BETTER?
OUT OF IT. TIRED.
DOCTOR SAID YOU MIGHT-- FIRST FEW DAYS, AT LEAST.
JUST YOUR BODY GETTING USED TO THE MEDICINE.
I JUST DON'T KNOW IF I LIKE THIS FEELING EITHER.
IF YOU DON'T LIKE 'EM, YOU DON'T HAVE TO KEEP TAKING THEM, SON.
I DON'T WANNA END UP RUNNING OUT OF SCHOOL LIKE A CRAZED PERSON EITHER.
THEN JUST HOLD ONTO THEM. YOU DON'T HAVE TO TAKE IT EVERY DAY.
JUST WHEN IT FEELS LIKE TOO MUCH...
...AIN'T A THING WRONG WITH TAKING SOME HELP EVERY ONCE IN A WHILE.

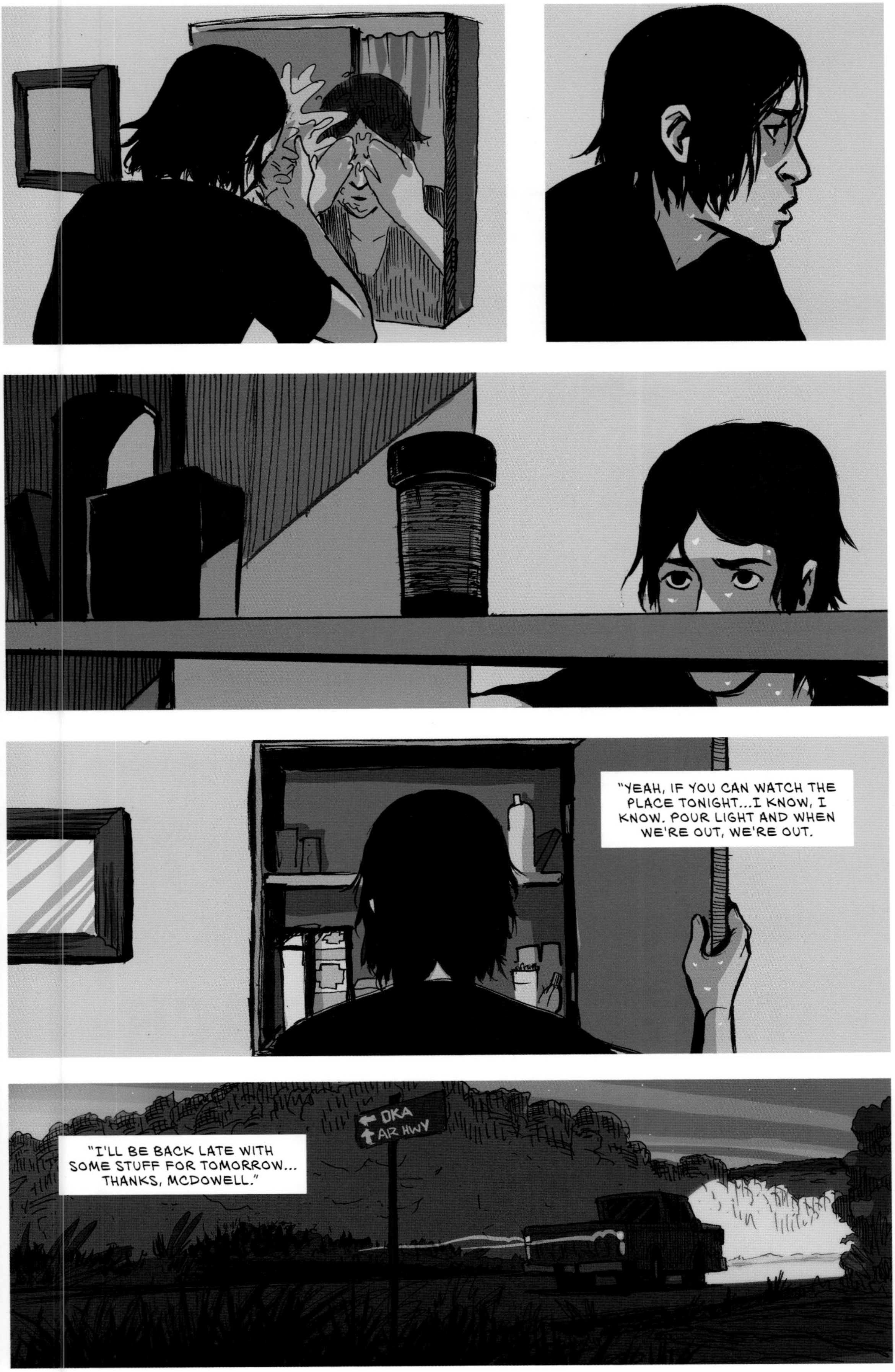
"YEAH, IF YOU CAN WATCH THE PLACE TONIGHT...I KNOW, I KNOW. POUR LIGHT AND WHEN WE'RE OUT, WE'RE OUT.
OKA
AR HWY
"I'LL BE BACK LATE WITH SOME STUFF FOR TOMORROW... THANKS, MCDOWELL."

# CHAPTER FOUR

# THESE ROOTS REACH
# THE RAFTERS

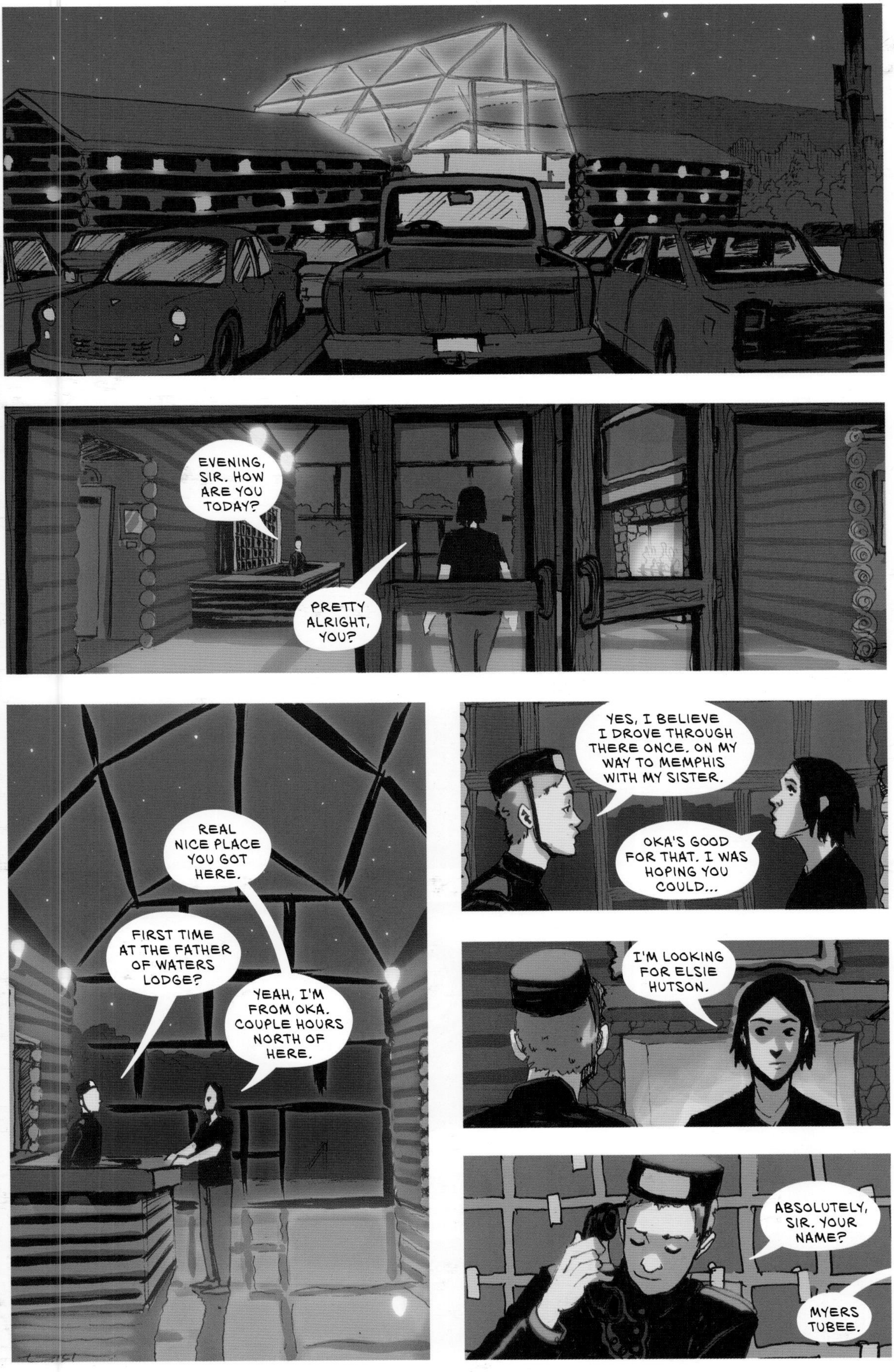
EVENING, SIR. HOW ARE YOU TODAY?
PRETTY ALRIGHT, YOU?
REAL NICE PLACE YOU GOT HERE.
FIRST TIME AT THE FATHER OF WATERS LODGE?
YEAH, I'M FROM OKA. COUPLE HOURS NORTH OF HERE.
YES, I BELIEVE I DROVE THROUGH THERE ONCE. ON MY WAY TO MEMPHIS WITH MY SISTER.
OKA'S GOOD FOR THAT. I WAS HOPING YOU COULD...
I'M LOOKING FOR ELSIE HUTSON.
ABSOLUTELY, SIR. YOUR NAME?
MYERS TUBEE.

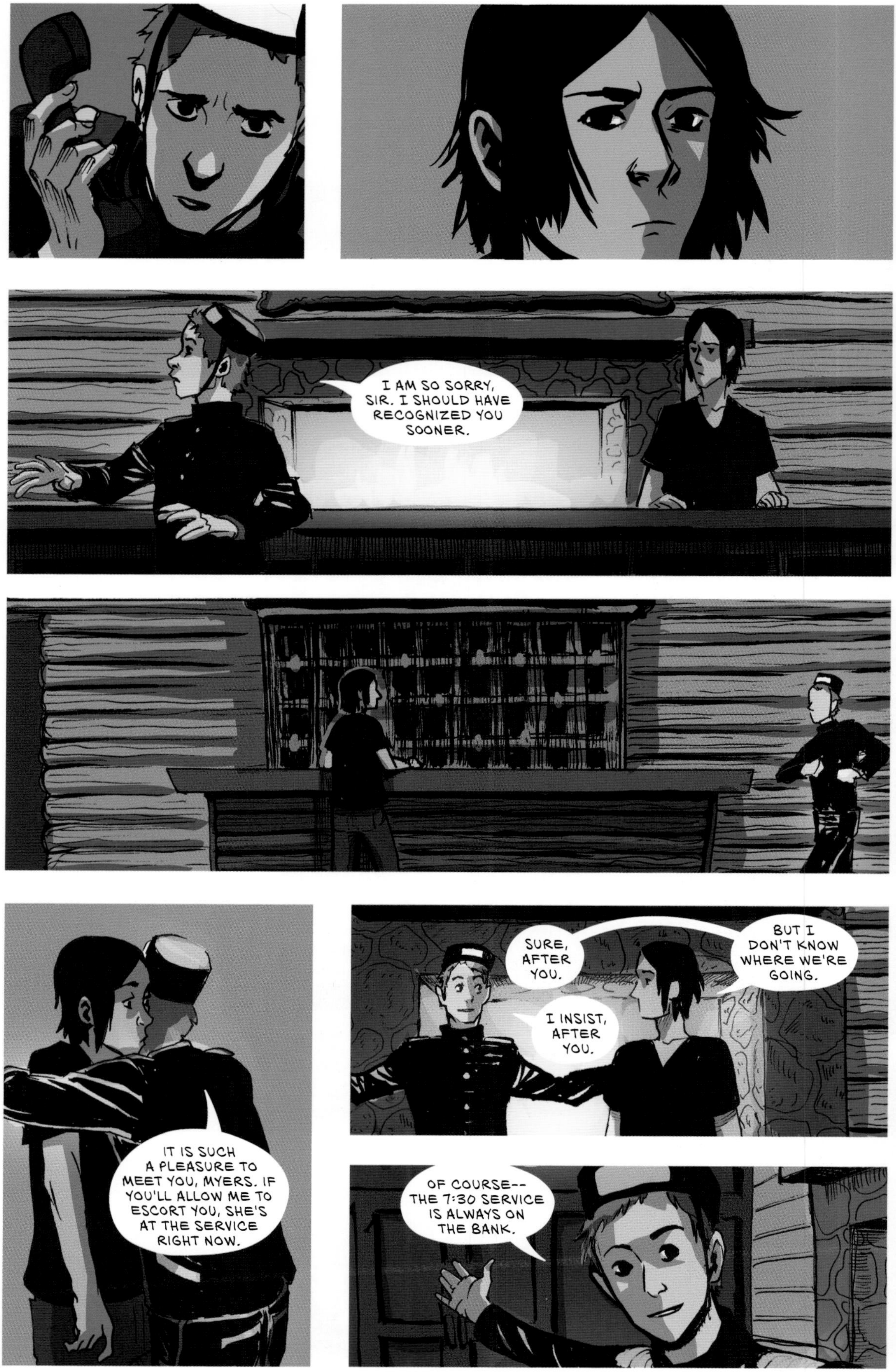
I AM SO SORRY, SIR. I SHOULD HAVE RECOGNIZED YOU SOONER.
IT IS SUCH A PLEASURE TO MEET YOU, MYERS. IF YOU'LL ALLOW ME TO ESCORT YOU, SHE'S AT THE SERVICE RIGHT NOW.
SURE, AFTER YOU.
BUT I DON'T KNOW WHERE WE'RE GOING.
I INSIST, AFTER YOU.
OF COURSE-- THE 7:30 SERVICE IS ALWAYS ON THE BANK.

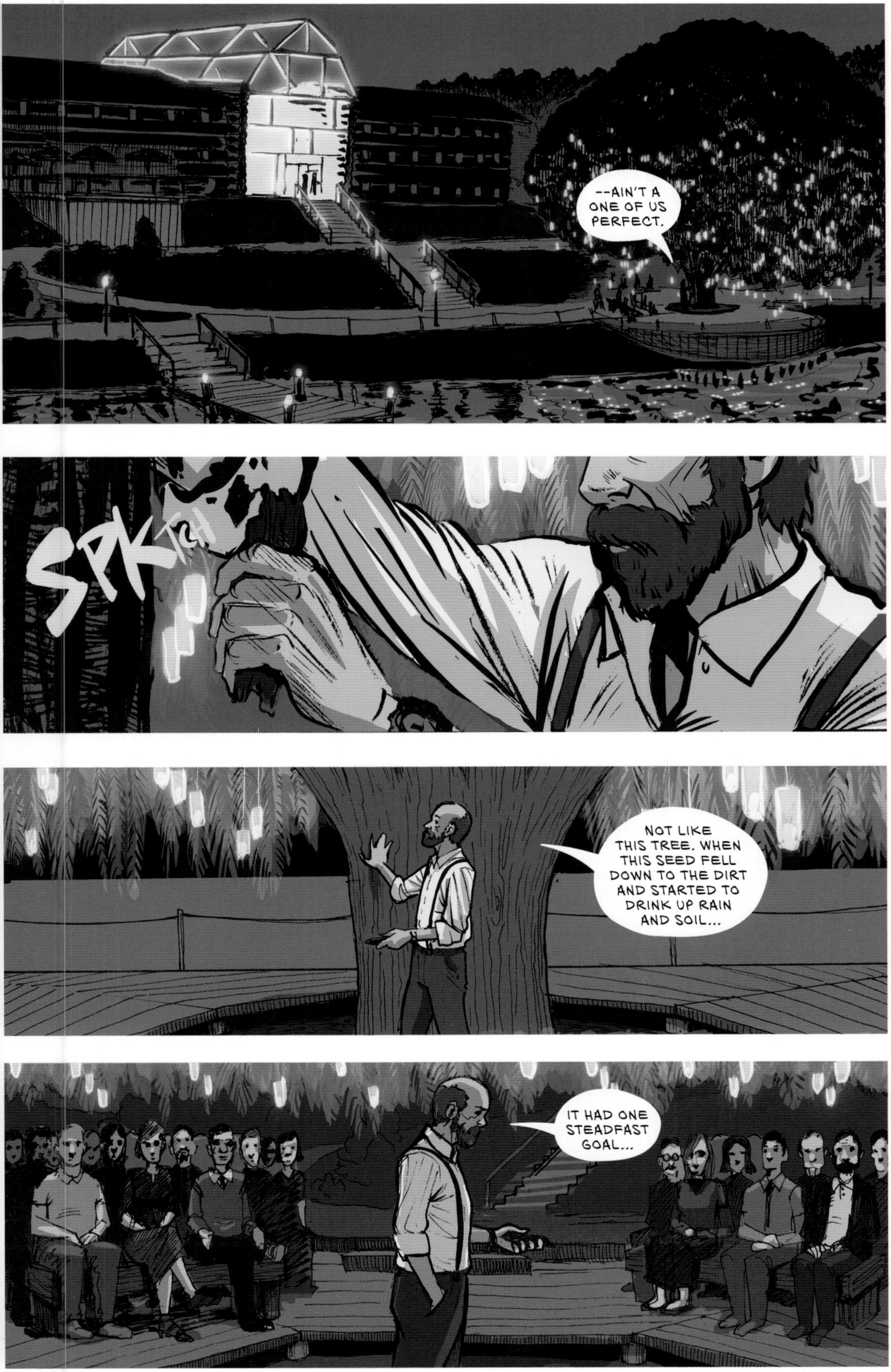
--AIN'T A ONE OF US PERFECT.
SPKTCH
NOT LIKE THIS TREE. WHEN THIS SEED FELL DOWN TO THE DIRT AND STARTED TO DRINK UP RAIN AND SOIL...
IT HAD ONE STEADFAST GOAL...

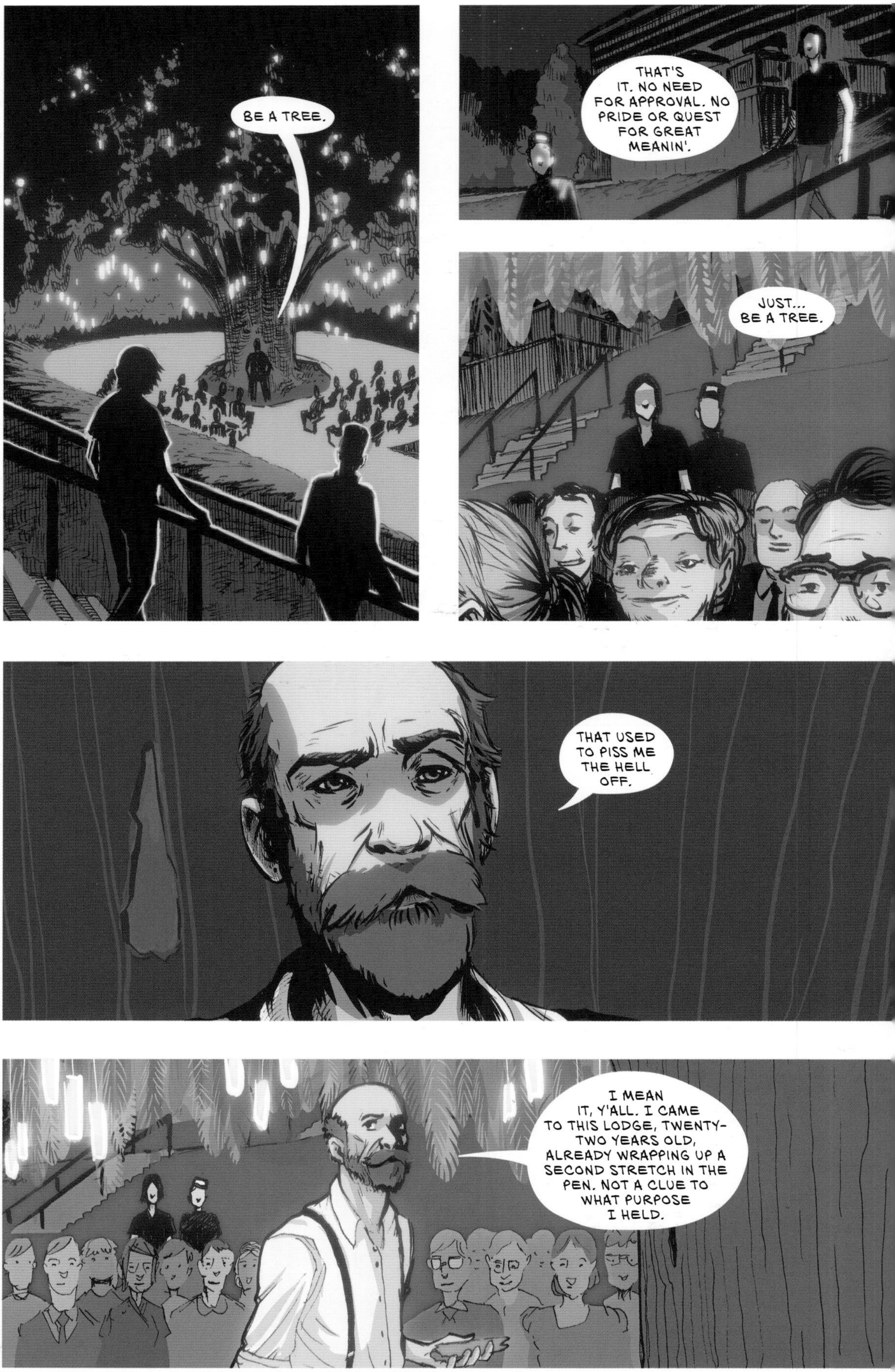
BE A TREE.
THAT'S IT. NO NEED FOR APPROVAL. NO PRIDE OR QUEST FOR GREAT MEANIN'.
JUST... BE A TREE.
THAT USED TO PISS ME THE HELL OFF.
I MEAN IT, Y'ALL. I CAME TO THIS LODGE, TWENTY-TWO YEARS OLD, ALREADY WRAPPING UP A SECOND STRETCH IN THE PEN. NOT A CLUE TO WHAT PURPOSE I HELD.

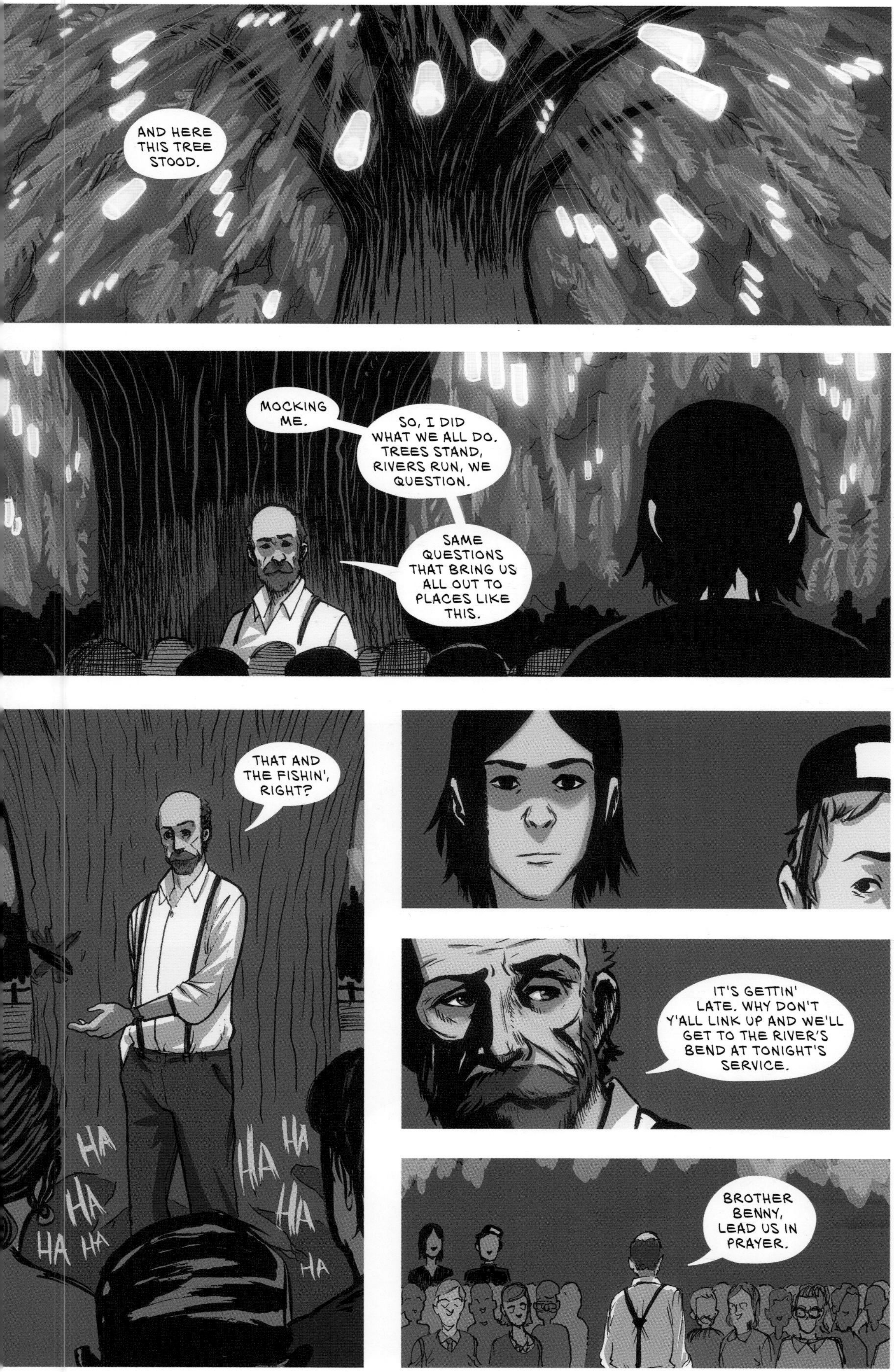
AND HERE THIS TREE STOOD.
MOCKING ME.
SO, I DID WHAT WE ALL DO. TREES STAND, RIVERS RUN, WE QUESTION.
SAME QUESTIONS THAT BRING US ALL OUT TO PLACES LIKE THIS.
THAT AND THE FISHIN', RIGHT?
HA HA HA HA HA HA HA HA HA
IT'S GETTIN' LATE. WHY DON'T Y'ALL LINK UP AND WE'LL GET TO THE RIVER'S BEND AT TONIGHT'S SERVICE.
BROTHER BENNY, LEAD US IN PRAYER.

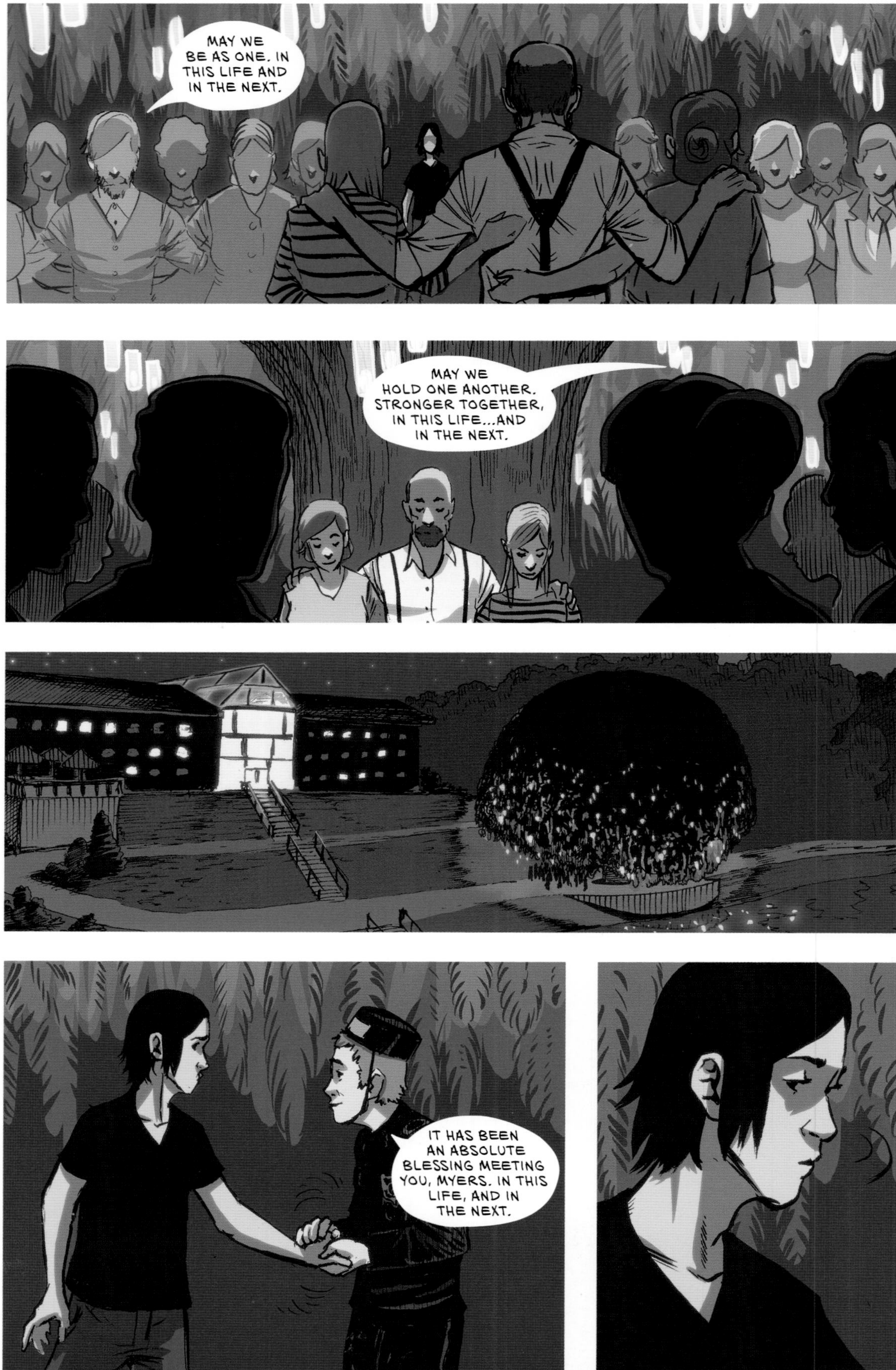
MAY WE BE AS ONE. IN THIS LIFE AND IN THE NEXT.
MAY WE HOLD ONE ANOTHER. STRONGER TOGETHER, IN THIS LIFE...AND IN THE NEXT.
IT HAS BEEN AN ABSOLUTE BLESSING MEETING YOU, MYERS. IN THIS LIFE, AND IN THE NEXT.

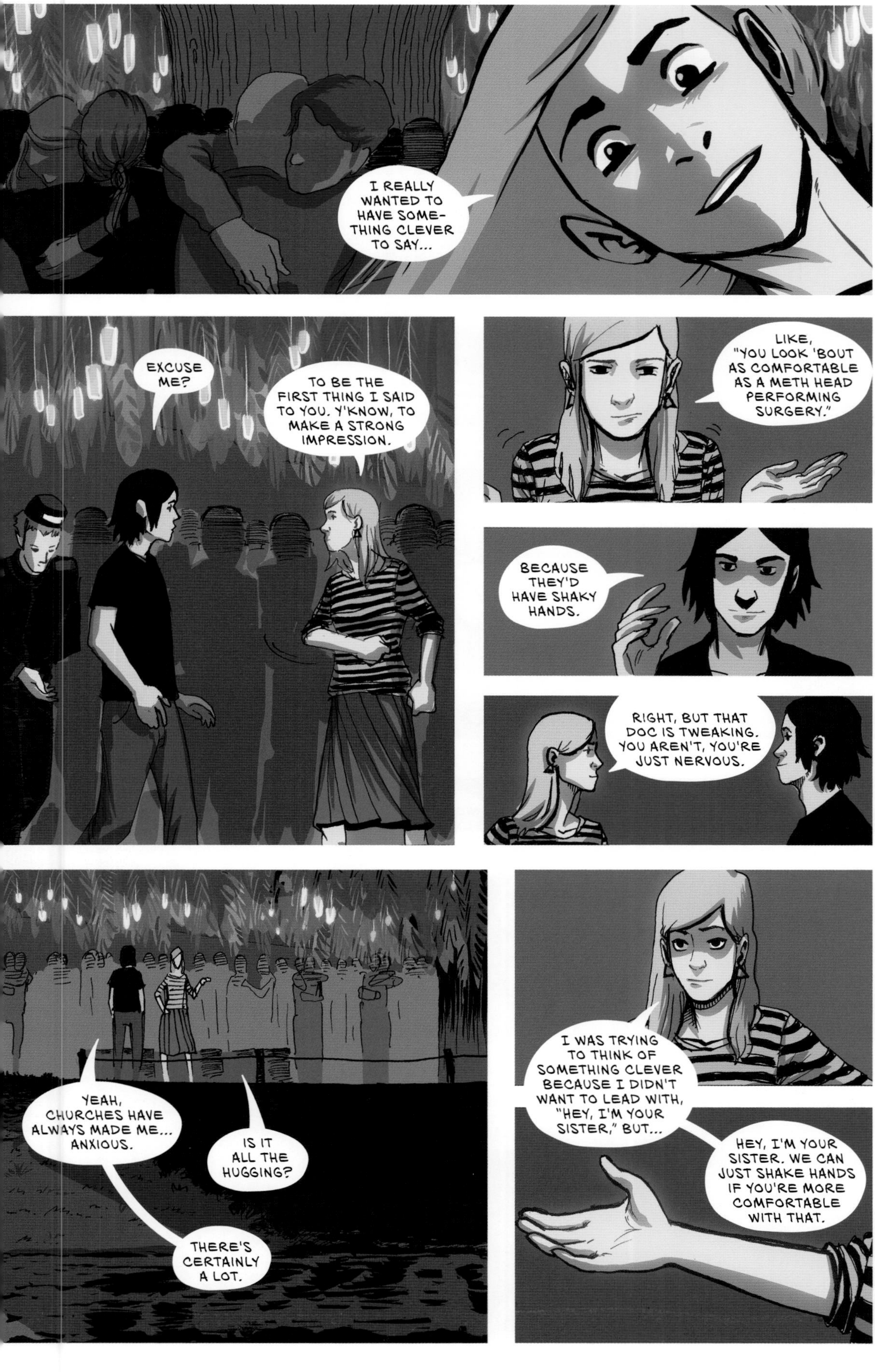
I REALLY WANTED TO HAVE SOME-THING CLEVER TO SAY...
EXCUSE ME?
TO BE THE FIRST THING I SAID TO YOU. Y'KNOW, TO MAKE A STRONG IMPRESSION.
LIKE, "YOU LOOK 'BOUT AS COMFORTABLE AS A METH HEAD PERFORMING SURGERY."
BECAUSE THEY'D HAVE SHAKY HANDS.
RIGHT, BUT THAT DOC IS TWEAKING. YOU AREN'T, YOU'RE JUST NERVOUS.
YEAH, CHURCHES HAVE ALWAYS MADE ME... ANXIOUS.
IS IT ALL THE HUGGING?
THERE'S CERTAINLY A LOT.
I WAS TRYING TO THINK OF SOMETHING CLEVER BECAUSE I DIDN'T WANT TO LEAD WITH, "HEY, I'M YOUR SISTER," BUT...
HEY, I'M YOUR SISTER. WE CAN JUST SHAKE HANDS IF YOU'RE MORE COMFORTABLE WITH THAT.

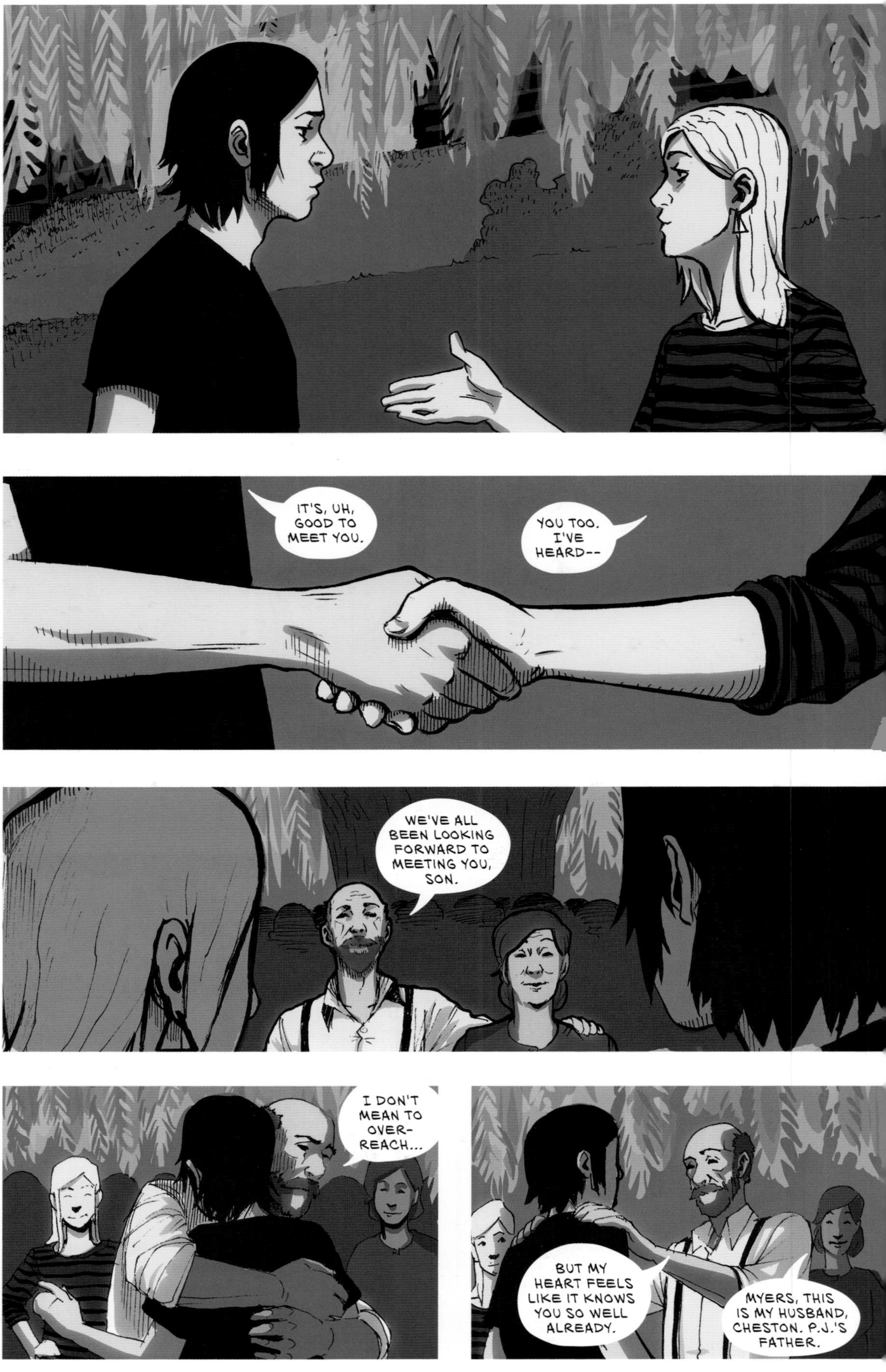
IT'S, UH, GOOD TO MEET YOU.
YOU TOO. I'VE HEARD--
WE'VE ALL BEEN LOOKING FORWARD TO MEETING YOU, SON.
I DON'T MEAN TO OVER-REACH...
BUT MY HEART FEELS LIKE IT KNOWS YOU SO WELL ALREADY.
MYERS, THIS IS MY HUSBAND, CHESTON. P.J.'S FATHER.

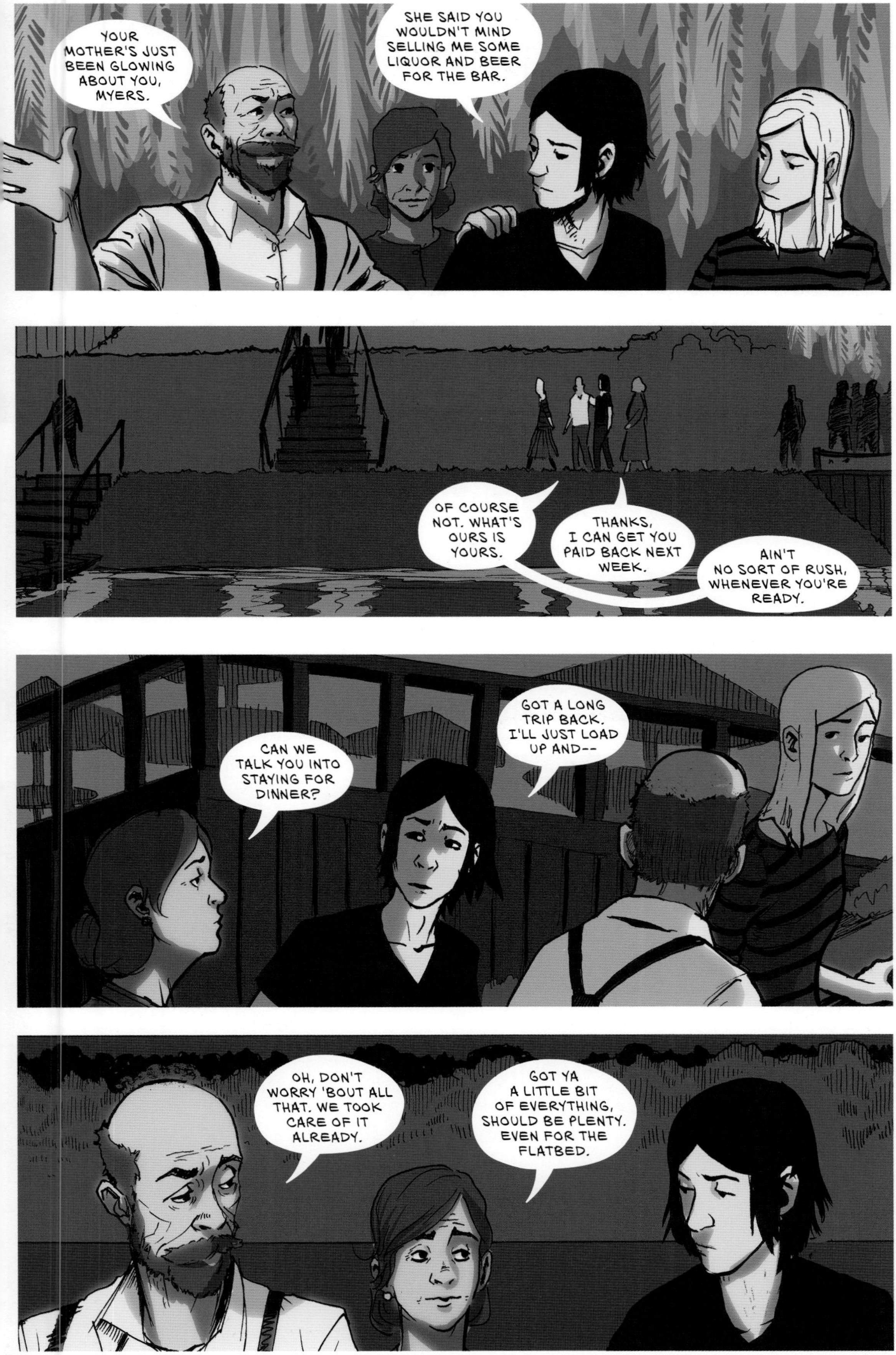
YOUR MOTHER'S JUST BEEN GLOWING ABOUT YOU, MYERS.
SHE SAID YOU WOULDN'T MIND SELLING ME SOME LIQUOR AND BEER FOR THE BAR.
OF COURSE NOT. WHAT'S OURS IS YOURS.
THANKS, I CAN GET YOU PAID BACK NEXT WEEK.
AIN'T NO SORT OF RUSH, WHENEVER YOU'RE READY.
CAN WE TALK YOU INTO STAYING FOR DINNER?
GOT A LONG TRIP BACK. I'LL JUST LOAD UP AND--
OH, DON'T WORRY 'BOUT ALL THAT. WE TOOK CARE OF IT ALREADY.
GOT YA A LITTLE BIT OF EVERYTHING, SHOULD BE PLENTY. EVEN FOR THE FLATBED.

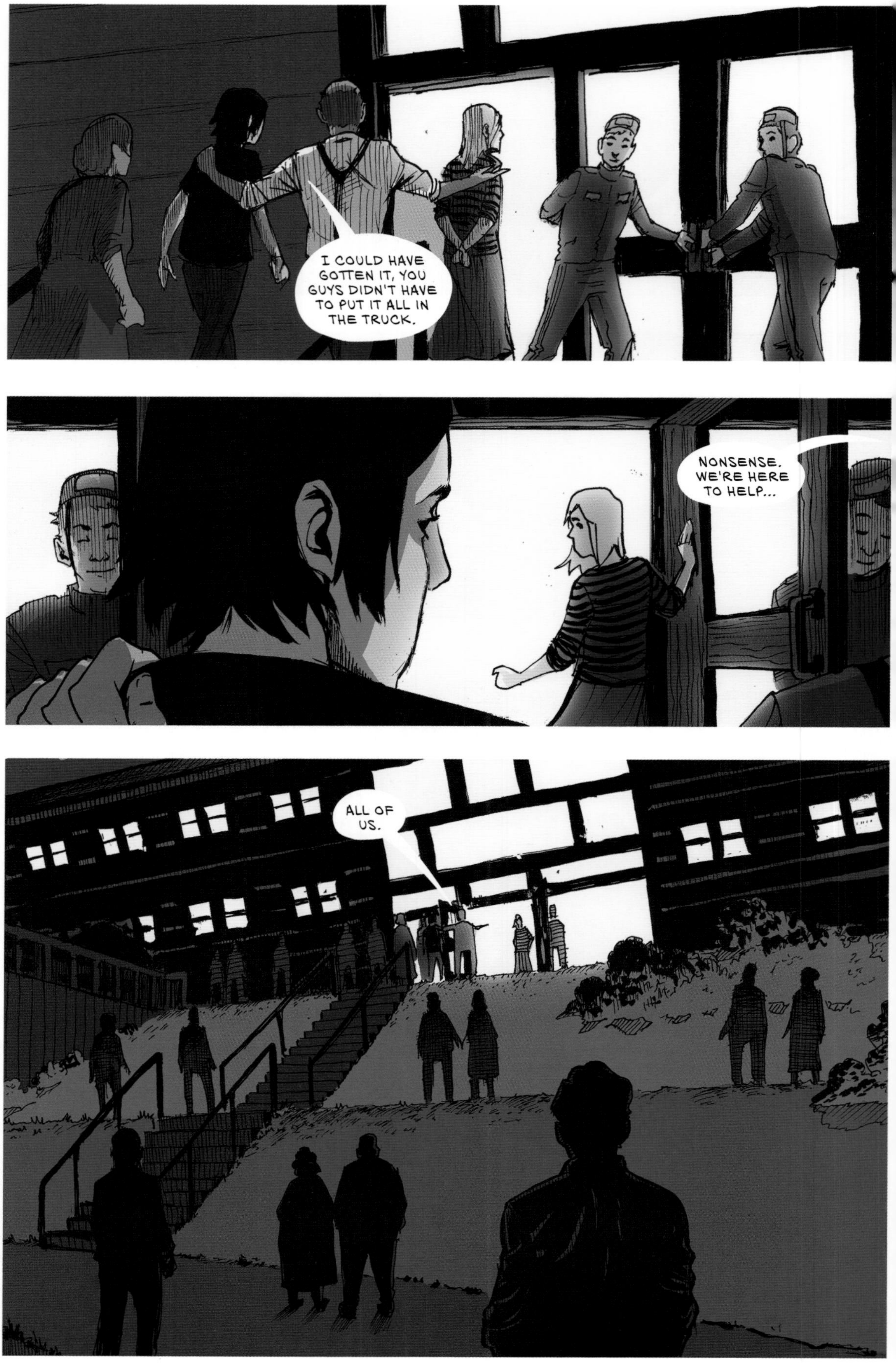
I COULD HAVE GOTTEN IT, YOU GUYS DIDN'T HAVE TO PUT IT ALL IN THE TRUCK.
NONSENSE. WE'RE HERE TO HELP...
ALL OF US.

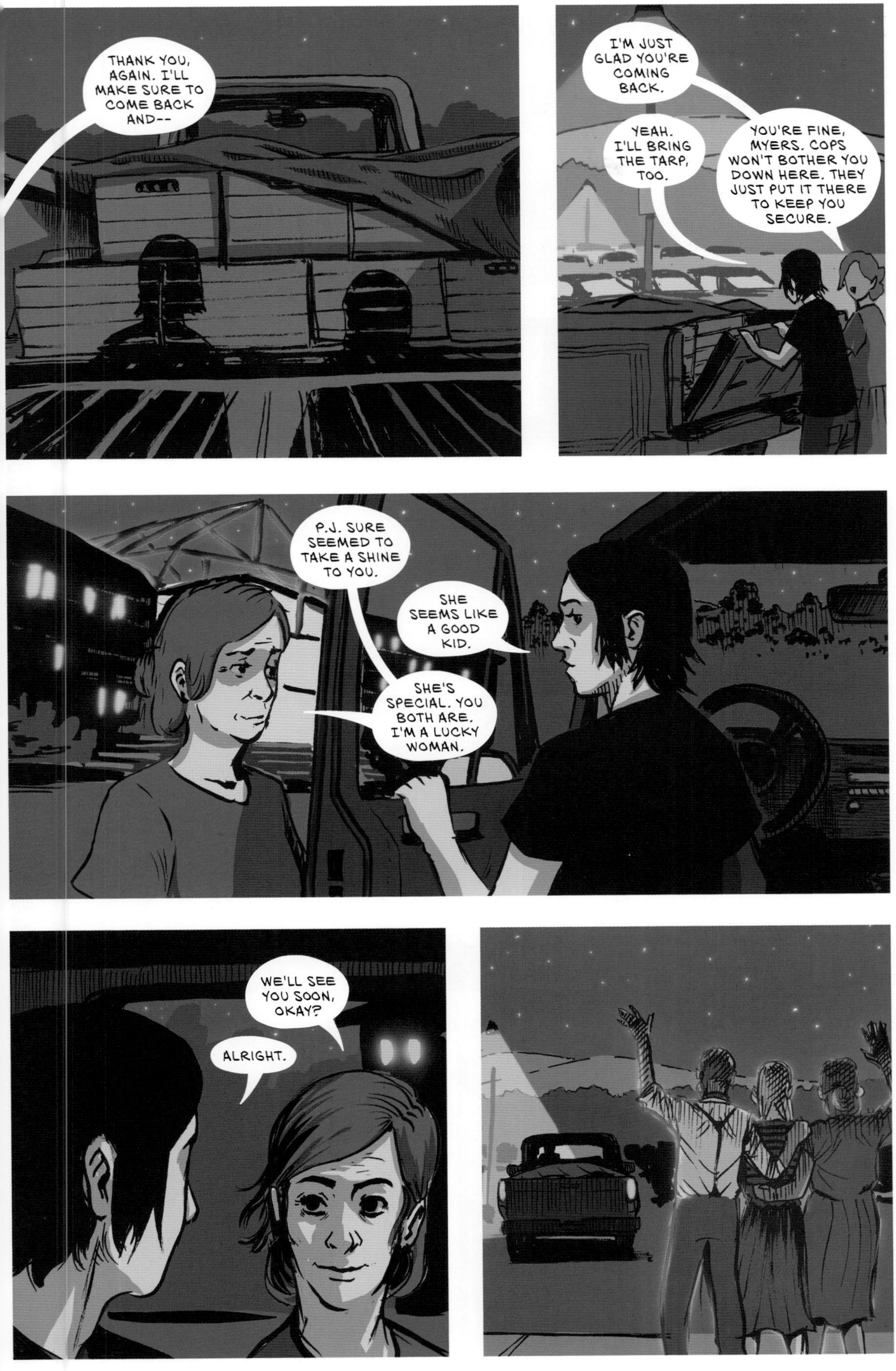
THANK YOU, AGAIN. I'LL MAKE SURE TO COME BACK AND--
I'M JUST GLAD YOU'RE COMING BACK.
YEAH. I'LL BRING THE TARP, TOO.
YOU'RE FINE, MYERS. COPS WON'T BOTHER YOU DOWN HERE. THEY JUST PUT IT THERE TO KEEP YOU SECURE.
P.J. SURE SEEMED TO TAKE A SHINE TO YOU.
SHE SEEMS LIKE A GOOD KID.
SHE'S SPECIAL. YOU BOTH ARE. I'M A LUCKY WOMAN.
WE'LL SEE YOU SOON, OKAY?
ALRIGHT.

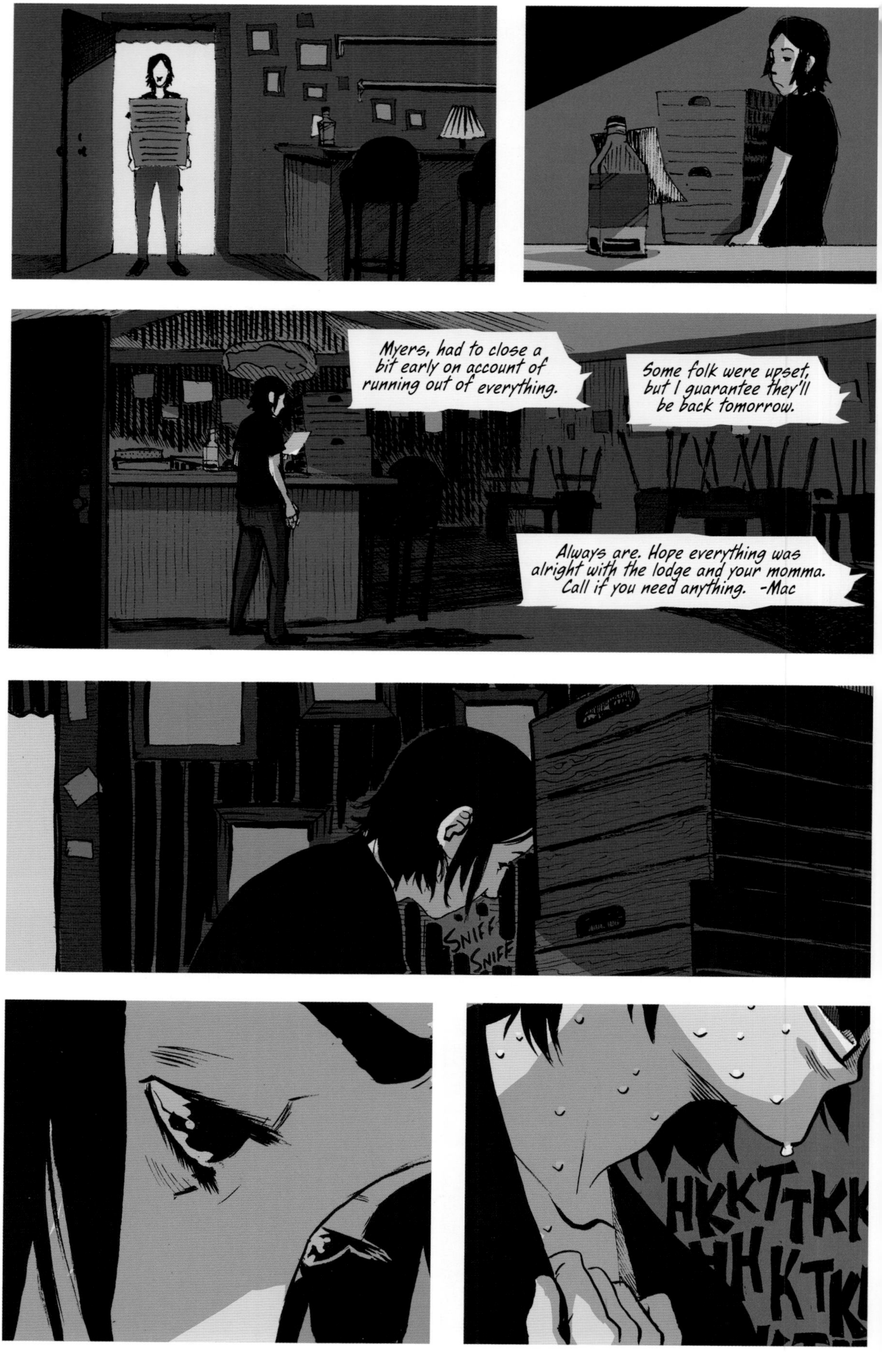
Myers, had to close a bit early on account of running out of everything.
Some folk were upset, but I guarantee they'll be back tomorrow.
Always are. Hope everything was alright with the lodge and your momma. Call if you need anything. -Mac
SNIFF
SNIFF
HKKTTKK
HHKTK

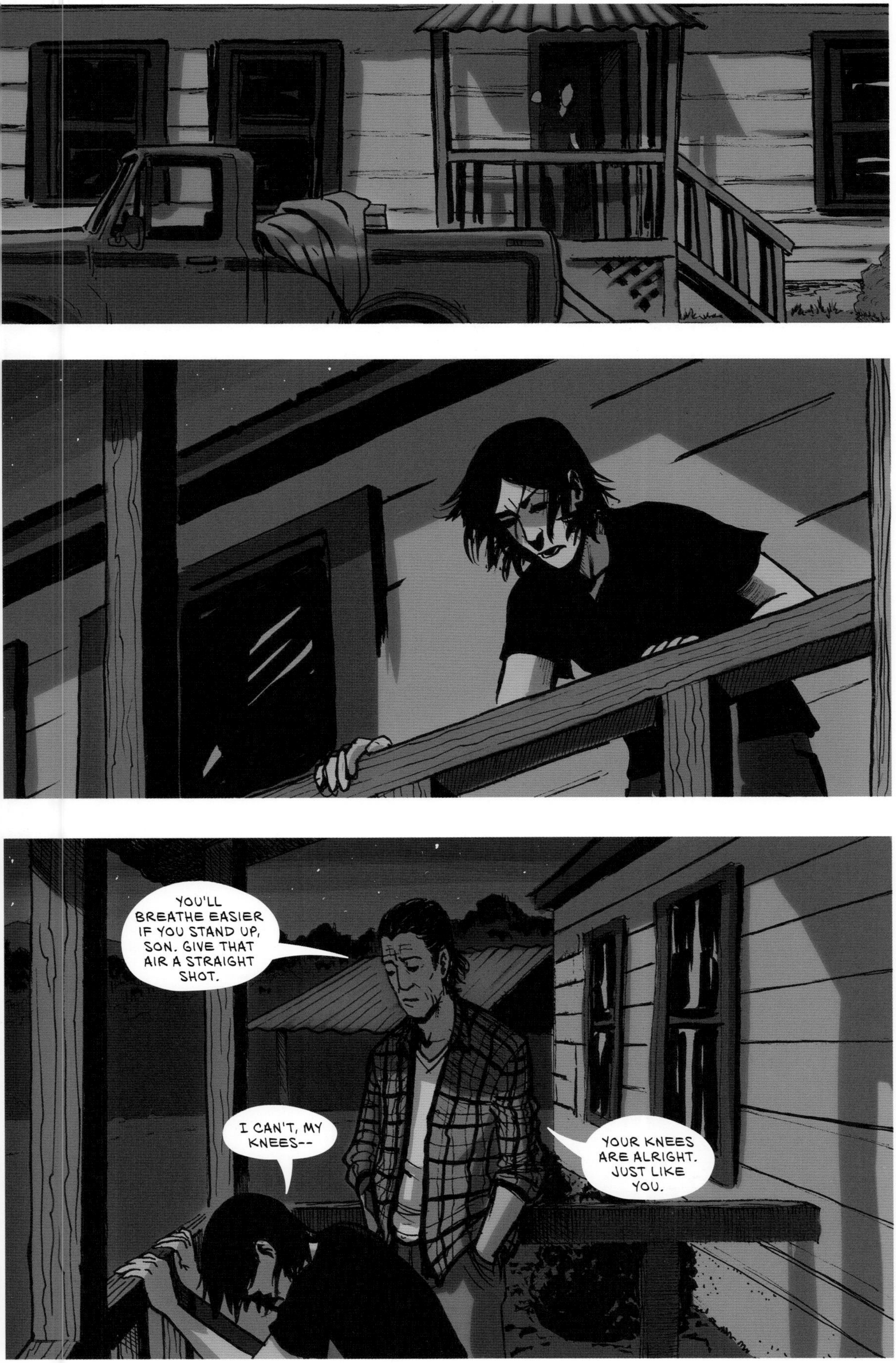
YOU'LL BREATHE EASIER IF YOU STAND UP, SON. GIVE THAT AIR A STRAIGHT SHOT.
I CAN'T, MY KNEES--
YOUR KNEES ARE ALRIGHT. JUST LIKE YOU.

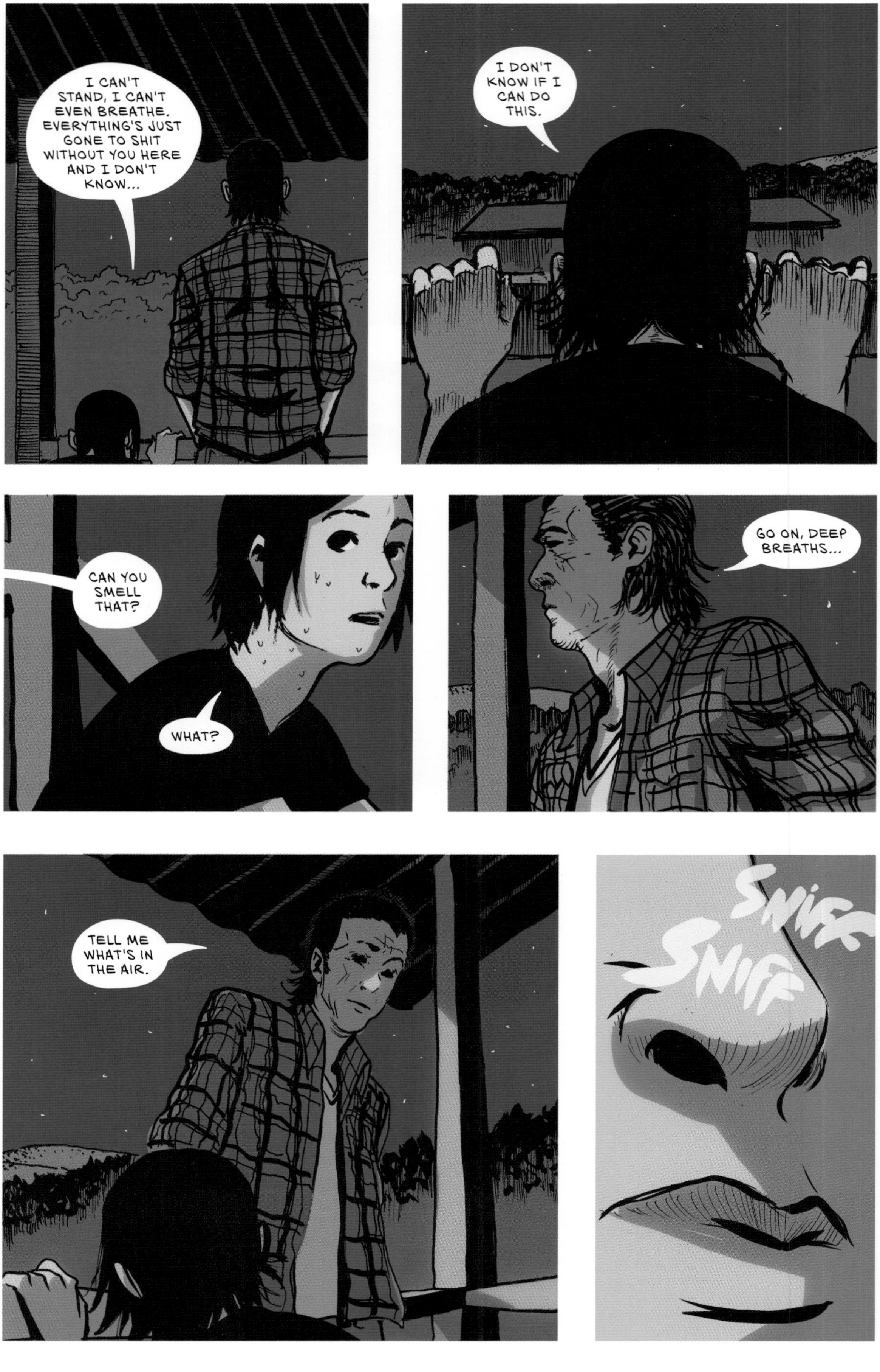
I CAN'T STAND, I CAN'T EVEN BREATHE. EVERYTHING'S JUST GONE TO SHIT WITHOUT YOU HERE AND I DON'T KNOW...
I DON'T KNOW IF I CAN DO THIS.
CAN YOU SMELL THAT?
WHAT?
GO ON, DEEP BREATHS...
TELL ME WHAT'S IN THE AIR.
SNIFF
SNIFF

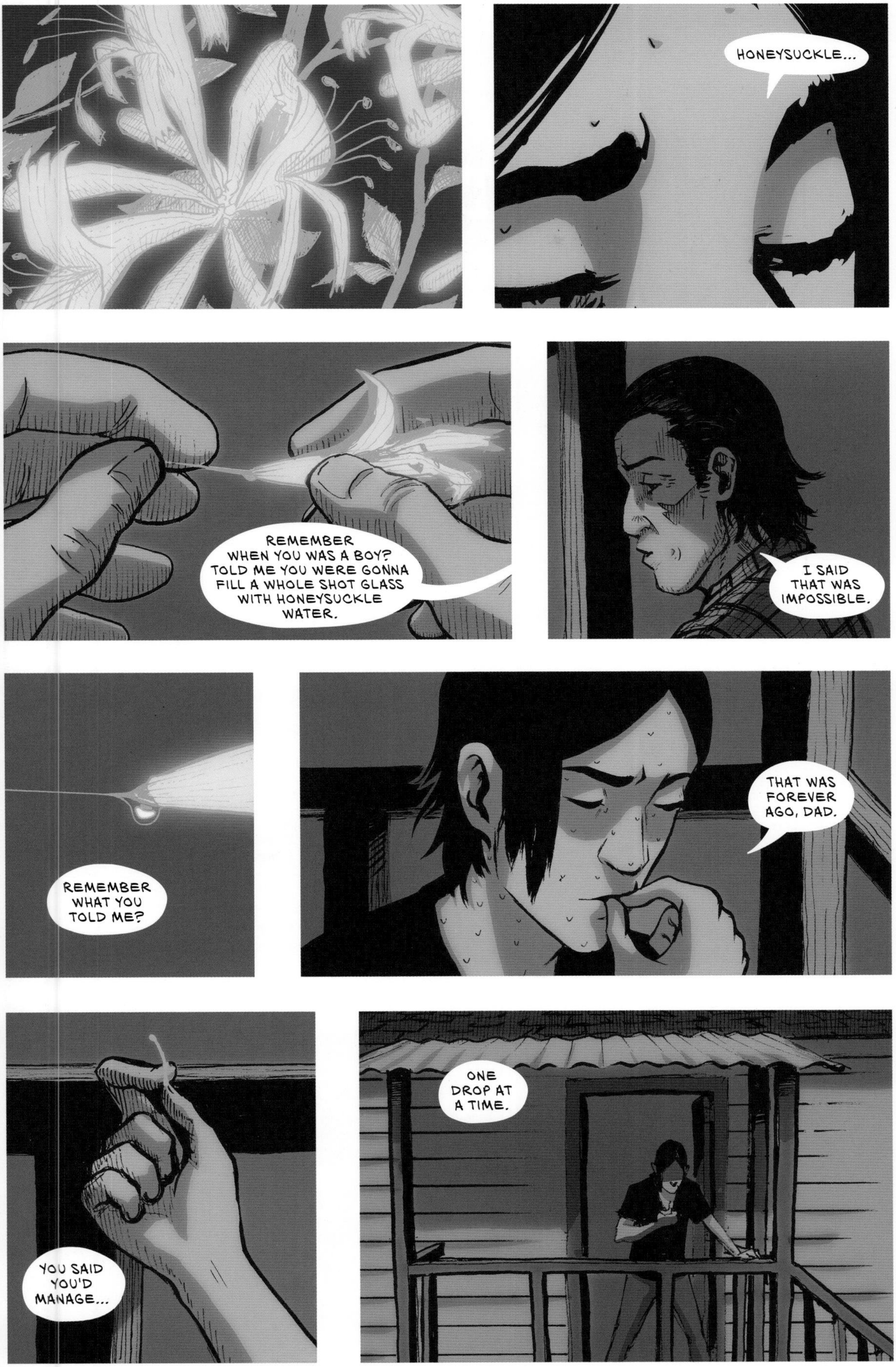
HONEYSUCKLE...
REMEMBER WHEN YOU WAS A BOY? TOLD ME YOU WERE GONNA FILL A WHOLE SHOT GLASS WITH HONEYSUCKLE WATER.
I SAID THAT WAS IMPOSSIBLE.
REMEMBER WHAT YOU TOLD ME?
THAT WAS FOREVER AGO, DAD.
YOU SAID YOU'D MANAGE...
ONE DROP AT A TIME.

# CHAPTER FIVE

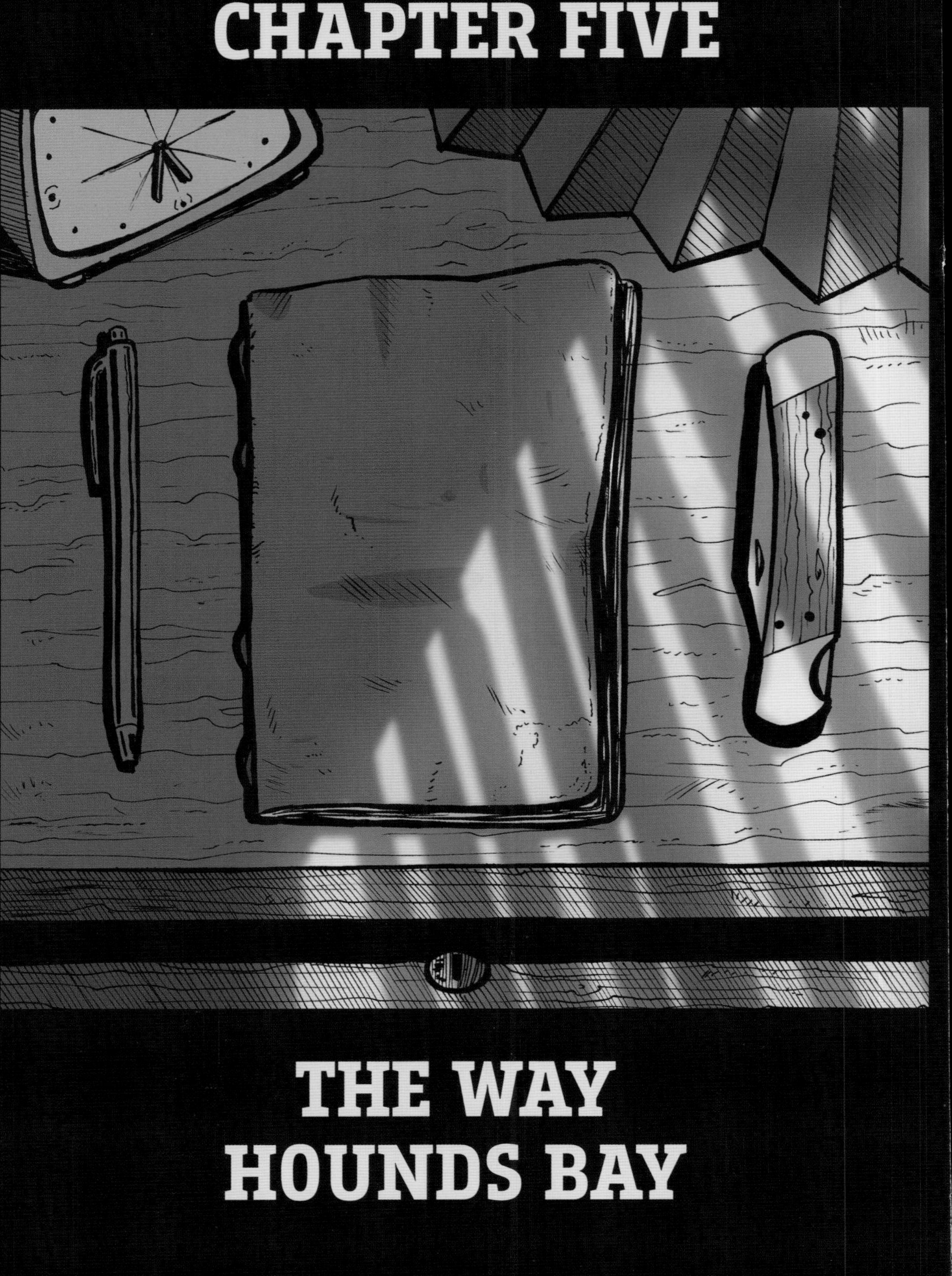

# THE WAY HOUNDS BAY

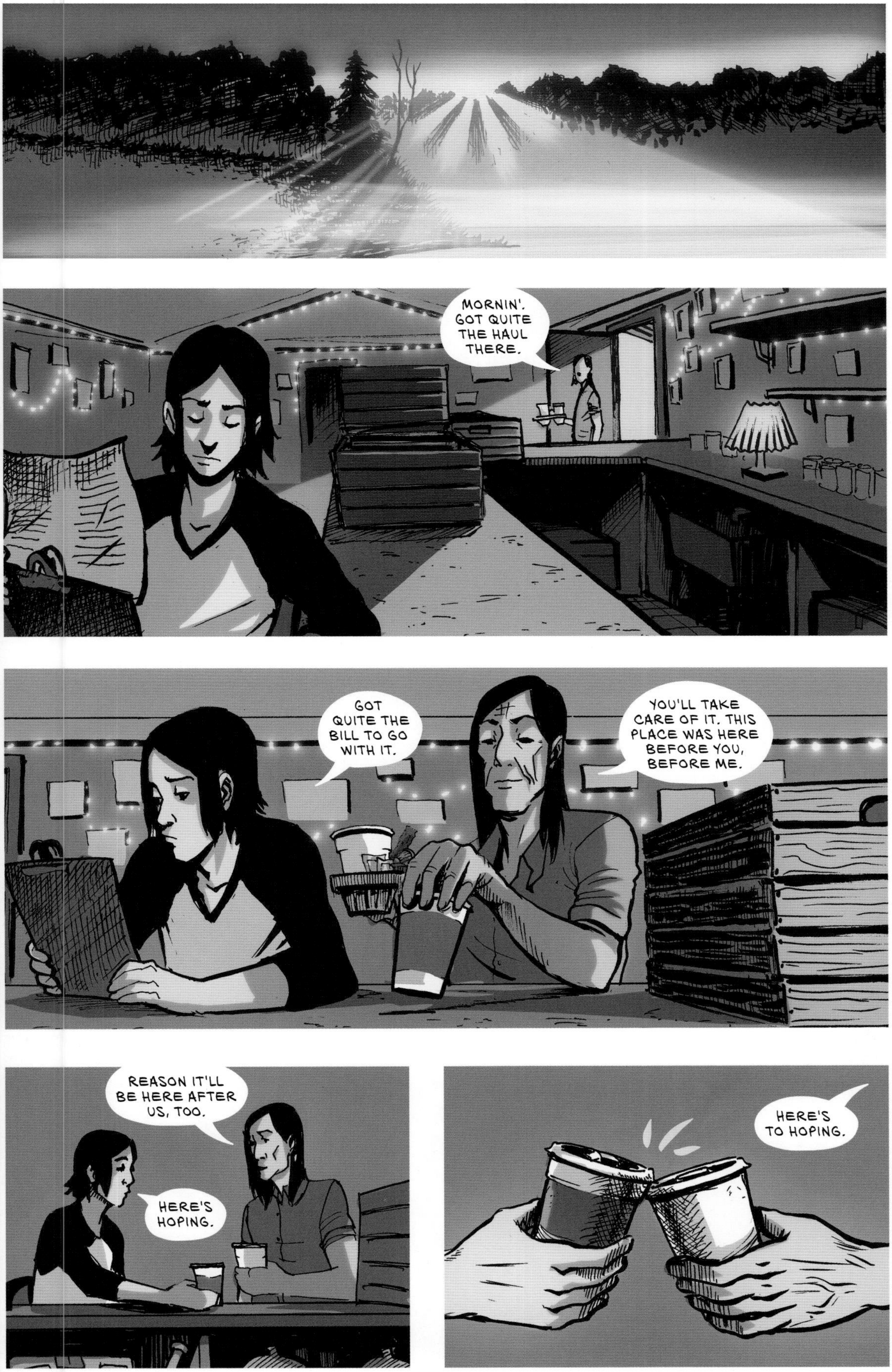
MORNIN'. GOT QUITE THE HAUL THERE.
GOT QUITE THE BILL TO GO WITH IT.
YOU'LL TAKE CARE OF IT. THIS PLACE WAS HERE BEFORE YOU, BEFORE ME.
REASON IT'LL BE HERE AFTER US, TOO.
HERE'S HOPING.
HERE'S TO HOPING.

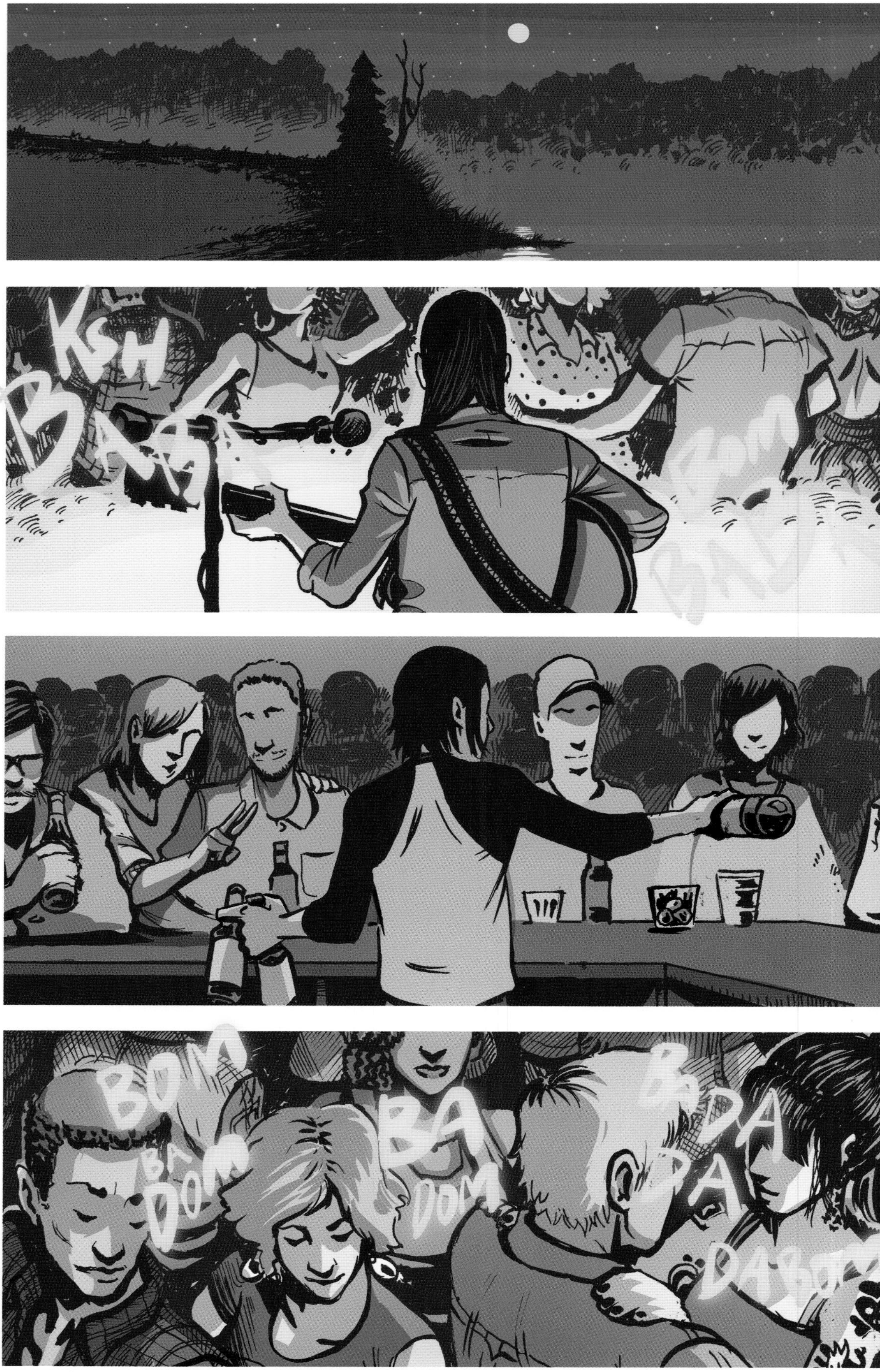
KSH
BOM
BOM
BA
DOM
BA
DOM
DA
DA

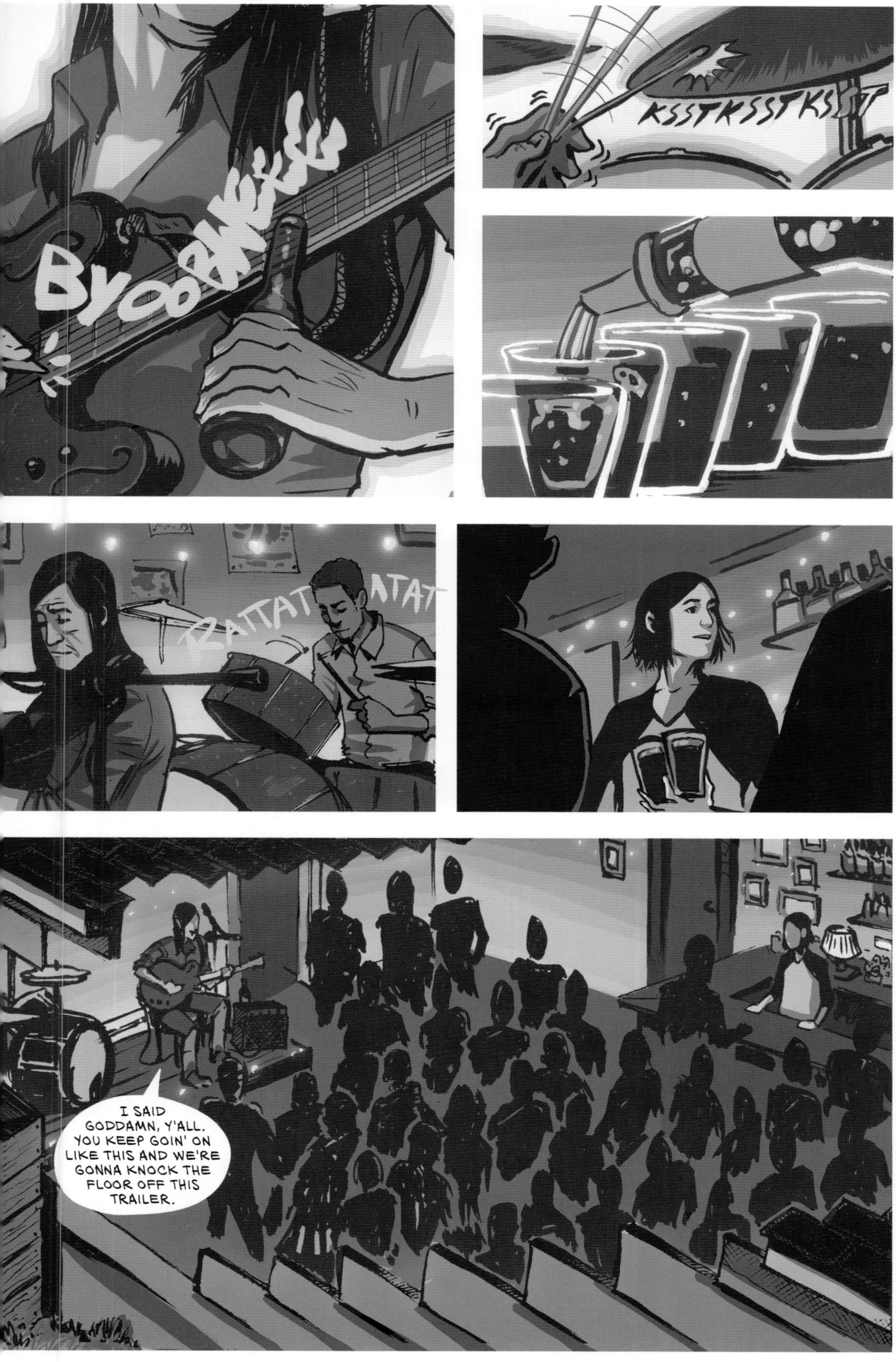
BYOOWEEEE
KSSTKSSTKSST
RATTATATAT
I SAID GODDAMN, Y'ALL. YOU KEEP GOIN' ON LIKE THIS AND WE'RE GONNA KNOCK THE FLOOR OFF THIS TRAILER.

ALRIGHT THEN, LET'S SEE IF WE CAN.

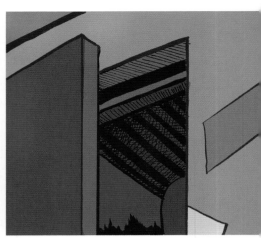

HEY THERE, SURE IS HOPPING IN HERE TONIGHT.

YEAH, MAC'S REALLY GOT 'EM RILED UP. HOW ARE YOU TWO?

'BOUT TO BE MUCH BETTER. THINK I COULD GET A RYE? DEALER'S CHOICE.

WHAT BRINGS YOU THREE UP HERE?

WELL, I WANTED TO DO SOME DANCIN'.

SO, WE DECIDED TO SPEND A NIGHT WITH OUR KIDS.

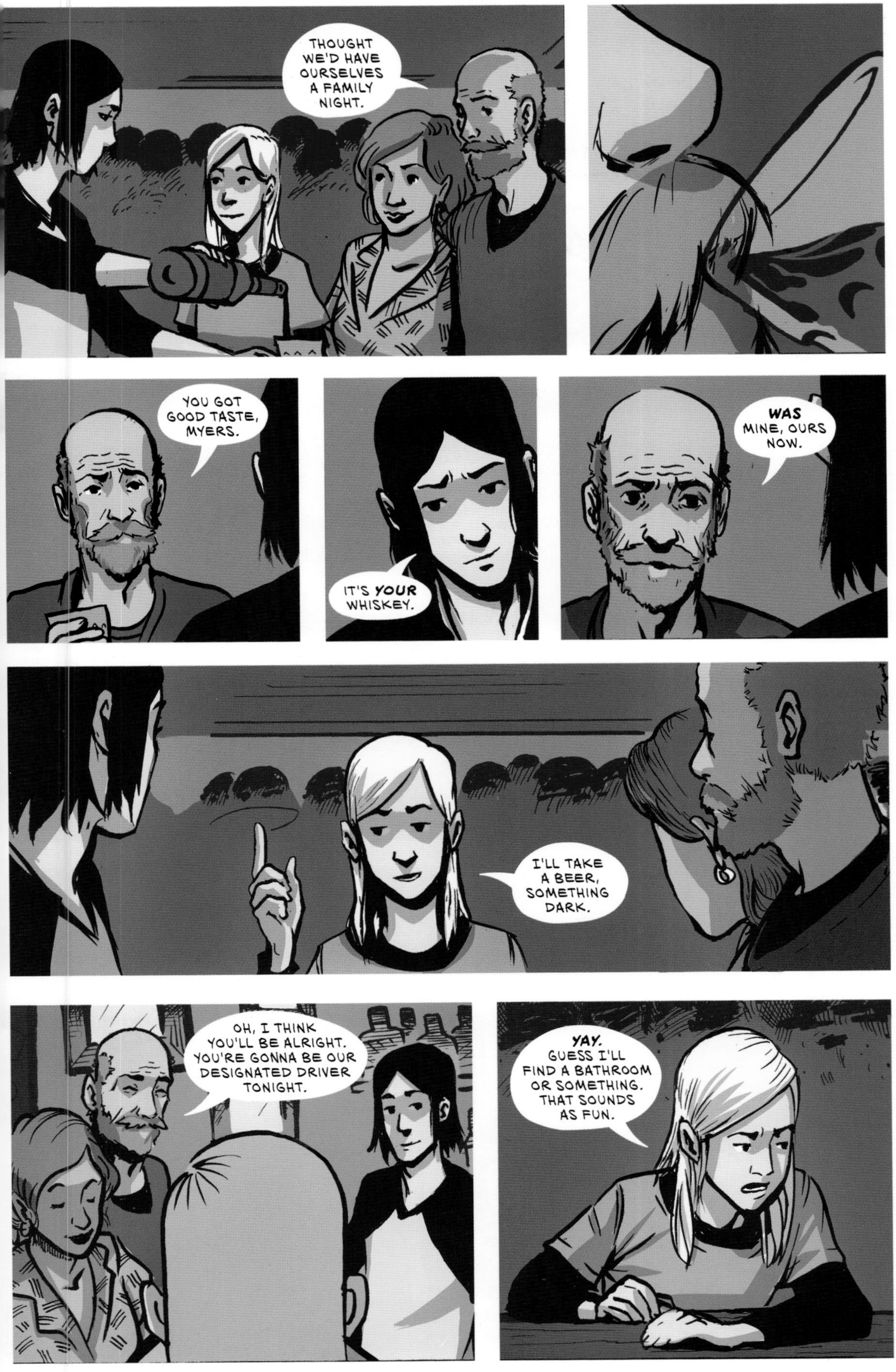
THOUGHT WE'D HAVE OURSELVES A FAMILY NIGHT.
YOU GOT GOOD TASTE, MYERS.
IT'S **YOUR** WHISKEY.
**WAS** MINE, OURS NOW.
I'LL TAKE A BEER, SOMETHING DARK.
OH, I THINK YOU'LL BE ALRIGHT. YOU'RE GONNA BE OUR DESIGNATED DRIVER TONIGHT.
**YAY.** GUESS I'LL FIND A BATHROOM OR SOMETHING. THAT SOUNDS AS FUN.

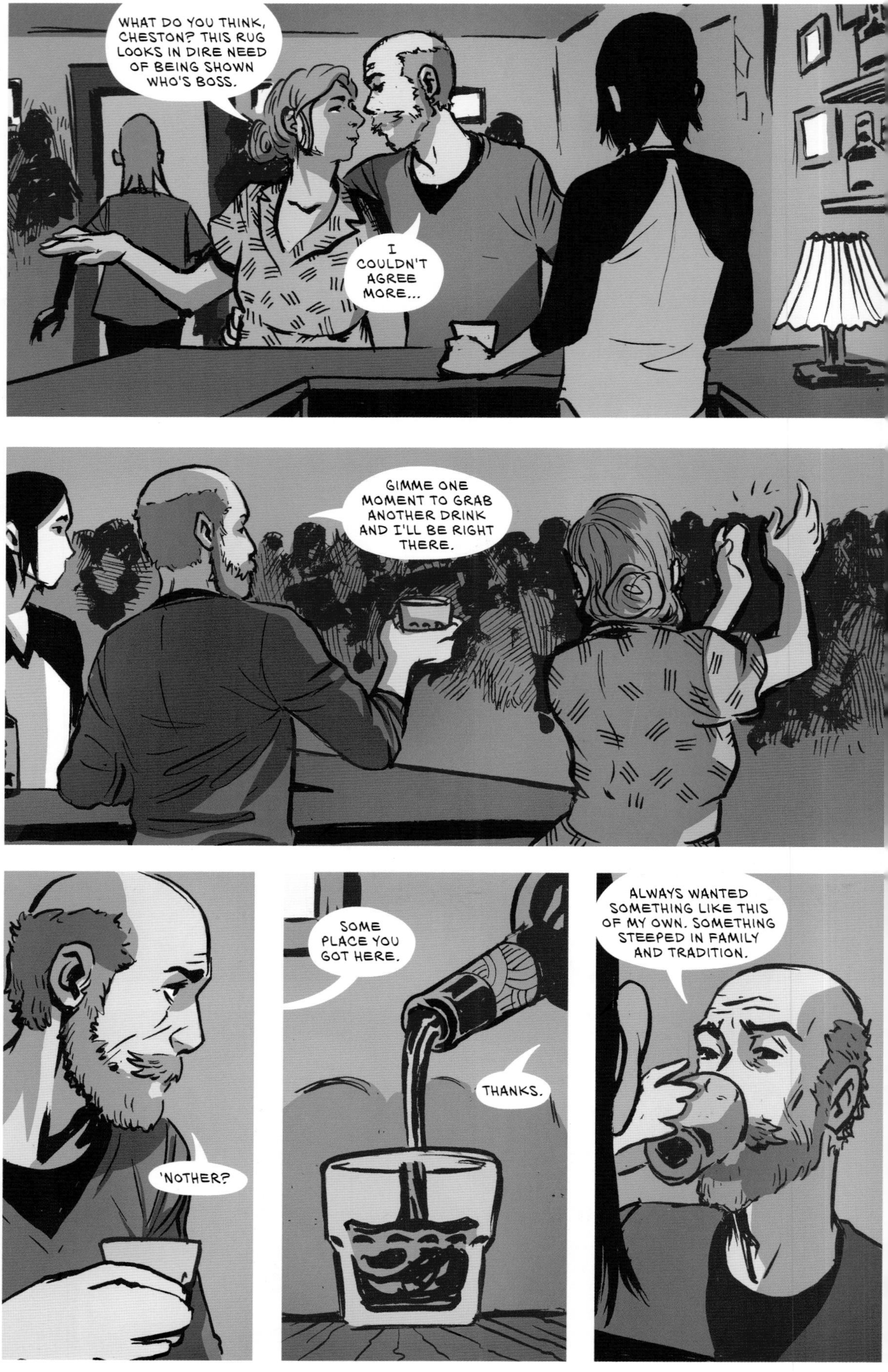
WHAT DO YOU THINK, CHESTON? THIS RUG LOOKS IN DIRE NEED OF BEING SHOWN WHO'S BOSS.
I COULDN'T AGREE MORE...
GIMME ONE MOMENT TO GRAB ANOTHER DRINK AND I'LL BE RIGHT THERE.
'NOTHER?
SOME PLACE YOU GOT HERE.
THANKS.
ALWAYS WANTED SOMETHING LIKE THIS OF MY OWN. SOMETHING STEEPED IN FAMILY AND TRADITION.

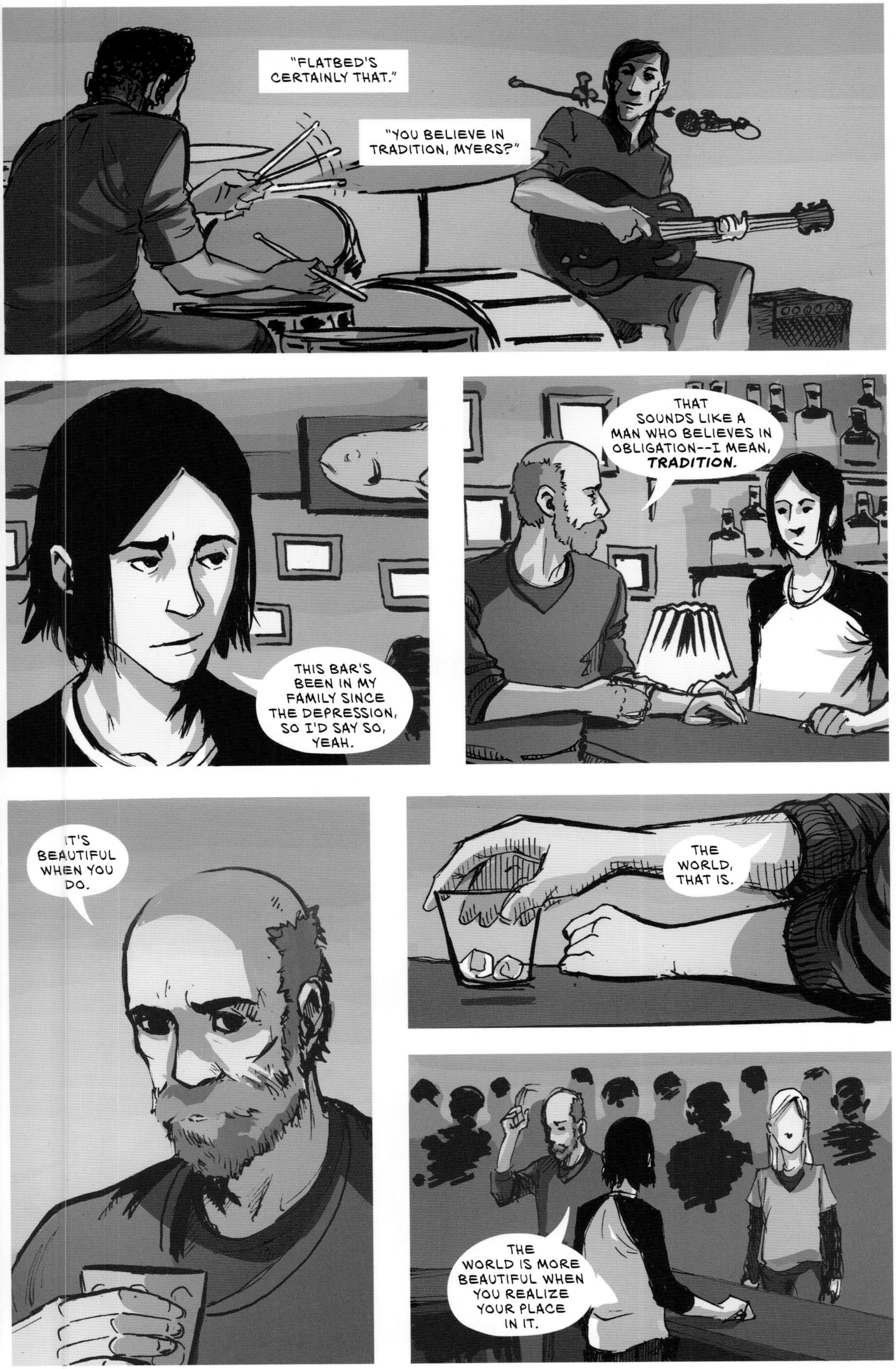
"FLATBED'S CERTAINLY THAT."
"YOU BELIEVE IN TRADITION, MYERS?"
THIS BAR'S BEEN IN MY FAMILY SINCE THE DEPRESSION, SO I'D SAY SO, YEAH.
THAT SOUNDS LIKE A MAN WHO BELIEVES IN OBLIGATION--I MEAN, TRADITION.
IT'S BEAUTIFUL WHEN YOU DO.
THE WORLD, THAT IS.
THE WORLD IS MORE BEAUTIFUL WHEN YOU REALIZE YOUR PLACE IN IT.

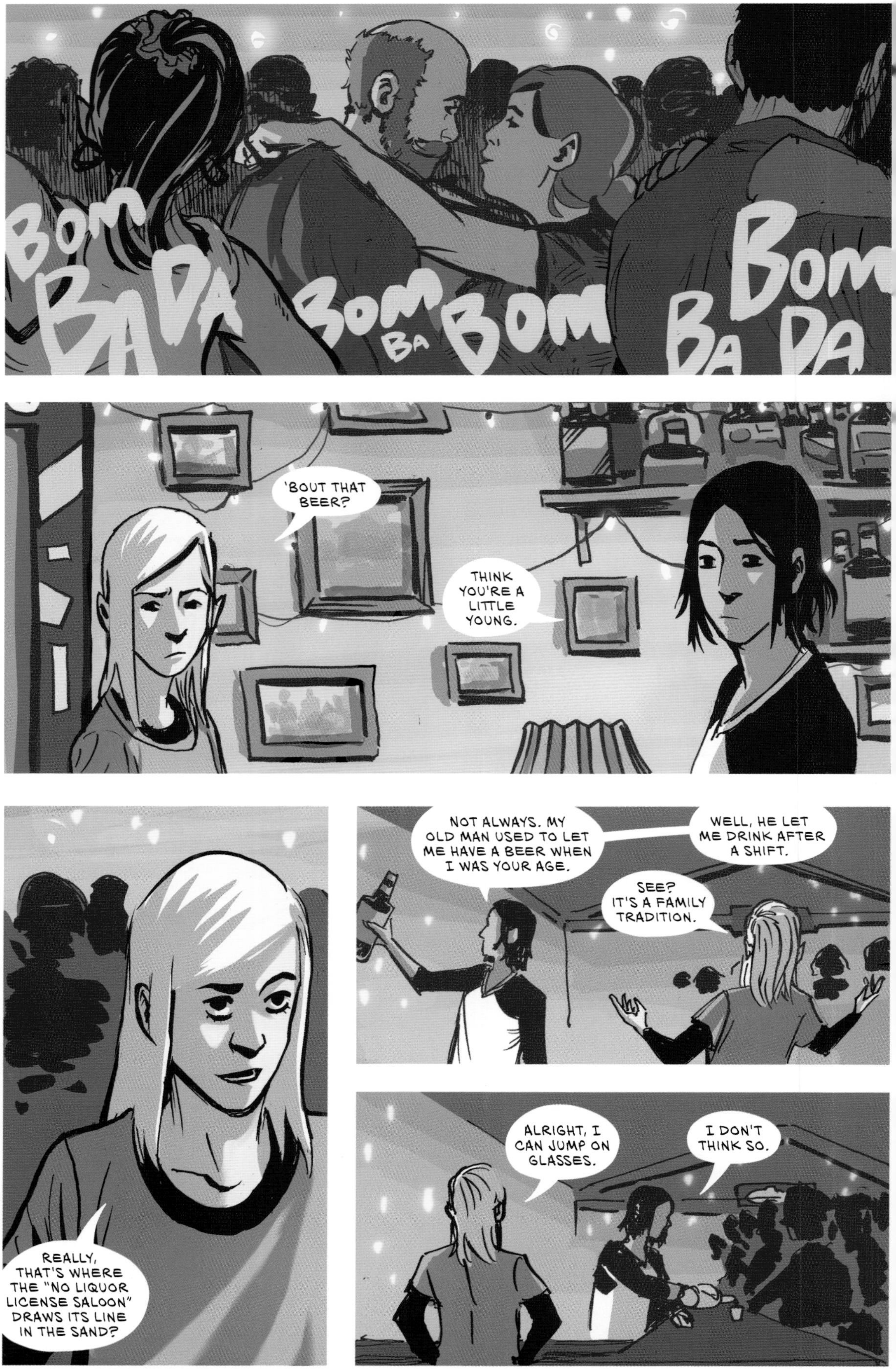
BOM BADA BOM BA BOM BOM BA DA
'BOUT THAT BEER?
THINK YOU'RE A LITTLE YOUNG.
REALLY, THAT'S WHERE THE "NO LIQUOR LICENSE SALOON" DRAWS ITS LINE IN THE SAND?
NOT ALWAYS. MY OLD MAN USED TO LET ME HAVE A BEER WHEN I WAS YOUR AGE.
WELL, HE LET ME DRINK AFTER A SHIFT.
SEE? IT'S A FAMILY TRADITION.
ALRIGHT, I CAN JUMP ON GLASSES.
I DON'T THINK SO.

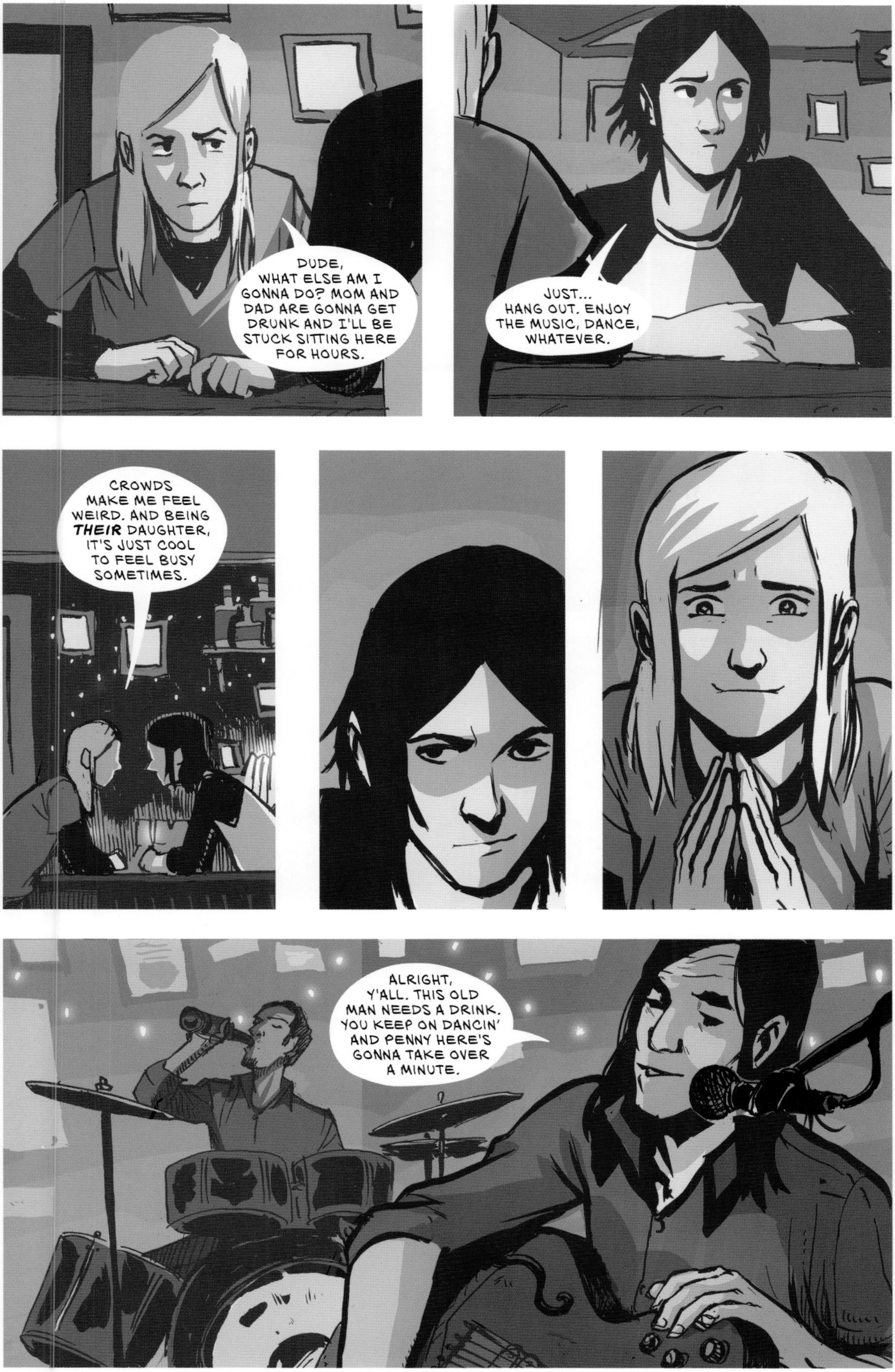
DUDE, WHAT ELSE AM I GONNA DO? MOM AND DAD ARE GONNA GET DRUNK AND I'LL BE STUCK SITTING HERE FOR HOURS.
JUST... HANG OUT. ENJOY THE MUSIC, DANCE, WHATEVER.
CROWDS MAKE ME FEEL WEIRD. AND BEING ***THEIR*** DAUGHTER, IT'S JUST COOL TO FEEL BUSY SOMETIMES.
ALRIGHT, Y'ALL. THIS OLD MAN NEEDS A DRINK. YOU KEEP ON DANCIN' AND PENNY HERE'S GONNA TAKE OVER A MINUTE.

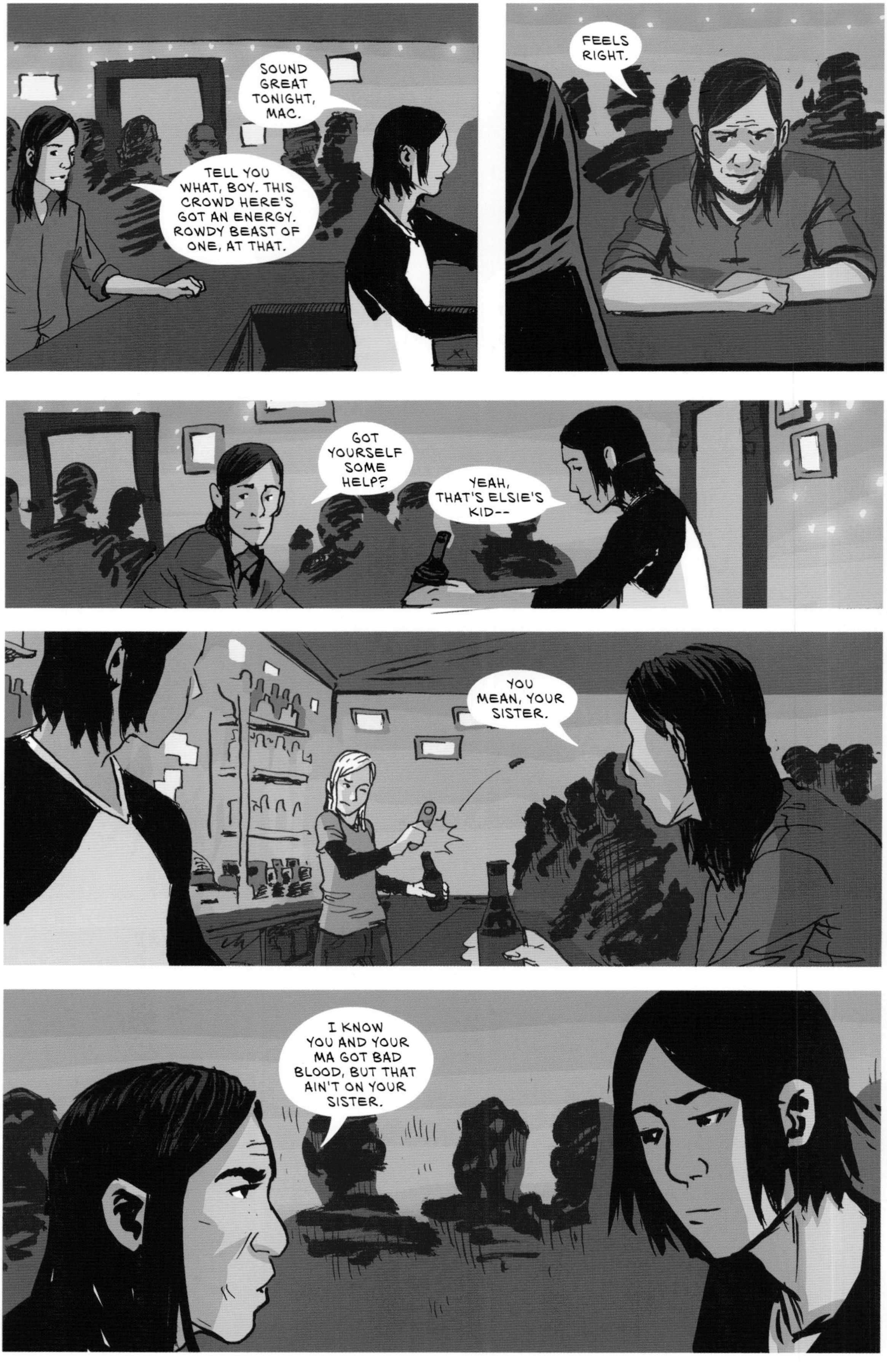
SOUND GREAT TONIGHT, MAC.
TELL YOU WHAT, BOY. THIS CROWD HERE'S GOT AN ENERGY. ROWDY BEAST OF ONE, AT THAT.
FEELS RIGHT.
GOT YOURSELF SOME HELP?
YEAH, THAT'S ELSIE'S KID--
YOU MEAN, YOUR SISTER.
I KNOW YOU AND YOUR MA GOT BAD BLOOD, BUT THAT AIN'T ON YOUR SISTER.

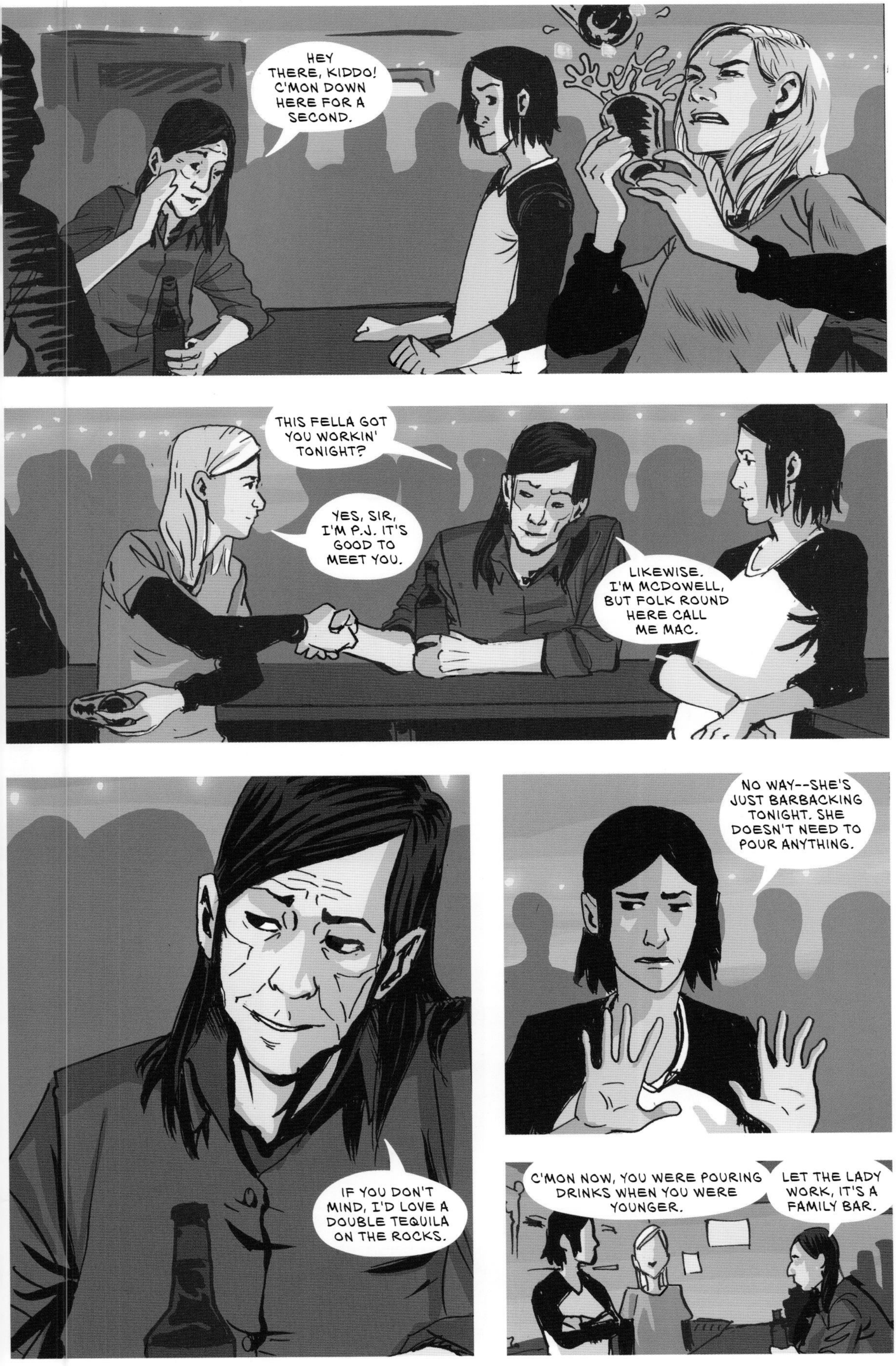
HEY THERE, KIDDO! C'MON DOWN HERE FOR A SECOND.
THIS FELLA GOT YOU WORKIN' TONIGHT?
YES, SIR, I'M P.J. IT'S GOOD TO MEET YOU.
LIKEWISE. I'M MCDOWELL, BUT FOLK ROUND HERE CALL ME MAC.
IF YOU DON'T MIND, I'D LOVE A DOUBLE TEQUILA ON THE ROCKS.
NO WAY--SHE'S JUST BARBACKING TONIGHT. SHE DOESN'T NEED TO POUR ANYTHING.
C'MON NOW, YOU WERE POURING DRINKS WHEN YOU WERE YOUNGER.
LET THE LADY WORK, IT'S A FAMILY BAR.

HOW MUCH?

'BOUT HERE.

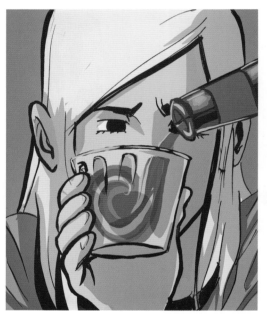

A LITTLE TOO FULL?

NO, MA'AM, THAT'S JUST ABOUT PERFECT FOR ME. GRANTED, DON'T GO GIVING ALL THESE OTHER FOLK THAT MUCH.

I DON'T THINK THERE'S ROOM.

THERE YOU GO. TRY TO STAY SOBER ENOUGH TO HOLD THAT GUITAR.

PLiSH

TAKE MORE TEQUILA THAN YOU GOT IN THIS JOINT TO MAKE ME DROP ROBERT.

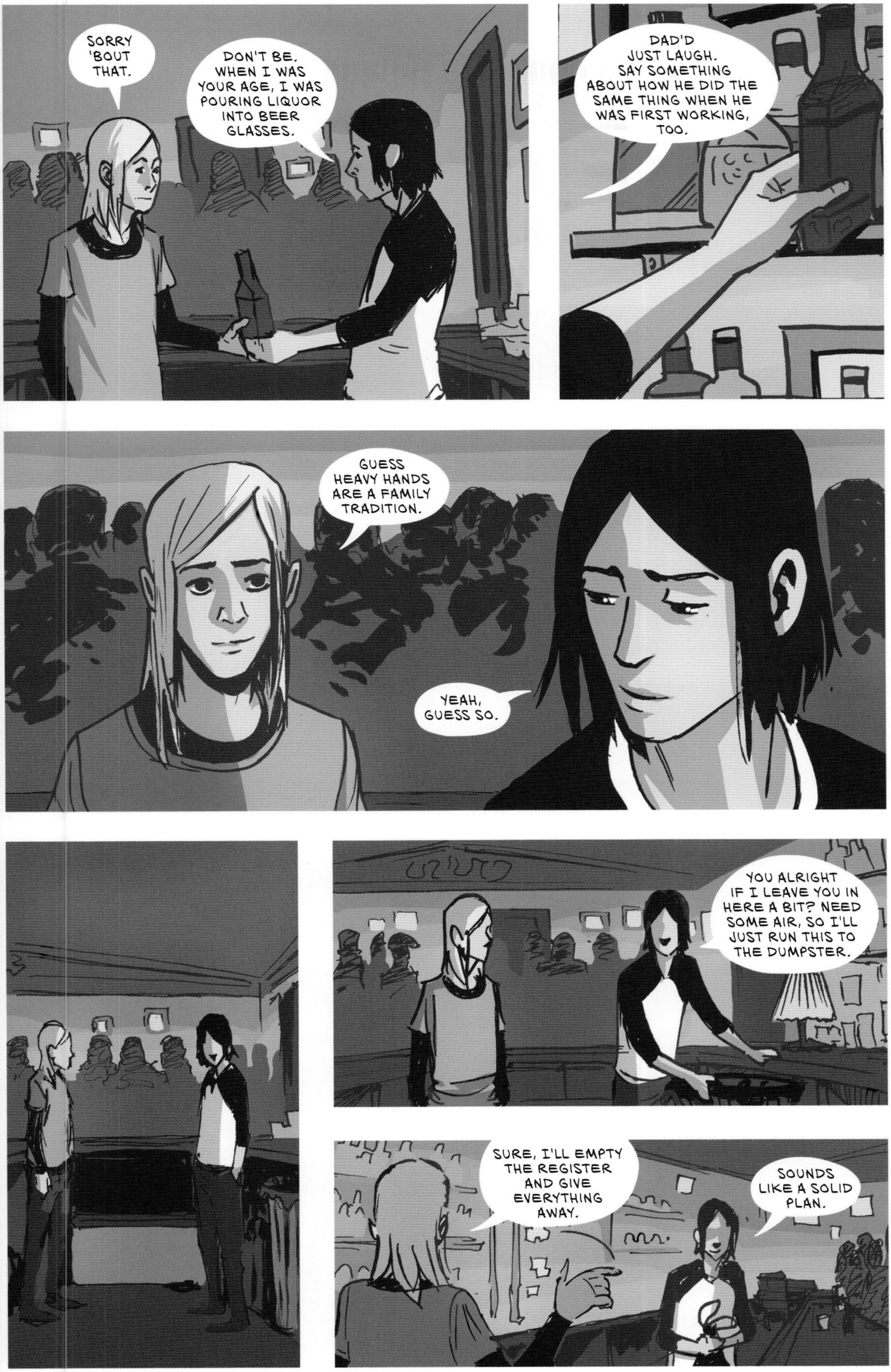
SORRY 'BOUT THAT.
DON'T BE. WHEN I WAS YOUR AGE, I WAS POURING LIQUOR INTO BEER GLASSES.
DAD'D JUST LAUGH. SAY SOMETHING ABOUT HOW HE DID THE SAME THING WHEN HE WAS FIRST WORKING, TOO.
GUESS HEAVY HANDS ARE A FAMILY TRADITION.
YEAH, GUESS SO.
YOU ALRIGHT IF I LEAVE YOU IN HERE A BIT? NEED SOME AIR, SO I'LL JUST RUN THIS TO THE DUMPSTER.
SURE, I'LL EMPTY THE REGISTER AND GIVE EVERYTHING AWAY.
SOUNDS LIKE A SOLID PLAN.

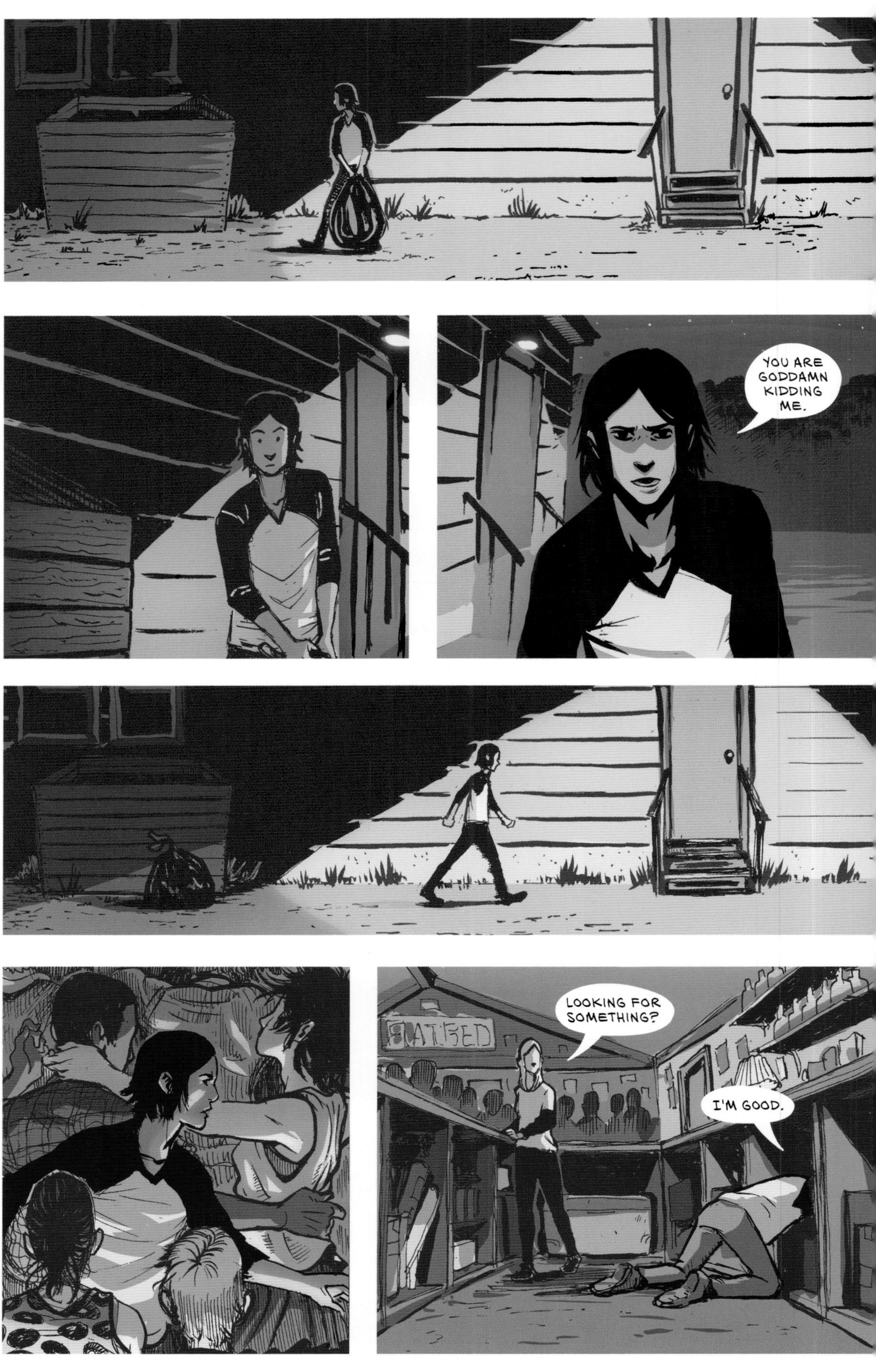
YOU ARE GODDAMN KIDDING ME.
LOOKING FOR SOMETHING?
I'M GOOD.

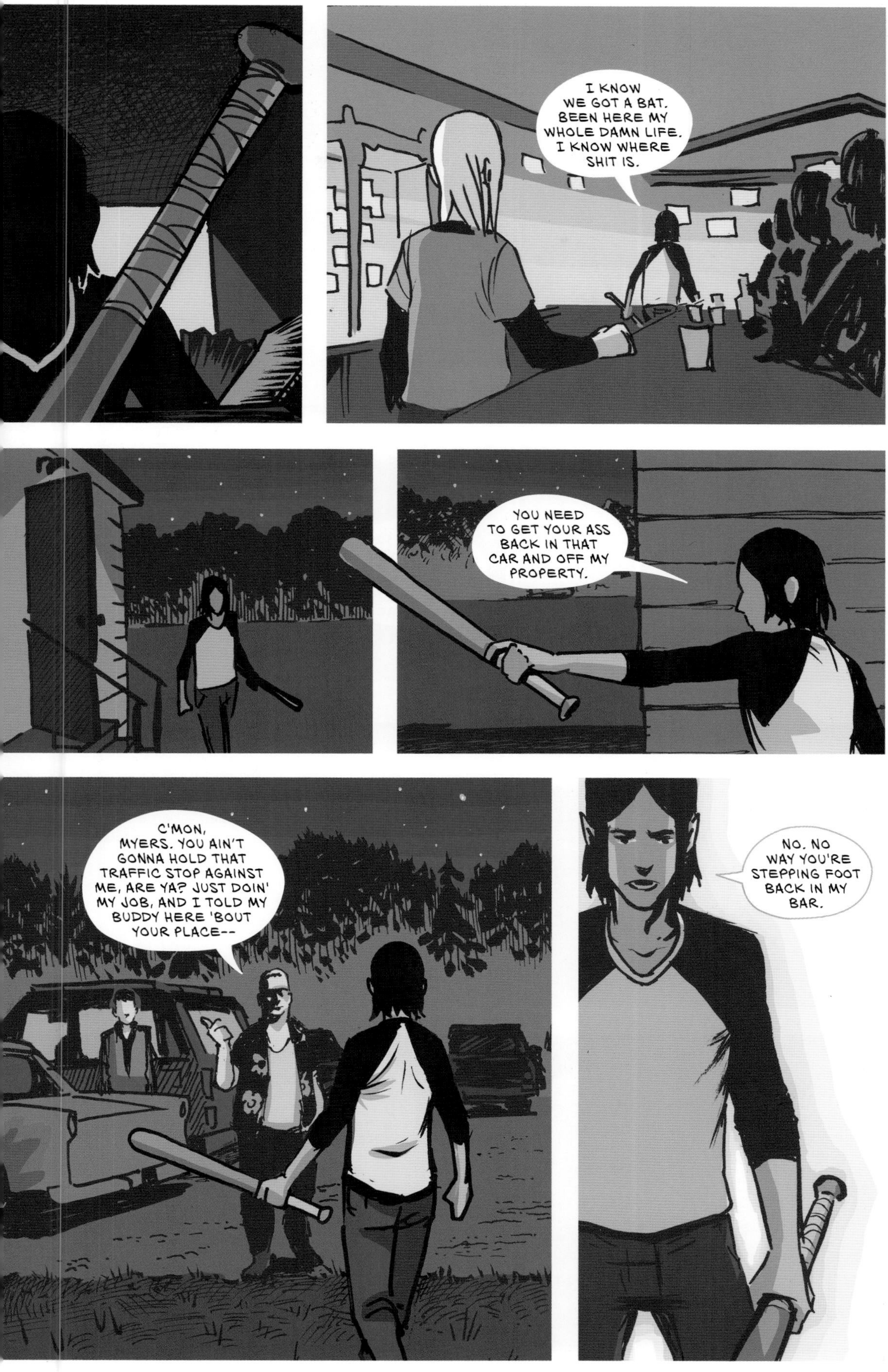
I KNOW WE GOT A BAT. BEEN HERE MY WHOLE DAMN LIFE. I KNOW WHERE SHIT IS.
YOU NEED TO GET YOUR ASS BACK IN THAT CAR AND OFF MY PROPERTY.
C'MON, MYERS. YOU AIN'T GONNA HOLD THAT TRAFFIC STOP AGAINST ME, ARE YA? JUST DOIN' MY JOB, AND I TOLD MY BUDDY HERE 'BOUT YOUR PLACE--
NO. NO WAY YOU'RE STEPPING FOOT BACK IN MY BAR.

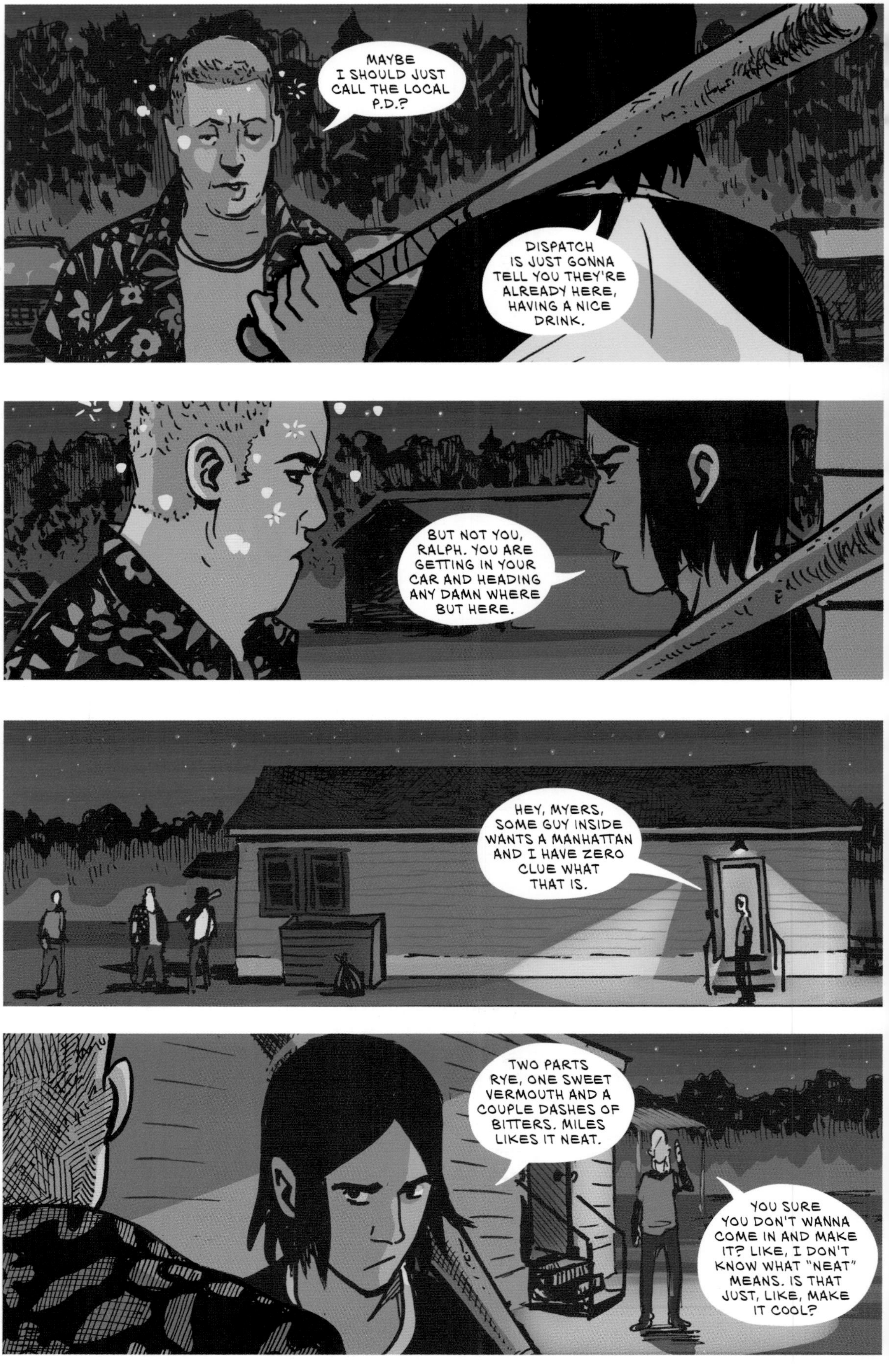
MAYBE I SHOULD JUST CALL THE LOCAL P.D.?
DISPATCH IS JUST GONNA TELL YOU THEY'RE ALREADY HERE, HAVING A NICE DRINK.
BUT NOT YOU, RALPH. YOU ARE GETTING IN YOUR CAR AND HEADING ANY DAMN WHERE BUT HERE.
HEY, MYERS, SOME GUY INSIDE WANTS A MANHATTAN AND I HAVE ZERO CLUE WHAT THAT IS.
TWO PARTS RYE, ONE SWEET VERMOUTH AND A COUPLE DASHES OF BITTERS. MILES LIKES IT NEAT.
YOU SURE YOU DON'T WANNA COME IN AND MAKE IT? LIKE, I DON'T KNOW WHAT "NEAT" MEANS. IS THAT JUST, LIKE, MAKE IT COOL?

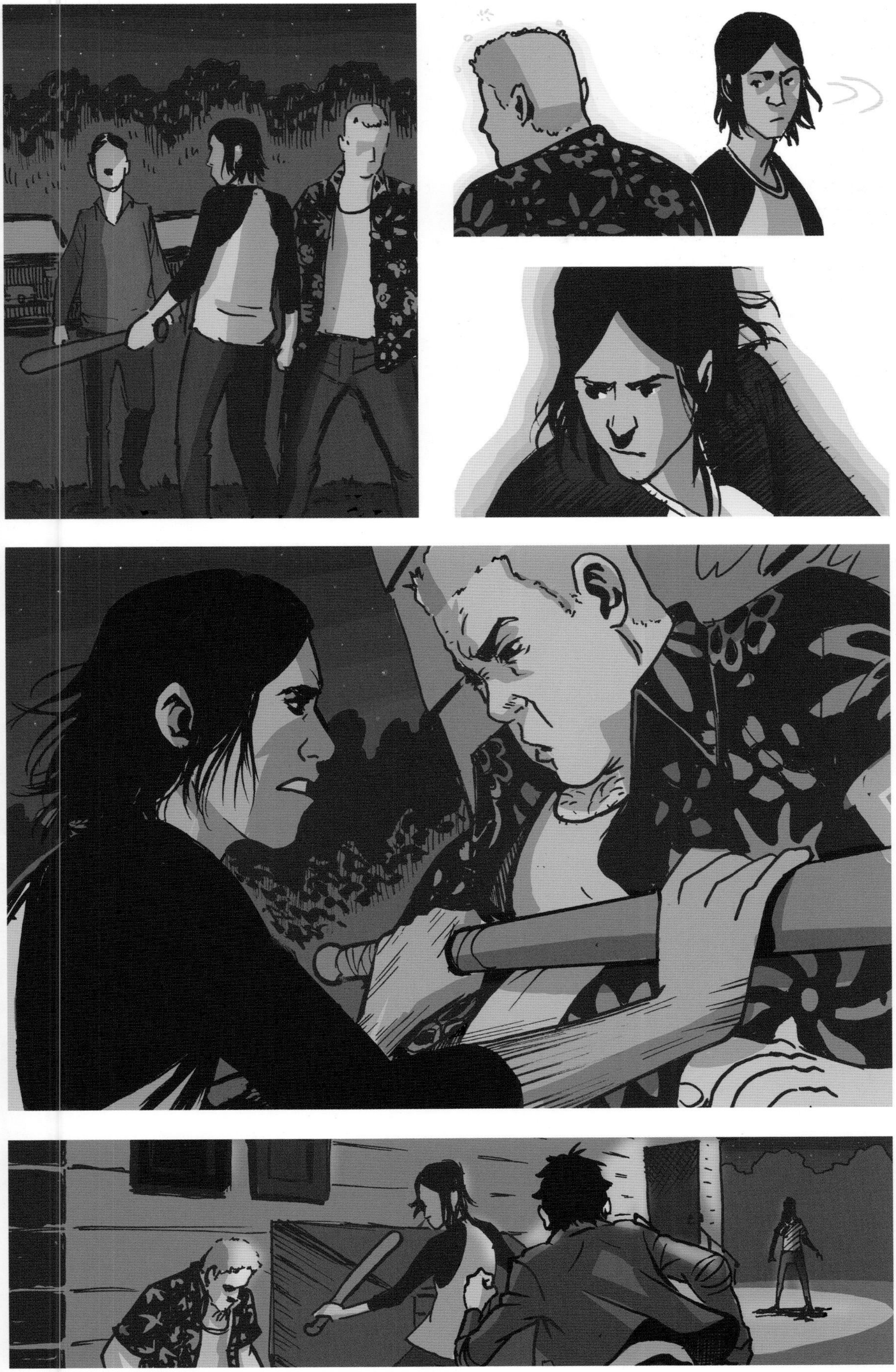

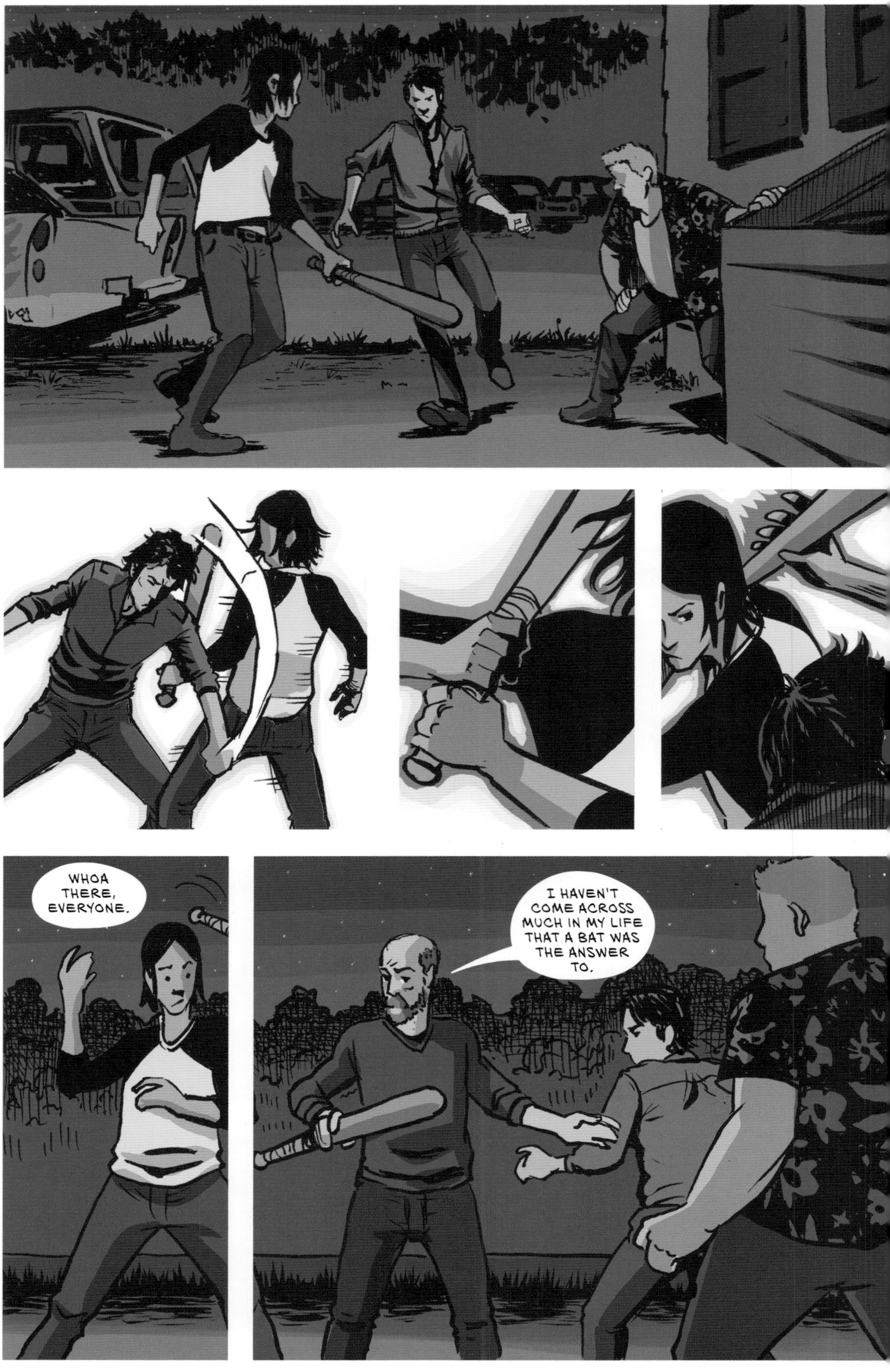
WHOA THERE, EVERYONE.
I HAVEN'T COME ACROSS MUCH IN MY LIFE THAT A BAT WAS THE ANSWER TO.

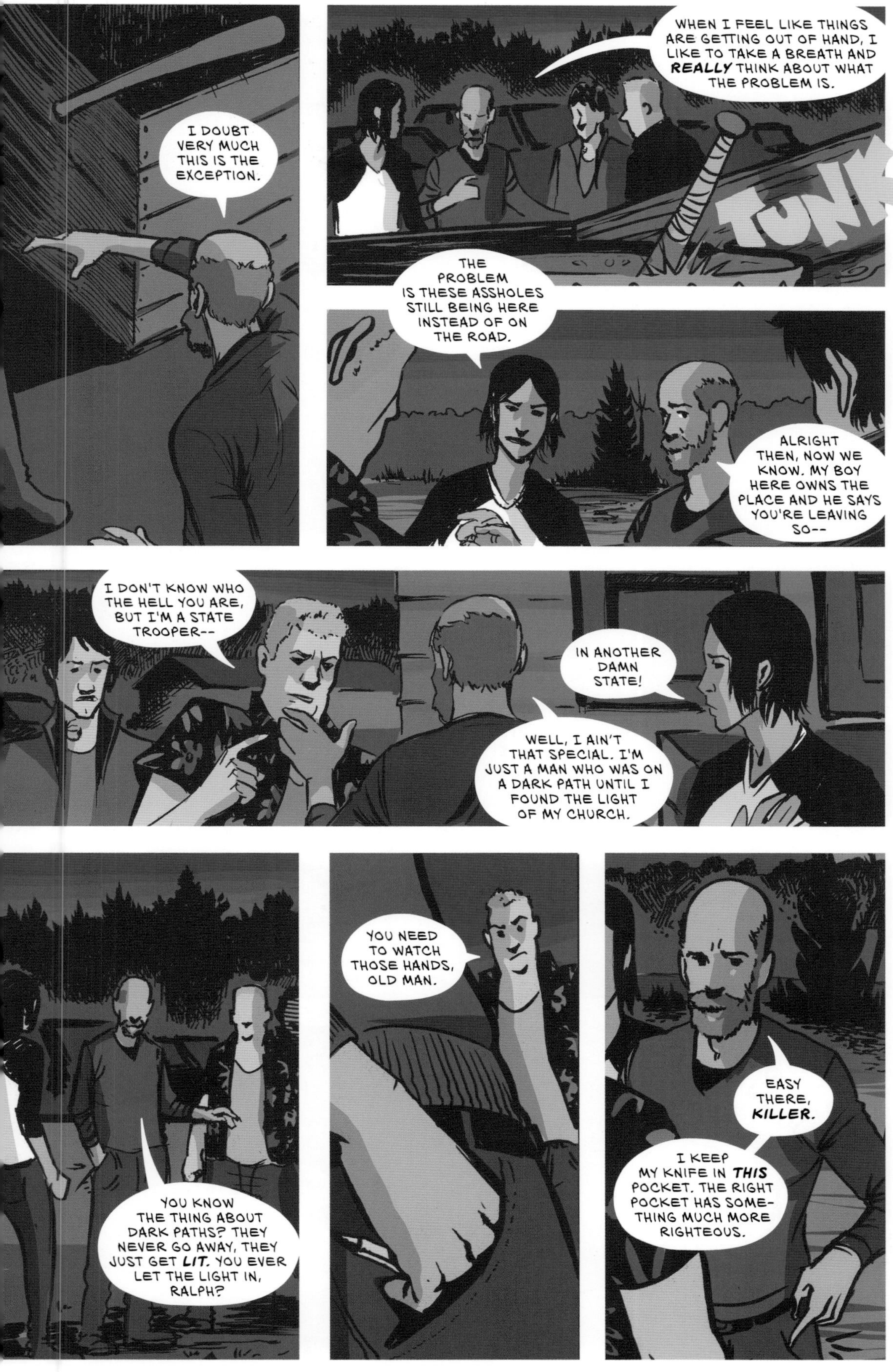
I DOUBT VERY MUCH THIS IS THE EXCEPTION.
WHEN I FEEL LIKE THINGS ARE GETTING OUT OF HAND, I LIKE TO TAKE A BREATH AND **REALLY** THINK ABOUT WHAT THE PROBLEM IS.
TUNK
THE PROBLEM IS THESE ASSHOLES STILL BEING HERE INSTEAD OF ON THE ROAD.
ALRIGHT THEN, NOW WE KNOW. MY BOY HERE OWNS THE PLACE AND HE SAYS YOU'RE LEAVING SO--
I DON'T KNOW WHO THE HELL YOU ARE, BUT I'M A STATE TROOPER--
IN ANOTHER DAMN STATE!
WELL, I AIN'T THAT SPECIAL. I'M JUST A MAN WHO WAS ON A DARK PATH UNTIL I FOUND THE LIGHT OF MY CHURCH.
YOU KNOW THE THING ABOUT DARK PATHS? THEY NEVER GO AWAY, THEY JUST GET **LIT.** YOU EVER LET THE LIGHT IN, RALPH?
YOU NEED TO WATCH THOSE HANDS, OLD MAN.
EASY THERE, **KILLER.**
I KEEP MY KNIFE IN **THIS** POCKET. THE RIGHT POCKET HAS SOMETHING MUCH MORE RIGHTEOUS.

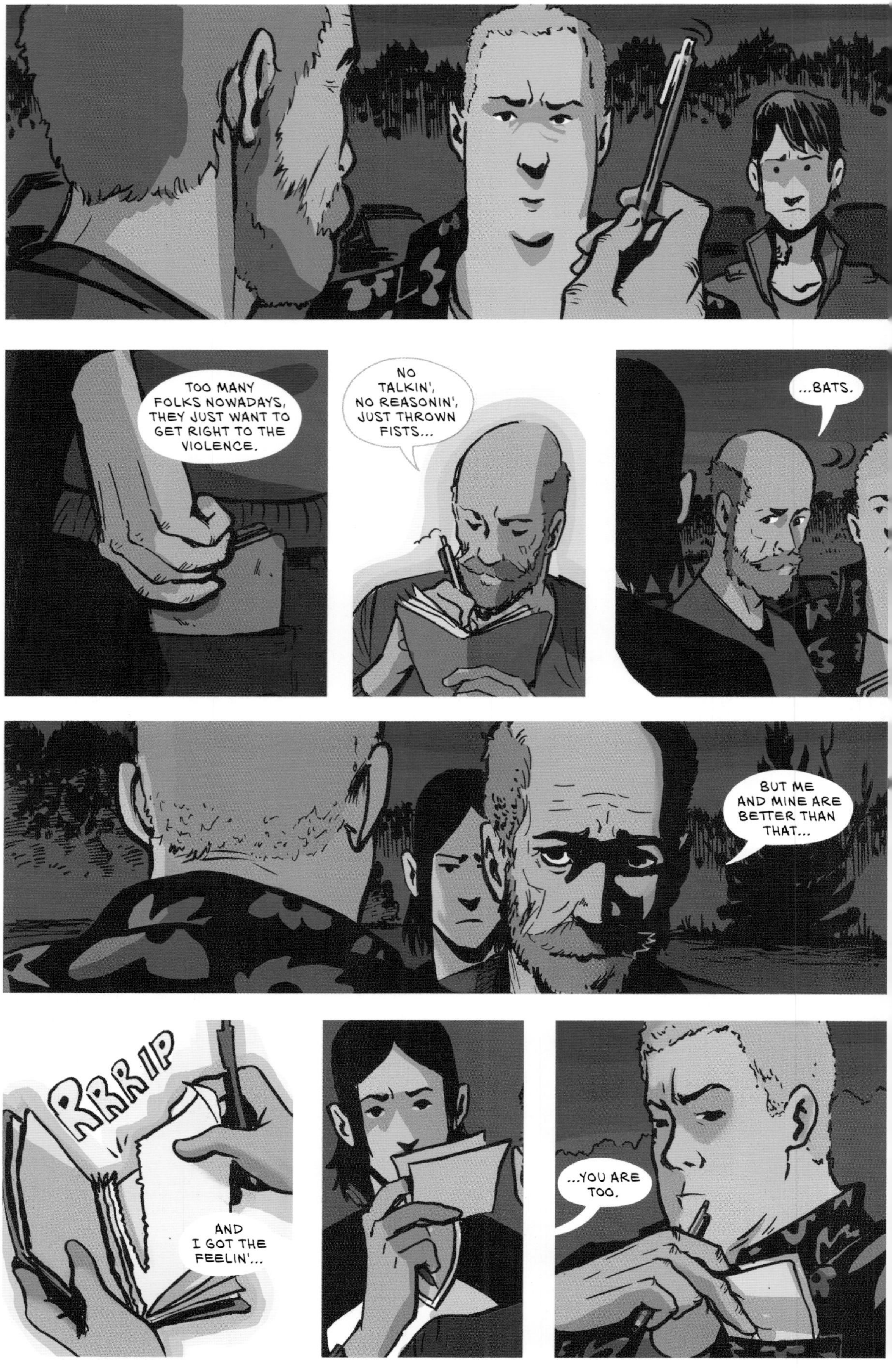
TOO MANY FOLKS NOWADAYS, THEY JUST WANT TO GET RIGHT TO THE VIOLENCE.
NO TALKIN', NO REASONIN', JUST THROWN FISTS...
...BATS.
BUT ME AND MINE ARE BETTER THAN THAT...
RRRIP
AND I GOT THE FEELIN'...
...YOU ARE TOO.

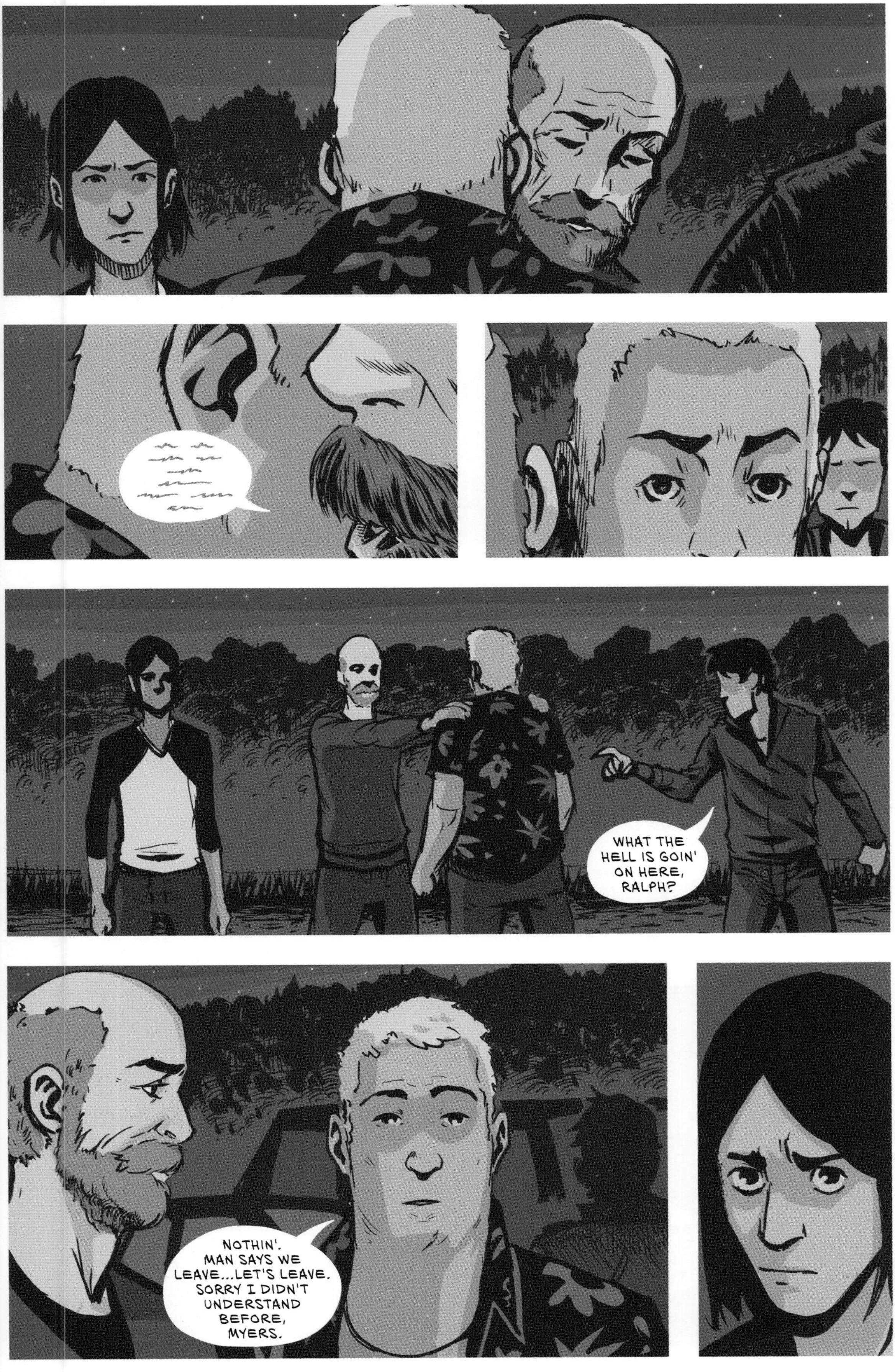
WHAT THE HELL IS GOIN' ON HERE, RALPH?
NOTHIN'. MAN SAYS WE LEAVE...LET'S LEAVE. SORRY I DIDN'T UNDERSTAND BEFORE, MYERS.

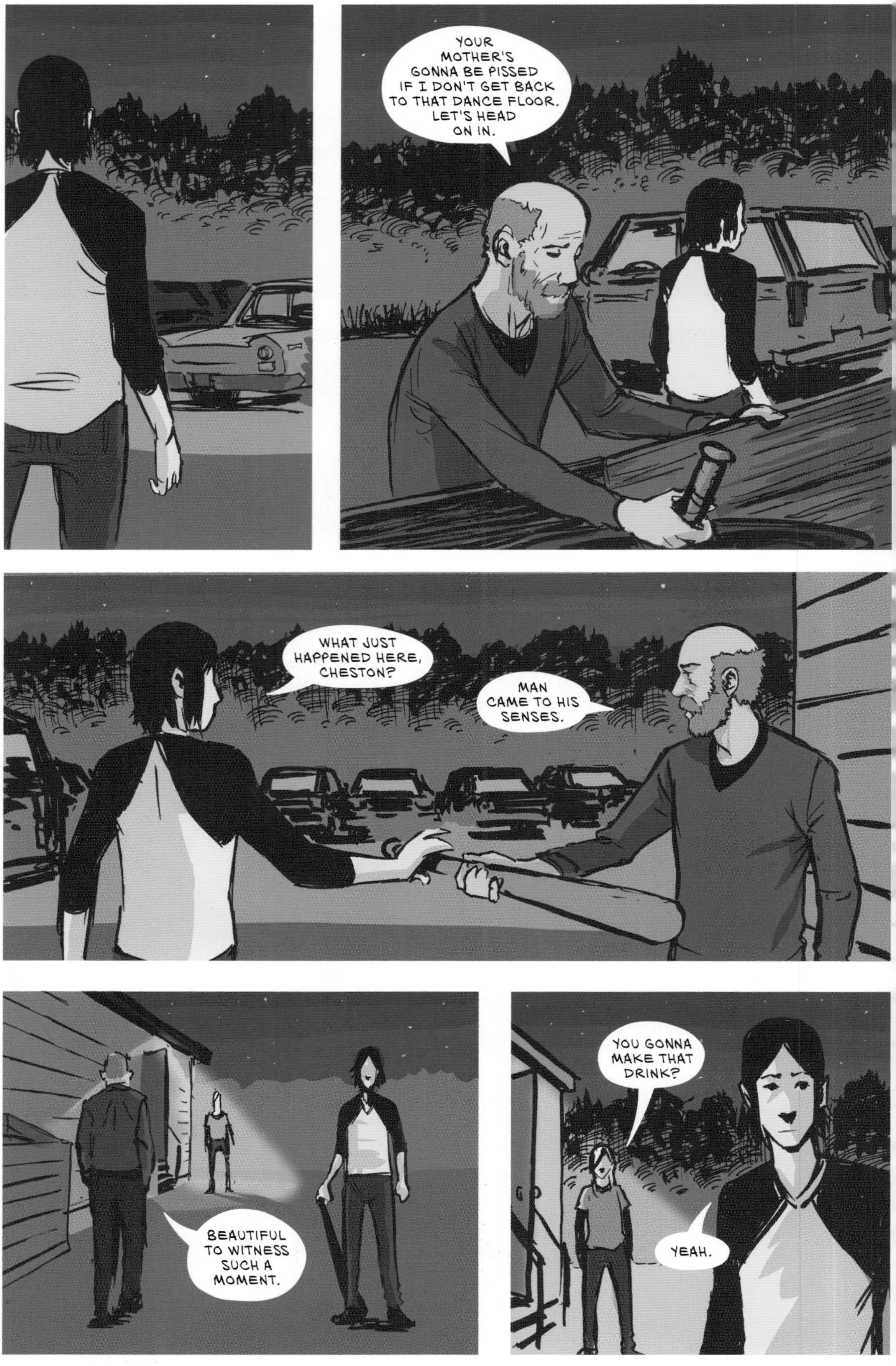
YOUR MOTHER'S GONNA BE PISSED IF I DON'T GET BACK TO THAT DANCE FLOOR. LET'S HEAD ON IN.
WHAT JUST HAPPENED HERE, CHESTON?
MAN CAME TO HIS SENSES.
BEAUTIFUL TO WITNESS SUCH A MOMENT.
YOU GONNA MAKE THAT DRINK?
YEAH.

# CHAPTER SIX

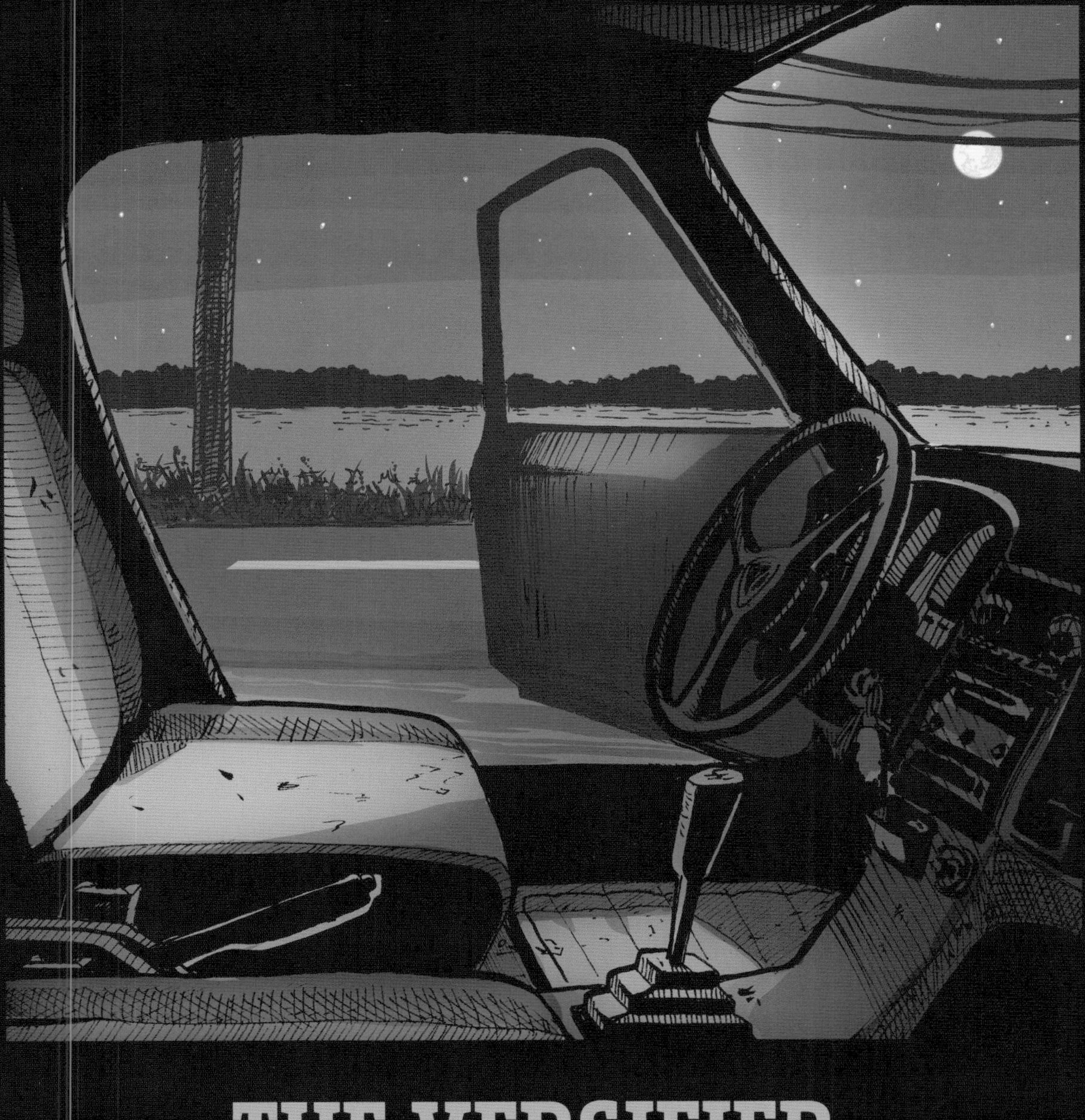

# THE VERSIFIER

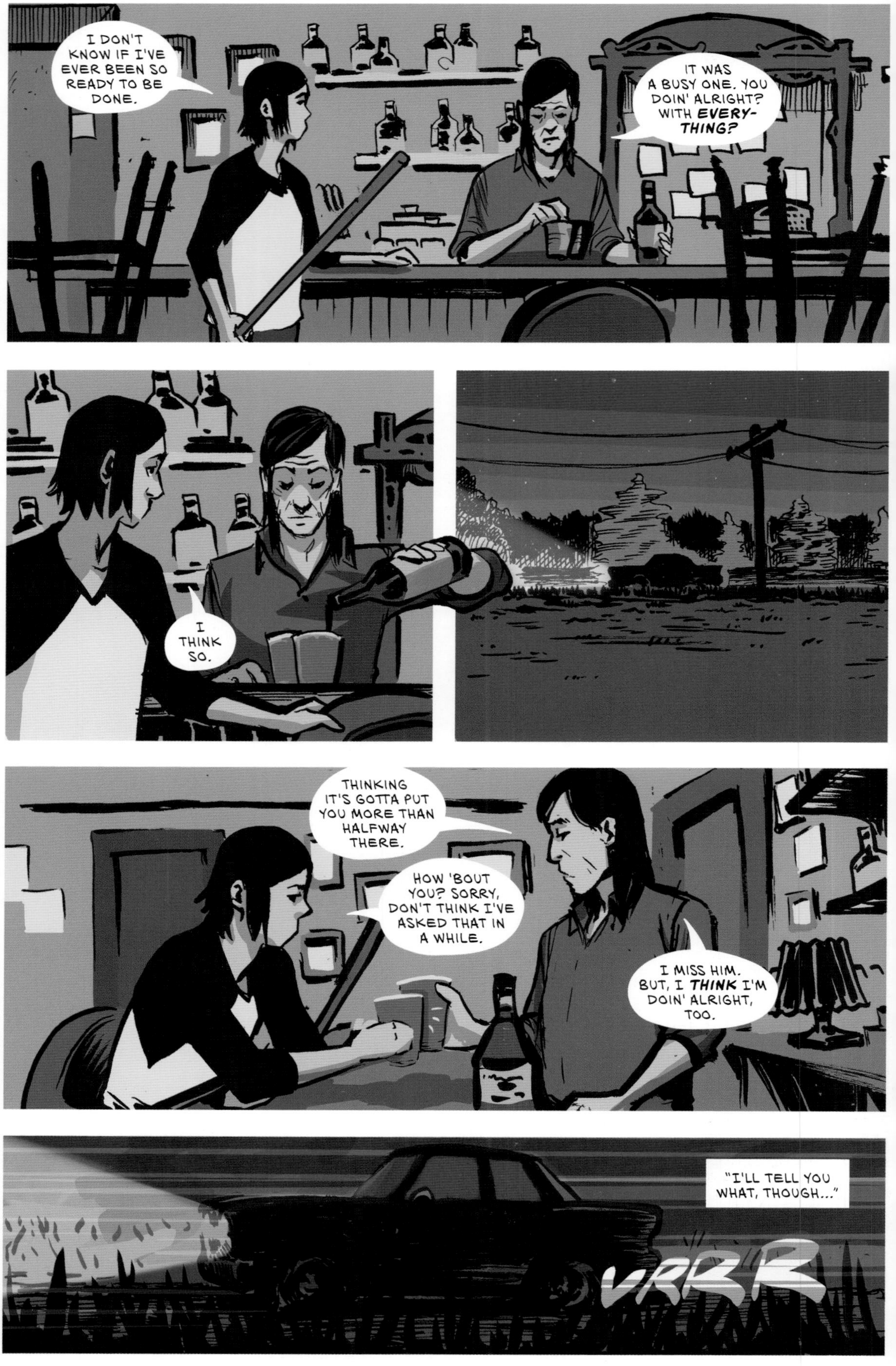
I DON'T KNOW IF I'VE EVER BEEN SO READY TO BE DONE.
IT WAS A BUSY ONE. YOU DOIN' ALRIGHT? WITH EVERYTHING?
I THINK SO.
THINKING IT'S GOTTA PUT YOU MORE THAN HALFWAY THERE.
HOW 'BOUT YOU? SORRY, DON'T THINK I'VE ASKED THAT IN A WHILE.
I MISS HIM. BUT, I THINK I'M DOIN' ALRIGHT, TOO.
"I'LL TELL YOU WHAT, THOUGH..."
VRRR

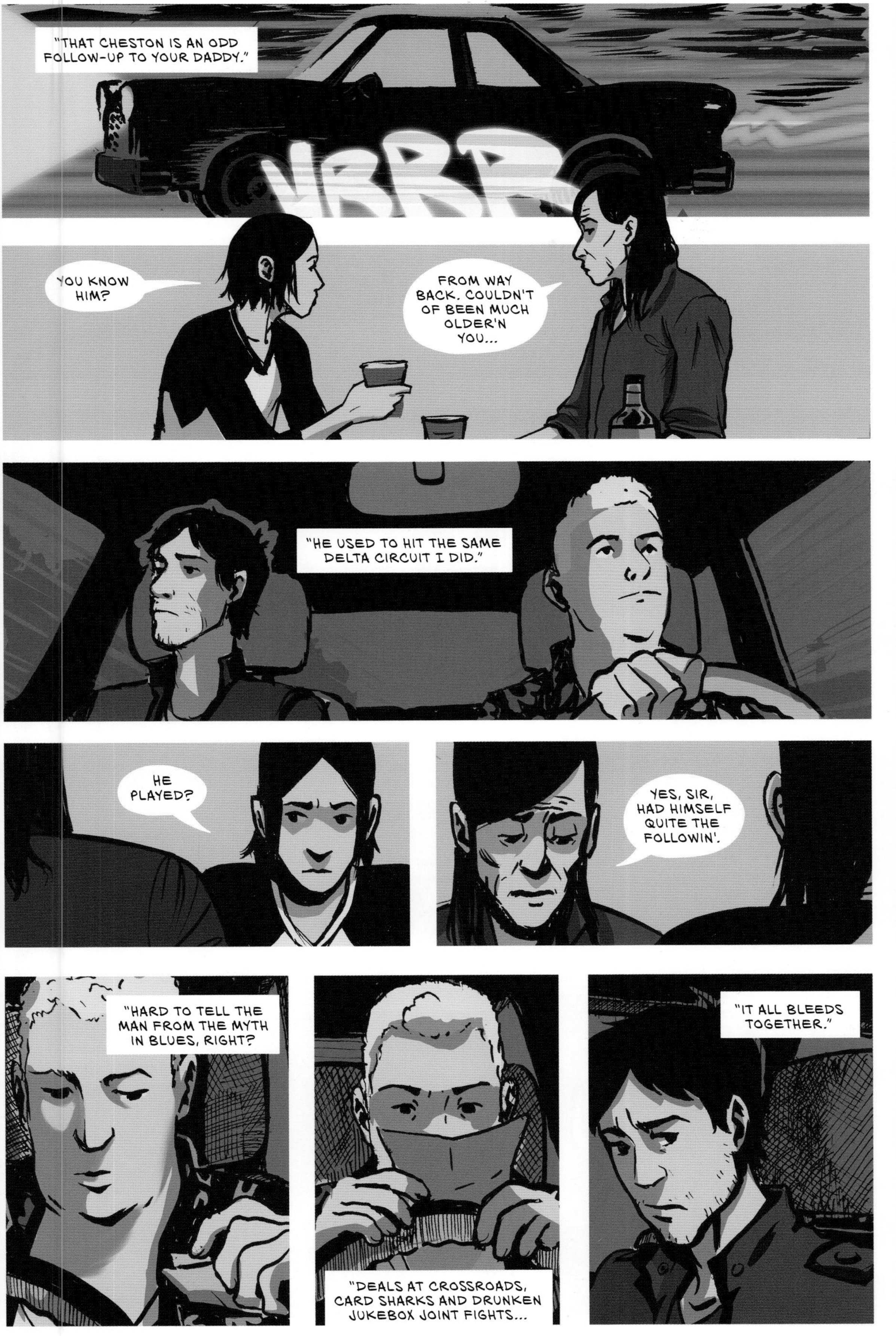
"THAT CHESTON IS AN ODD FOLLOW-UP TO YOUR DADDY."
VRRR
YOU KNOW HIM?
FROM WAY BACK. COULDN'T OF BEEN MUCH OLDER'N YOU...
"HE USED TO HIT THE SAME DELTA CIRCUIT I DID."
HE PLAYED?
YES, SIR, HAD HIMSELF QUITE THE FOLLOWIN'.
"HARD TO TELL THE MAN FROM THE MYTH IN BLUES, RIGHT?
"DEALS AT CROSSROADS, CARD SHARKS AND DRUNKEN JUKEBOX JOINT FIGHTS...
"IT ALL BLEEDS TOGETHER."

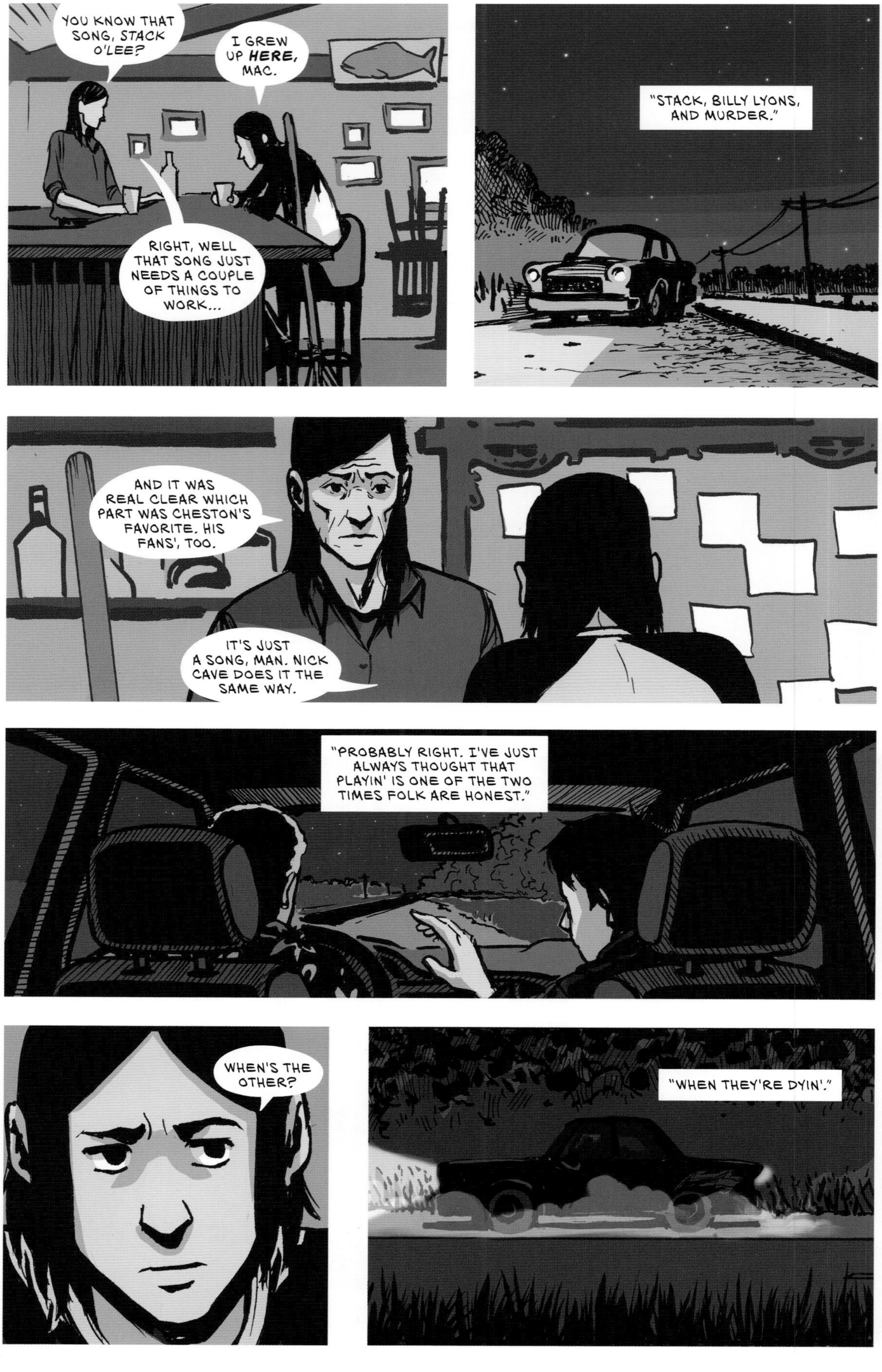
YOU KNOW THAT SONG, STACK O'LEE?
I GREW UP **HERE,** MAC.
RIGHT, WELL THAT SONG JUST NEEDS A COUPLE OF THINGS TO WORK...
"STACK, BILLY LYONS, AND MURDER."
AND IT WAS REAL CLEAR WHICH PART WAS CHESTON'S FAVORITE. HIS FANS', TOO.
IT'S JUST A SONG, MAN. NICK CAVE DOES IT THE SAME WAY.
"PROBABLY RIGHT. I'VE JUST ALWAYS THOUGHT THAT PLAYIN' IS ONE OF THE TWO TIMES FOLK ARE HONEST."
WHEN'S THE OTHER?
"WHEN THEY'RE DYIN'."

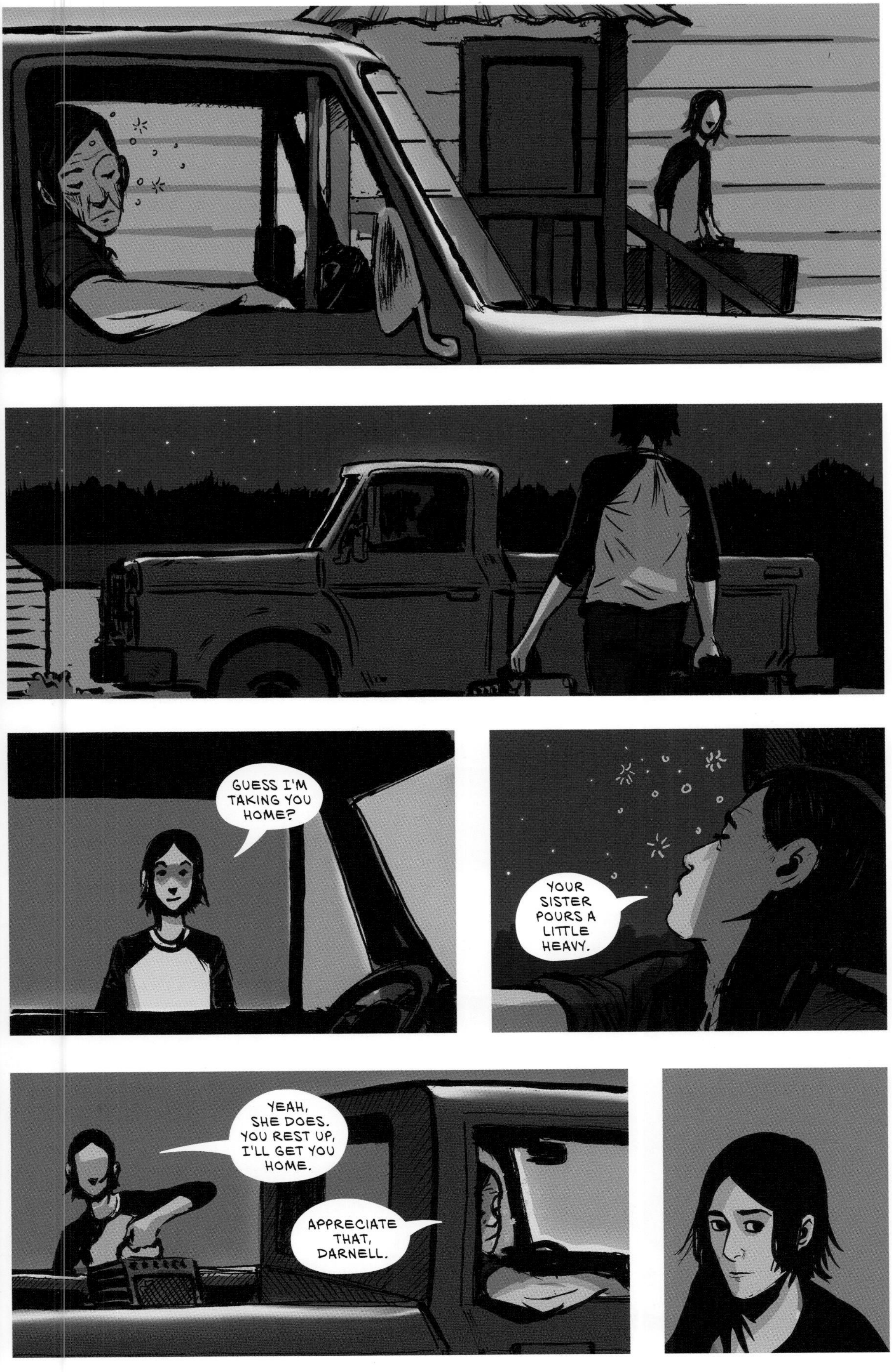
GUESS I'M TAKING YOU HOME?
YOUR SISTER POURS A LITTLE HEAVY.
YEAH, SHE DOES. YOU REST UP, I'LL GET YOU HOME.
APPRECIATE THAT, DARNELL.

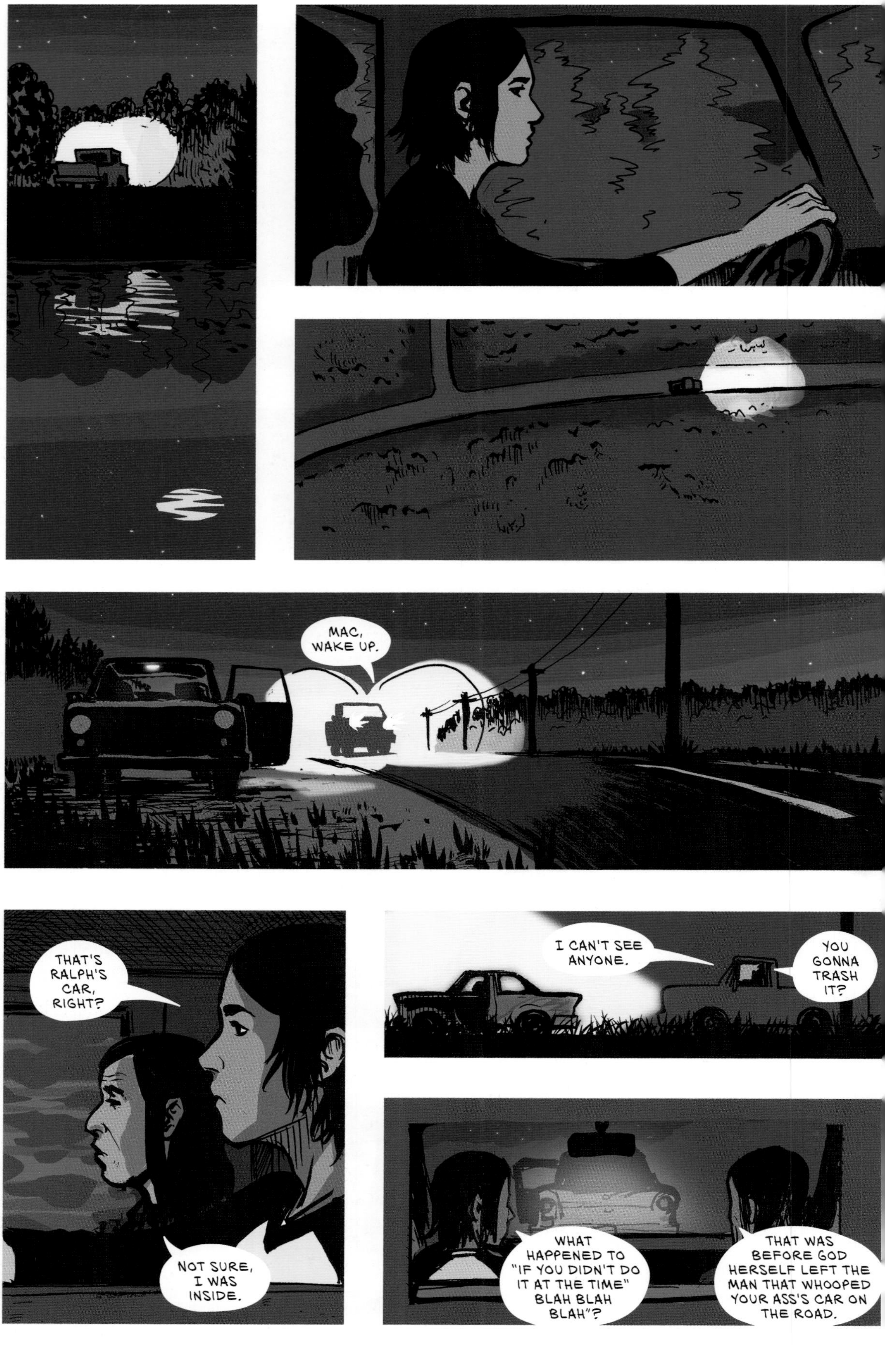
MAC, WAKE UP.
THAT'S RALPH'S CAR, RIGHT?
NOT SURE, I WAS INSIDE.
I CAN'T SEE ANYONE.
YOU GONNA TRASH IT?
WHAT HAPPENED TO "IF YOU DIDN'T DO IT AT THE TIME" BLAH BLAH BLAH"?
THAT WAS BEFORE GOD HERSELF LEFT THE MAN THAT WHOOPED YOUR ASS'S CAR ON THE ROAD.

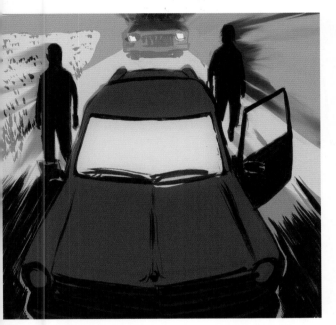

WE NEED TO CALL THE COPS.

# CHAPTER SEVEN

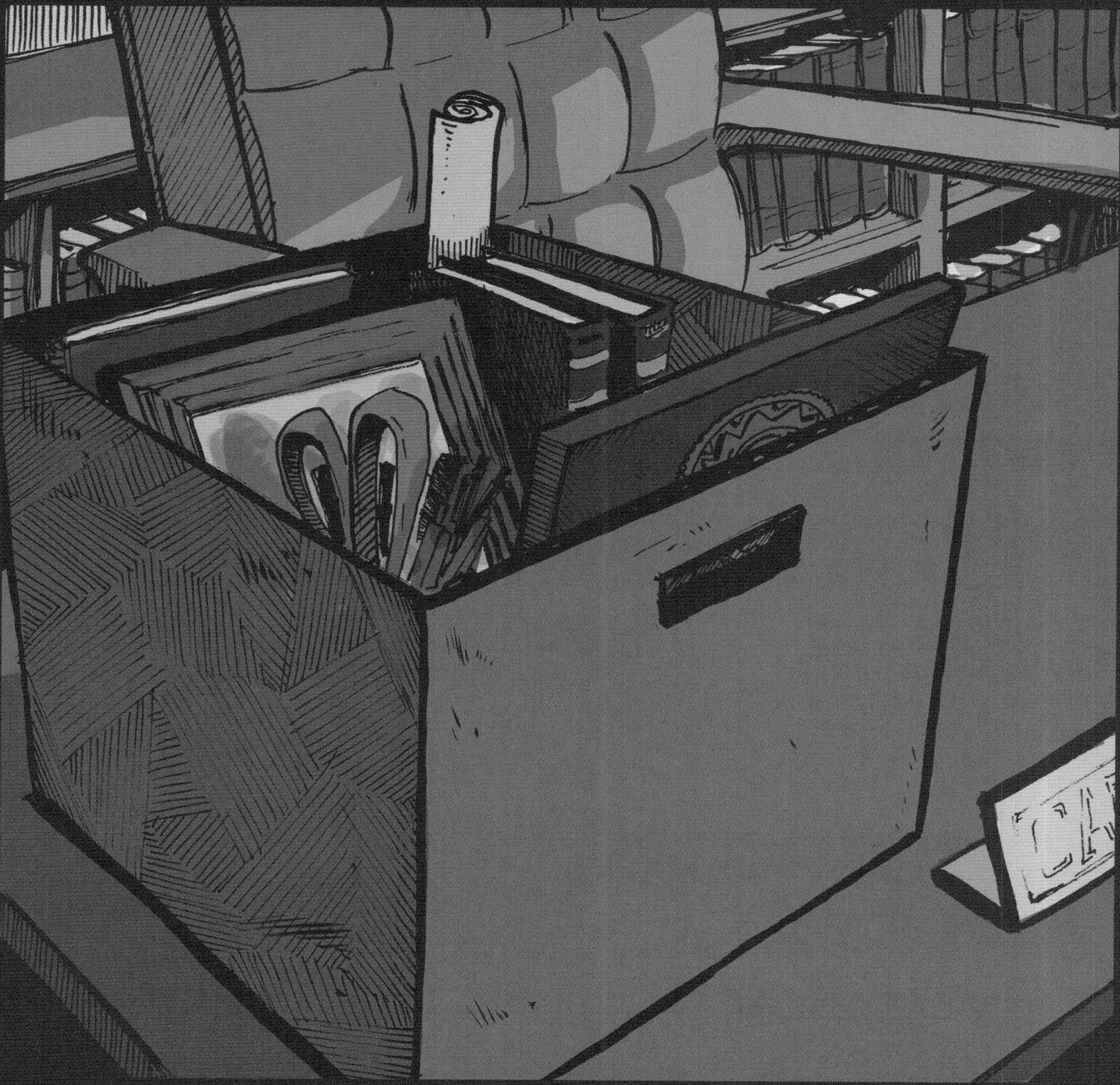

# A PLACE FOR EVERYTHING

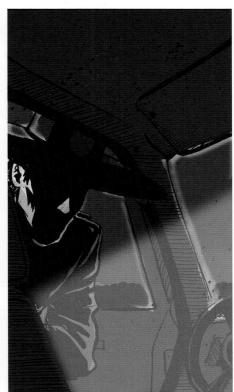

AND Y'ALL SAID BOTH DOORS WERE SHUT?

NO, SIR, THE DRIVER'S SIDE WAS OPEN.

AND THE...VICTIM, HE WAS ALREADY, UH--

YEAH.

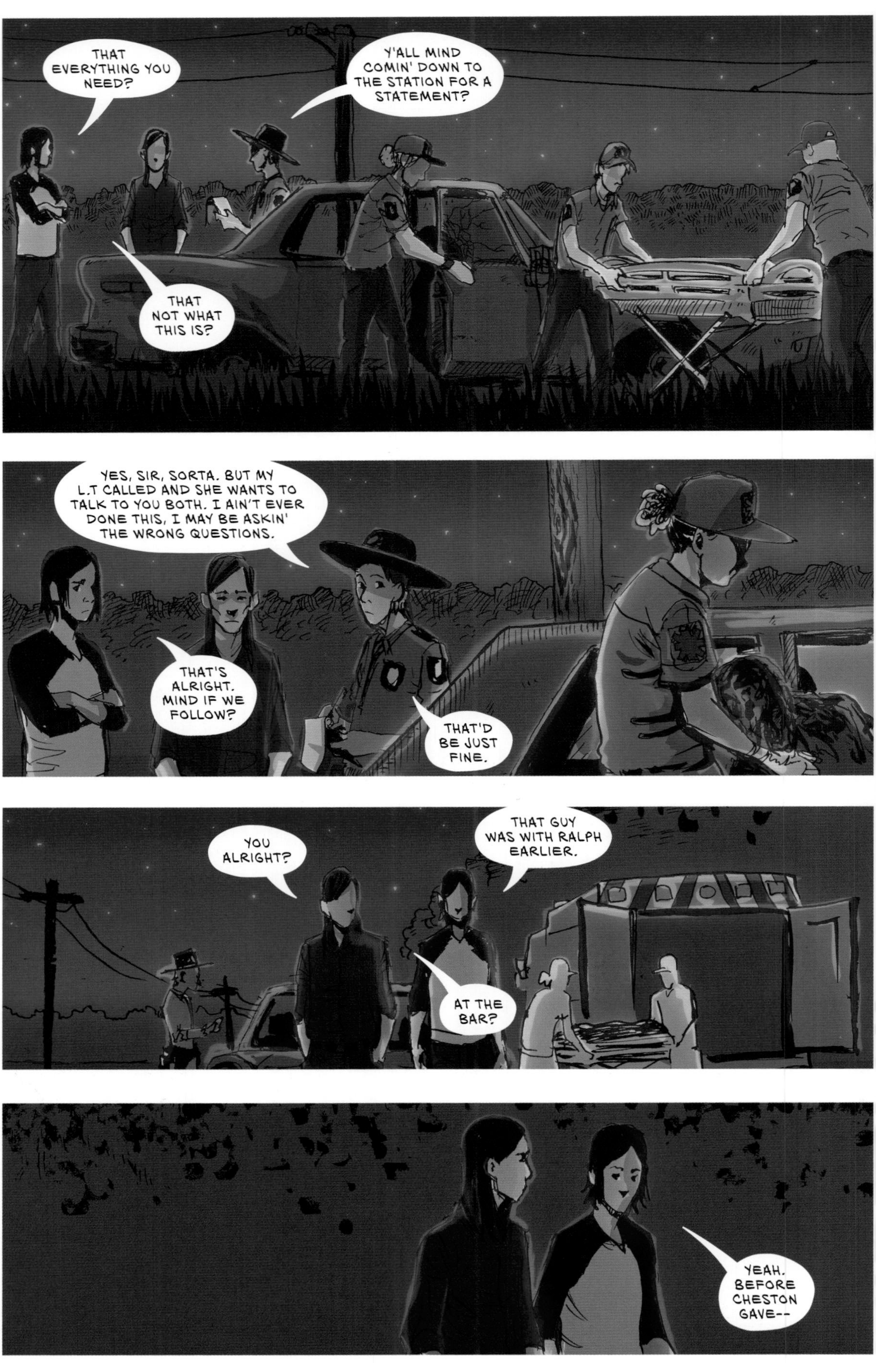
THAT EVERYTHING YOU NEED?
Y'ALL MIND COMIN' DOWN TO THE STATION FOR A STATEMENT?
THAT NOT WHAT THIS IS?
YES, SIR, SORTA. BUT MY L.T CALLED AND SHE WANTS TO TALK TO YOU BOTH. I AIN'T EVER DONE THIS, I MAY BE ASKIN' THE WRONG QUESTIONS.
THAT'S ALRIGHT. MIND IF WE FOLLOW?
THAT'D BE JUST FINE.
YOU ALRIGHT?
THAT GUY WAS WITH RALPH EARLIER.
AT THE BAR?
YEAH. BEFORE CHESTON GAVE--

SSH!

WHATEVER FIGHT THEY GOT INTO AFTER THEY LEFT AIN'T GOT A DAMN THING TO DO WITH YOU. THEY ASK, YOU ANSWER. THEY DON'T NEED MORE THAN THAT.

EVERYTHING ALRIGHT, FELLAS?

YES, SIR, JUST TIRED IS ALL.

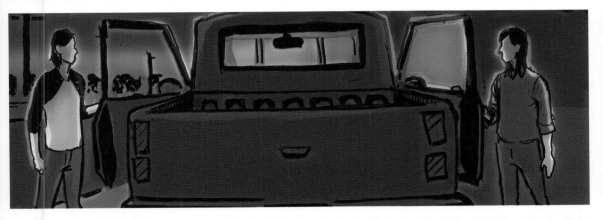

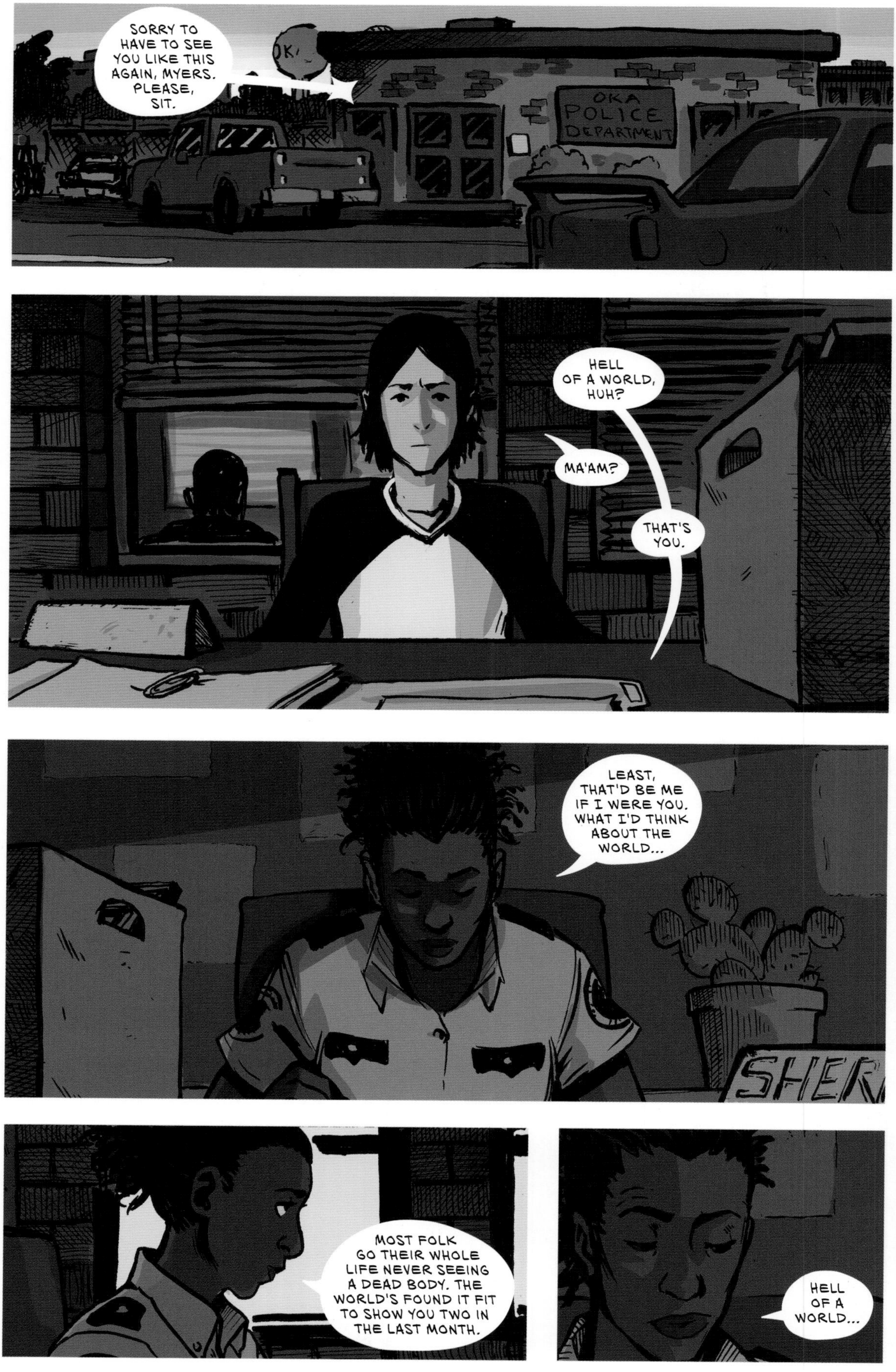
SORRY TO HAVE TO SEE YOU LIKE THIS AGAIN, MYERS. PLEASE, SIT.
OKA POLICE DEPARTMENT
HELL OF A WORLD, HUH?
MA'AM?
THAT'S YOU.
LEAST, THAT'D BE ME IF I WERE YOU. WHAT I'D THINK ABOUT THE WORLD...
MOST FOLK GO THEIR WHOLE LIFE NEVER SEEING A DEAD BODY. THE WORLD'S FOUND IT FIT TO SHOW YOU TWO IN THE LAST MONTH.
HELL OF A WORLD...

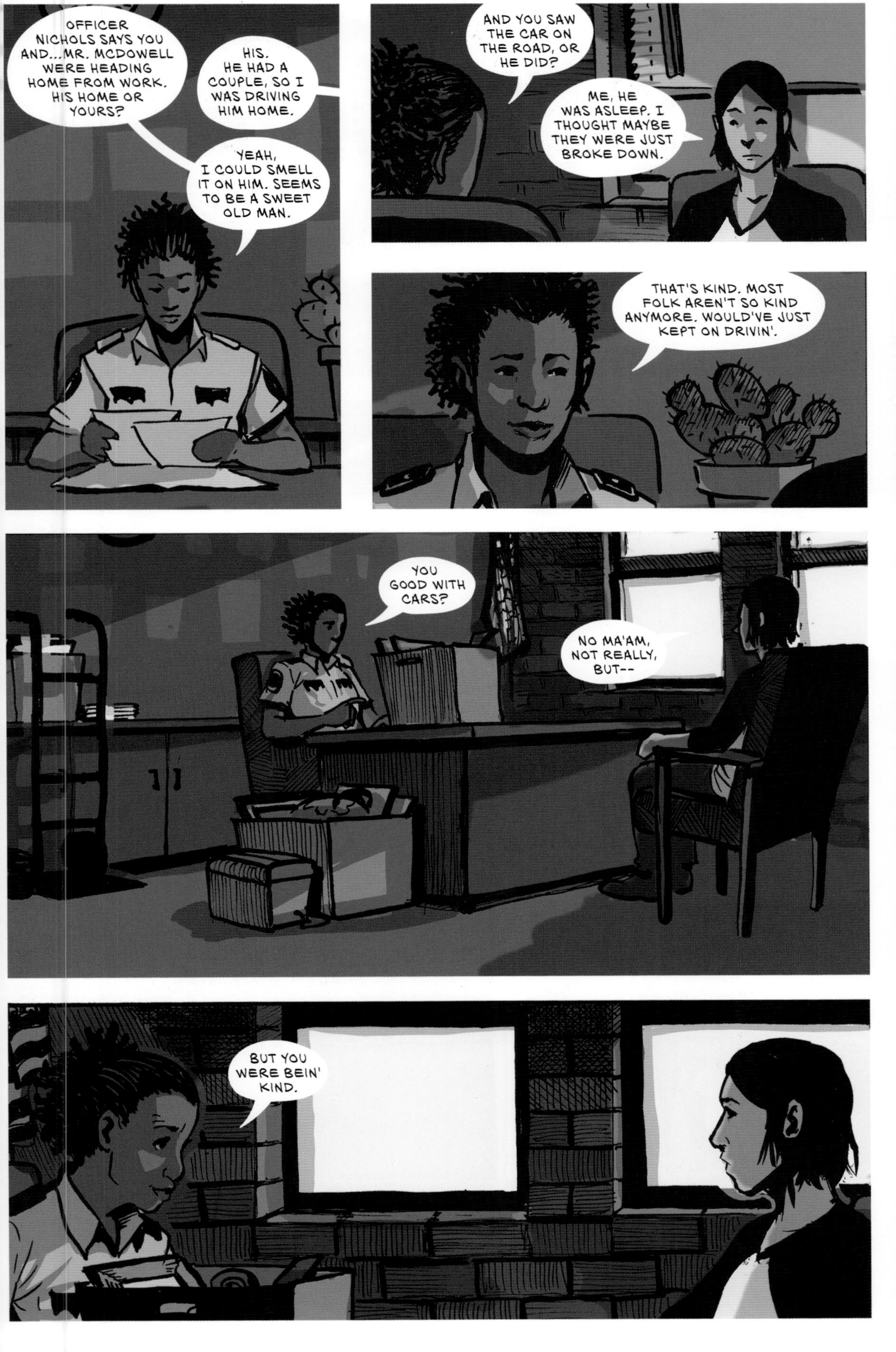
OFFICER NICHOLS SAYS YOU AND...MR. MCDOWELL WERE HEADING HOME FROM WORK. HIS HOME OR YOURS?
HIS. HE HAD A COUPLE, SO I WAS DRIVING HIM HOME.
YEAH, I COULD SMELL IT ON HIM. SEEMS TO BE A SWEET OLD MAN.
AND YOU SAW THE CAR ON THE ROAD, OR HE DID?
ME, HE WAS ASLEEP. I THOUGHT MAYBE THEY WERE JUST BROKE DOWN.
THAT'S KIND. MOST FOLK AREN'T SO KIND ANYMORE. WOULD'VE JUST KEPT ON DRIVIN'.
YOU GOOD WITH CARS?
NO MA'AM, NOT REALLY, BUT--
BUT YOU WERE BEIN' KIND.

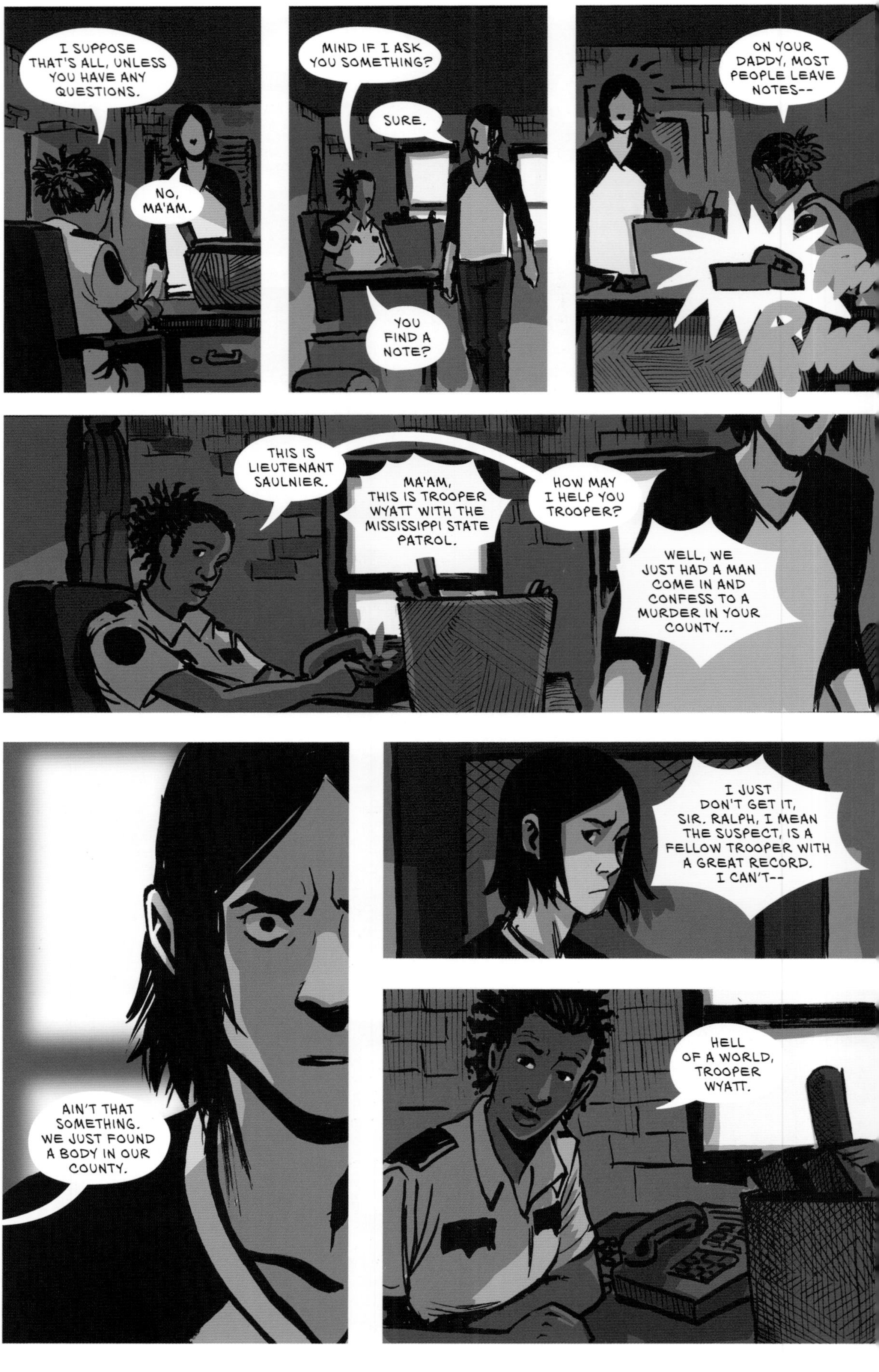
I SUPPOSE THAT'S ALL, UNLESS YOU HAVE ANY QUESTIONS.
NO, MA'AM.
MIND IF I ASK YOU SOMETHING?
SURE.
YOU FIND A NOTE?
ON YOUR DADDY, MOST PEOPLE LEAVE NOTES--
THIS IS LIEUTENANT SAULNIER.
MA'AM, THIS IS TROOPER WYATT WITH THE MISSISSIPPI STATE PATROL.
HOW MAY I HELP YOU TROOPER?
WELL, WE JUST HAD A MAN COME IN AND CONFESS TO A MURDER IN YOUR COUNTY...
AIN'T THAT SOMETHING. WE JUST FOUND A BODY IN OUR COUNTY.
I JUST DON'T GET IT, SIR. RALPH, I MEAN THE SUSPECT, IS A FELLOW TROOPER WITH A GREAT RECORD. I CAN'T--
HELL OF A WORLD, TROOPER WYATT.

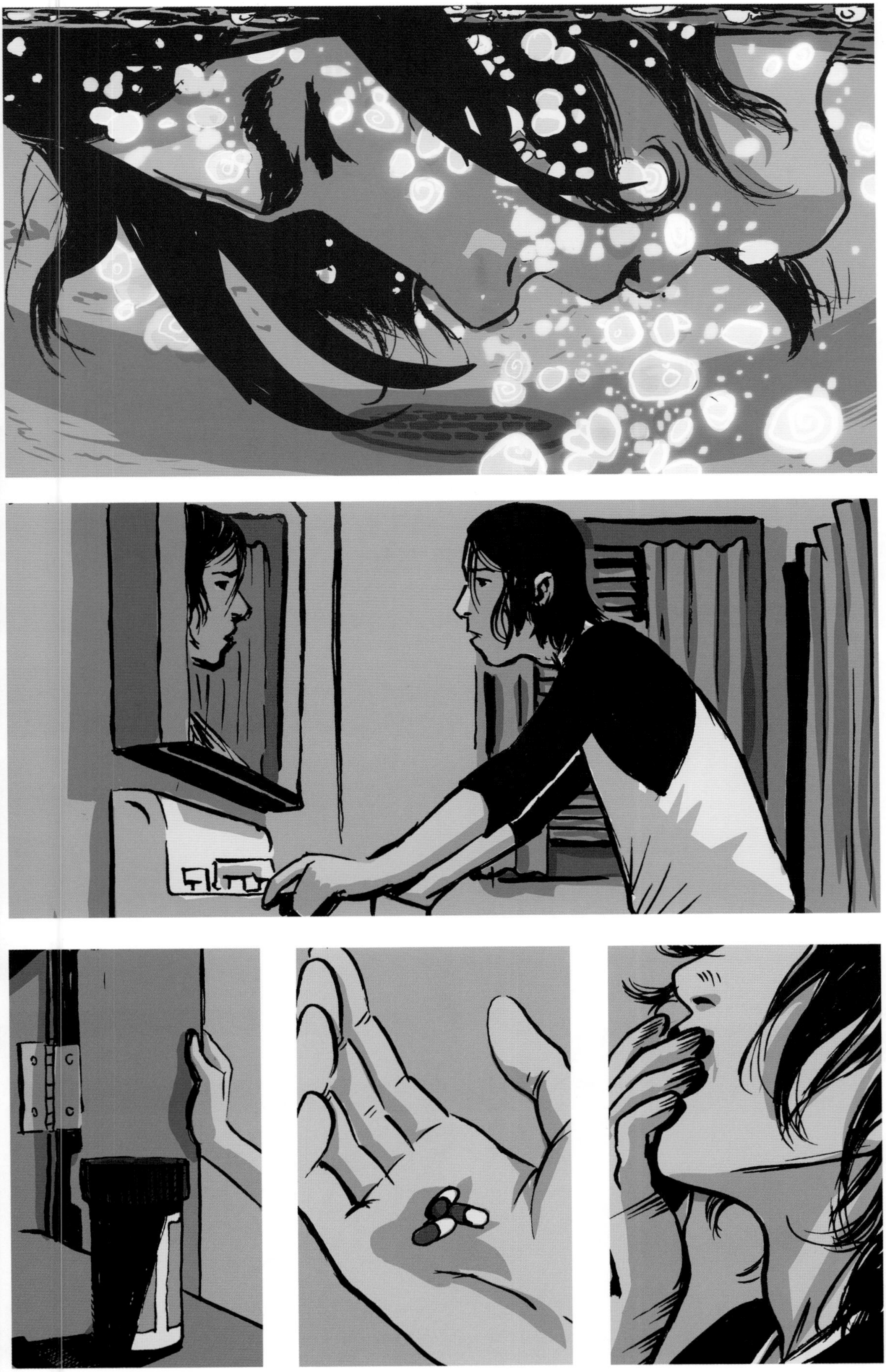

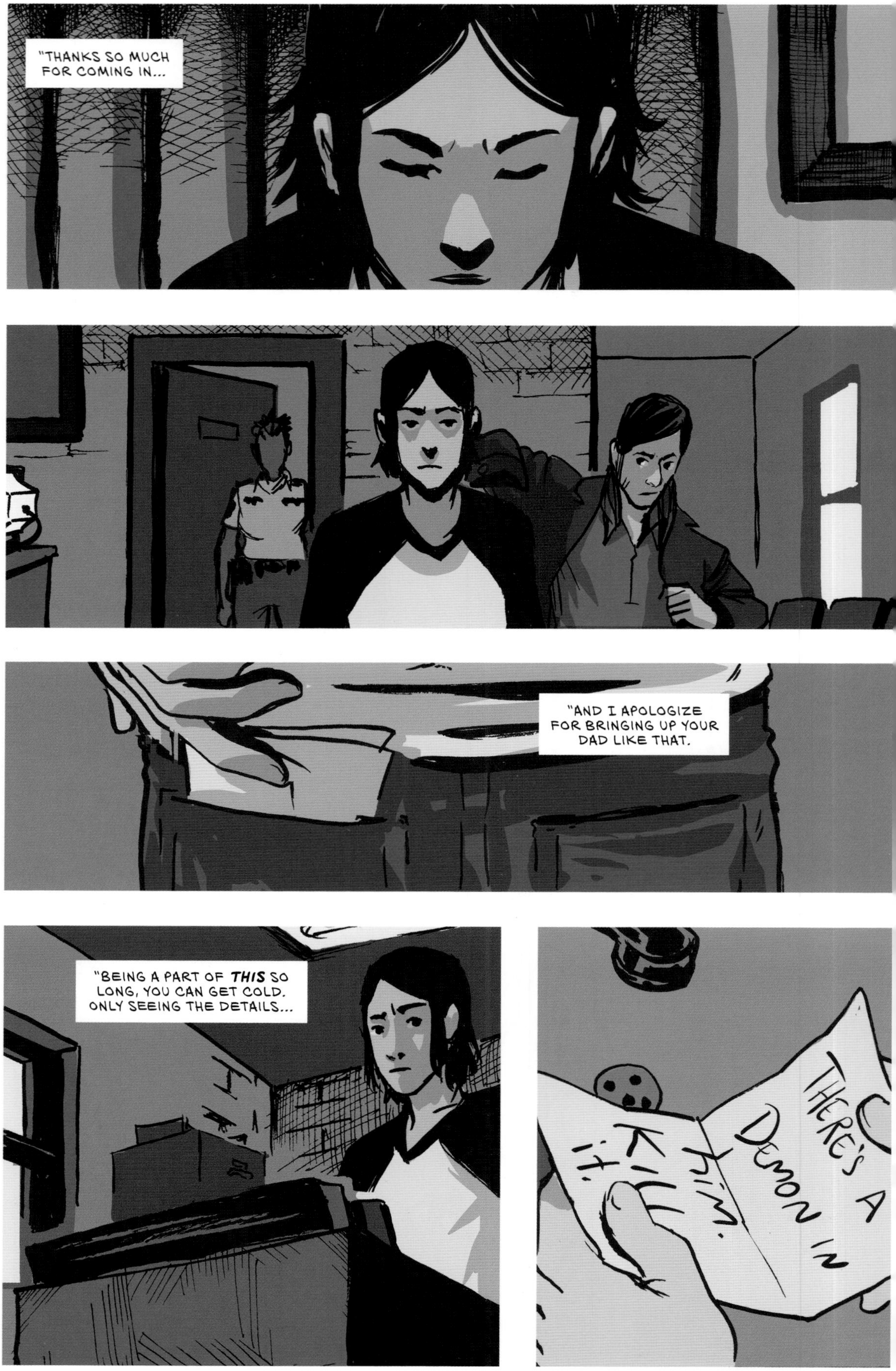
"THANKS SO MUCH FOR COMING IN...
"AND I APOLOGIZE FOR BRINGING UP YOUR DAD LIKE THAT.
"BEING A PART OF ***THIS*** SO LONG, YOU CAN GET COLD. ONLY SEEING THE DETAILS...
THERE'S A DEMON IN HIM.
KILL IT.

"BUT IN TIMES LIKE THESE, I'VE ALWAYS FOUND WARMTH IN FAMILY...

"IF IT GETS TO BE TOO MUCH...

"OR YOU DON'T WANT TO BE ALONE...

"FAMILY IS NEVER TOO FAR."

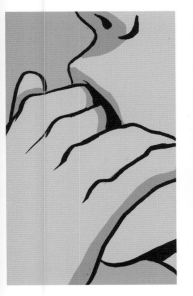

GHYUUK

# CHAPTER EIGHT

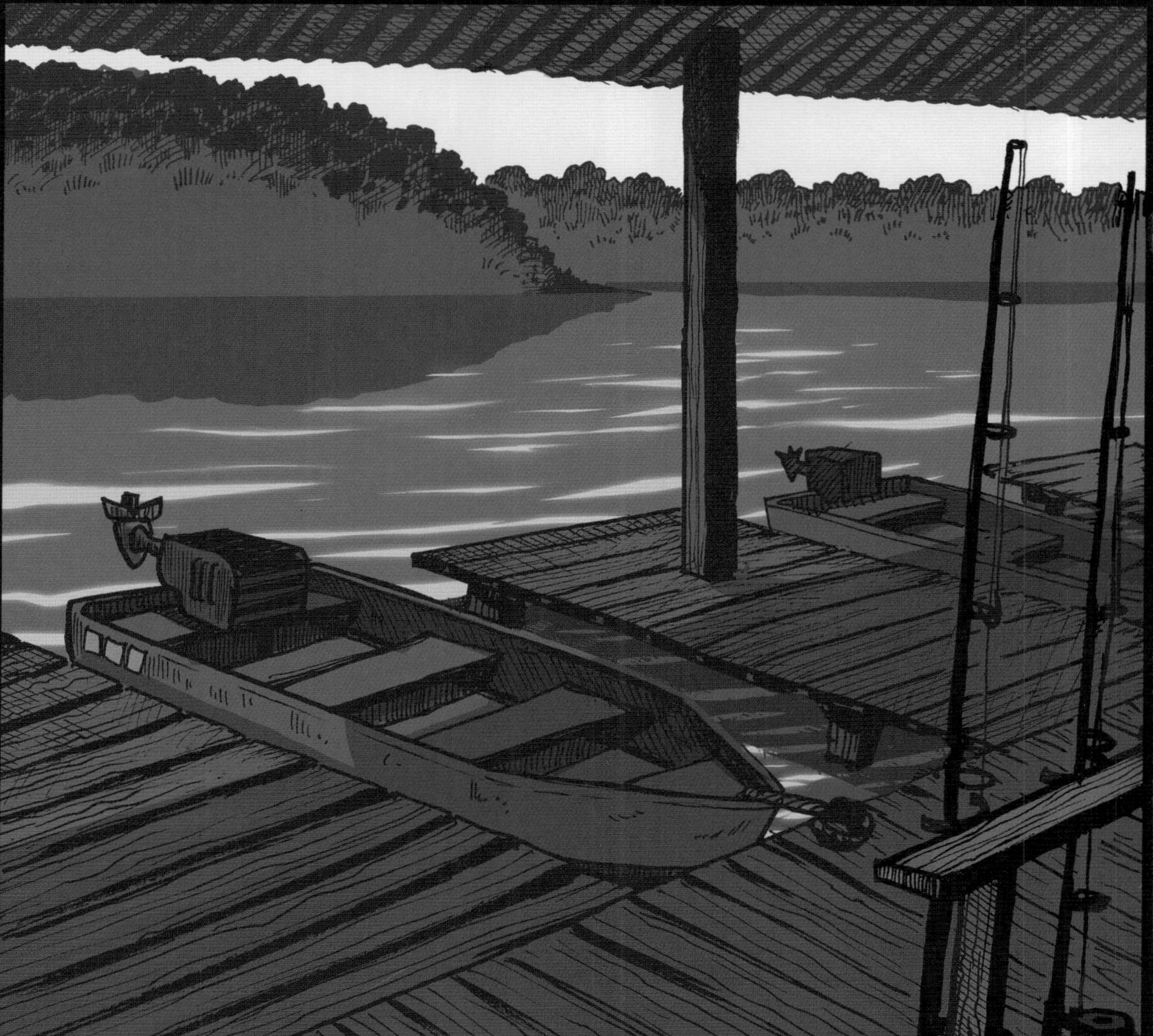

# TWILIGHT TO DAWN

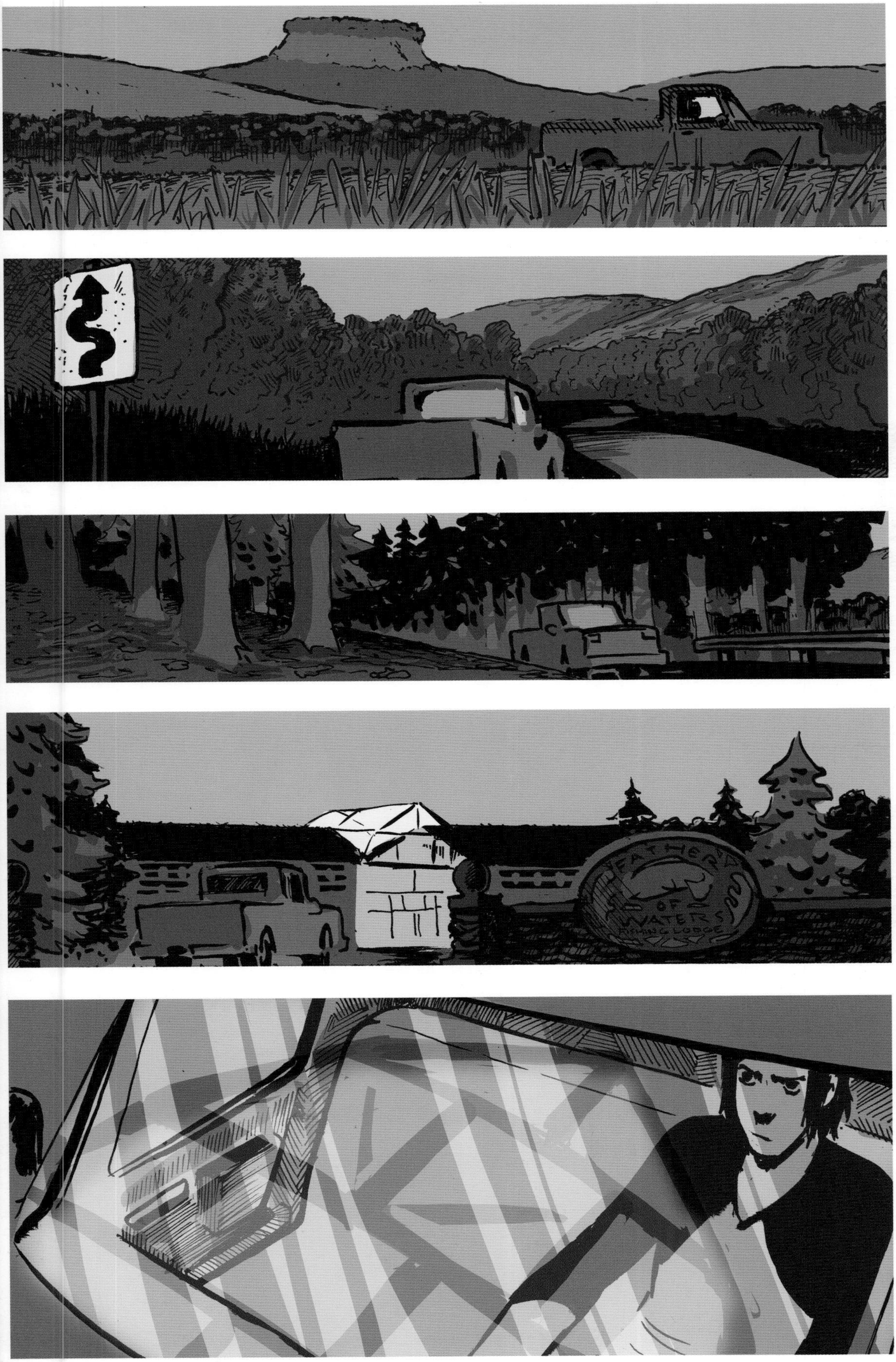
FATHER
OF
WATERS
FISHING LODGE

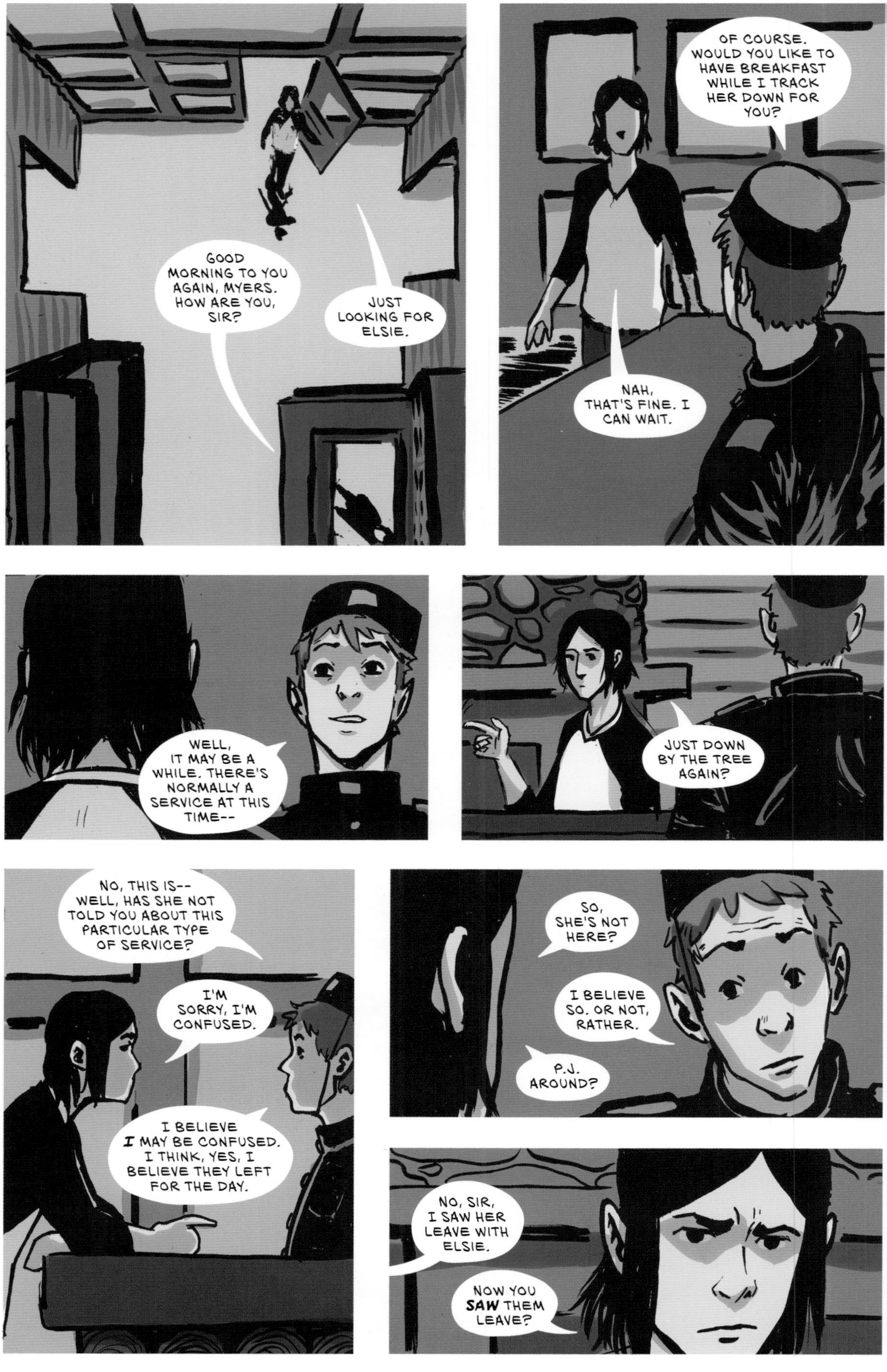
GOOD MORNING TO YOU AGAIN, MYERS. HOW ARE YOU, SIR?
JUST LOOKING FOR ELSIE.
OF COURSE. WOULD YOU LIKE TO HAVE BREAKFAST WHILE I TRACK HER DOWN FOR YOU?
NAH, THAT'S FINE. I CAN WAIT.
WELL, IT MAY BE A WHILE. THERE'S NORMALLY A SERVICE AT THIS TIME--
JUST DOWN BY THE TREE AGAIN?
NO, THIS IS-- WELL, HAS SHE NOT TOLD YOU ABOUT THIS PARTICULAR TYPE OF SERVICE?
I'M SORRY, I'M CONFUSED.
I BELIEVE *I* MAY BE CONFUSED. I THINK, YES, I BELIEVE THEY LEFT FOR THE DAY.
SO, SHE'S NOT HERE?
I BELIEVE SO. OR NOT, RATHER.
P.J. AROUND?
NO, SIR, I SAW HER LEAVE WITH ELSIE.
NOW YOU **SAW** THEM LEAVE?

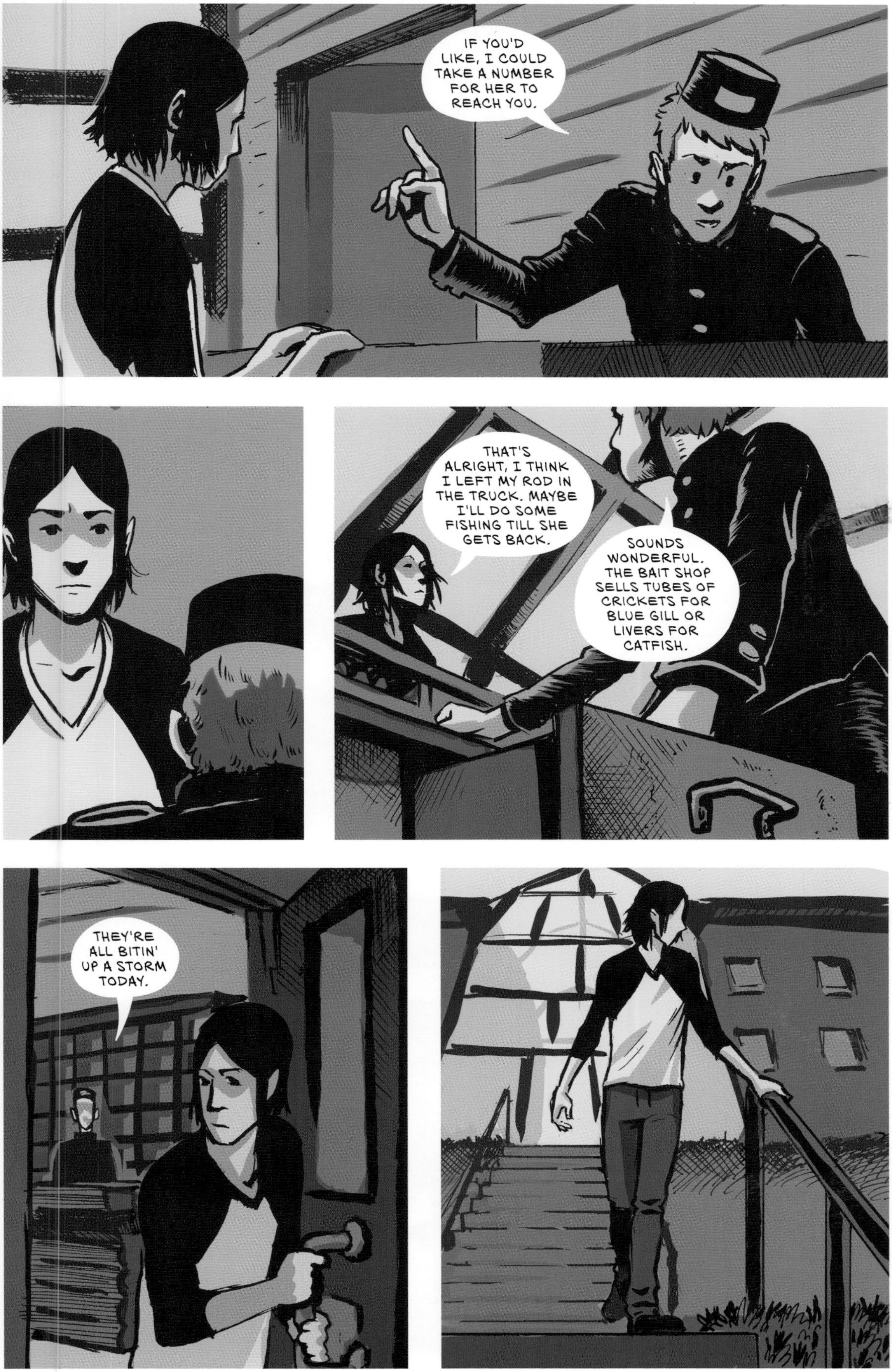
IF YOU'D LIKE, I COULD TAKE A NUMBER FOR HER TO REACH YOU.
THAT'S ALRIGHT, I THINK I LEFT MY ROD IN THE TRUCK. MAYBE I'LL DO SOME FISHING TILL SHE GETS BACK.
SOUNDS WONDERFUL. THE BAIT SHOP SELLS TUBES OF CRICKETS FOR BLUE GILL OR LIVERS FOR CATFISH.
THEY'RE ALL BITIN' UP A STORM TODAY.

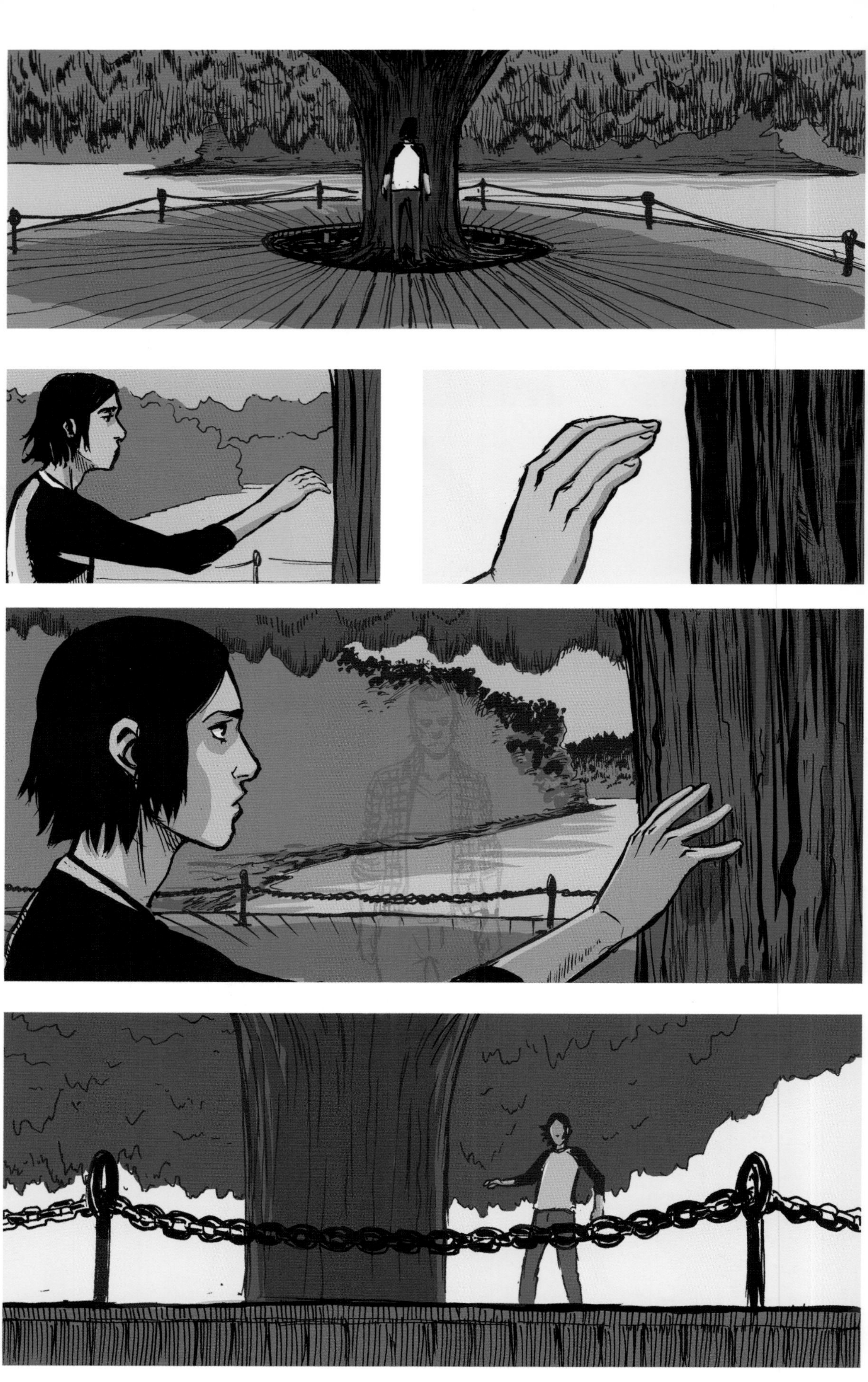

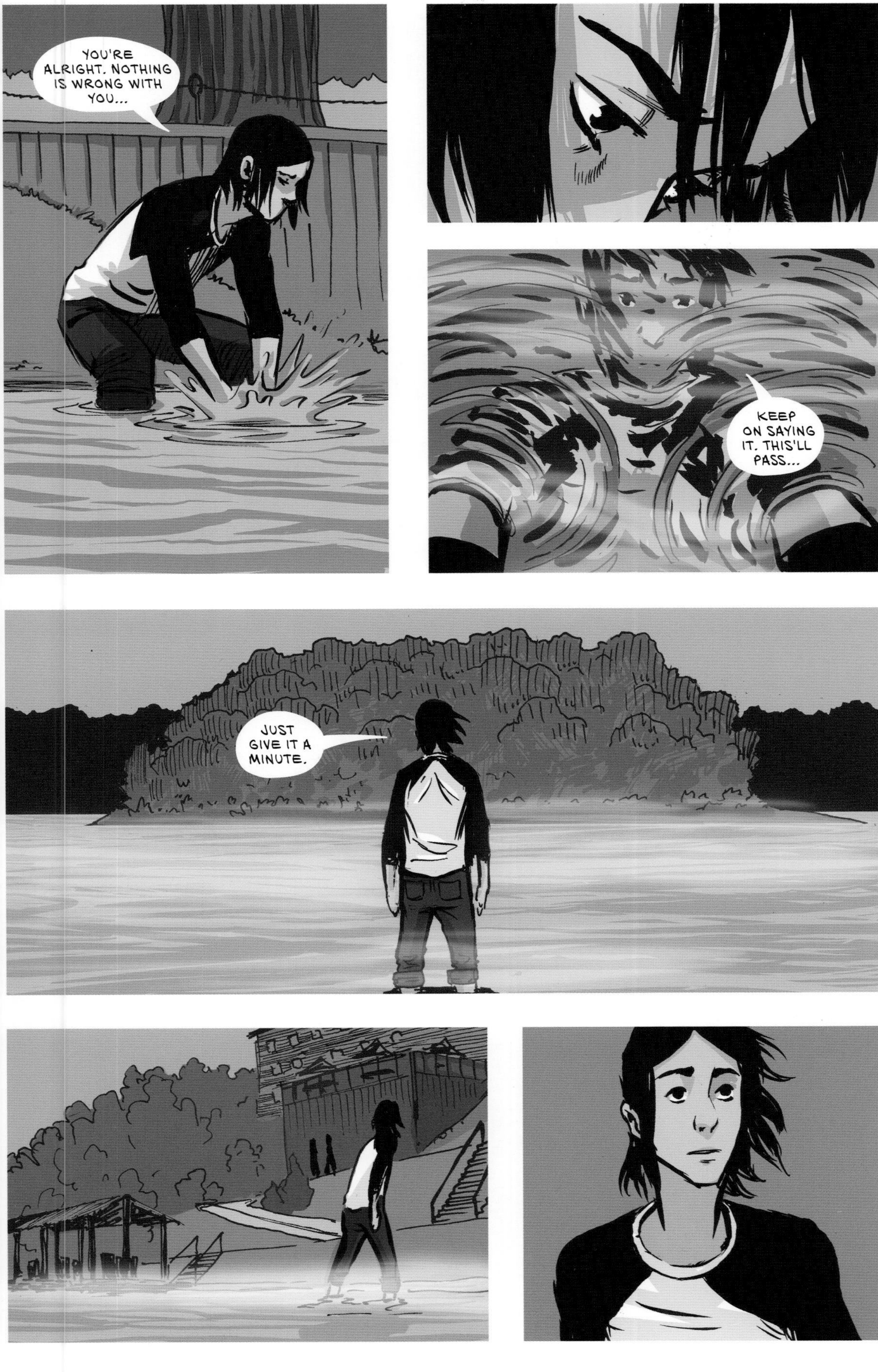
YOU'RE ALRIGHT. NOTHING IS WRONG WITH YOU...
KEEP ON SAYING IT. THIS'LL PASS...
JUST GIVE IT A MINUTE.

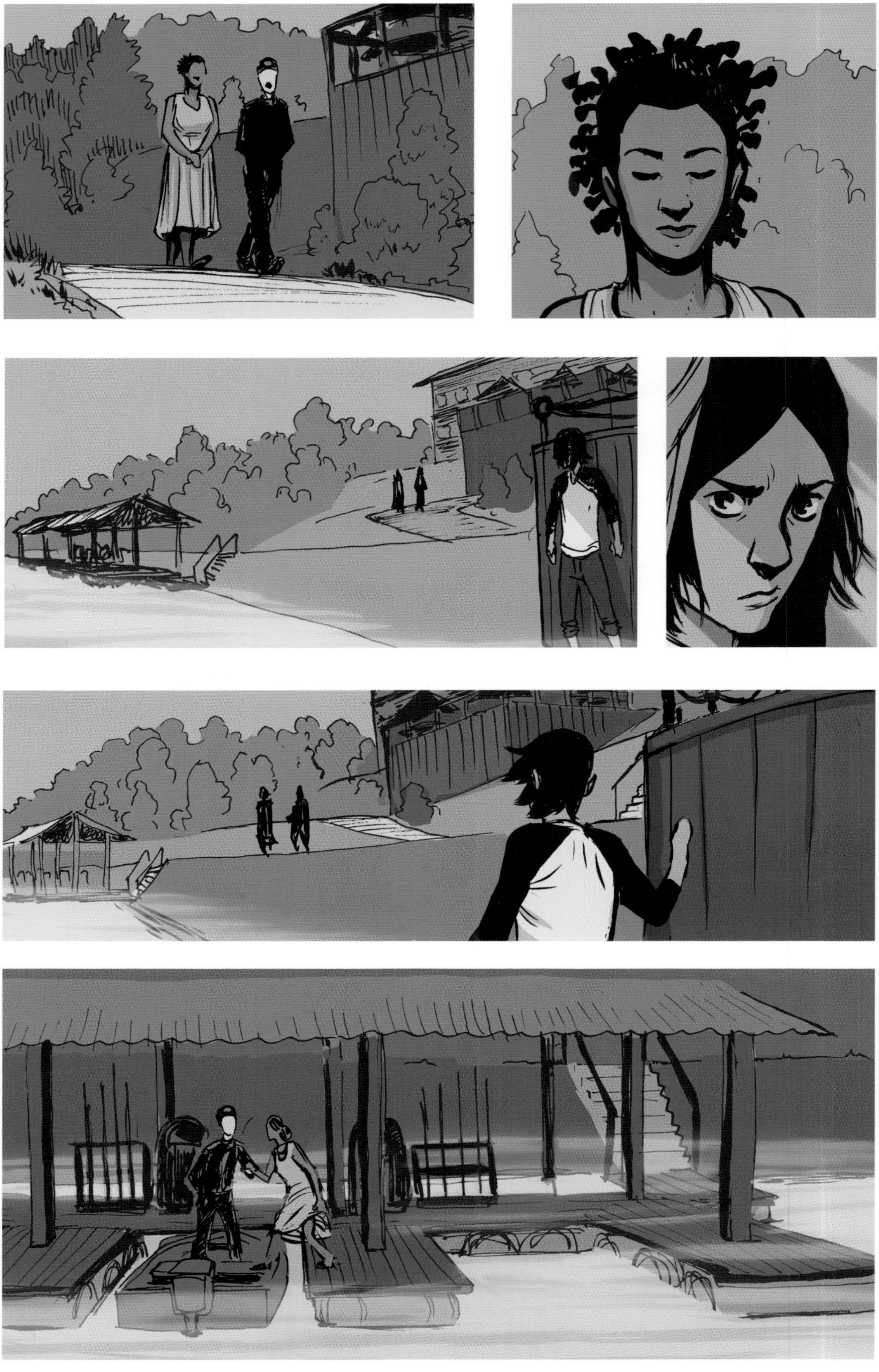

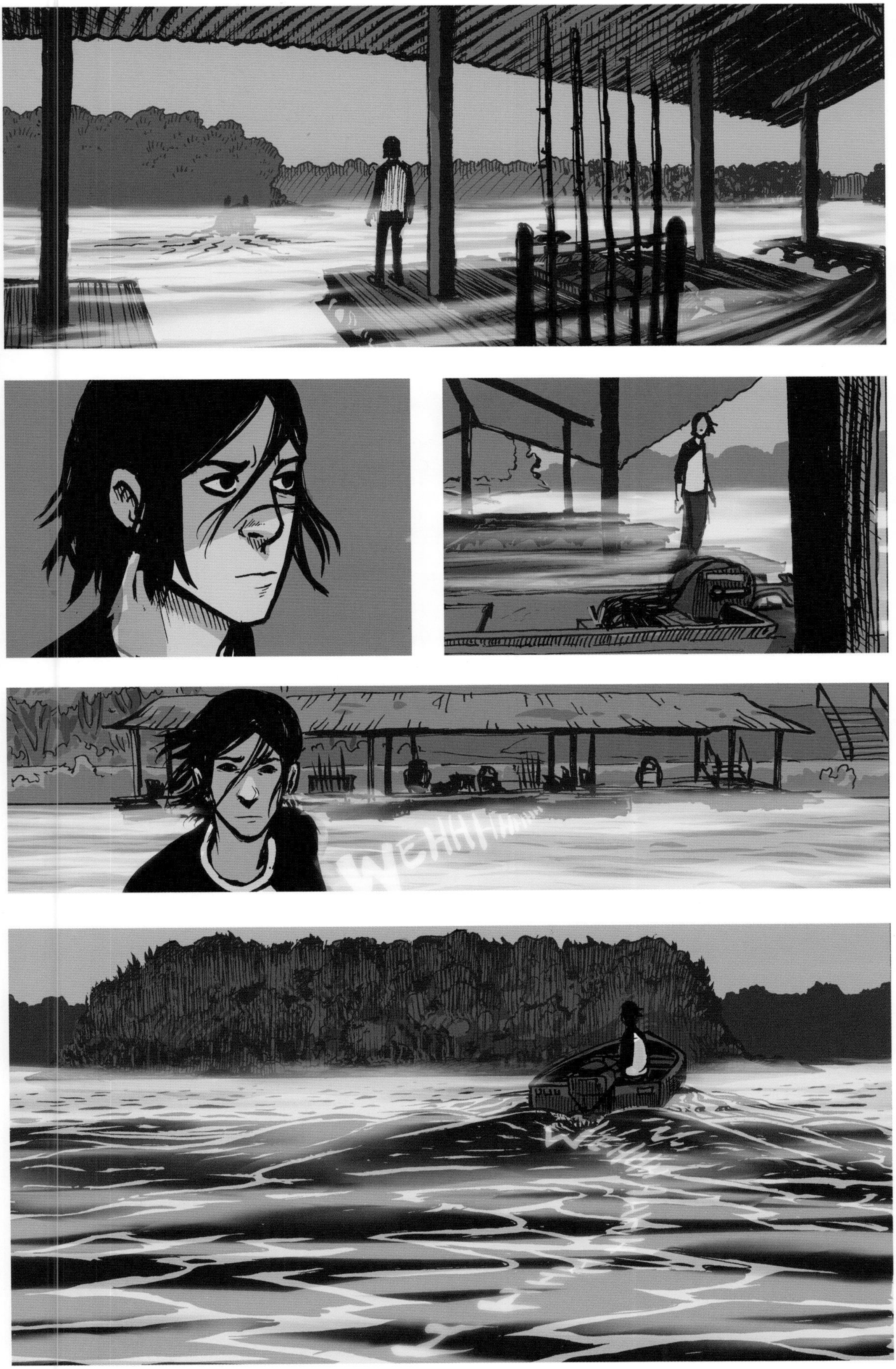
WEHHH

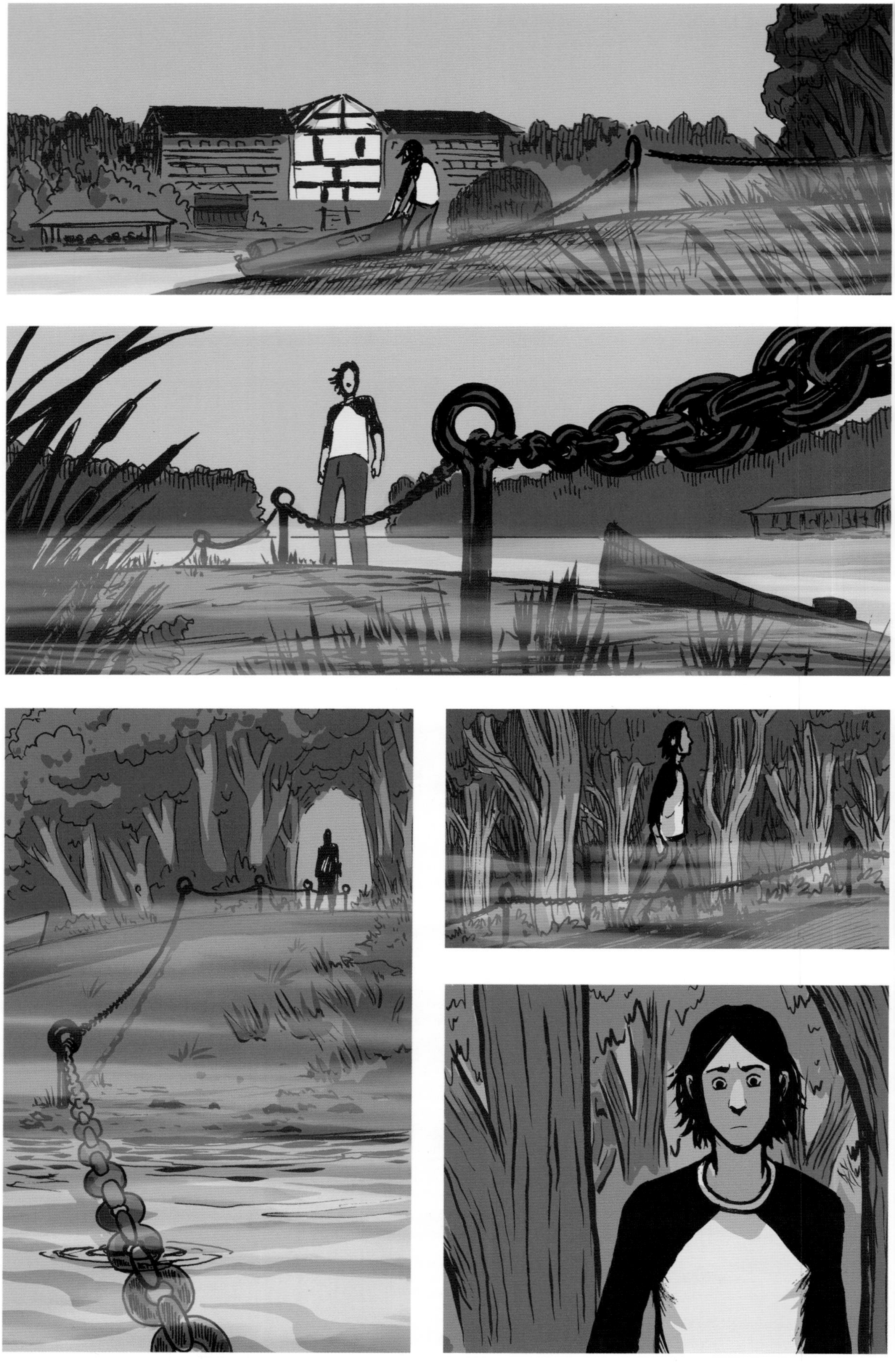

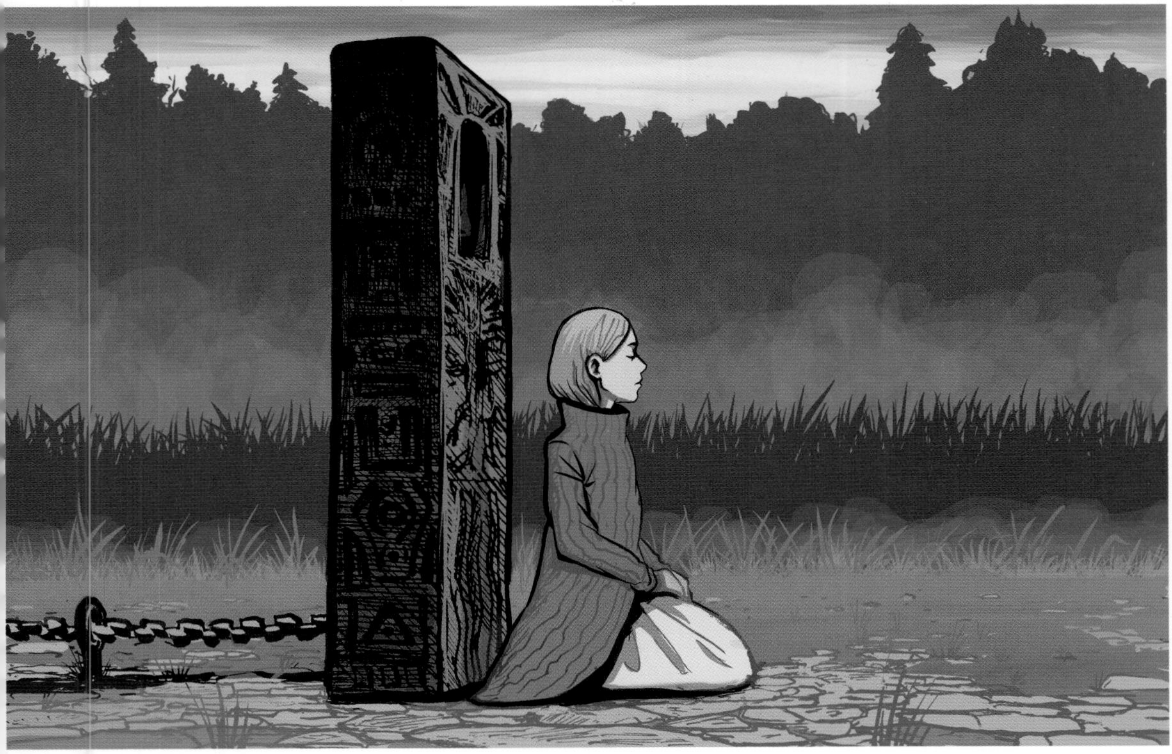

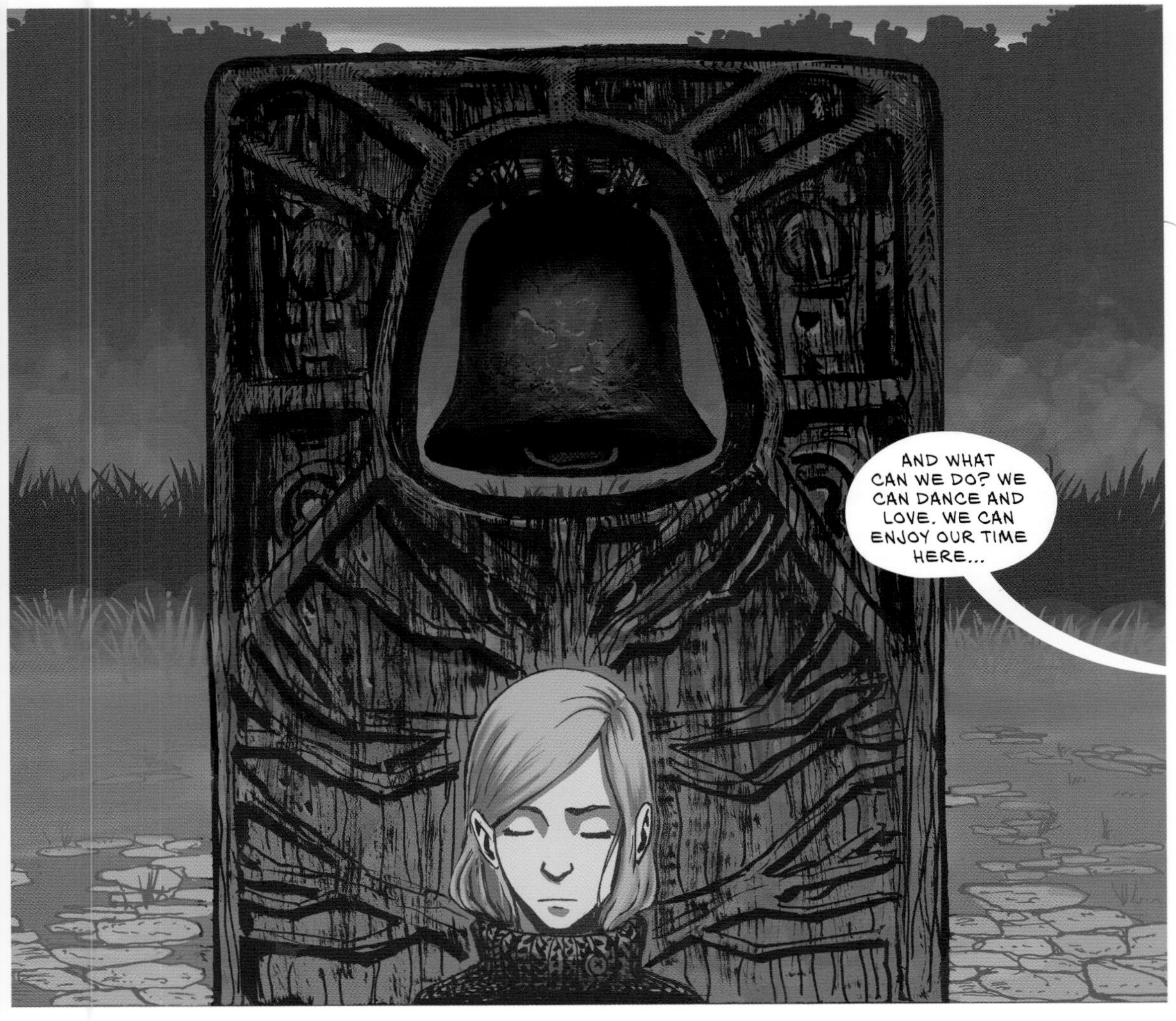
AND WHAT CAN WE DO? WE CAN DANCE AND LOVE. WE CAN ENJOY OUR TIME HERE...

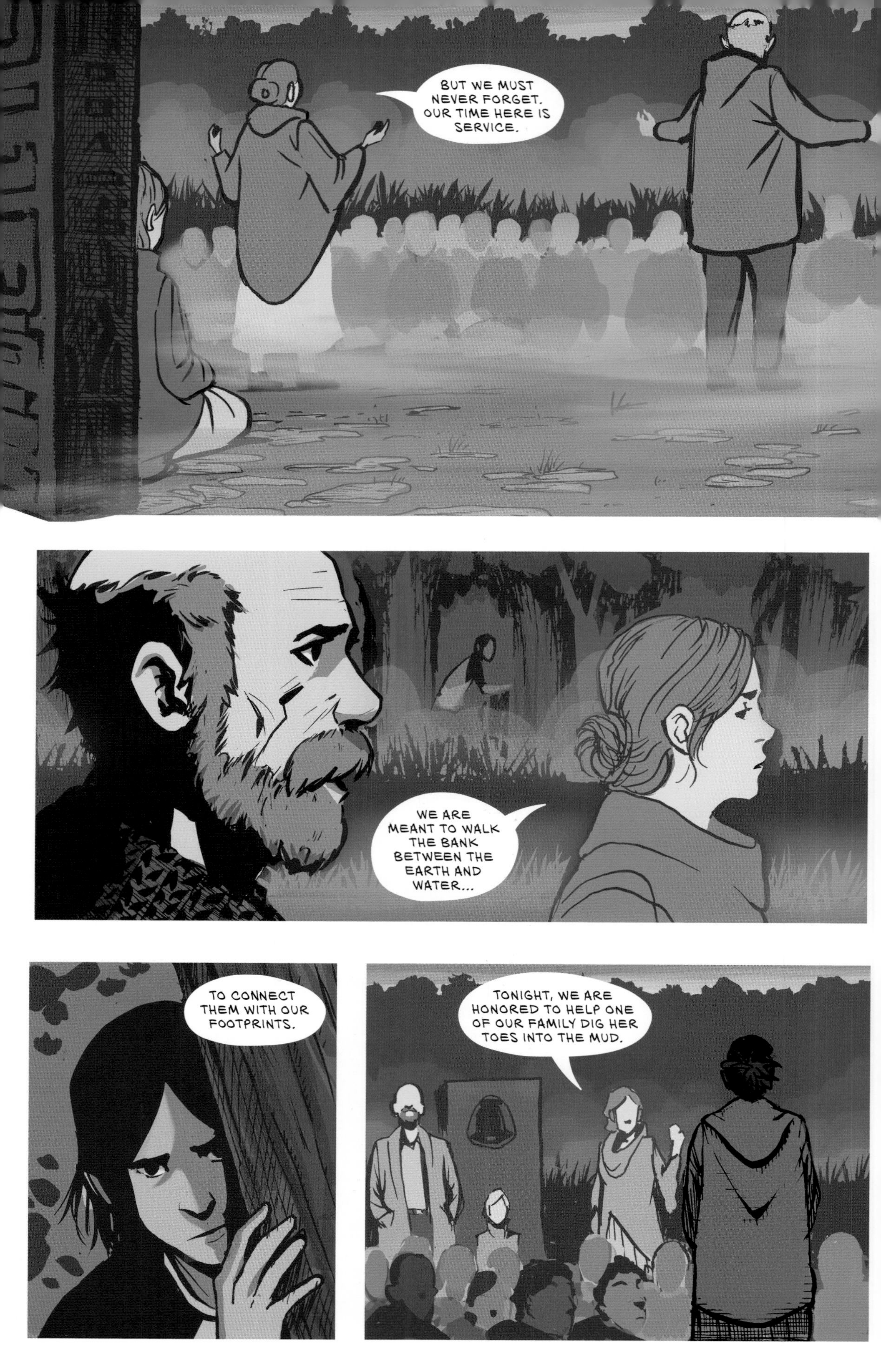
BUT WE MUST NEVER FORGET. OUR TIME HERE IS SERVICE.
WE ARE MEANT TO WALK THE BANK BETWEEN THE EARTH AND WATER...
TO CONNECT THEM WITH OUR FOOTPRINTS.
TONIGHT, WE ARE HONORED TO HELP ONE OF OUR FAMILY DIG HER TOES INTO THE MUD.

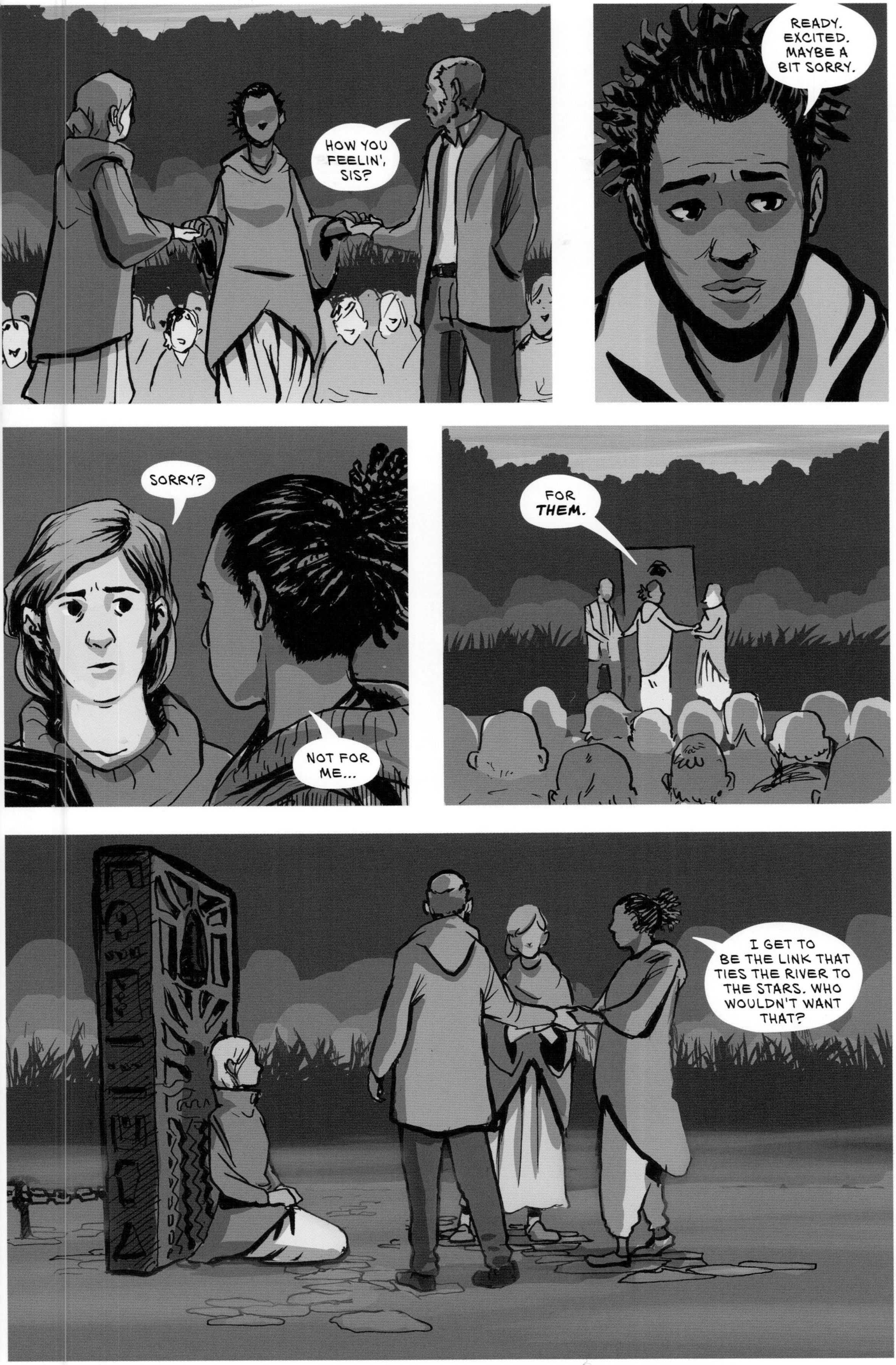
HOW YOU FEELIN', SIS?
READY. EXCITED. MAYBE A BIT SORRY.
SORRY?
NOT FOR ME...
FOR *THEM.*
I GET TO BE THE LINK THAT TIES THE RIVER TO THE STARS. WHO WOULDN'T WANT THAT?

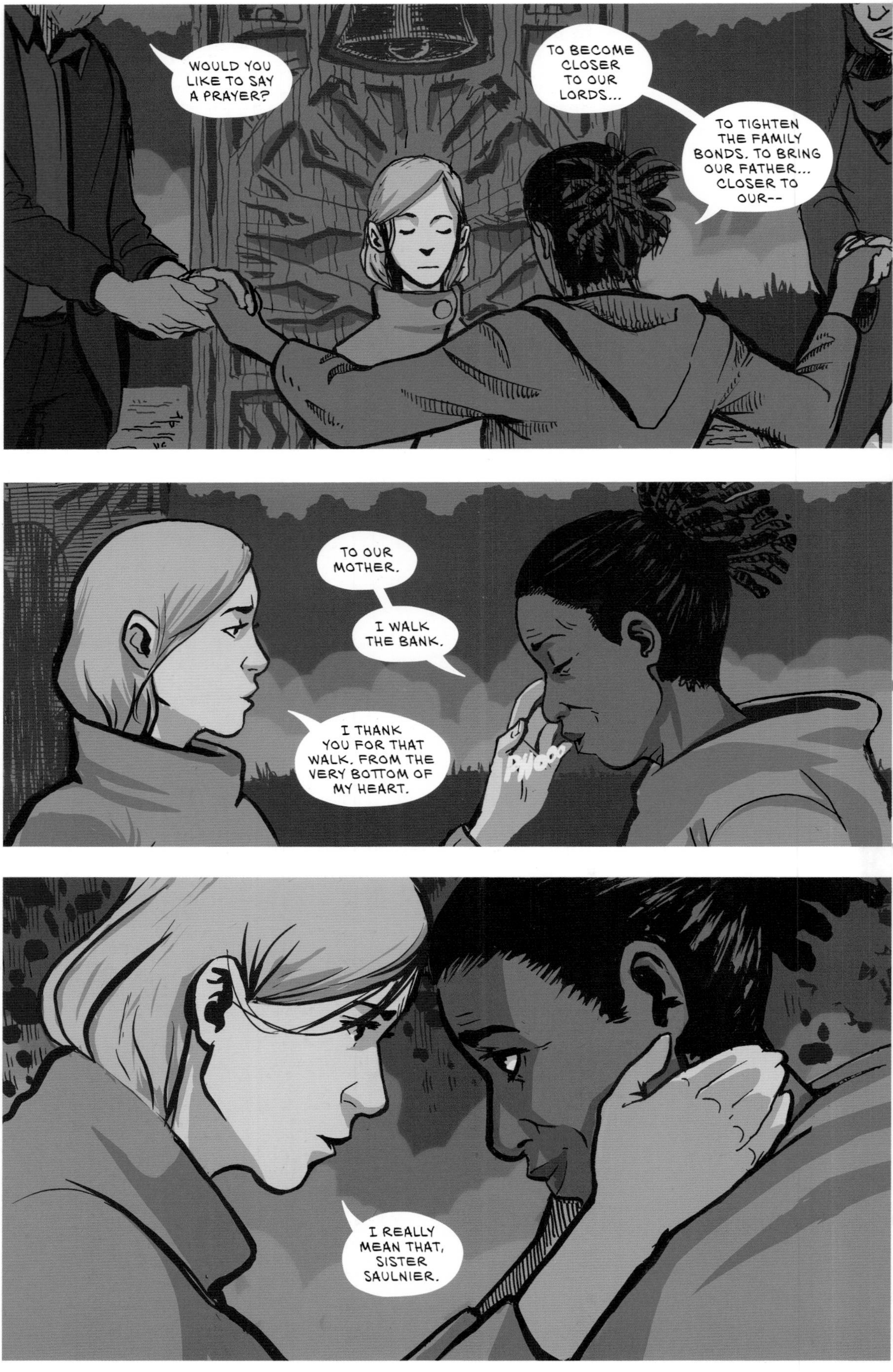
WOULD YOU LIKE TO SAY A PRAYER?
TO BECOME CLOSER TO OUR LORDS...
TO TIGHTEN THE FAMILY BONDS. TO BRING OUR FATHER... CLOSER TO OUR--
TO OUR MOTHER.
I WALK THE BANK.
I THANK YOU FOR THAT WALK. FROM THE VERY BOTTOM OF MY HEART.
PHOO
I REALLY MEAN THAT, SISTER SAULNIER.

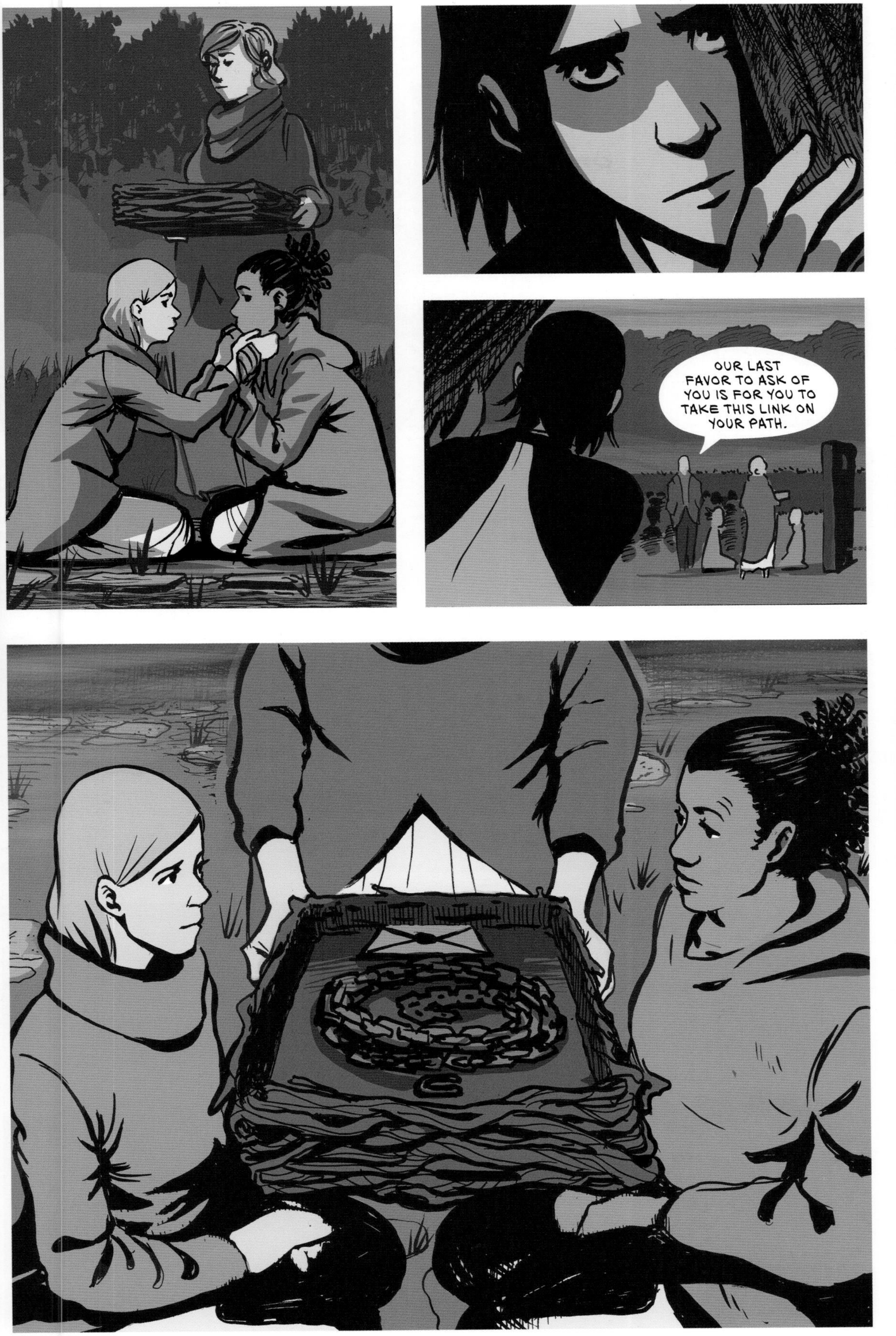
OUR LAST FAVOR TO ASK OF YOU IS FOR YOU TO TAKE THIS LINK ON YOUR PATH.

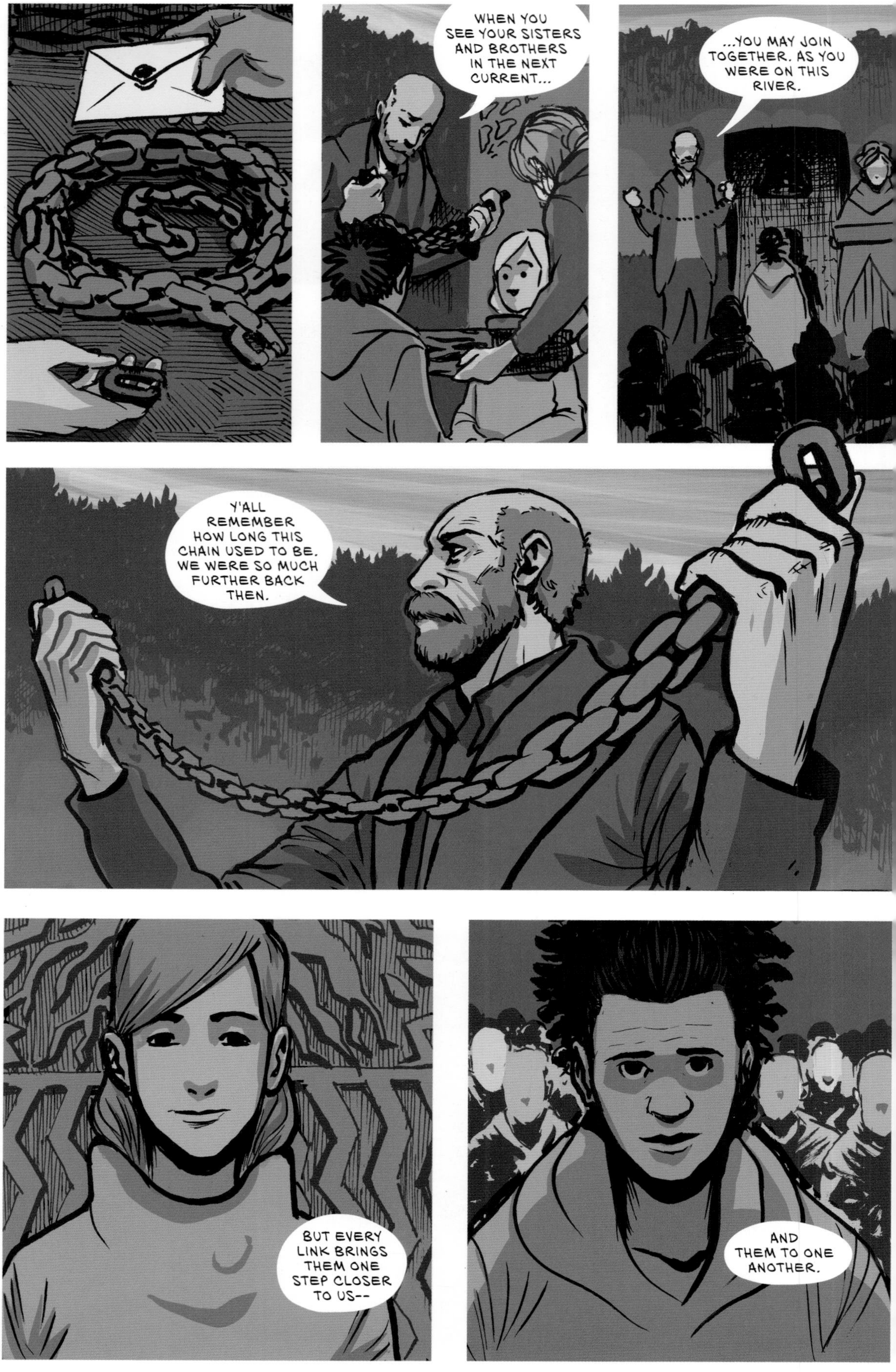
WHEN YOU SEE YOUR SISTERS AND BROTHERS IN THE NEXT CURRENT...
...YOU MAY JOIN TOGETHER. AS YOU WERE ON THIS RIVER.
Y'ALL REMEMBER HOW LONG THIS CHAIN USED TO BE. WE WERE SO MUCH FURTHER BACK THEN.
BUT EVERY LINK BRINGS THEM ONE STEP CLOSER TO US--
AND THEM TO ONE ANOTHER.

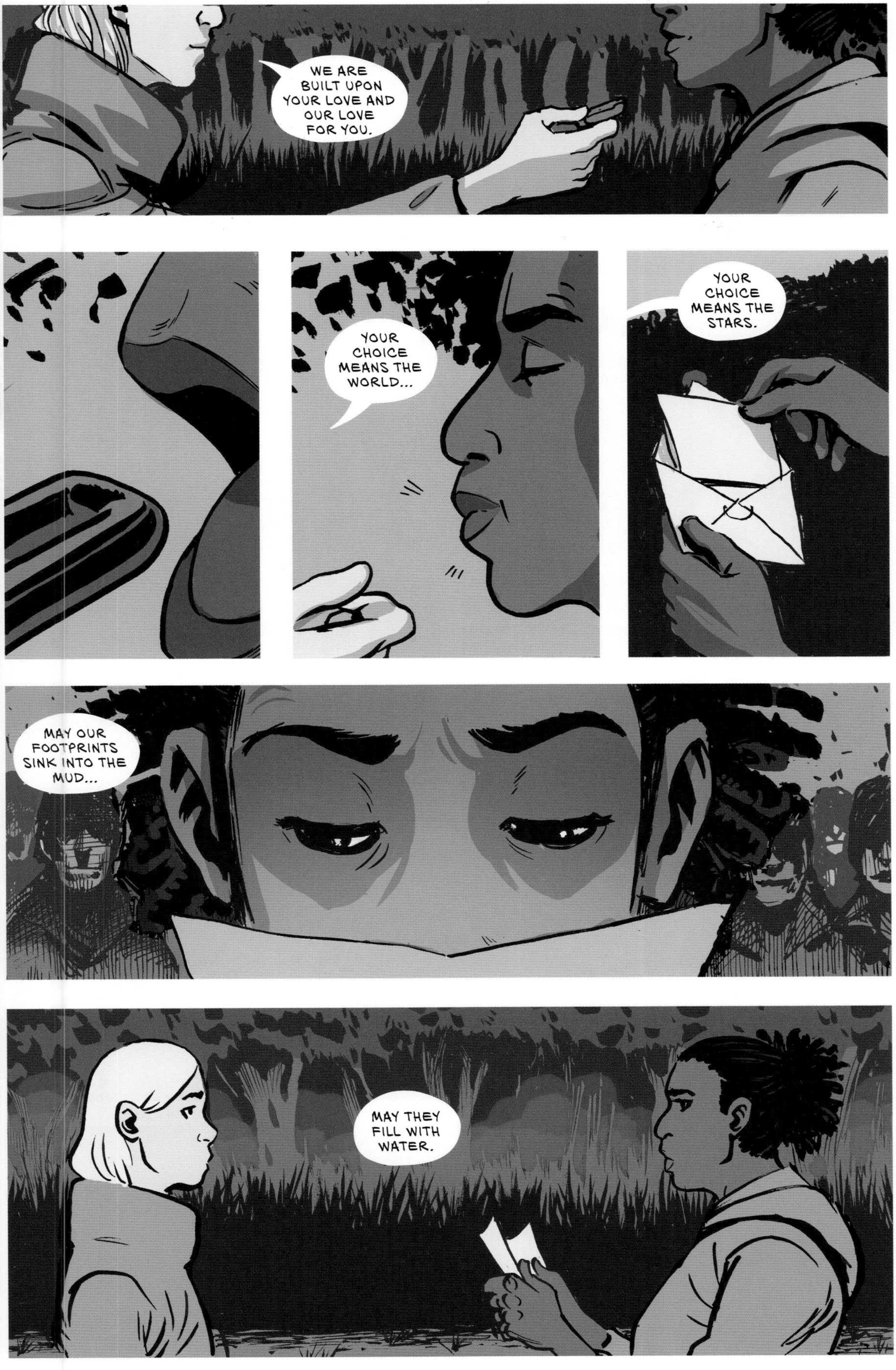
WE ARE BUILT UPON YOUR LOVE AND OUR LOVE FOR YOU.
YOUR CHOICE MEANS THE WORLD...
YOUR CHOICE MEANS THE STARS.
MAY OUR FOOTPRINTS SINK INTO THE MUD...
MAY THEY FILL WITH WATER.

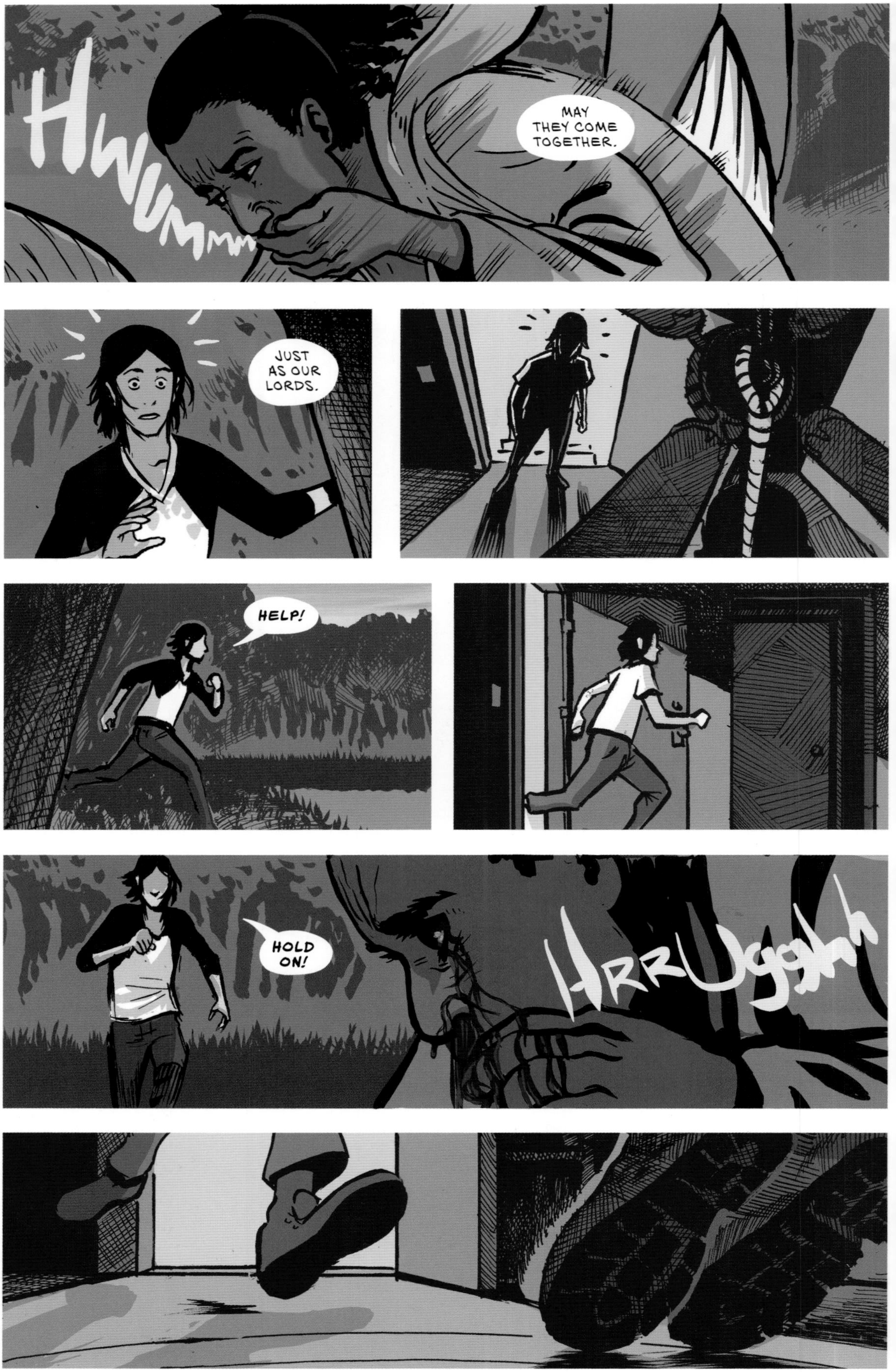
HWUMmmm
MAY THEY COME TOGETHER.
JUST AS OUR LORDS.
HELP!
HOLD ON!
HRRUgghh

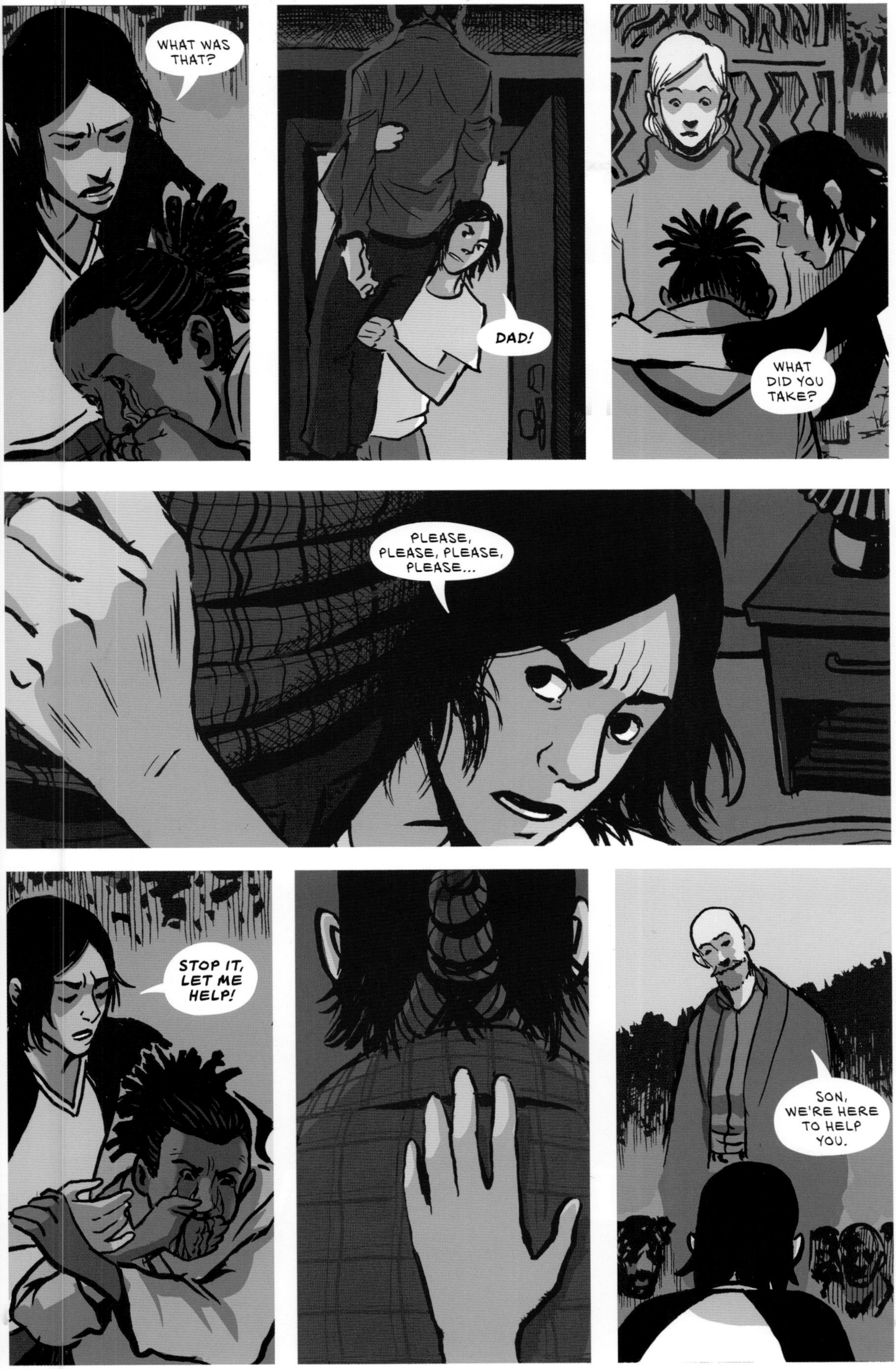
WHAT WAS THAT?
DAD!
WHAT DID YOU TAKE?
PLEASE, PLEASE, PLEASE, PLEASE...
STOP IT, LET ME HELP!
SON, WE'RE HERE TO HELP YOU.

# CHAPTER NINE

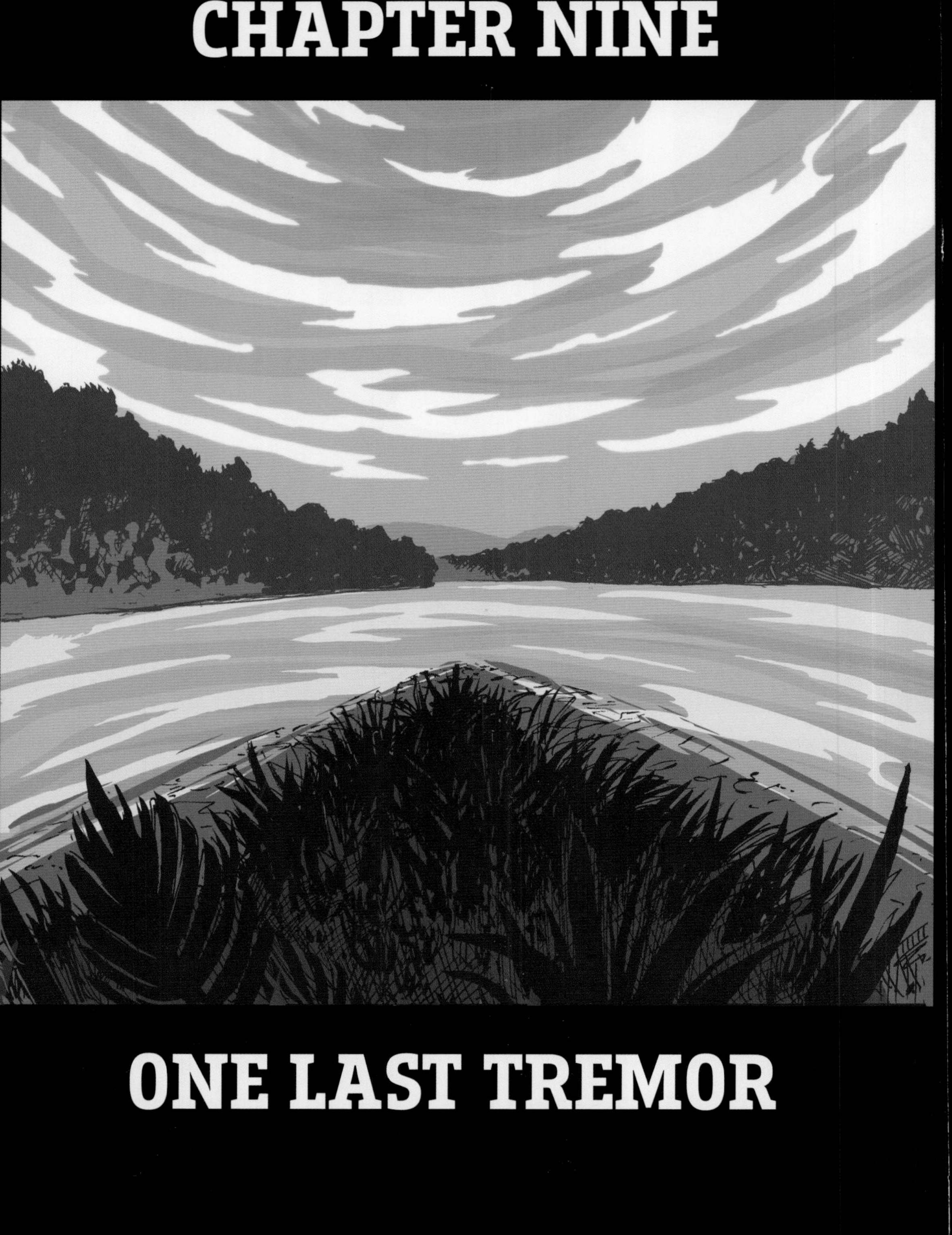

# ONE LAST TREMOR

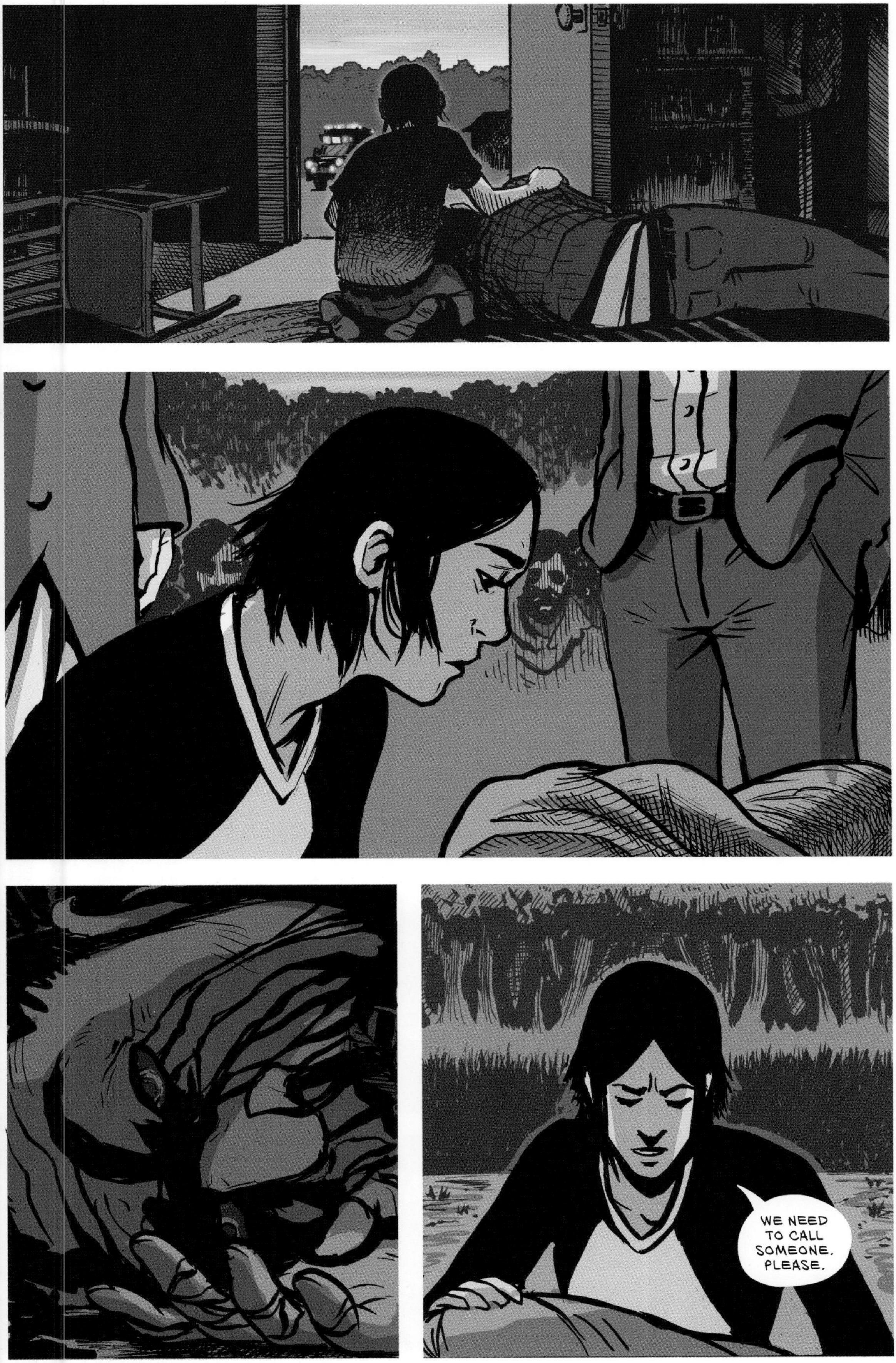
WE NEED TO CALL SOMEONE. PLEASE.

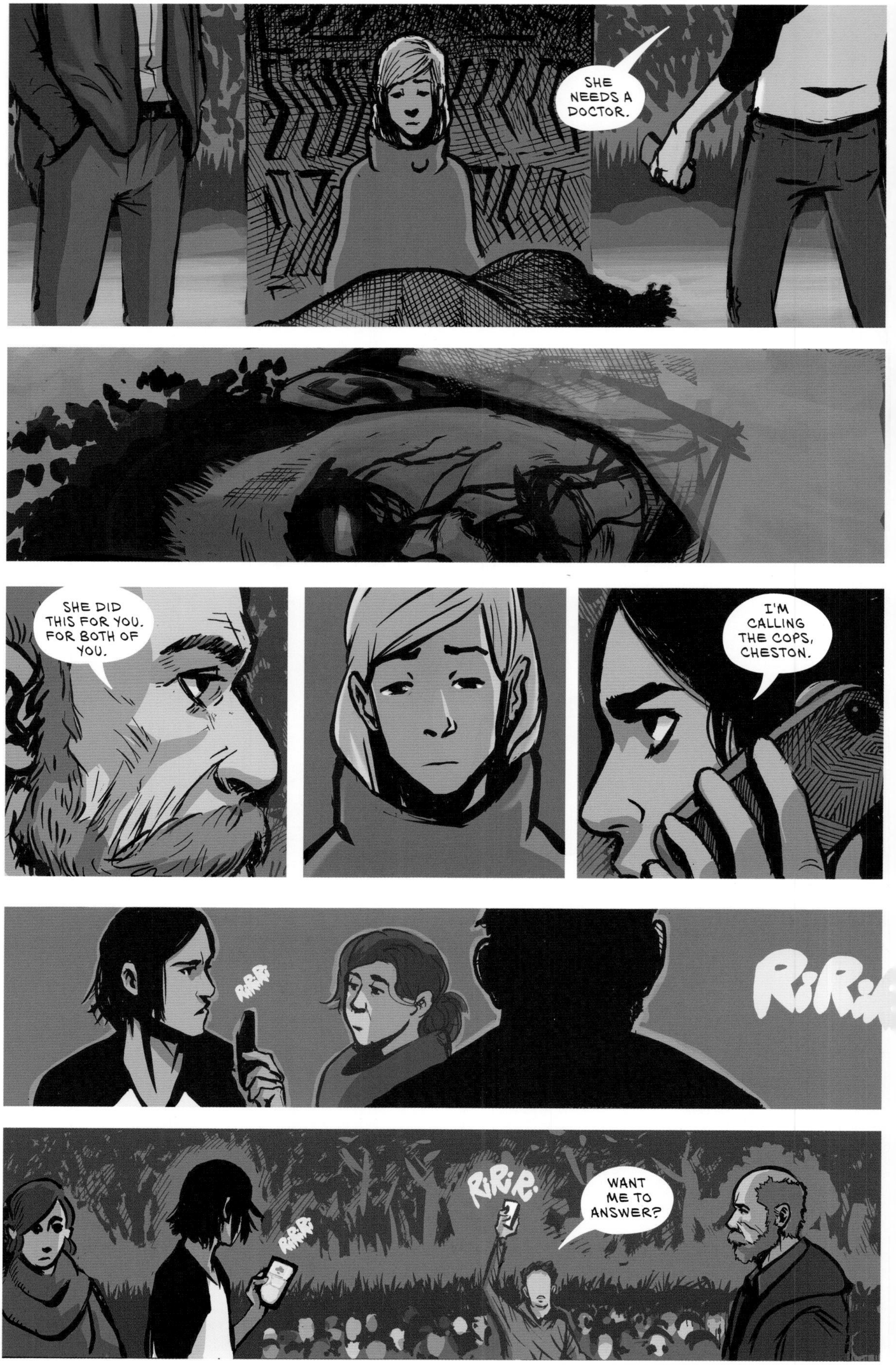
SHE NEEDS A DOCTOR.
SHE DID THIS FOR YOU. FOR BOTH OF YOU.
I'M CALLING THE COPS, CHESTON.
RiRiR
RiRi
RiRiR.
RiRiR
WANT ME TO ANSWER?

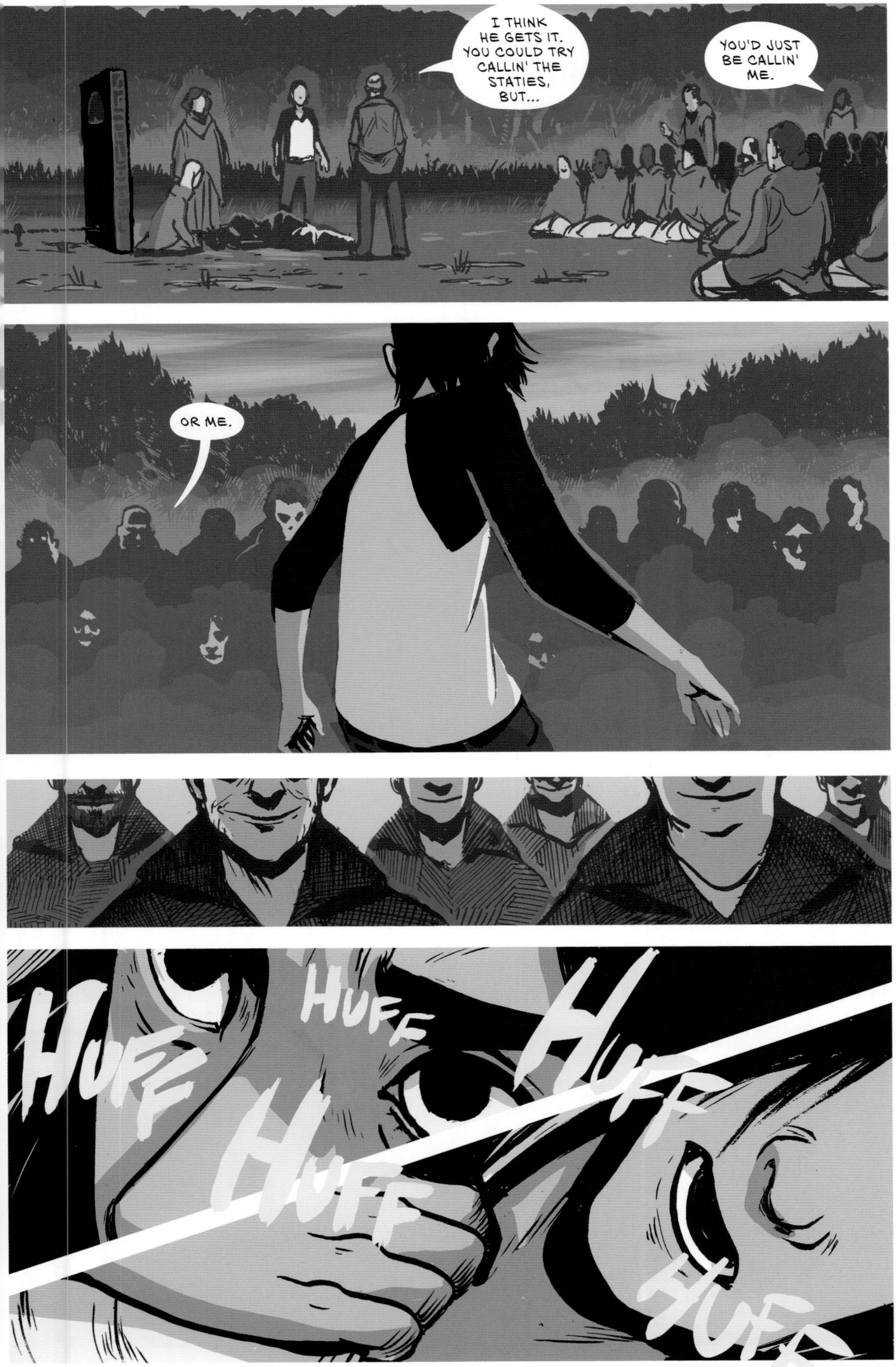
I THINK HE GETS IT. YOU COULD TRY CALLIN' THE STATIES, BUT...
YOU'D JUST BE CALLIN' ME.
OR ME.
HUFF
HUFF
HUFF
HUFF
HUFF

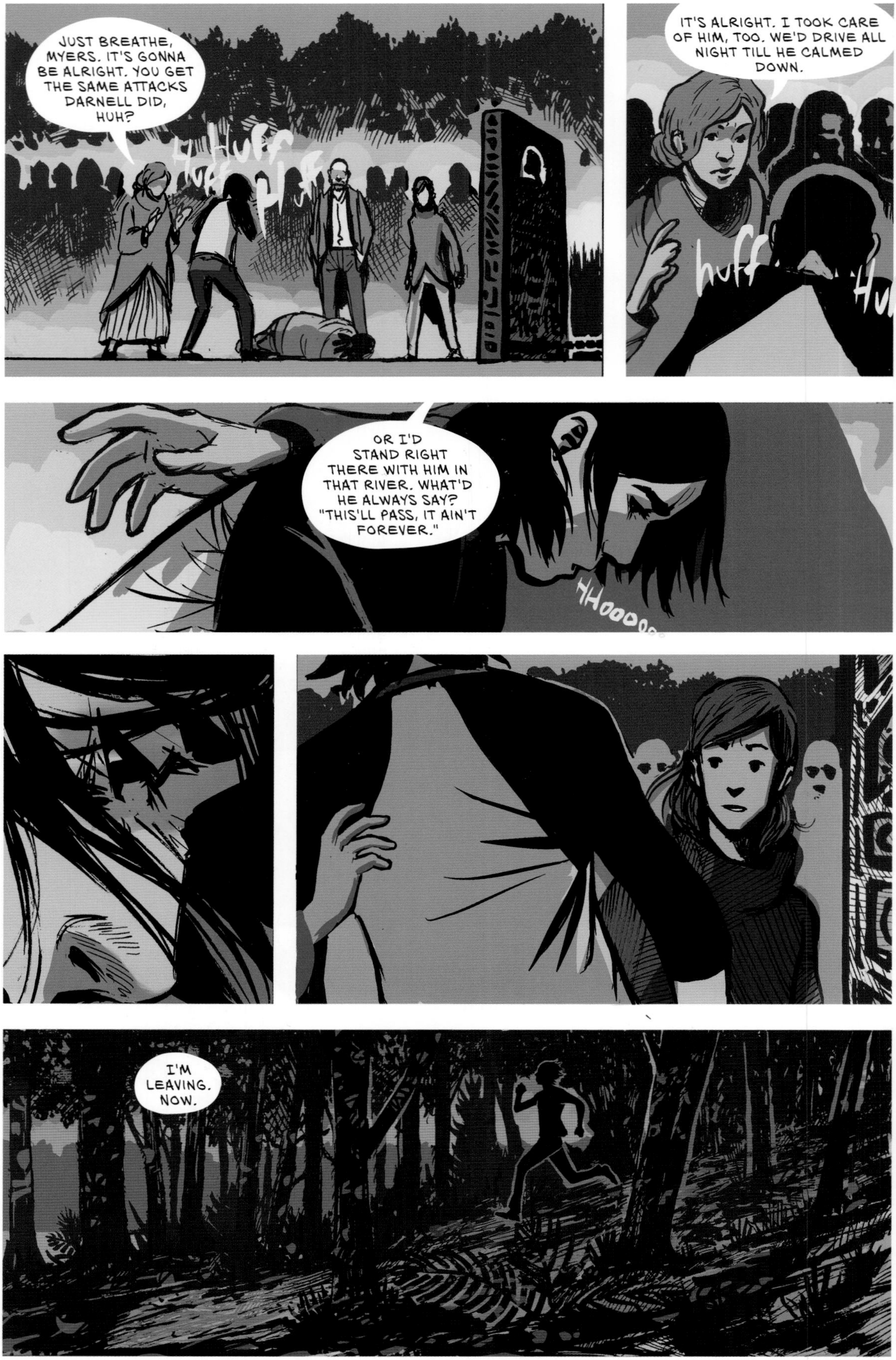
JUST BREATHE, MYERS. IT'S GONNA BE ALRIGHT. YOU GET THE SAME ATTACKS DARNELL DID, HUH?
HUFF HUFF HUF
IT'S ALRIGHT. I TOOK CARE OF HIM, TOO. WE'D DRIVE ALL NIGHT TILL HE CALMED DOWN.
huff HUF
OR I'D STAND RIGHT THERE WITH HIM IN THAT RIVER. WHAT'D HE ALWAYS SAY? "THIS'LL PASS, IT AIN'T FOREVER."
HHOOOO
I'M LEAVING. NOW.

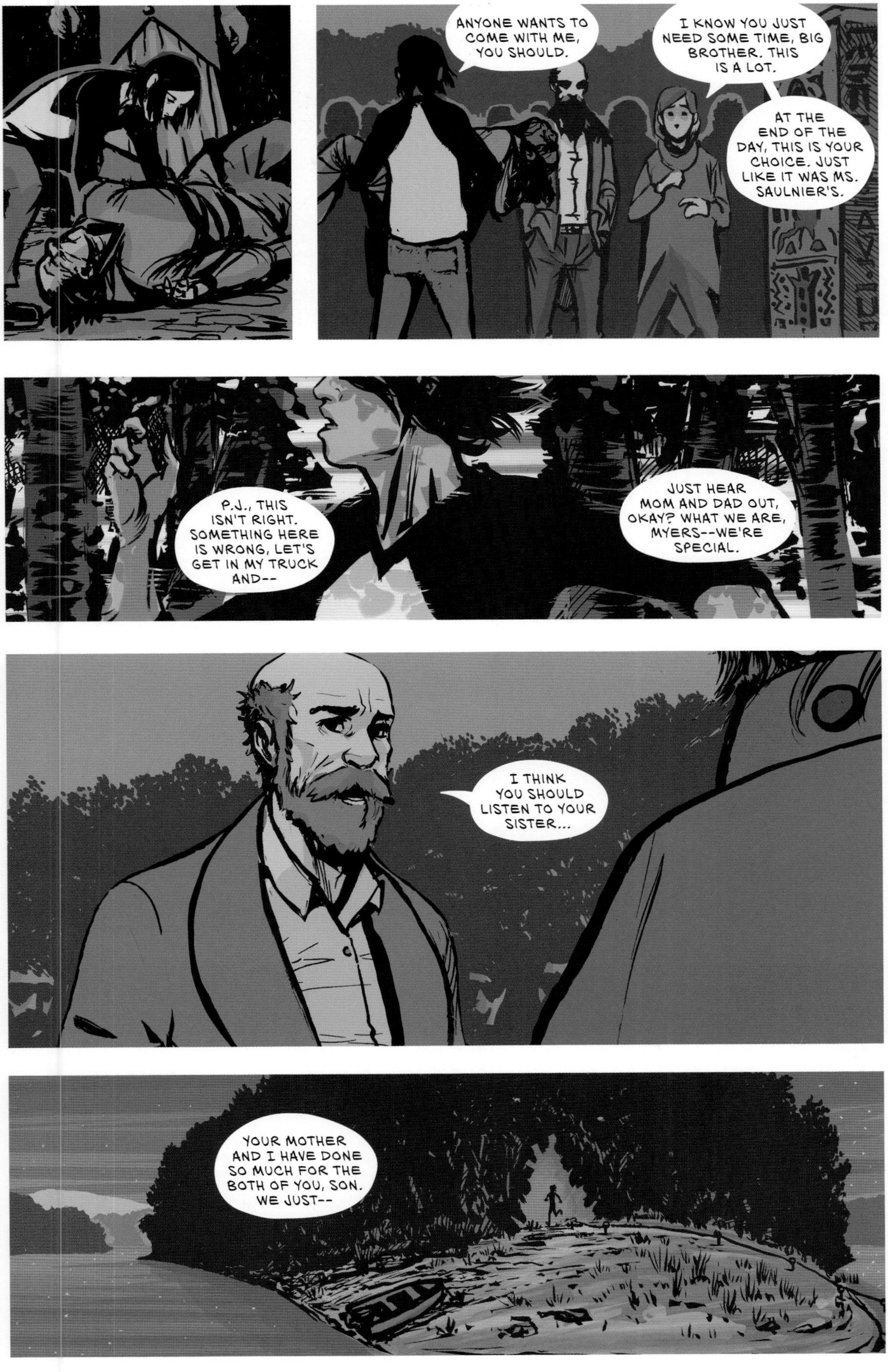
ANYONE WANTS TO COME WITH ME, YOU SHOULD.
I KNOW YOU JUST NEED SOME TIME, BIG BROTHER. THIS IS A LOT.
AT THE END OF THE DAY, THIS IS YOUR CHOICE. JUST LIKE IT WAS MS. SAULNIER'S.
P.J., THIS ISN'T RIGHT. SOMETHING HERE IS WRONG, LET'S GET IN MY TRUCK AND--
JUST HEAR MOM AND DAD OUT, OKAY? WHAT WE ARE, MYERS--WE'RE SPECIAL.
I THINK YOU SHOULD LISTEN TO YOUR SISTER...
YOUR MOTHER AND I HAVE DONE SO MUCH FOR THE BOTH OF YOU, SON. WE JUST--

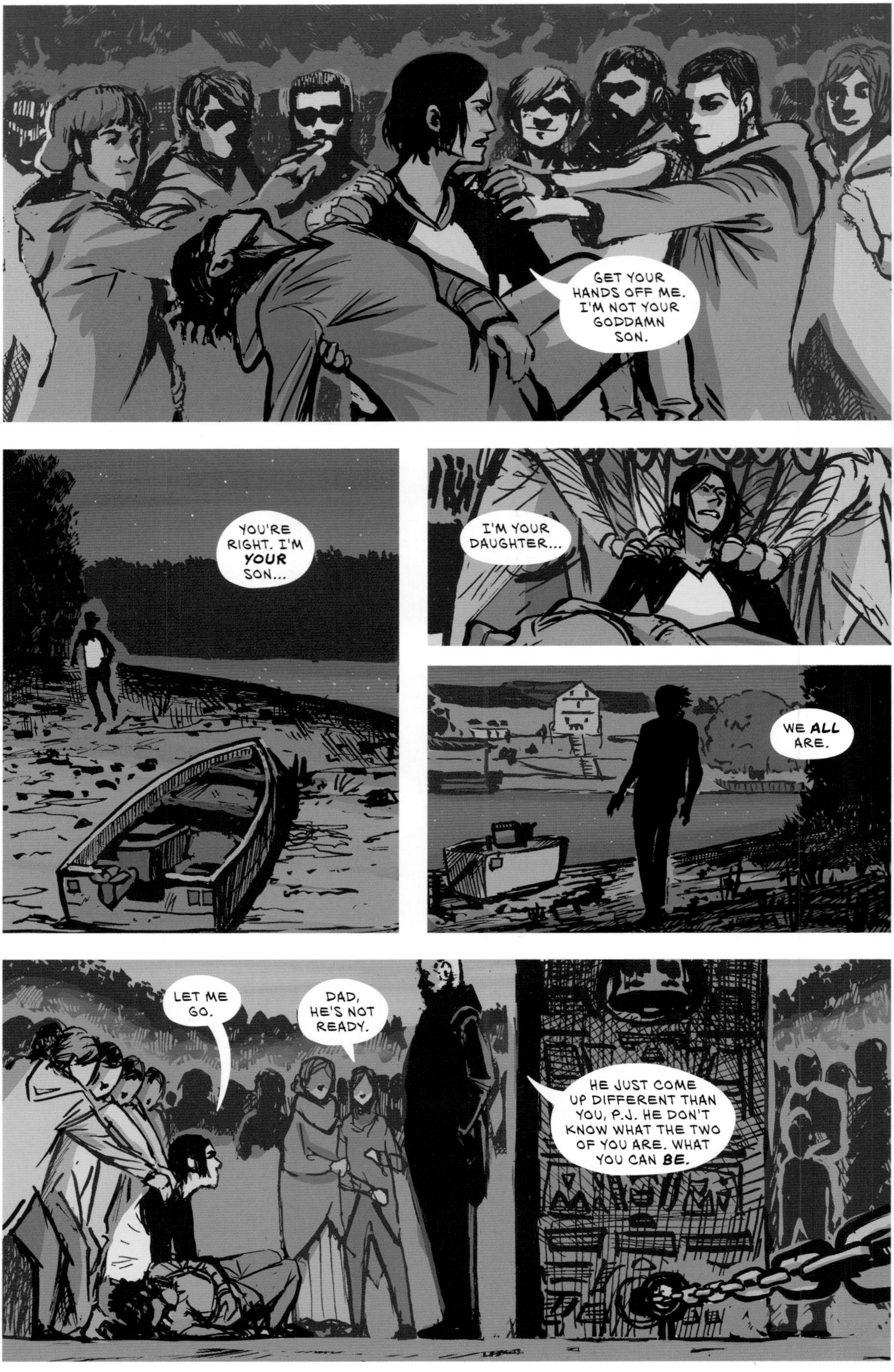
GET YOUR HANDS OFF ME. I'M NOT YOUR GODDAMN SON.
YOU'RE RIGHT. I'M **YOUR** SON...
I'M YOUR DAUGHTER...
WE **ALL** ARE.
LET ME GO.
DAD, HE'S NOT READY.
HE JUST COME UP DIFFERENT THAN YOU, P.J. HE DON'T KNOW WHAT THE TWO OF YOU ARE. WHAT YOU CAN **BE.**

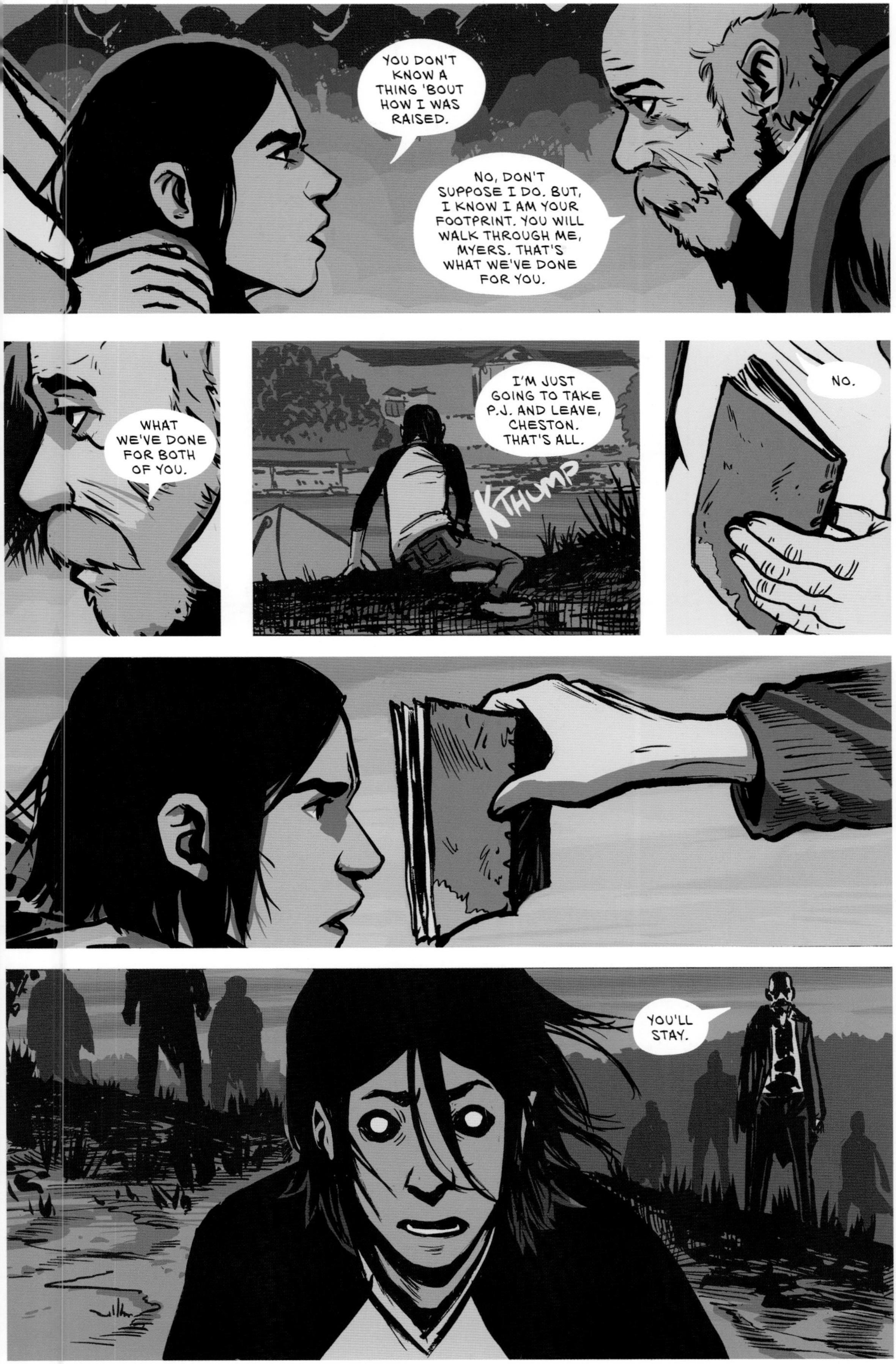
YOU DON'T KNOW A THING 'BOUT HOW I WAS RAISED.
NO, DON'T SUPPOSE I DO. BUT, I KNOW I AM YOUR FOOTPRINT. YOU WILL WALK THROUGH ME, MYERS. THAT'S WHAT WE'VE DONE FOR YOU.
WHAT WE'VE DONE FOR BOTH OF YOU.
I'M JUST GOING TO TAKE P.J. AND LEAVE, CHESTON. THAT'S ALL.
KTHUMP
NO.
YOU'LL STAY.

# CHAPTER TEN

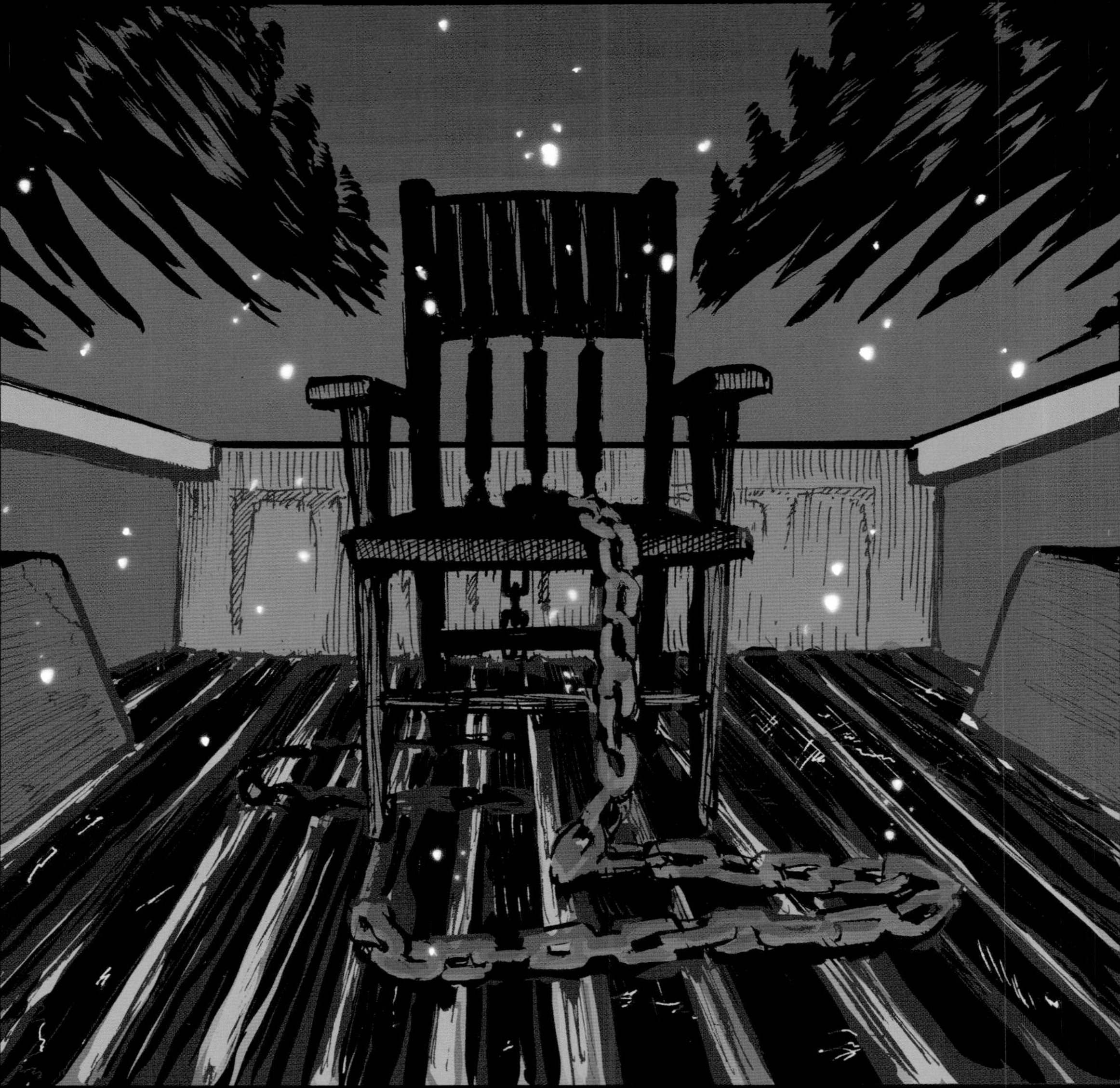

# THE RIVER: PART ONE

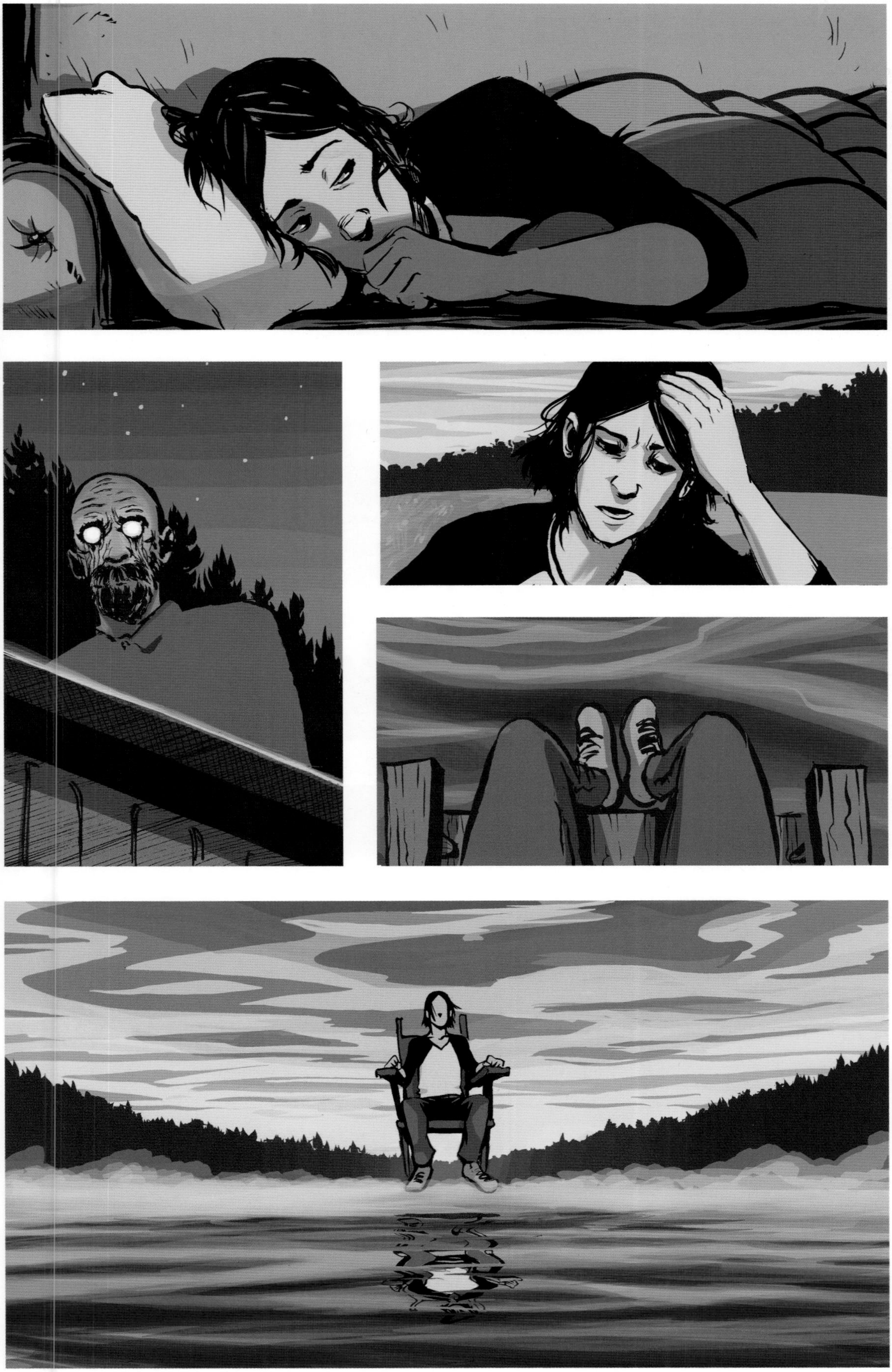

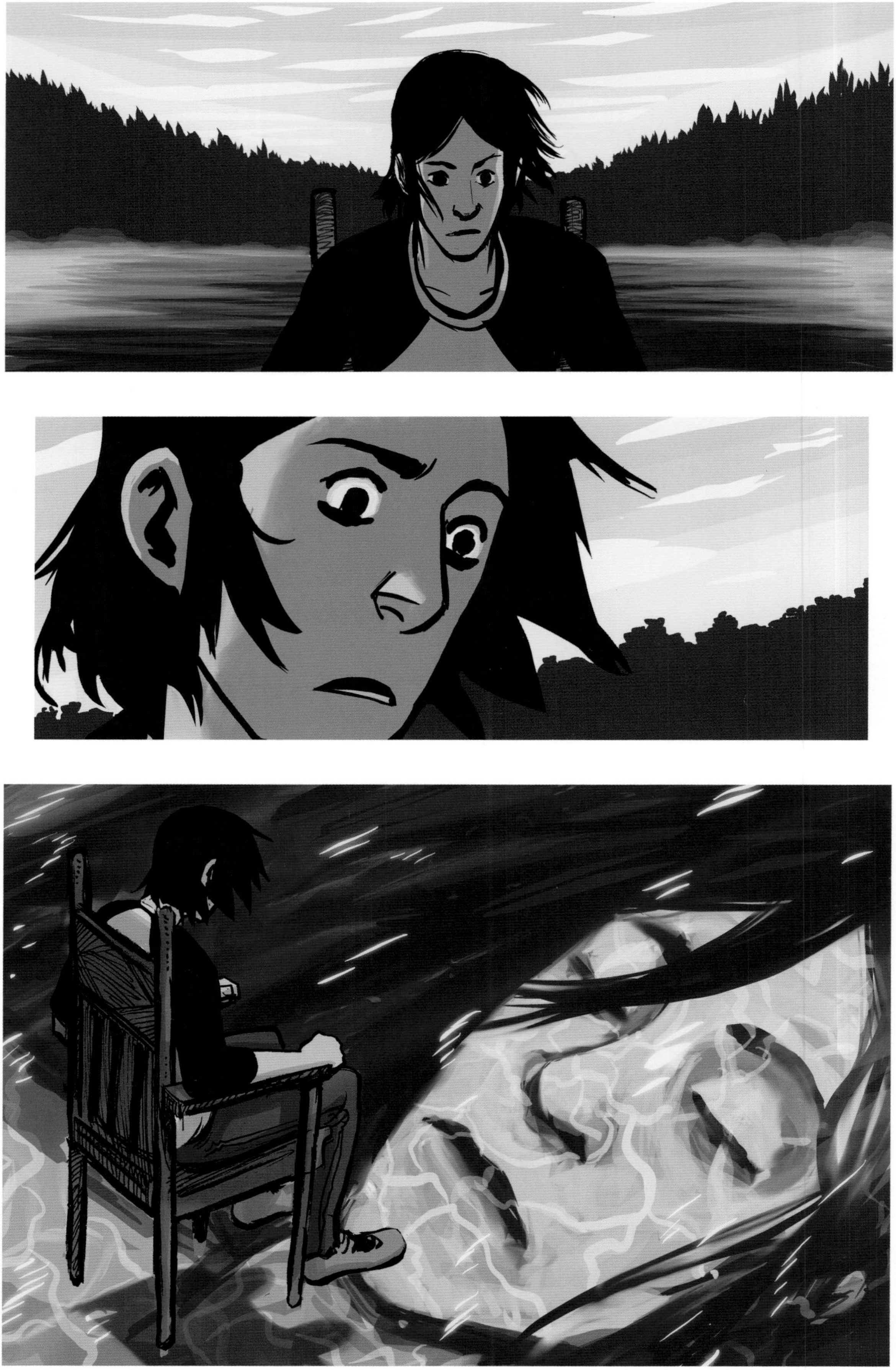

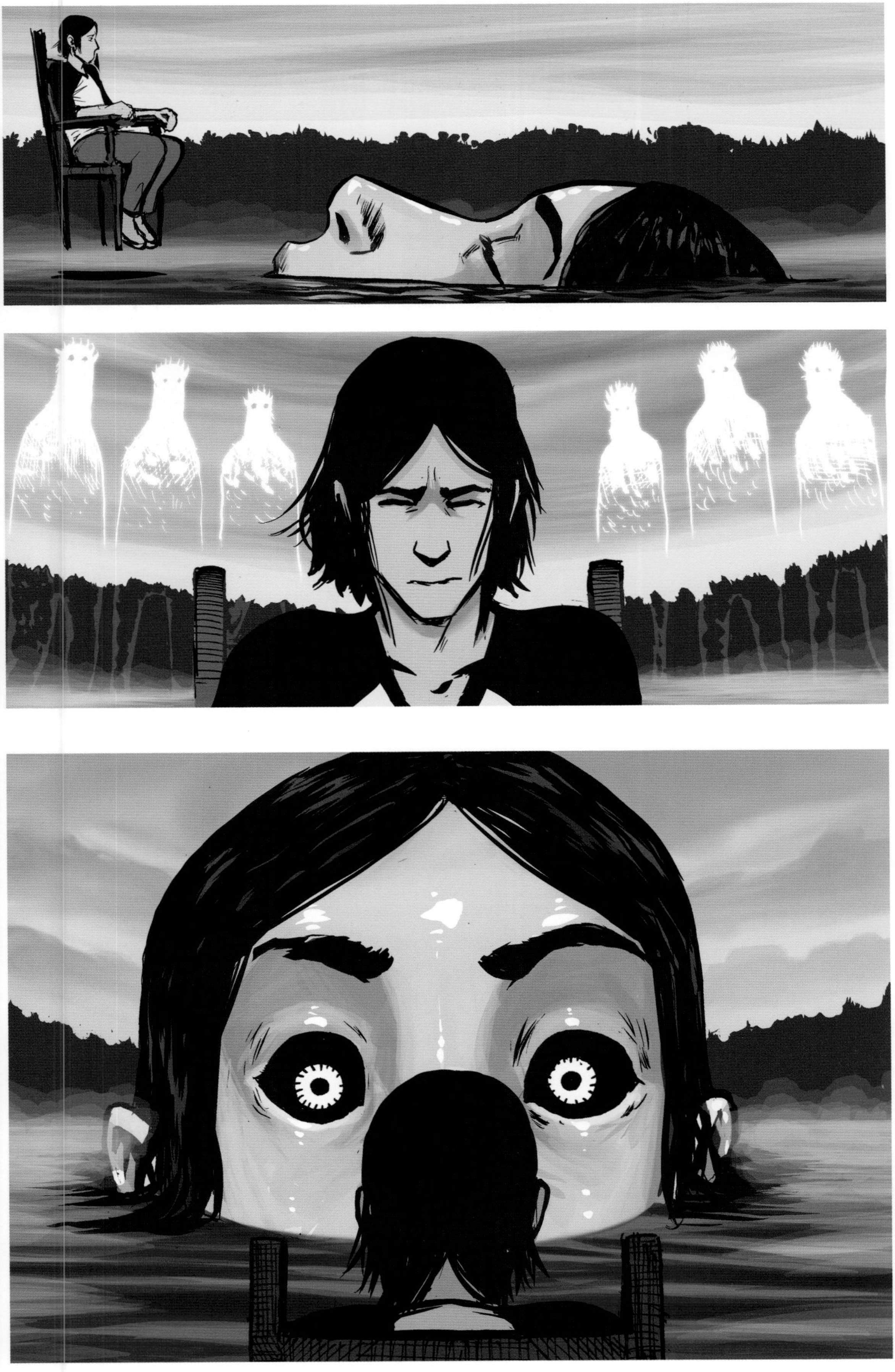

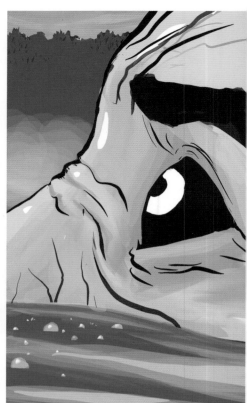

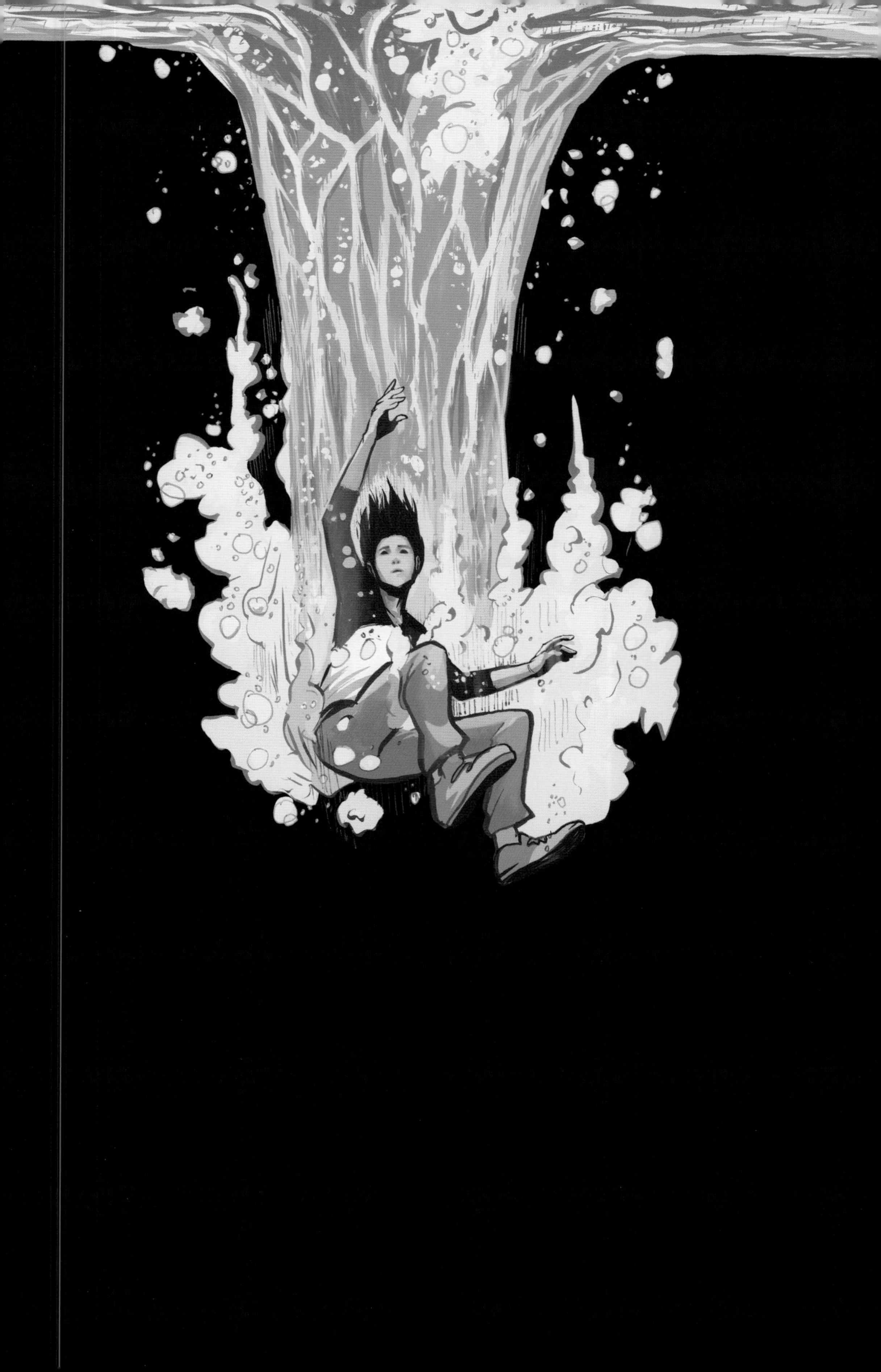

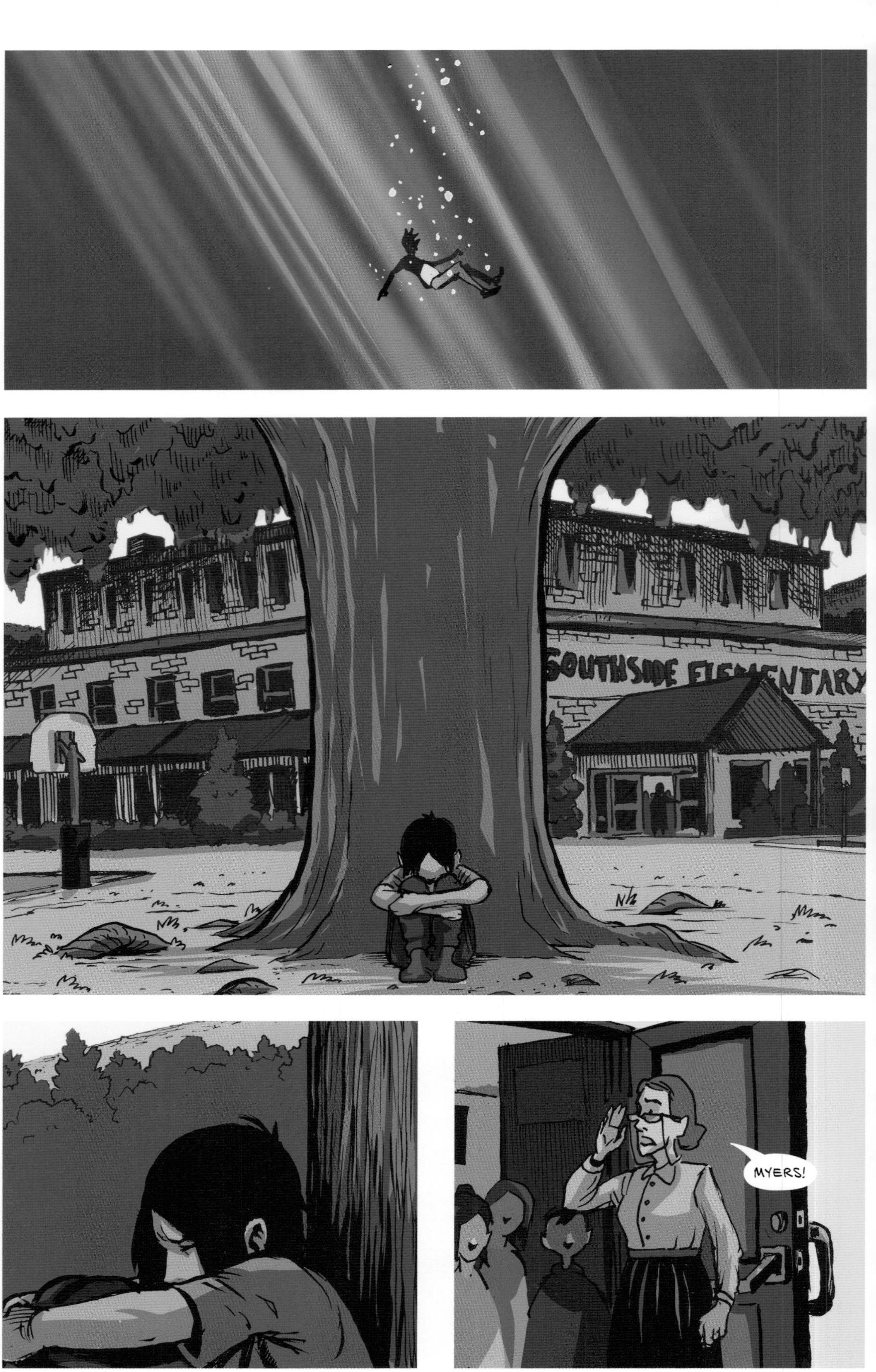
SOUTHSIDE ELEMENTARY
MYERS!

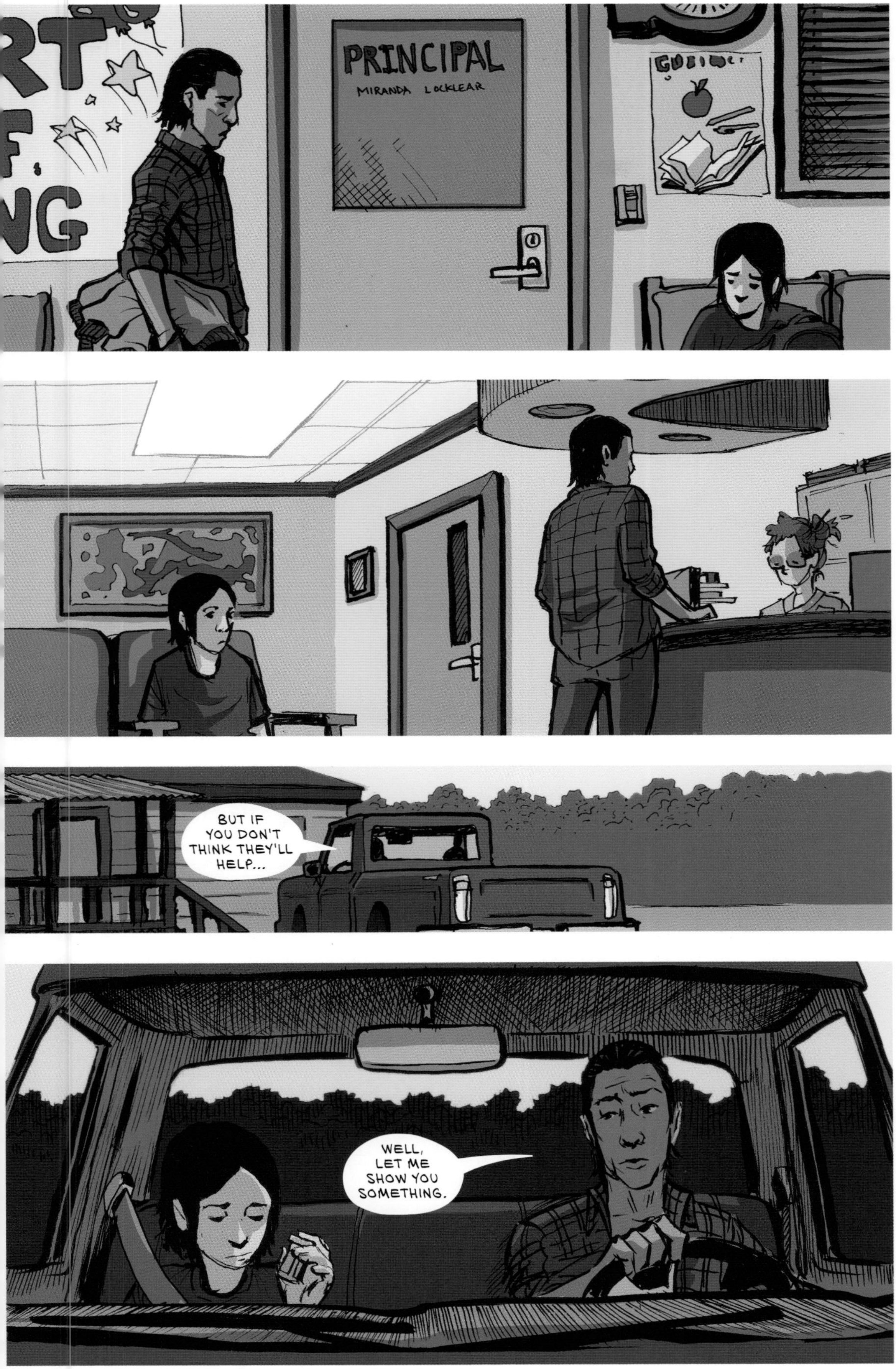
PRINCIPAL
MIRANDA LOCKLEAR
BUT IF YOU DON'T THINK THEY'LL HELP...
WELL, LET ME SHOW YOU SOMETHING.

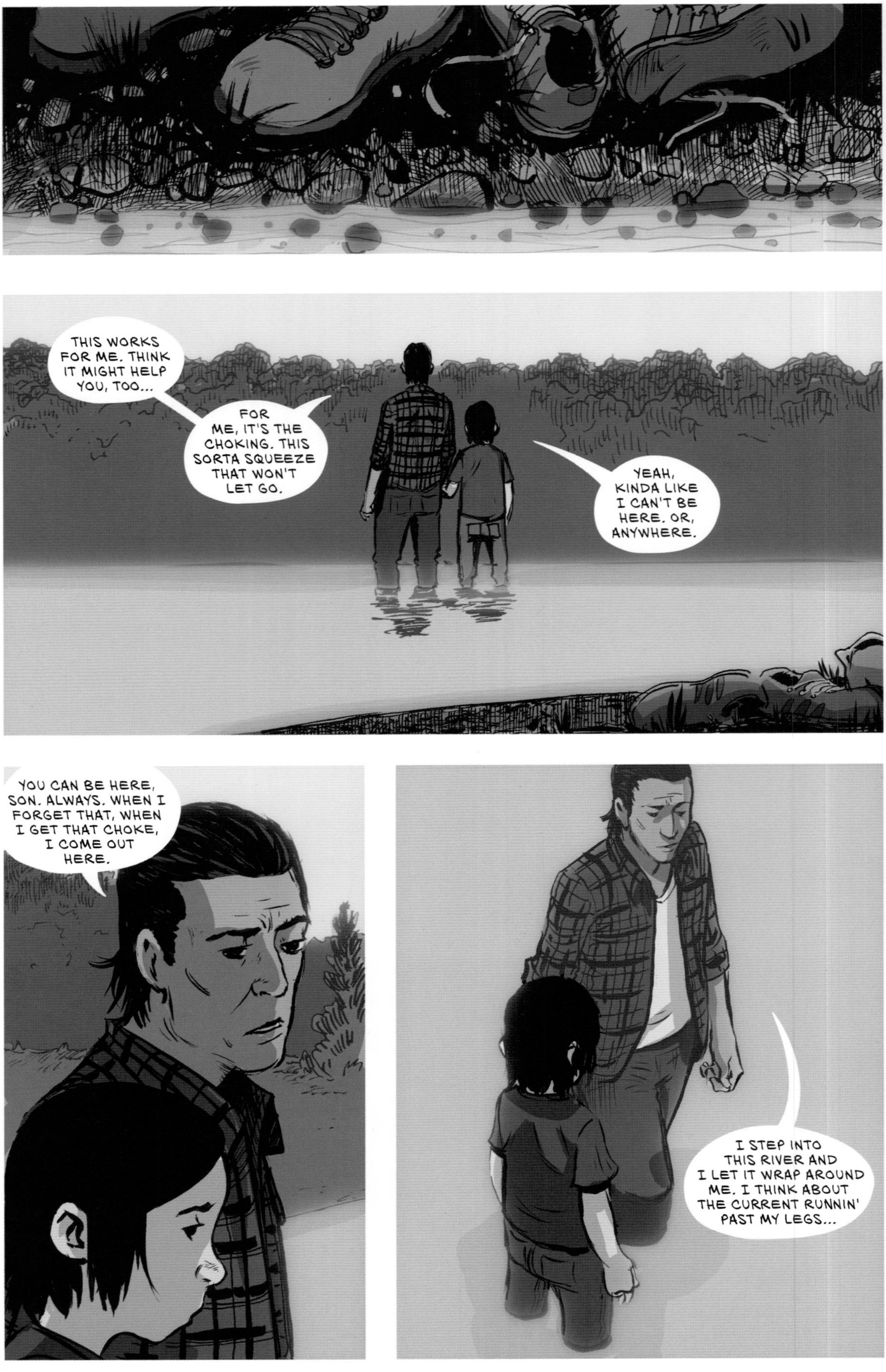
THIS WORKS FOR ME. THINK IT MIGHT HELP YOU, TOO...
FOR ME, IT'S THE CHOKING. THIS SORTA SQUEEZE THAT WON'T LET GO.
YEAH, KINDA LIKE I CAN'T BE HERE. OR, ANYWHERE.
YOU CAN BE HERE, SON. ALWAYS. WHEN I FORGET THAT, WHEN I GET THAT CHOKE, I COME OUT HERE.
I STEP INTO THIS RIVER AND I LET IT WRAP AROUND ME. I THINK ABOUT THE CURRENT RUNNIN' PAST MY LEGS...

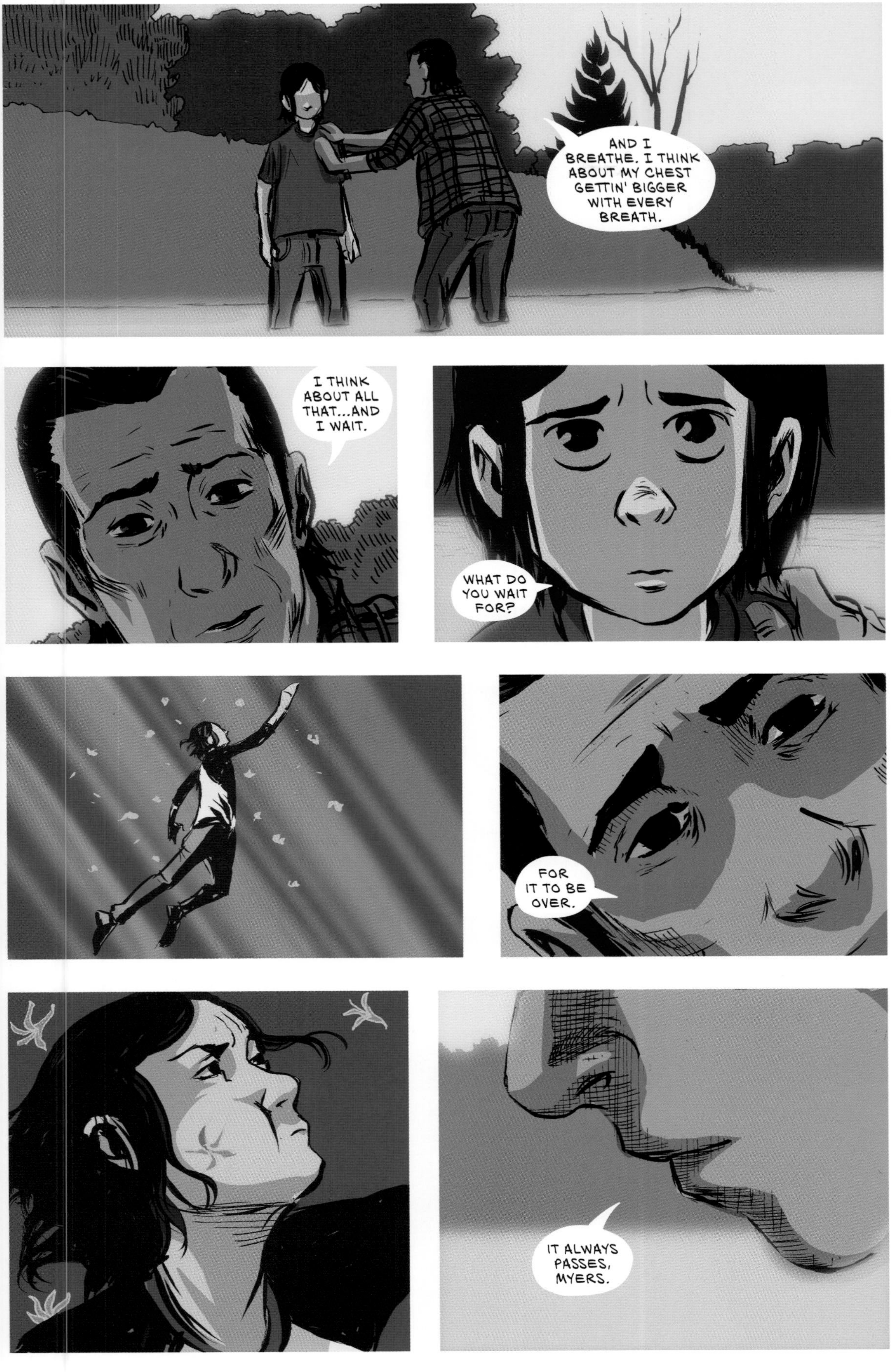
AND I BREATHE. I THINK ABOUT MY CHEST GETTIN' BIGGER WITH EVERY BREATH.
I THINK ABOUT ALL THAT...AND I WAIT.
WHAT DO YOU WAIT FOR?
FOR IT TO BE OVER.
IT ALWAYS PASSES, MYERS.

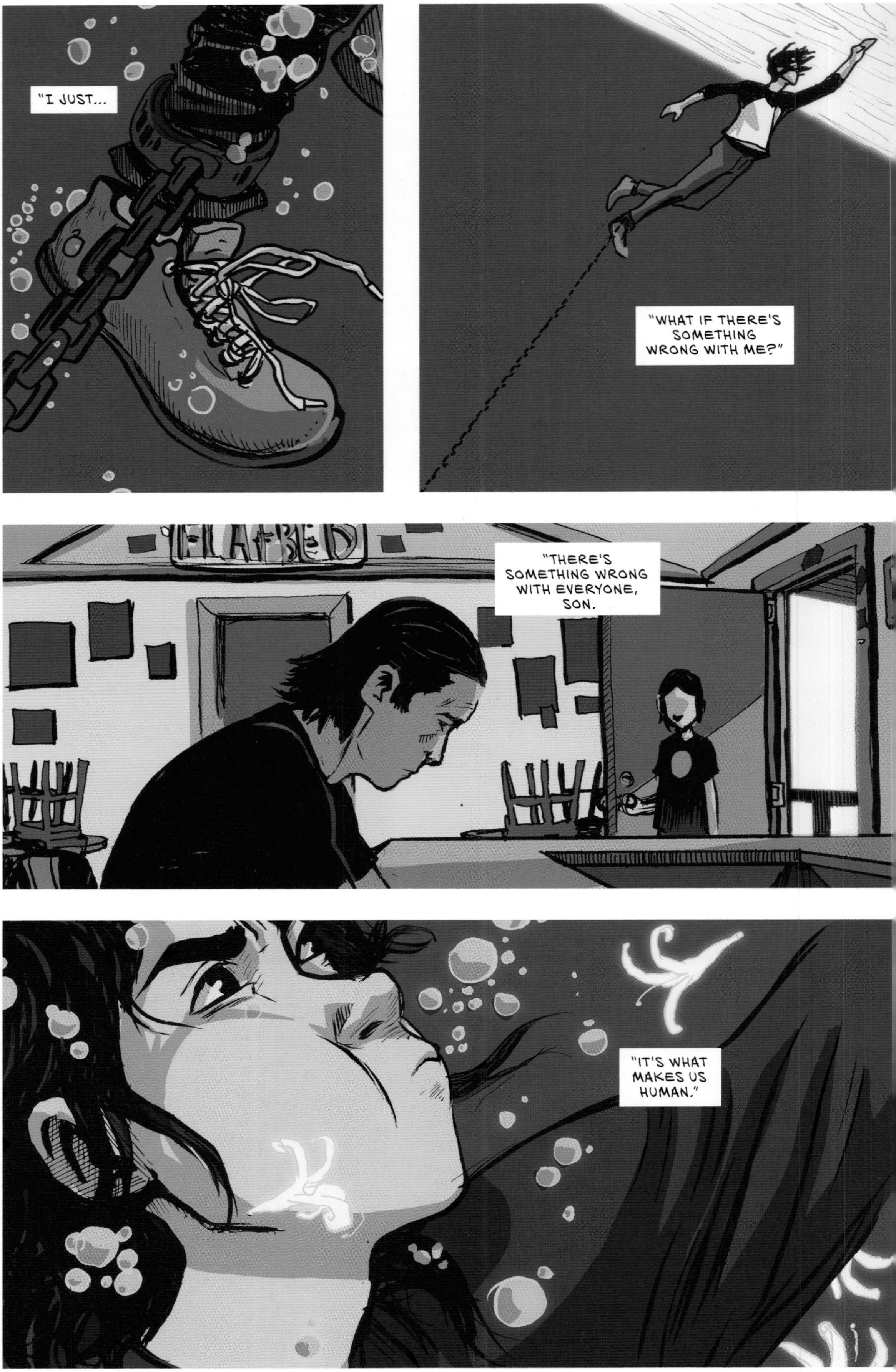
"I JUST...
"WHAT IF THERE'S SOMETHING WRONG WITH ME?"
"THERE'S SOMETHING WRONG WITH EVERYONE, SON.
"IT'S WHAT MAKES US HUMAN."

"BUT YOU CAN'T FOCUS ON THE WRONG...

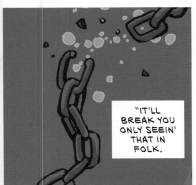

"IT'LL BREAK YOU ONLY SEEIN' THAT IN FOLK.

"YOU FOCUS ON THE ONES WHO LOVE YOU.

"AND YOU TRY YOUR DAMNDEST..."

TO GIVE AS MUCH LOVE BACK AS YOU CAN.

I LOVE YOU, DAD.

I LOVE YOU TOO, SON. THAT WON'T EVER PASS.

# CHAPTER ELEVEN

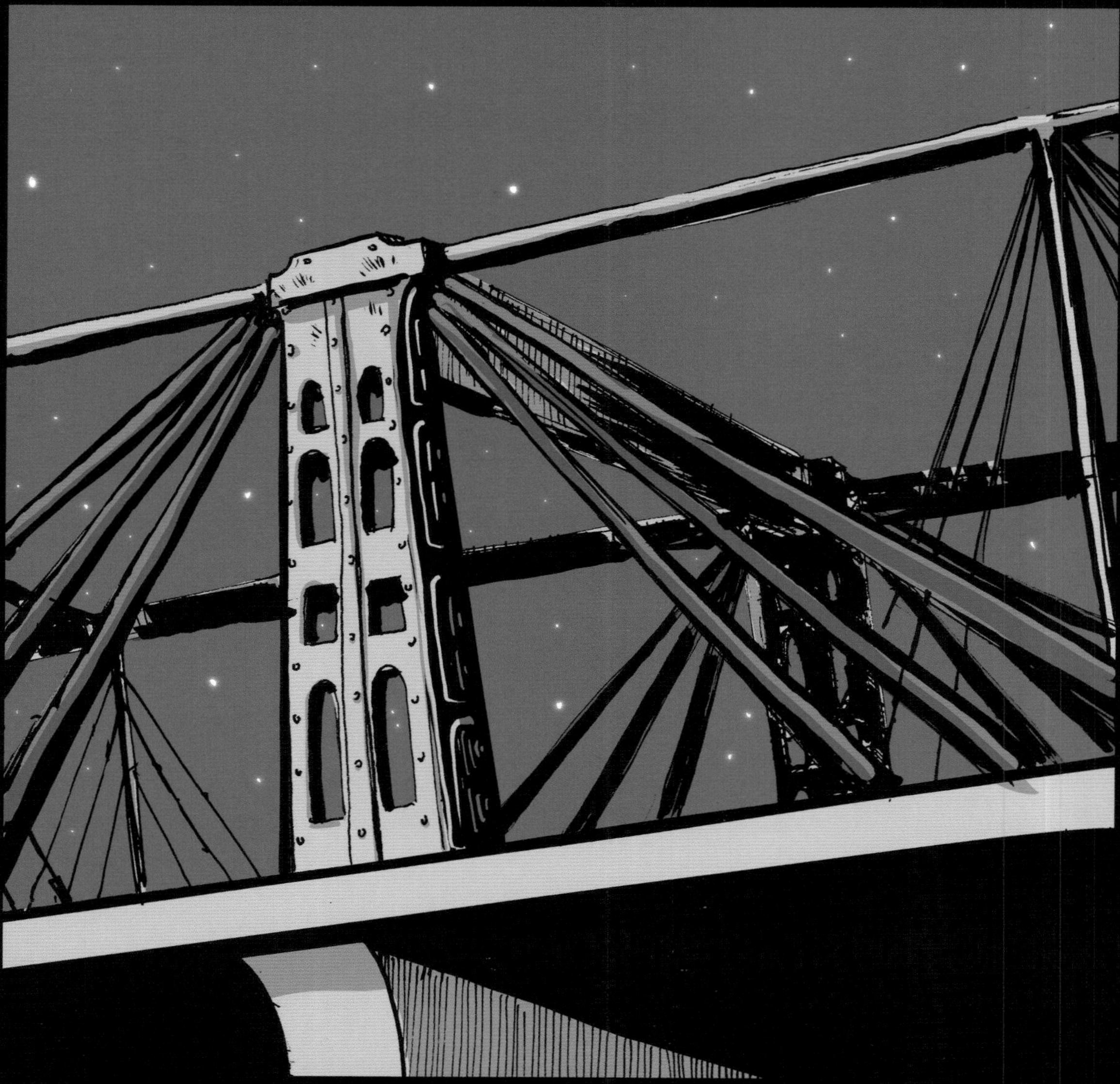

# CELESTES INSIPIENS

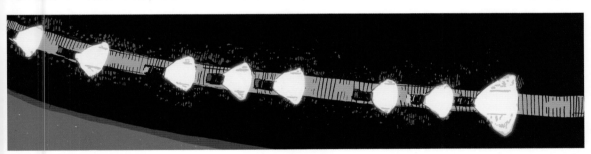

HOW YOU FEELIN'?

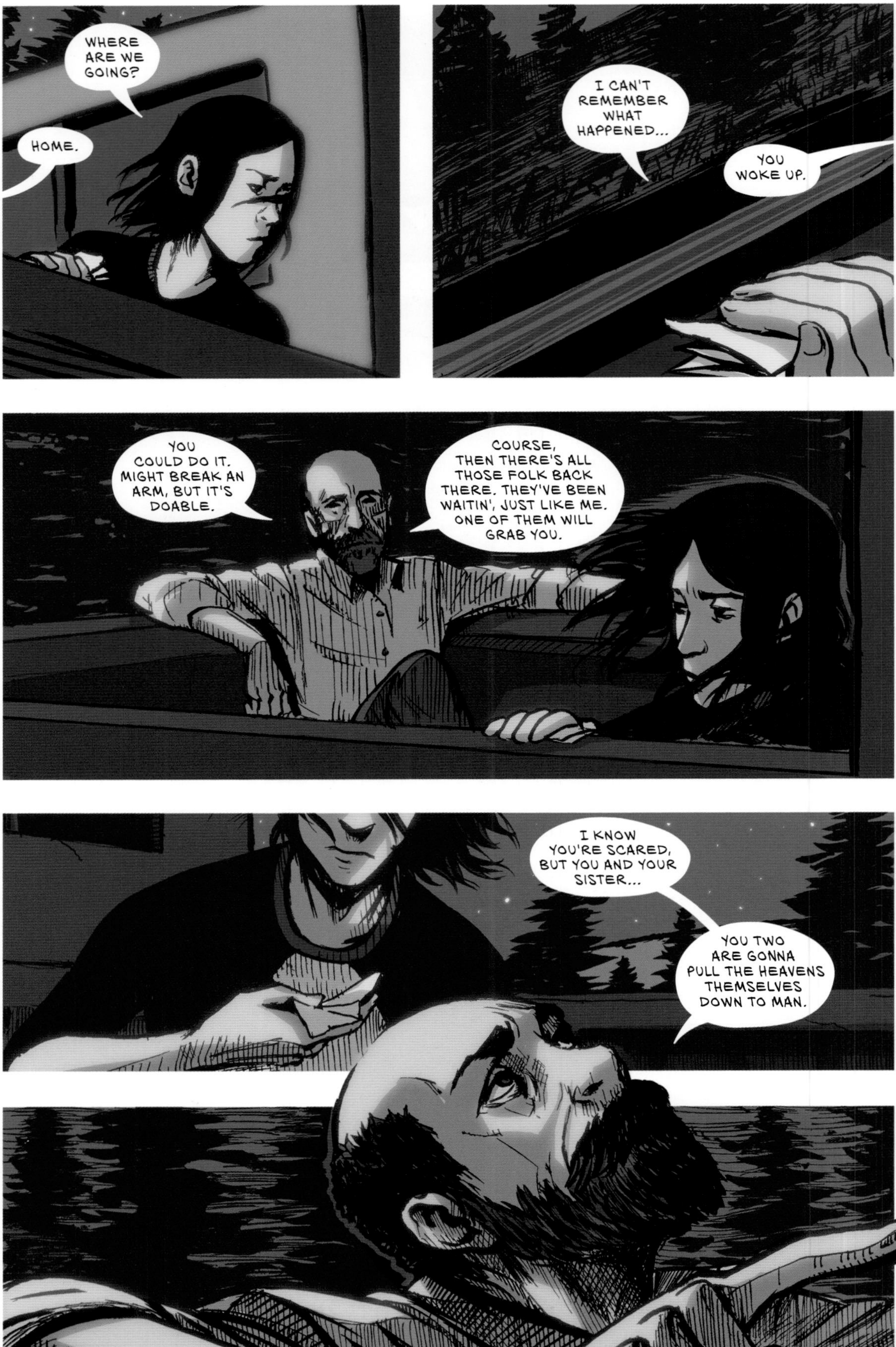
WHERE ARE WE GOING?
HOME.
I CAN'T REMEMBER WHAT HAPPENED...
YOU WOKE UP.
YOU COULD DO IT. MIGHT BREAK AN ARM, BUT IT'S DOABLE.
COURSE, THEN THERE'S ALL THOSE FOLK BACK THERE. THEY'VE BEEN WAITIN', JUST LIKE ME. ONE OF THEM WILL GRAB YOU.
I KNOW YOU'RE SCARED, BUT YOU AND YOUR SISTER...
YOU TWO ARE GONNA PULL THE HEAVENS THEMSELVES DOWN TO MAN.

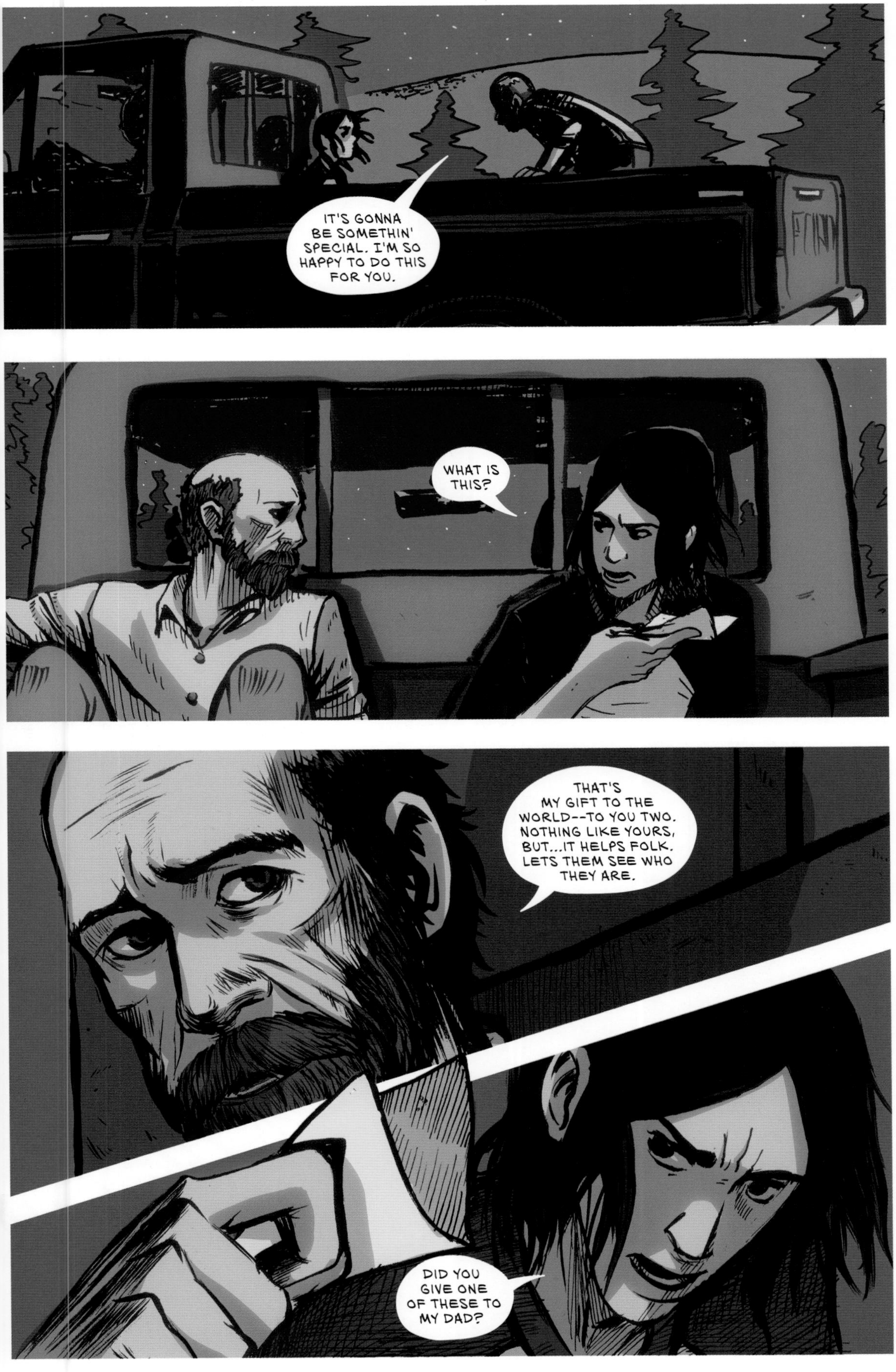
IT'S GONNA BE SOMETHIN' SPECIAL. I'M SO HAPPY TO DO THIS FOR YOU.
WHAT IS THIS?
THAT'S MY GIFT TO THE WORLD--TO YOU TWO. NOTHING LIKE YOURS, BUT...IT HELPS FOLK. LETS THEM SEE WHO THEY ARE.
DID YOU GIVE ONE OF THESE TO MY DAD?

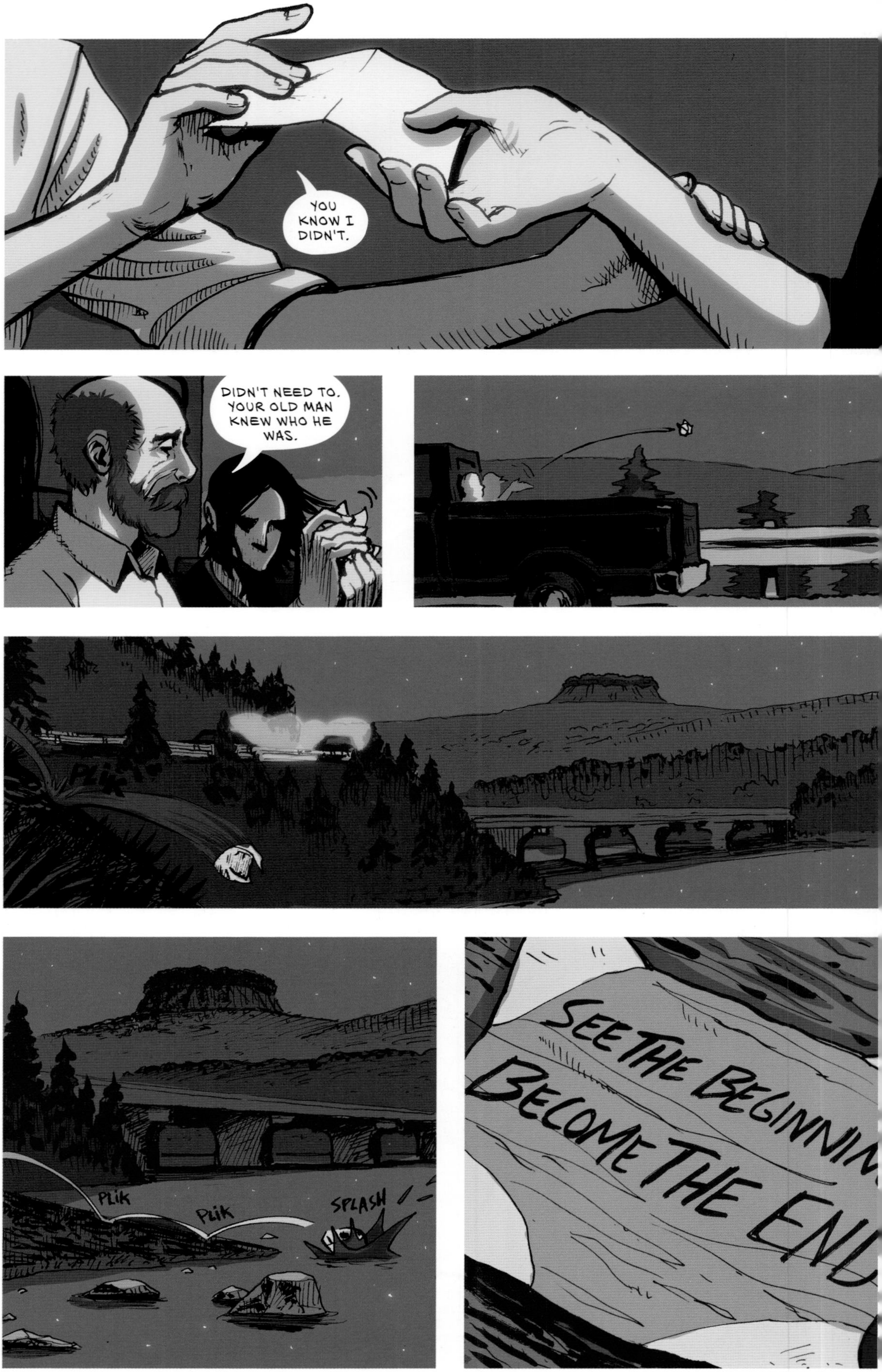

YOU KNOW I DIDN'T.
DIDN'T NEED TO. YOUR OLD MAN KNEW WHO HE WAS.
PLIK
PLIK
PLIK
SPLASH
SEE THE BEGINNIN
BECOME THE EN

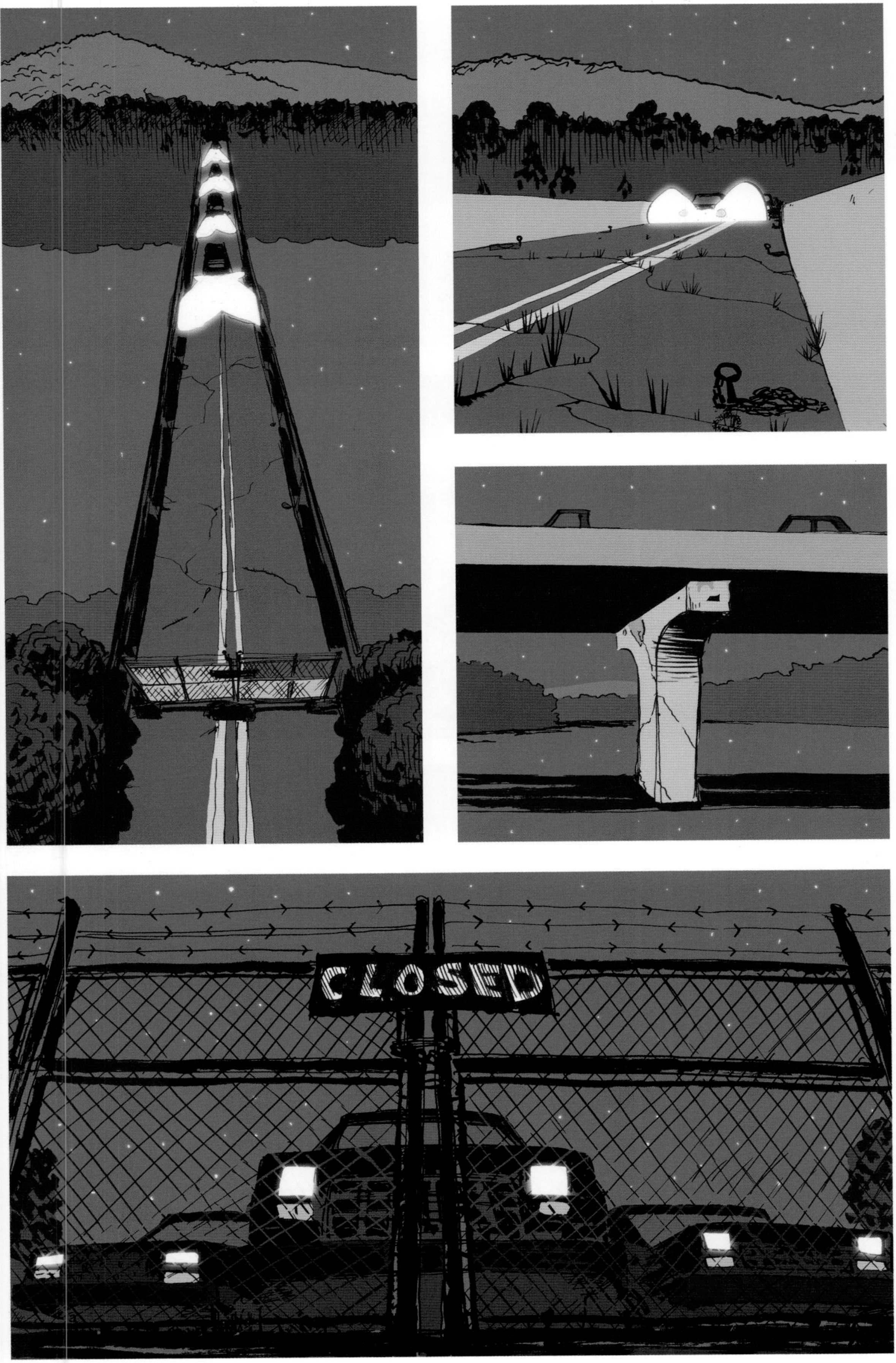
CLOSED

YOU GO AHEAD AND GET MISS SAULNIER READY, PAULA JEAN. WE'LL GET HER LINKS.

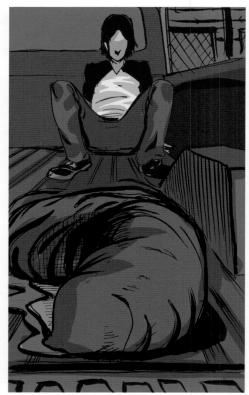

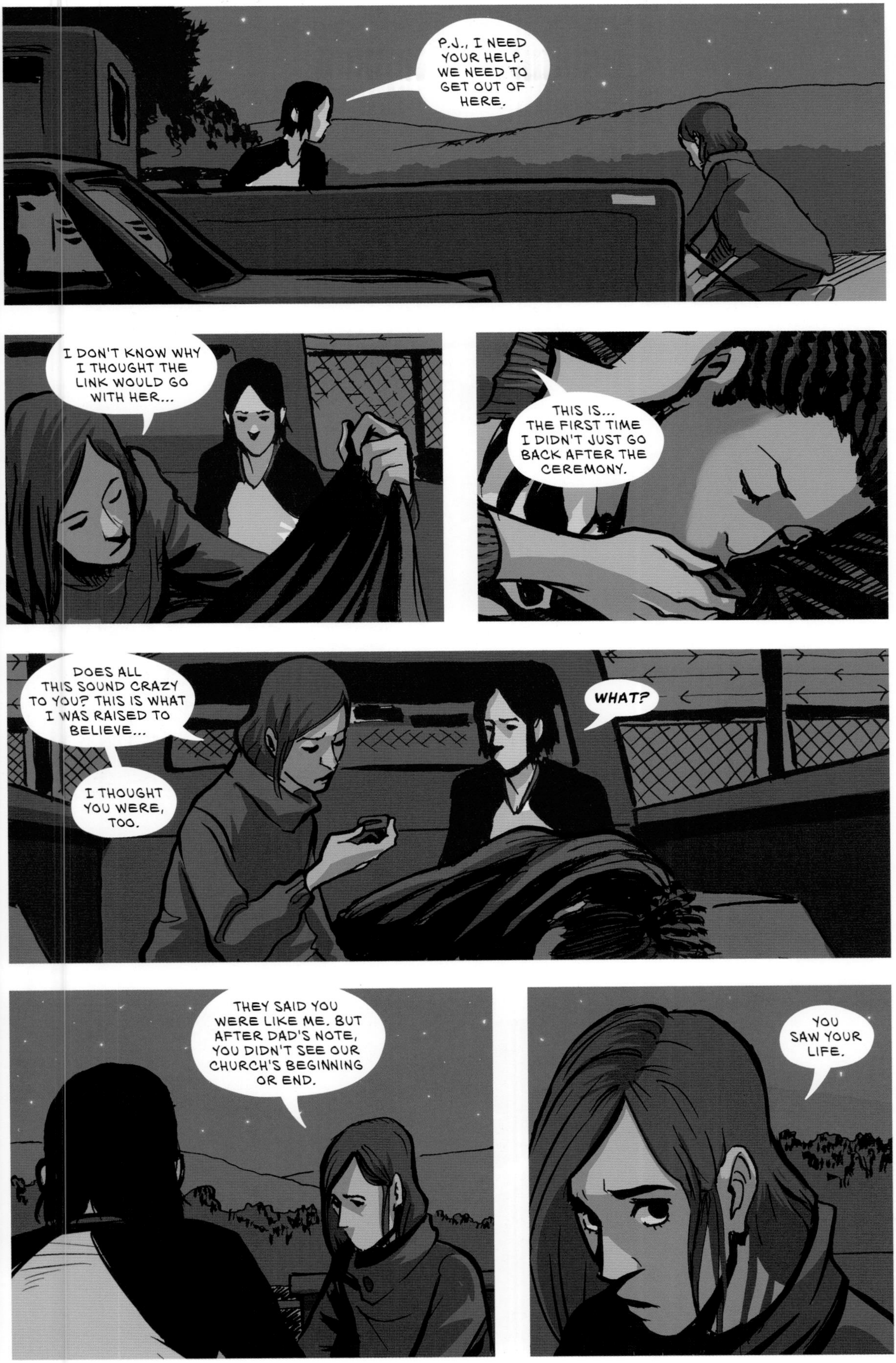
P.J., I NEED YOUR HELP. WE NEED TO GET OUT OF HERE.
I DON'T KNOW WHY I THOUGHT THE LINK WOULD GO WITH HER...
THIS IS... THE FIRST TIME I DIDN'T JUST GO BACK AFTER THE CEREMONY.
DOES ALL THIS SOUND CRAZY TO YOU? THIS IS WHAT I WAS RAISED TO BELIEVE...
I THOUGHT YOU WERE, TOO.
WHAT?
THEY SAID YOU WERE LIKE ME. BUT AFTER DAD'S NOTE, YOU DIDN'T SEE OUR CHURCH'S BEGINNING OR END.
YOU SAW YOUR LIFE.

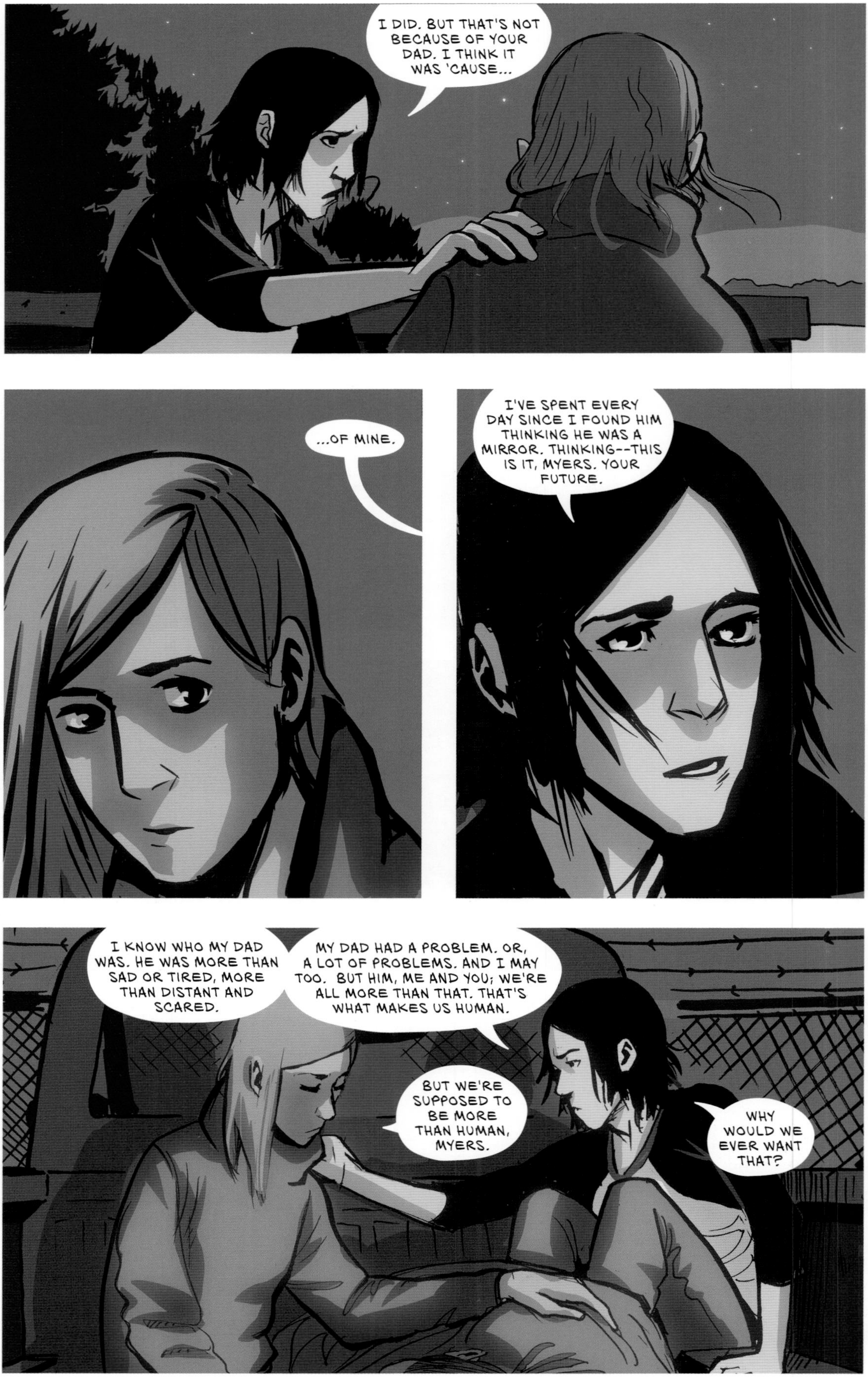
I DID. BUT THAT'S NOT BECAUSE OF YOUR DAD. I THINK IT WAS 'CAUSE...
...OF MINE.
I'VE SPENT EVERY DAY SINCE I FOUND HIM THINKING HE WAS A MIRROR. THINKING--THIS IS IT, MYERS. YOUR FUTURE.
I KNOW WHO MY DAD WAS. HE WAS MORE THAN SAD OR TIRED, MORE THAN DISTANT AND SCARED.
MY DAD HAD A PROBLEM. OR, A LOT OF PROBLEMS. AND I MAY TOO. BUT HIM, ME AND YOU; WE'RE ALL MORE THAN THAT. THAT'S WHAT MAKES US HUMAN.
BUT WE'RE SUPPOSED TO BE MORE THAN HUMAN, MYERS.
WHY WOULD WE EVER WANT THAT?

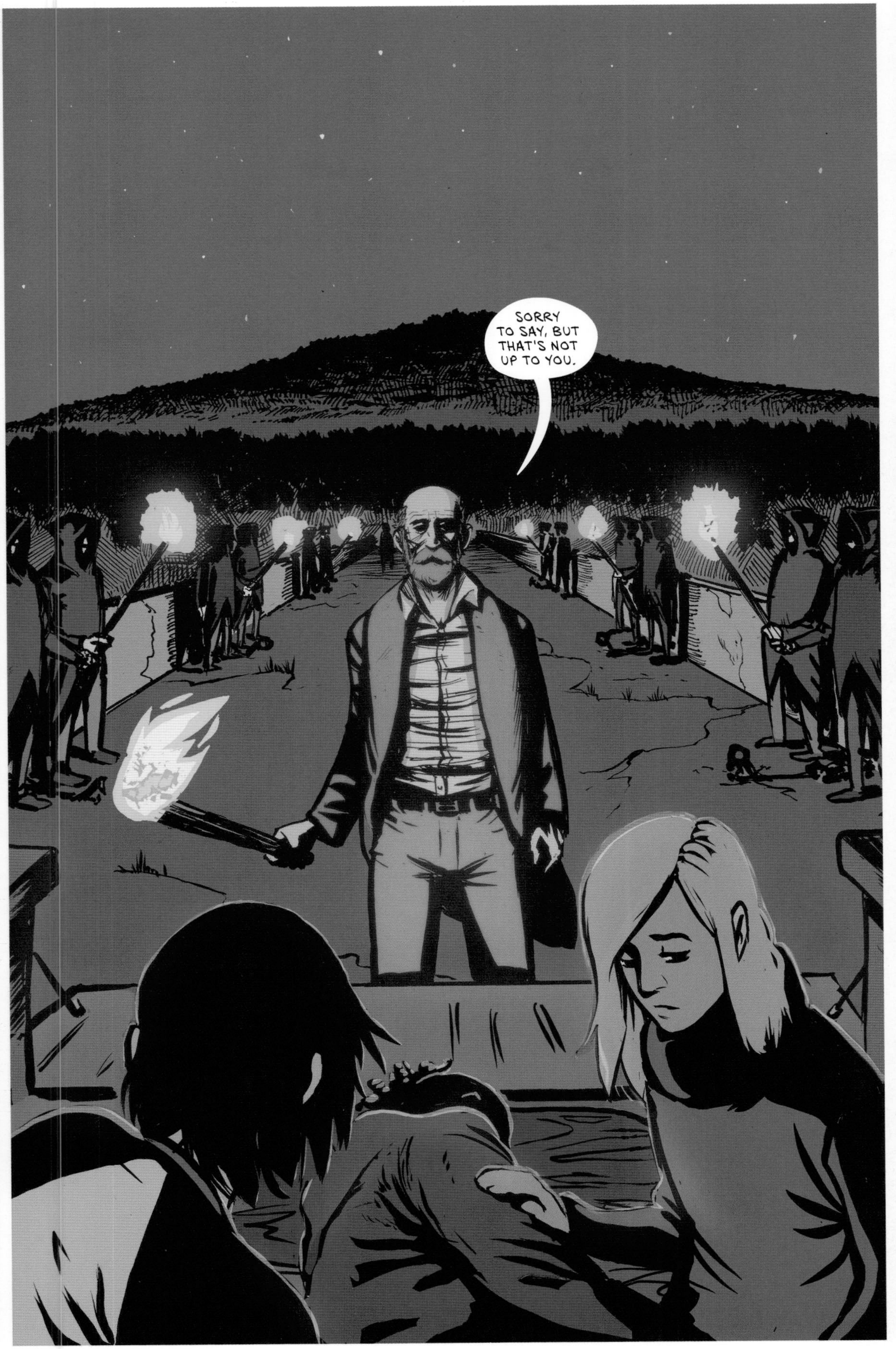
SORRY TO SAY, BUT THAT'S NOT UP TO YOU.

# CHAPTER TWELVE

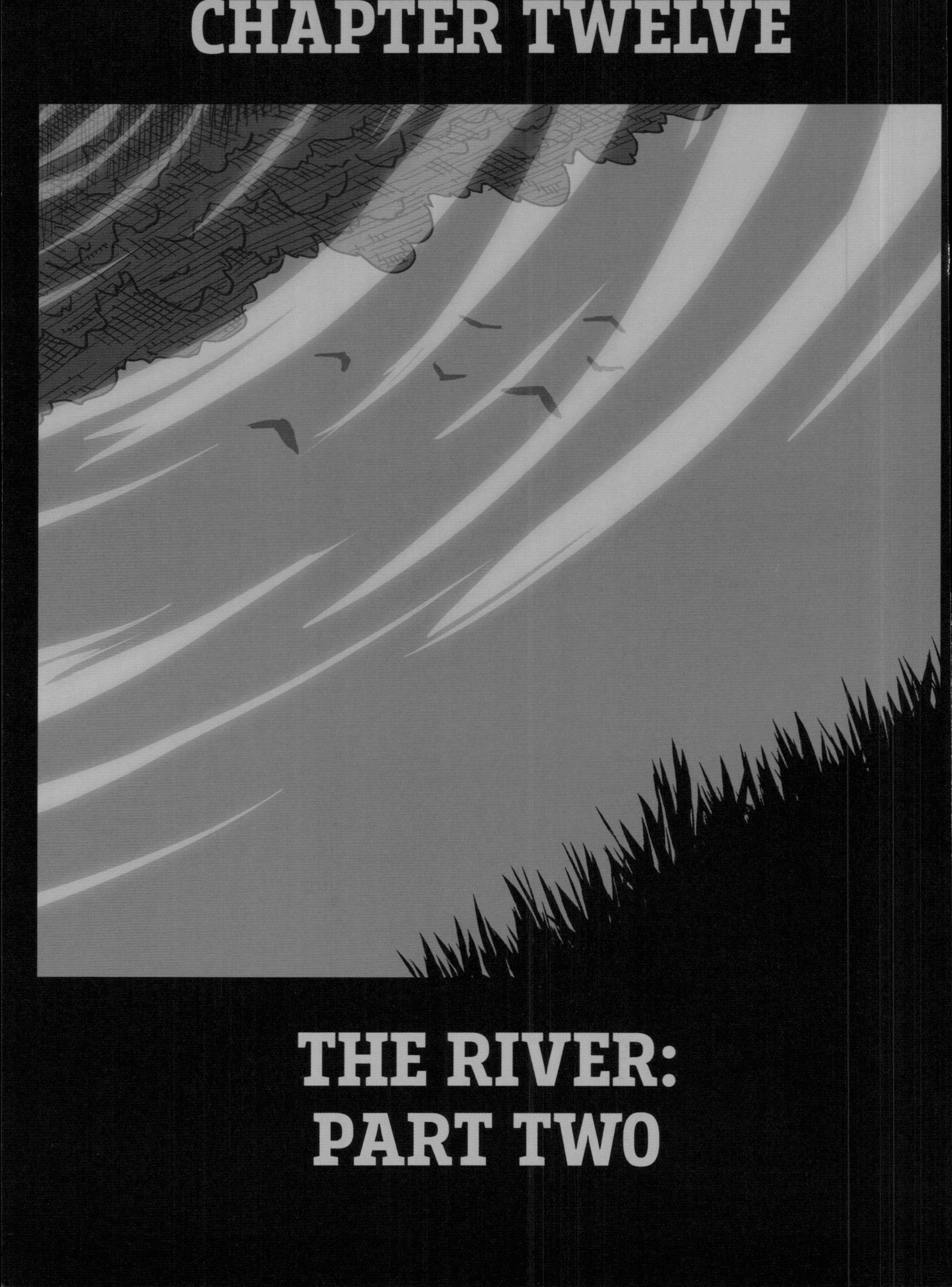

# THE RIVER: PART TWO

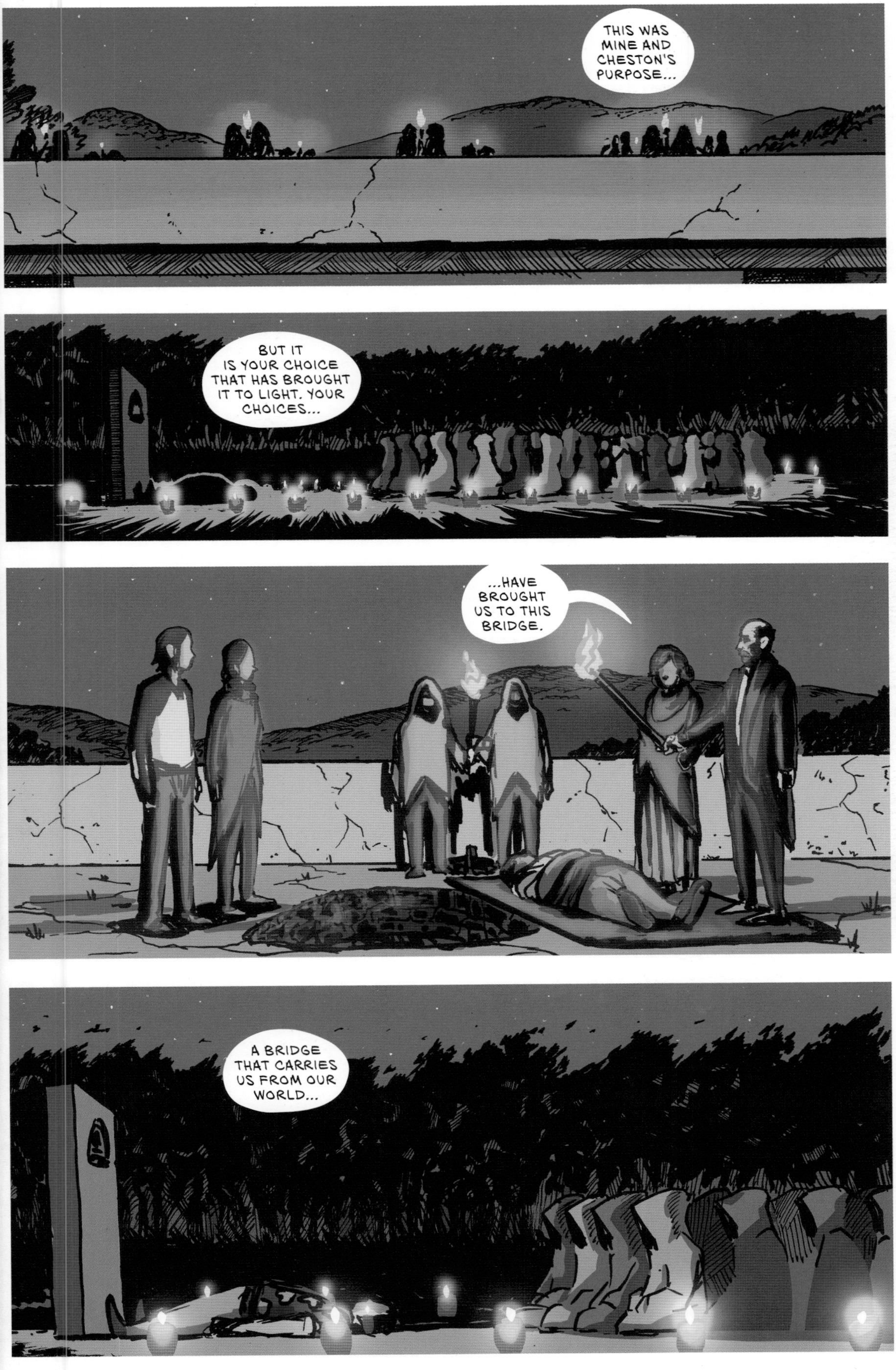
THIS WAS MINE AND CHESTON'S PURPOSE...
BUT IT IS YOUR CHOICE THAT HAS BROUGHT IT TO LIGHT. YOUR CHOICES...
...HAVE BROUGHT US TO THIS BRIDGE.
A BRIDGE THAT CARRIES US FROM OUR WORLD...

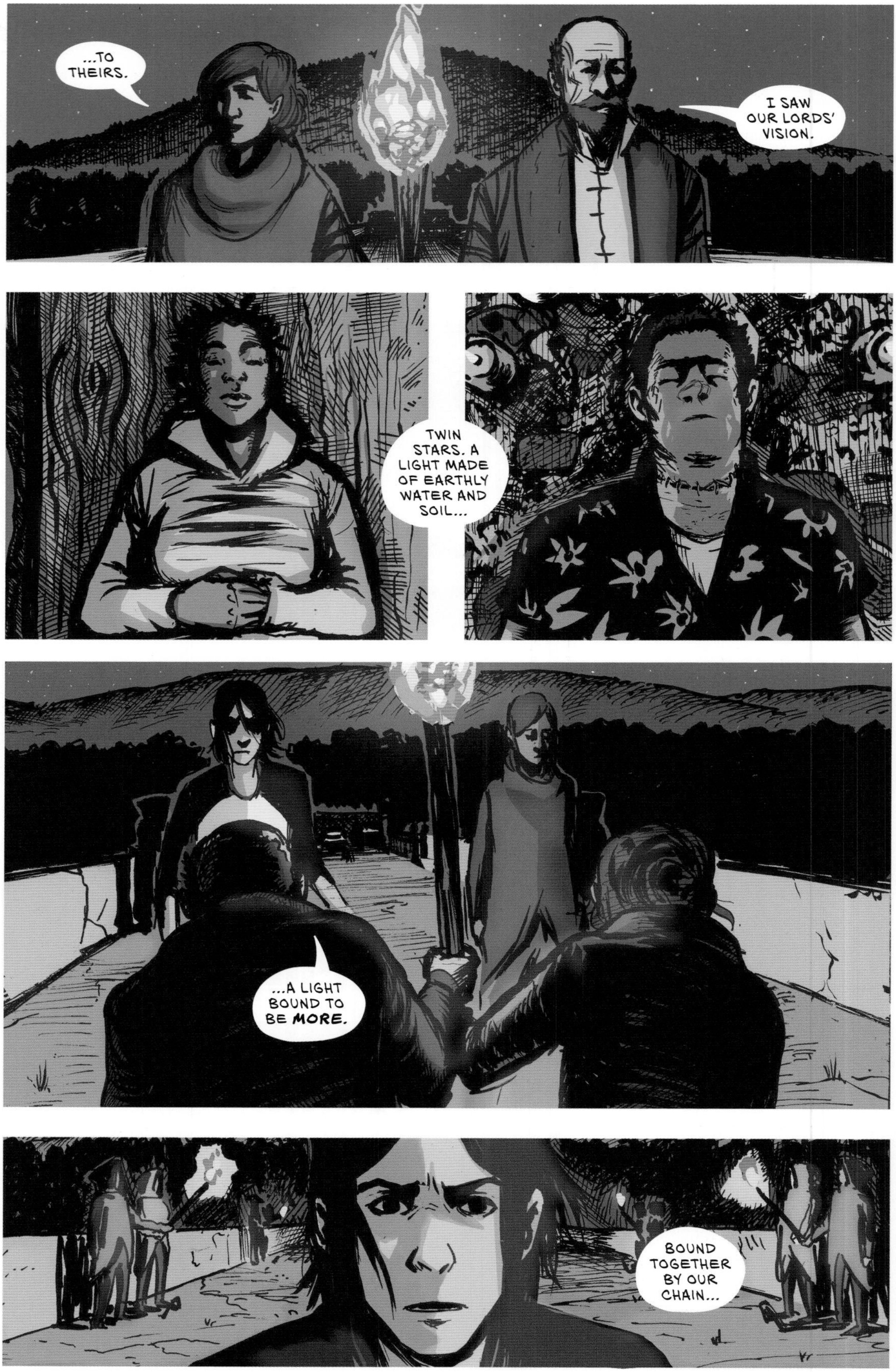
...TO THEIRS.
I SAW OUR LORDS' VISION.
TWIN STARS. A LIGHT MADE OF EARTHLY WATER AND SOIL...
...A LIGHT BOUND TO BE **MORE.**
BOUND TOGETHER BY OUR CHAIN...

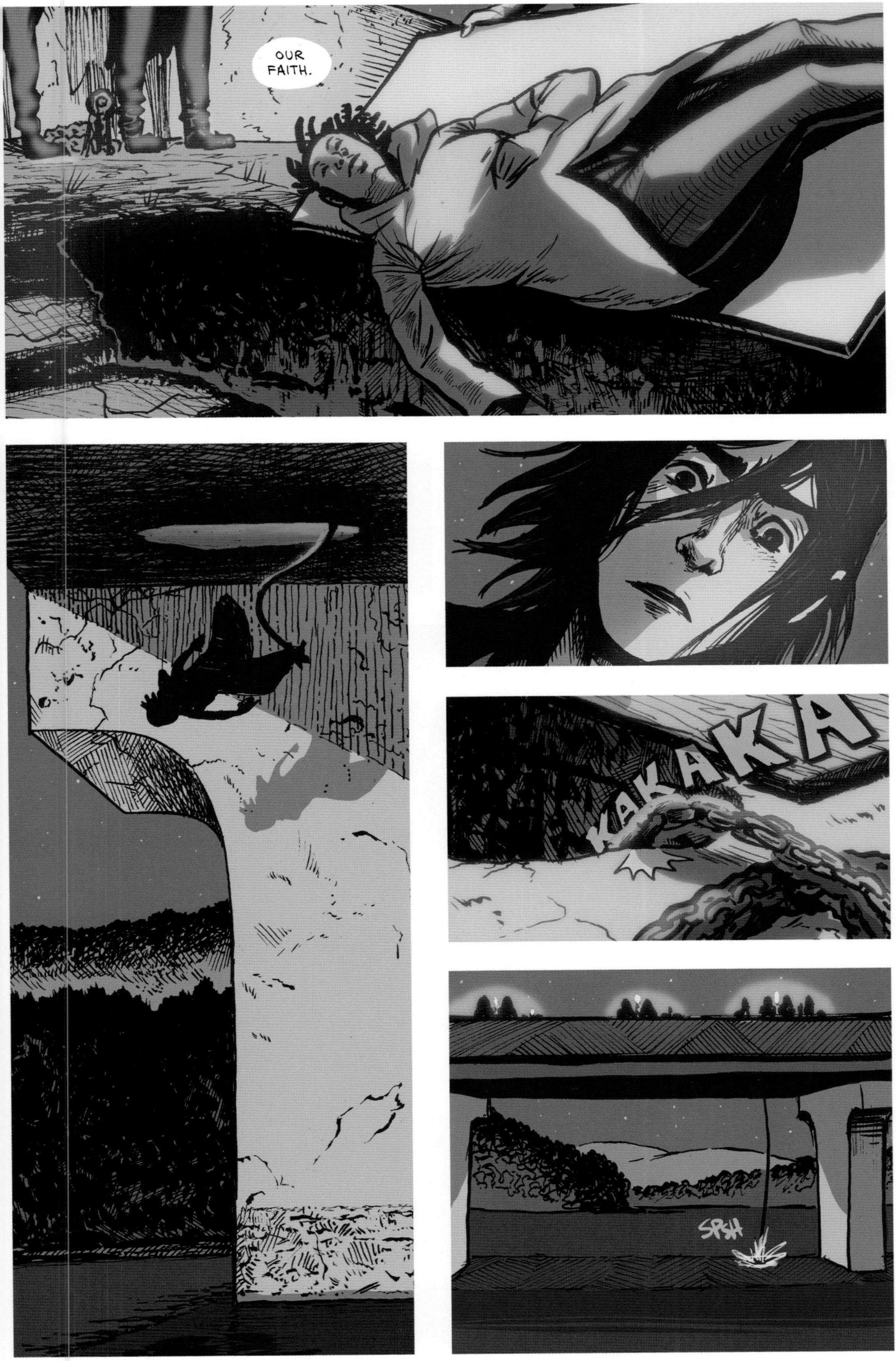
OUR FAITH.
KAKAKA
SPSH

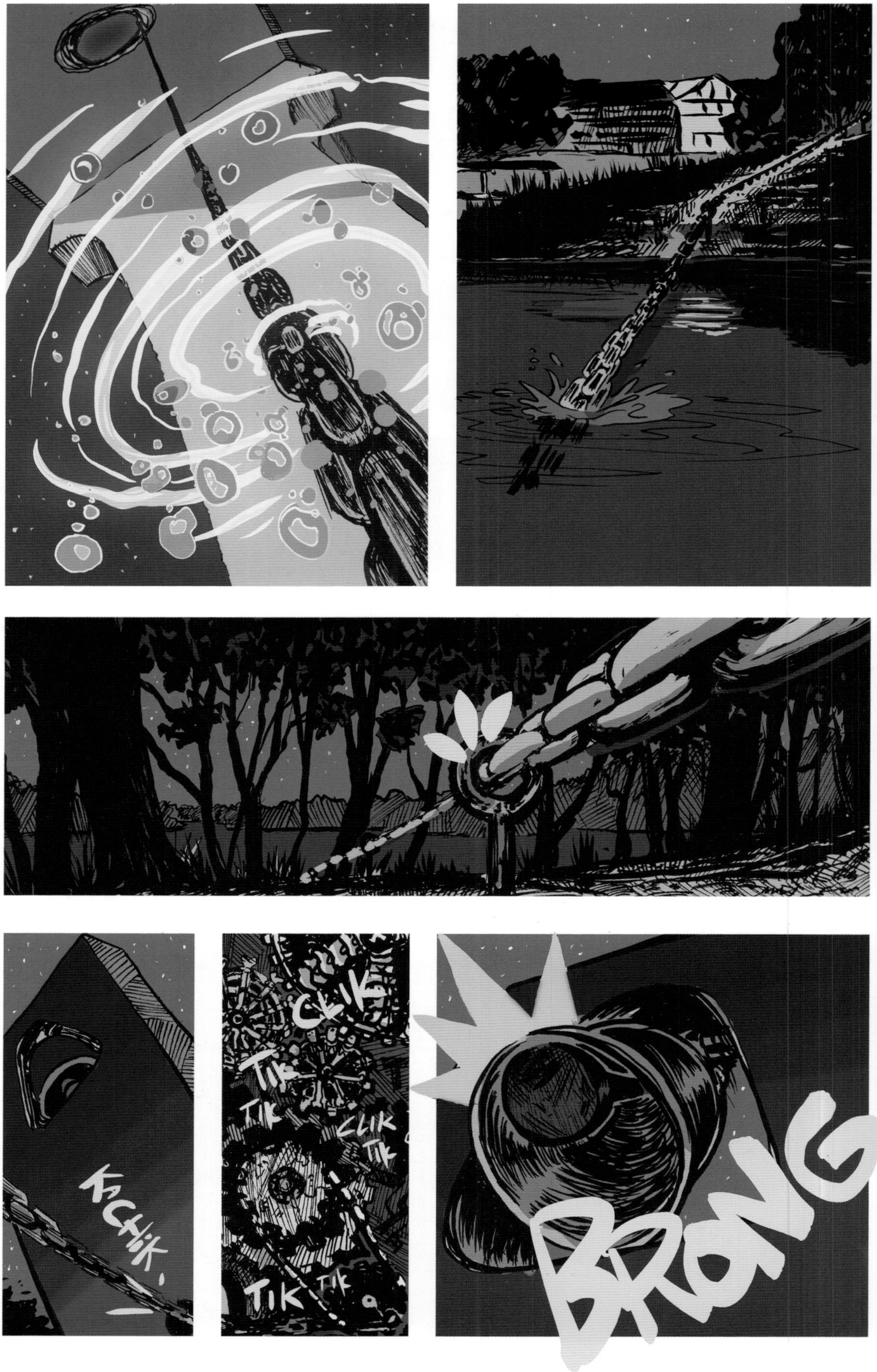
KaCHiK
CLIK
TIK
TIK
CLIK
TIK
TIK
TIK
BRONG

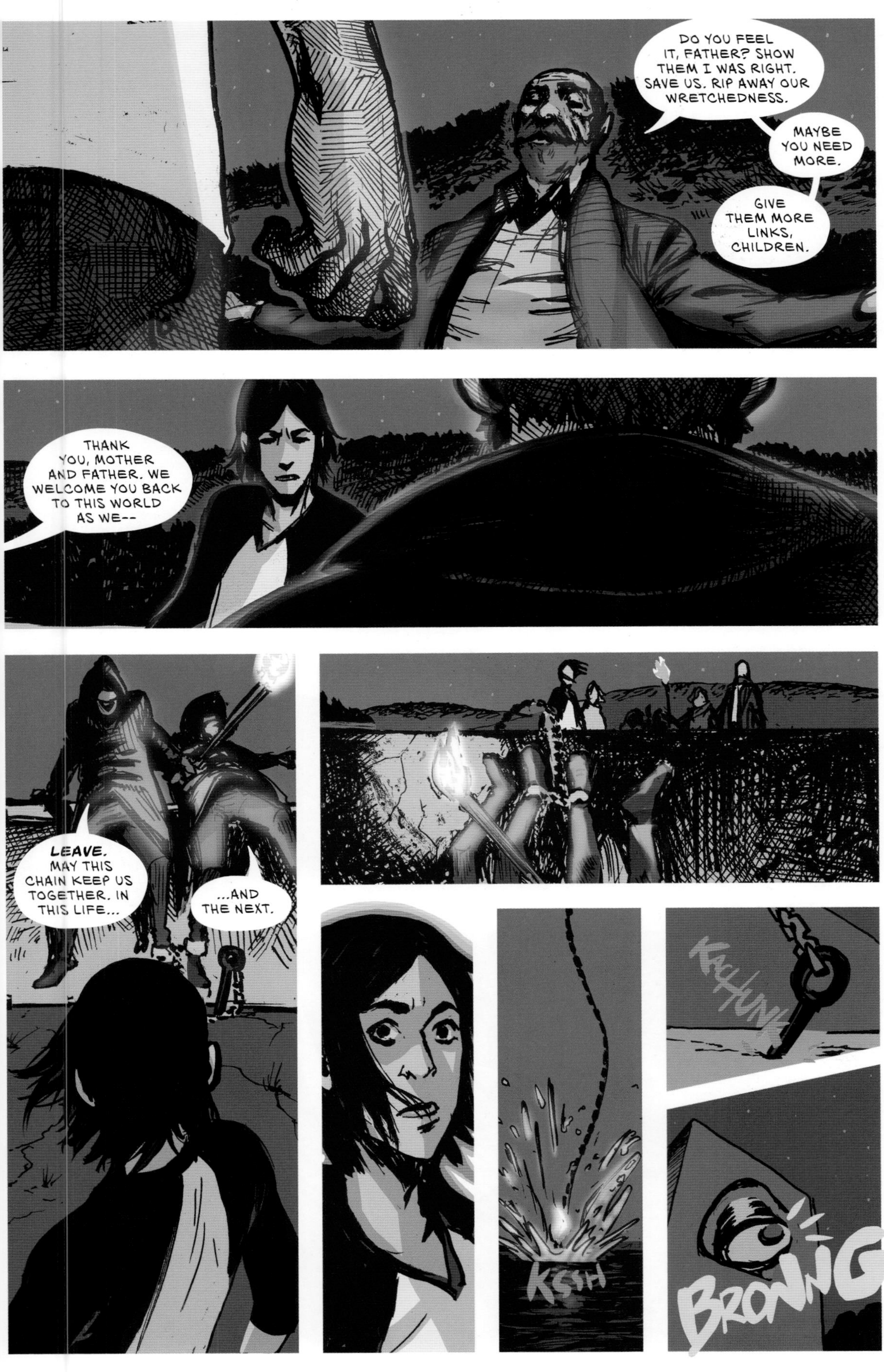
DO YOU FEEL IT, FATHER? SHOW THEM I WAS RIGHT. SAVE US. RIP AWAY OUR WRETCHEDNESS.
MAYBE YOU NEED MORE.
GIVE THEM MORE LINKS, CHILDREN.
THANK YOU, MOTHER AND FATHER. WE WELCOME YOU BACK TO THIS WORLD AS WE--
LEAVE. MAY THIS CHAIN KEEP US TOGETHER. IN THIS LIFE...
...AND THE NEXT.
KSSH
KACHUNK
BRONNG

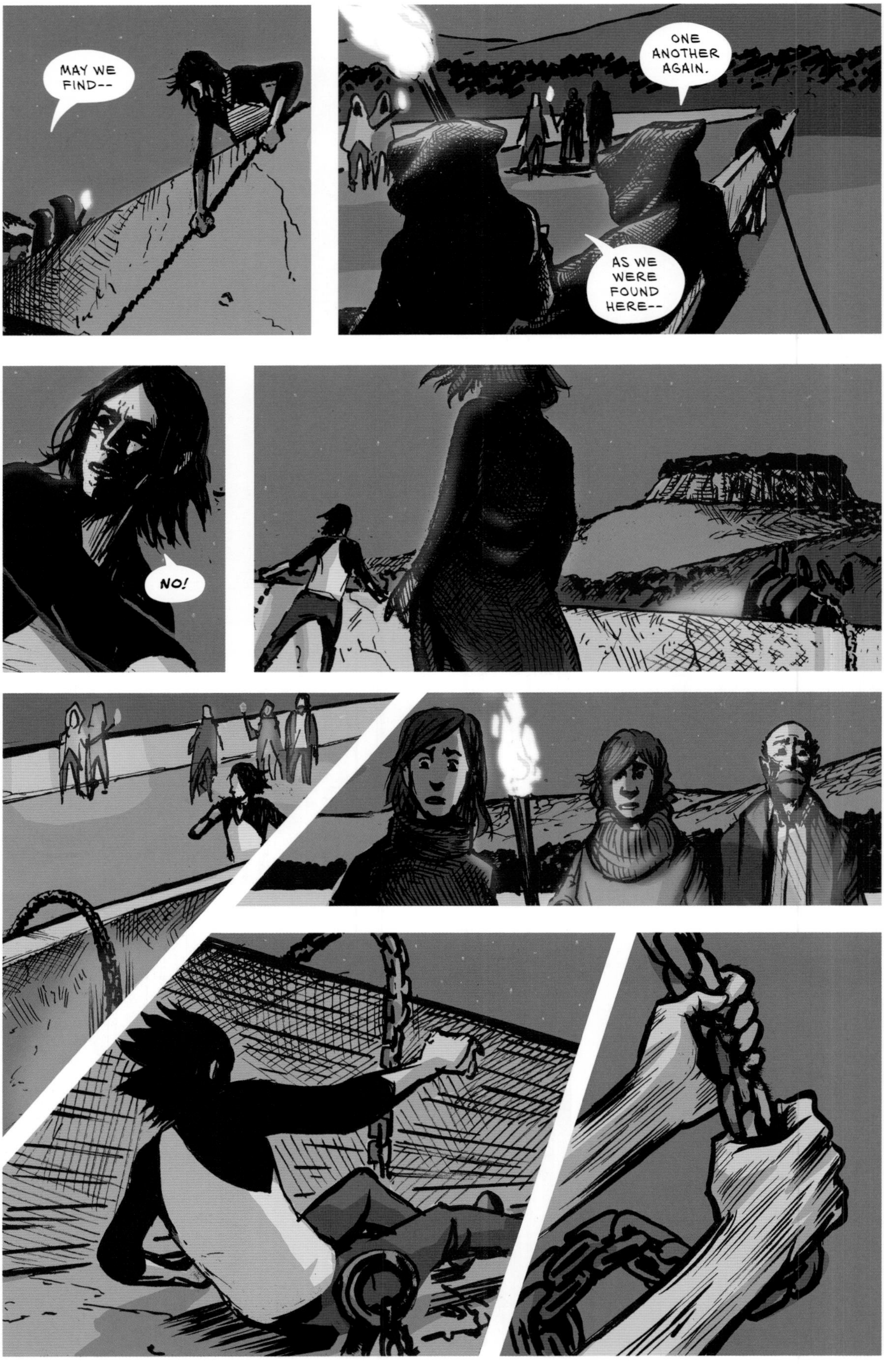
MAY WE FIND--
ONE ANOTHER AGAIN.
AS WE WERE FOUND HERE--
NO!

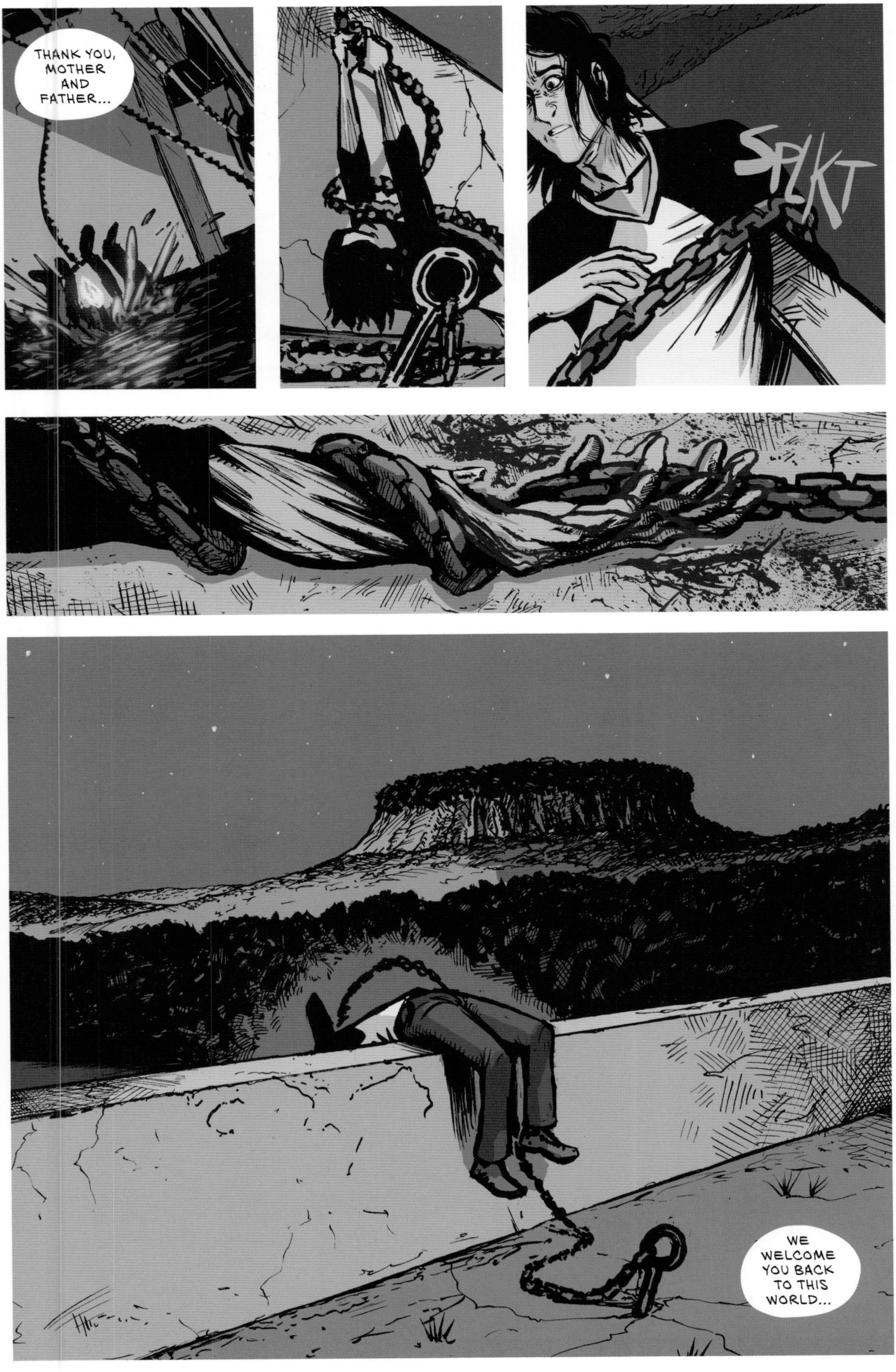
THANK YOU, MOTHER AND FATHER...
SPLKT
WE WELCOME YOU BACK TO THIS WORLD...

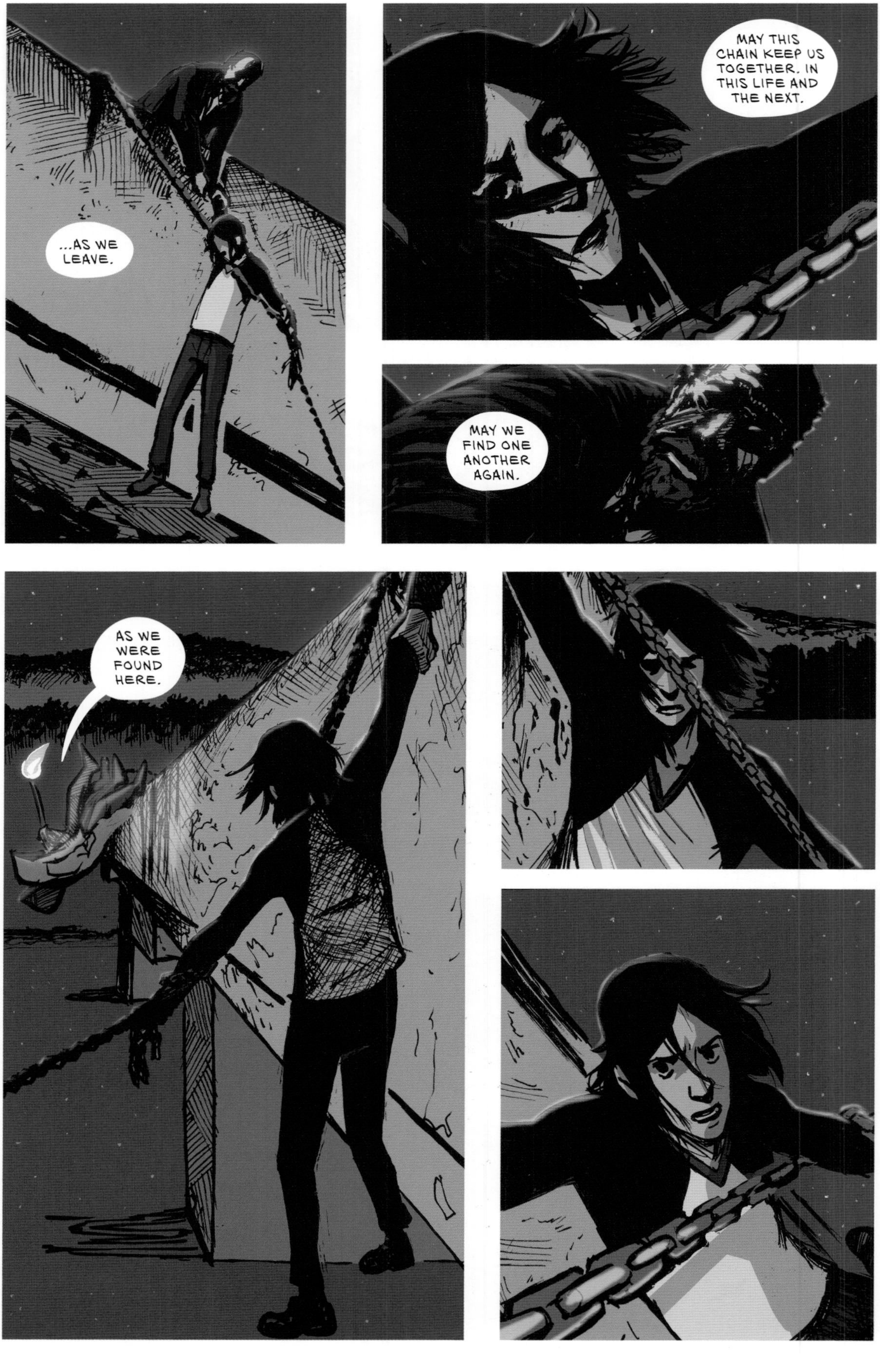
...AS WE LEAVE.
MAY THIS CHAIN KEEP US TOGETHER. IN THIS LIFE AND THE NEXT.
MAY WE FIND ONE ANOTHER AGAIN.
AS WE WERE FOUND HERE.

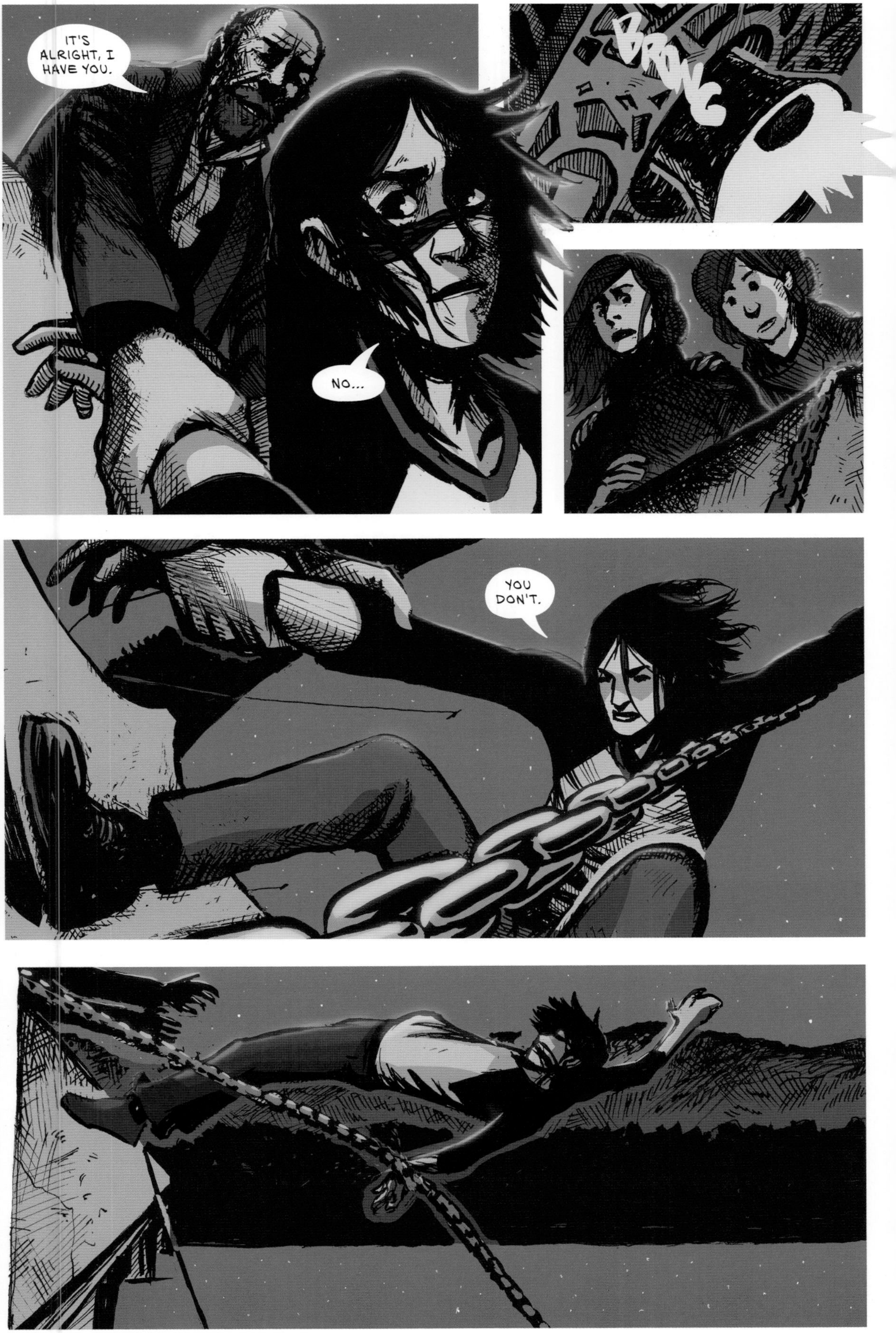
IT'S ALRIGHT, I HAVE YOU.
BRONG
NO...
YOU DON'T.

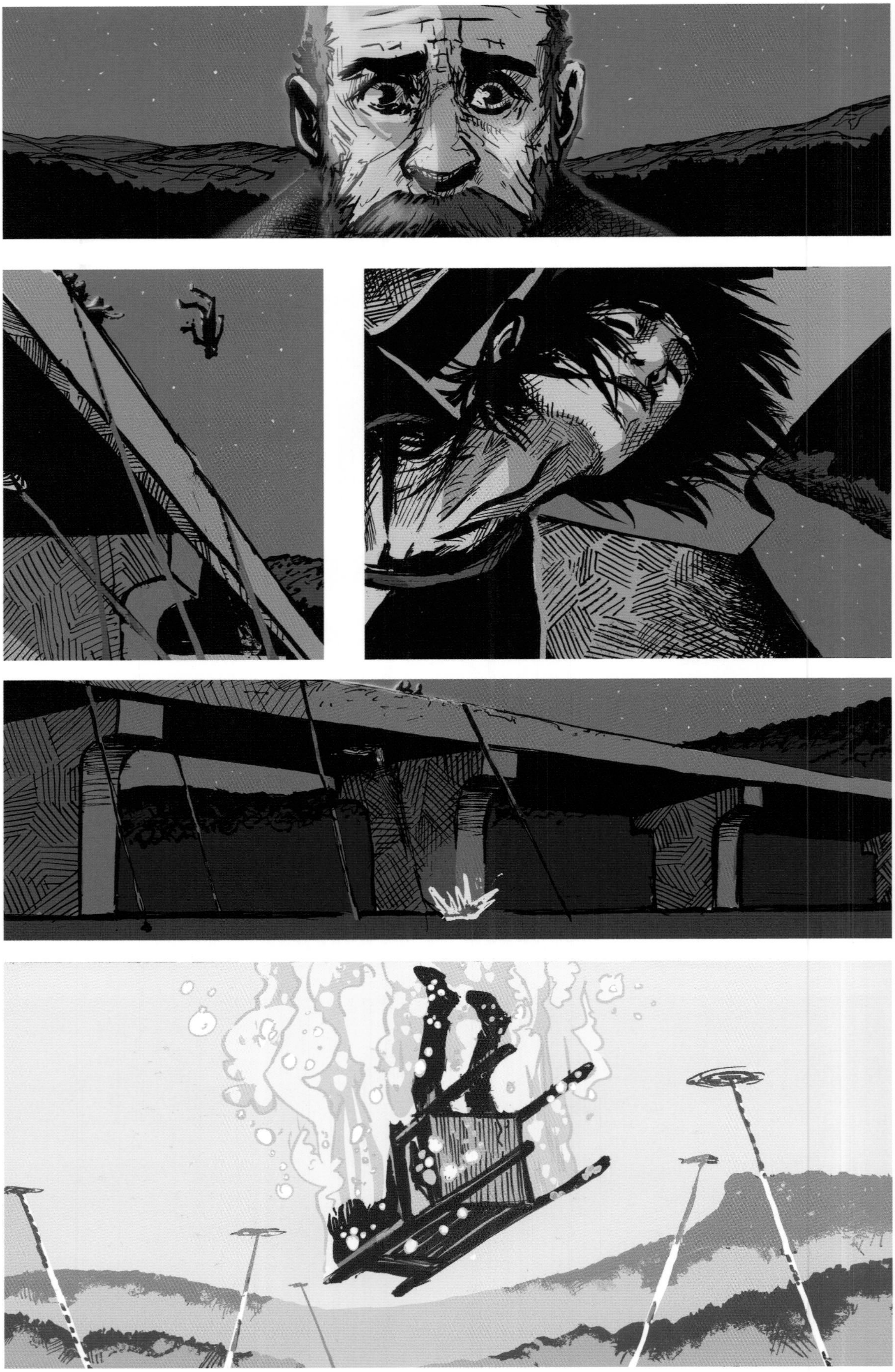

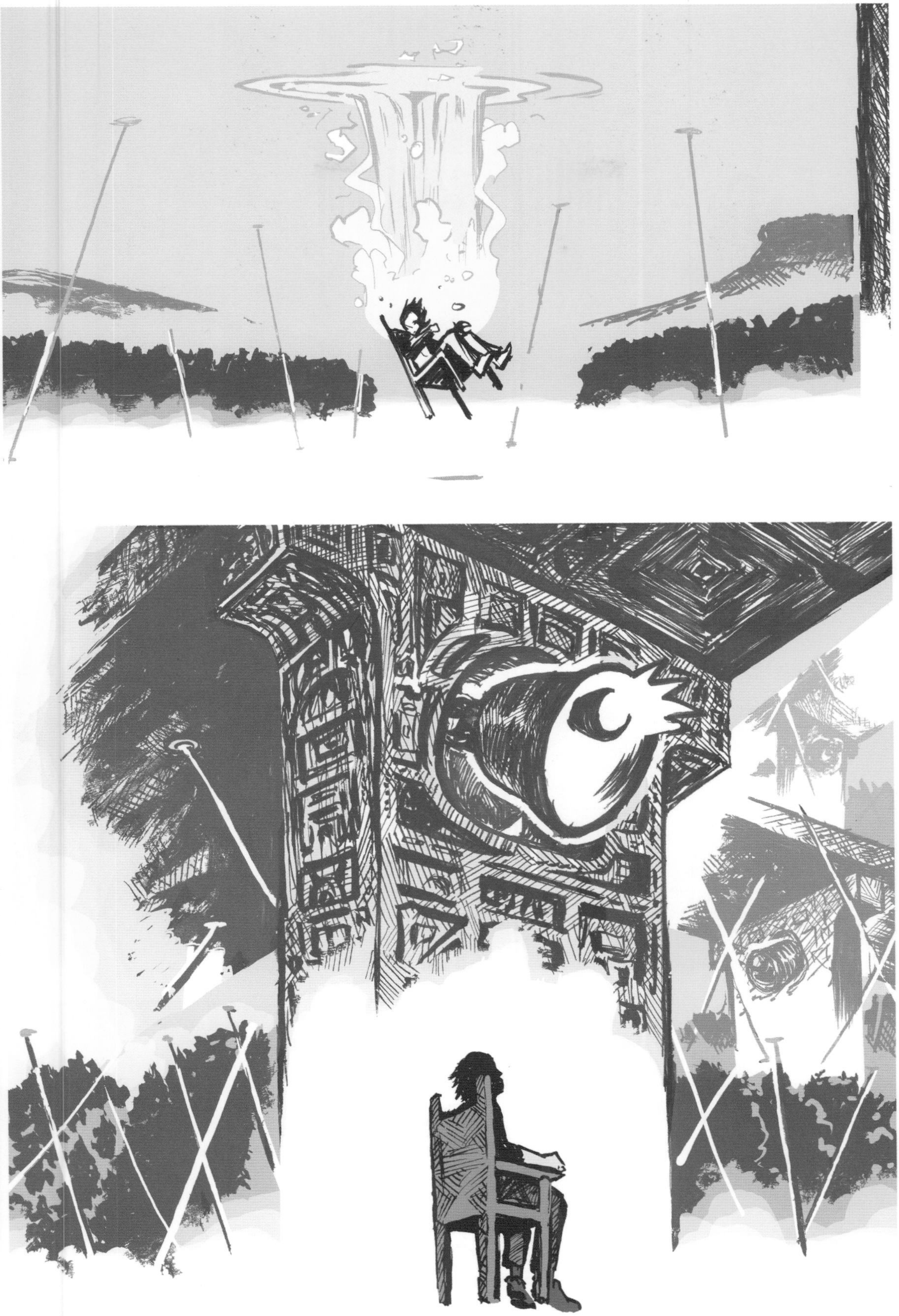

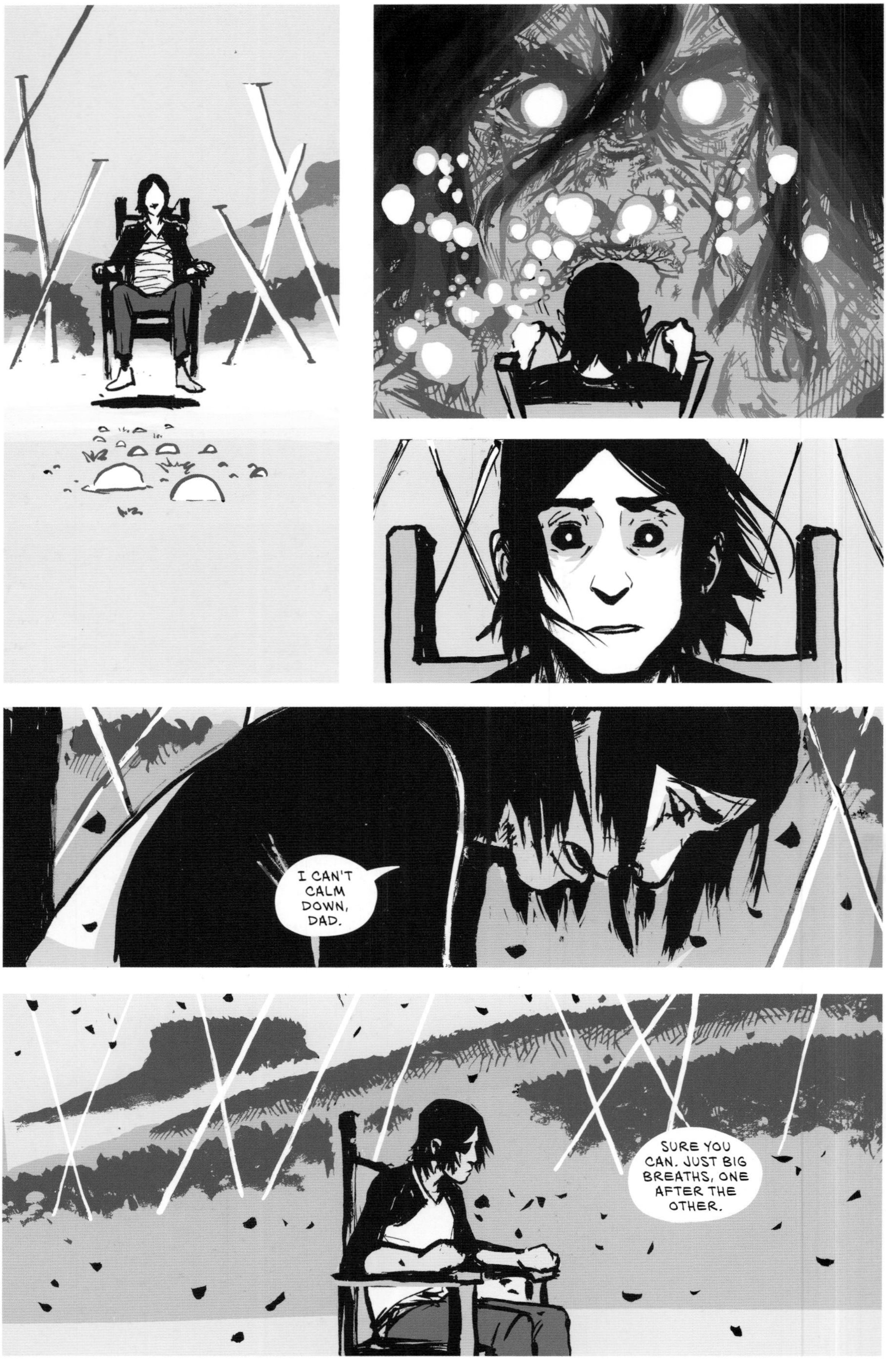
I CAN'T CALM DOWN, DAD.
SURE YOU CAN. JUST BIG BREATHS, ONE AFTER THE OTHER.

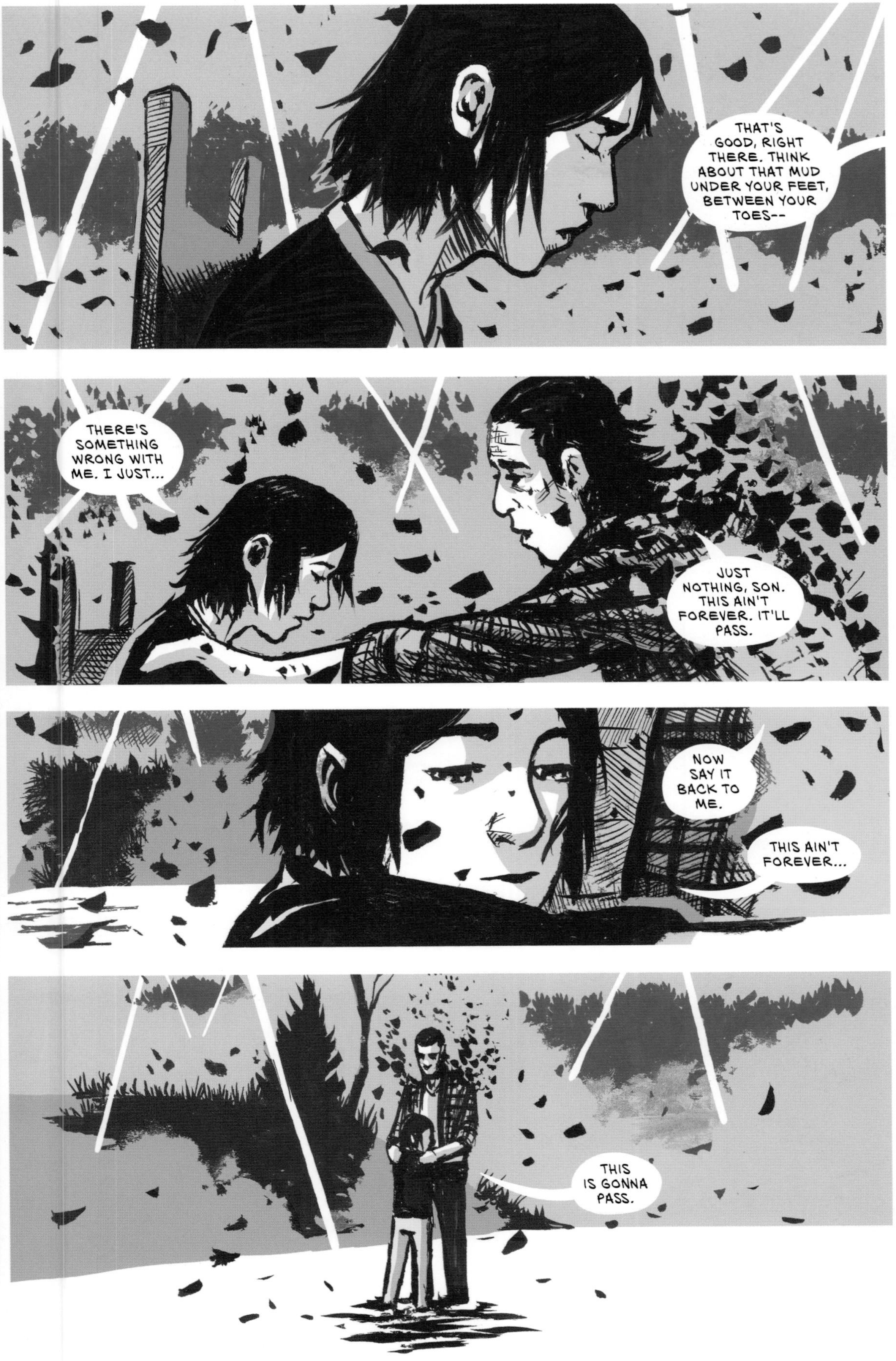
THAT'S GOOD, RIGHT THERE. THINK ABOUT THAT MUD UNDER YOUR FEET, BETWEEN YOUR TOES--
THERE'S SOMETHING WRONG WITH ME. I JUST...
JUST NOTHING, SON. THIS AIN'T FOREVER. IT'LL PASS.
NOW SAY IT BACK TO ME.
THIS AIN'T FOREVER...
THIS IS GONNA PASS.

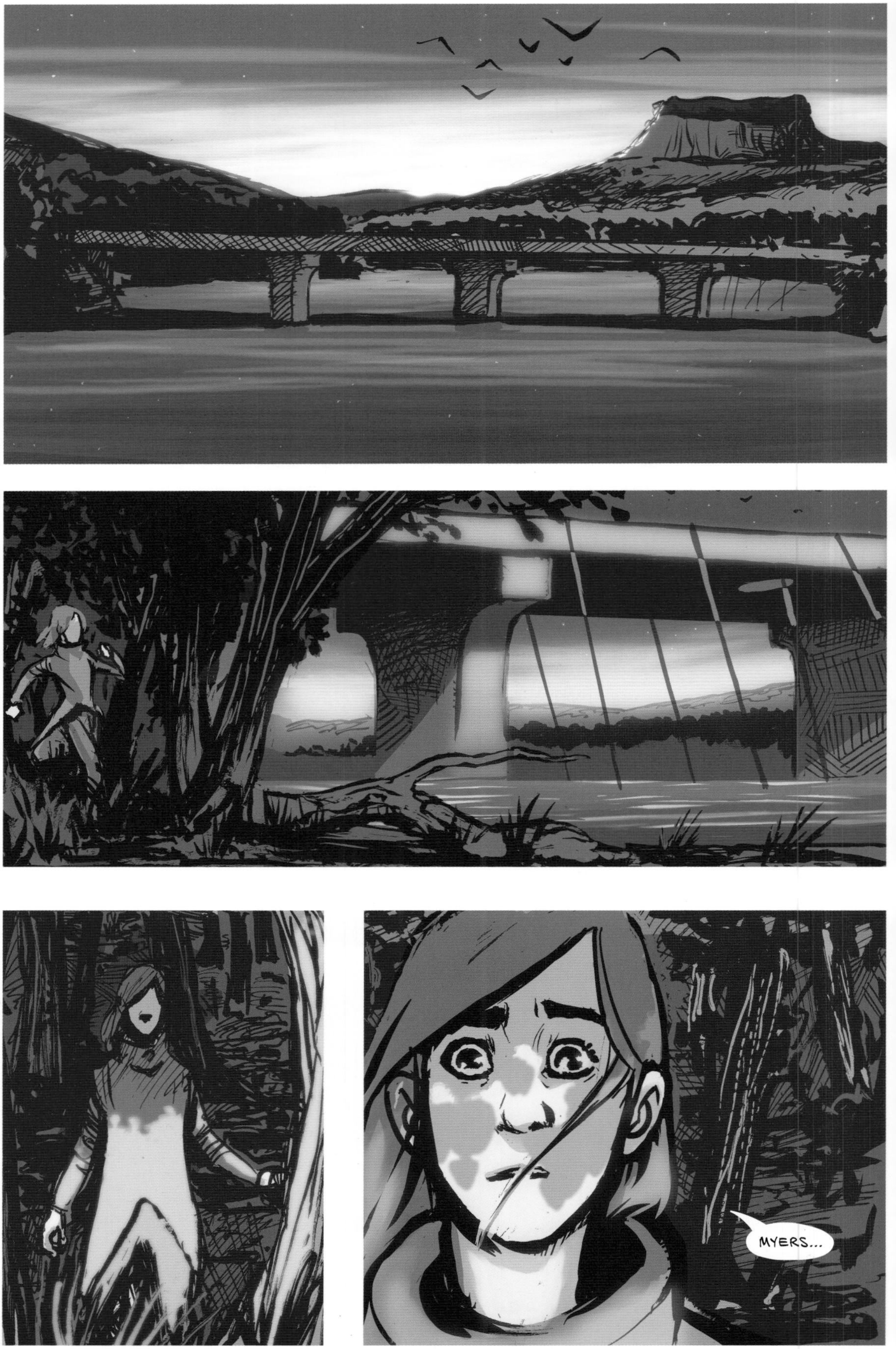
MYERS...

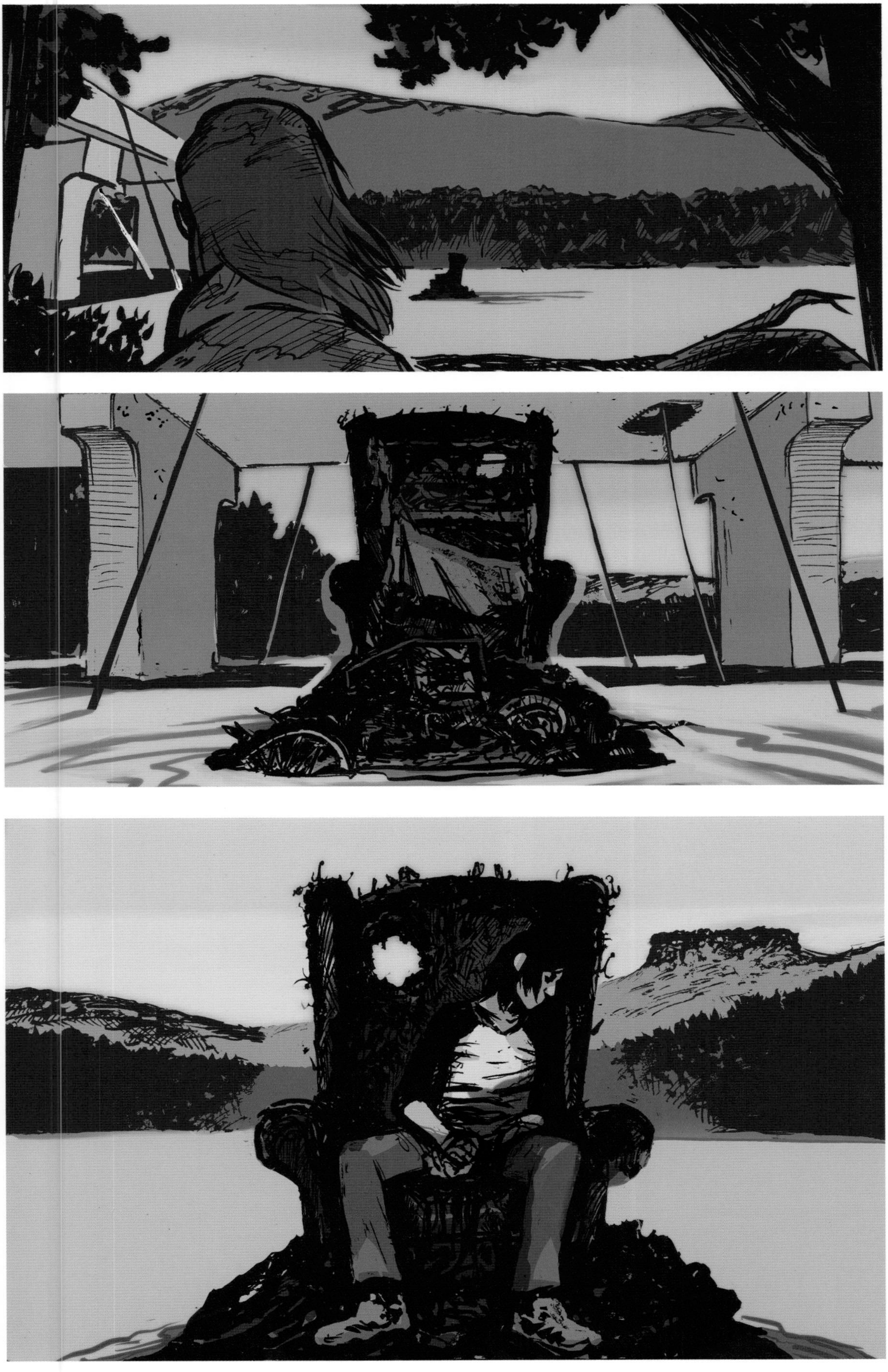

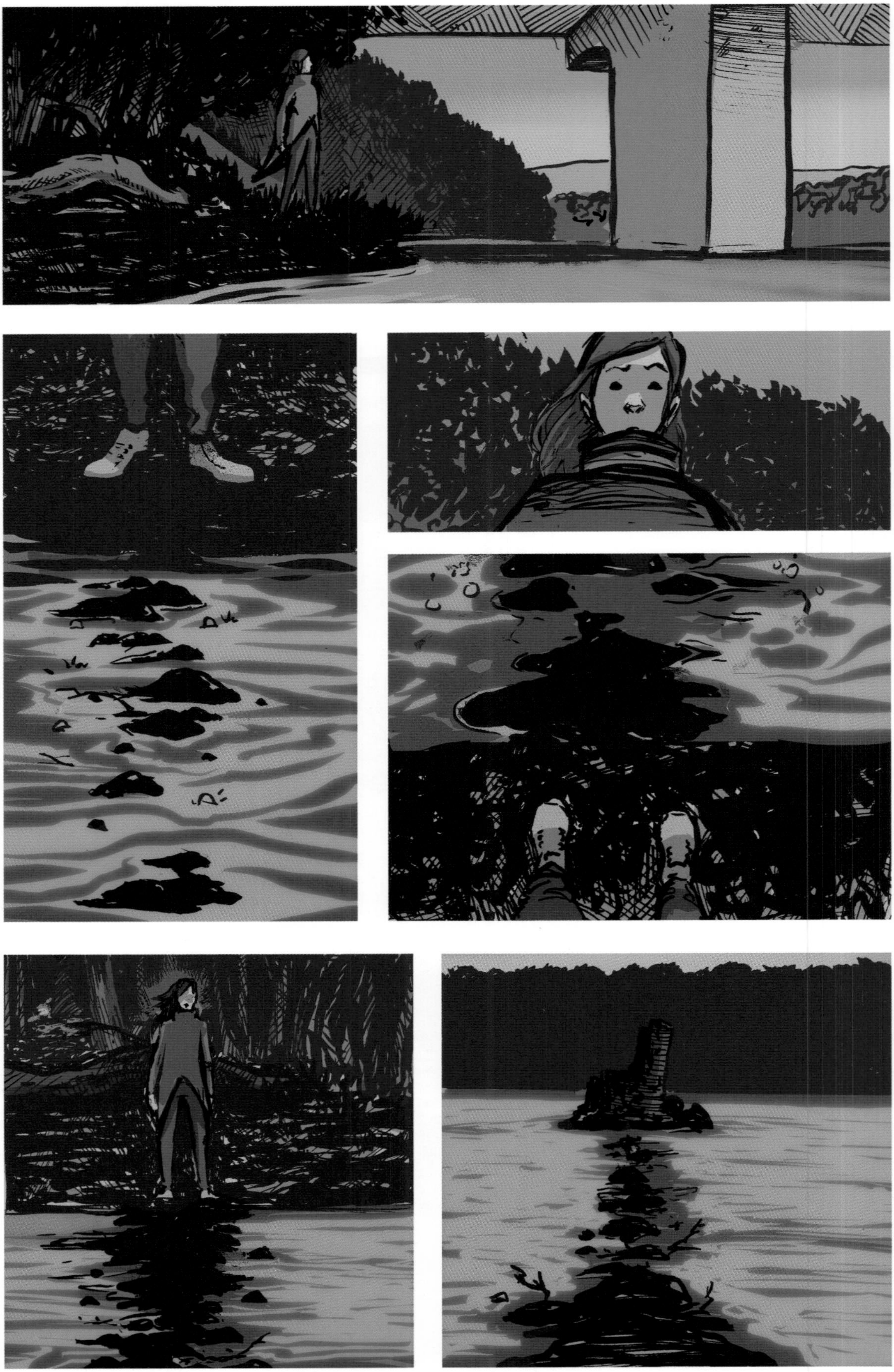

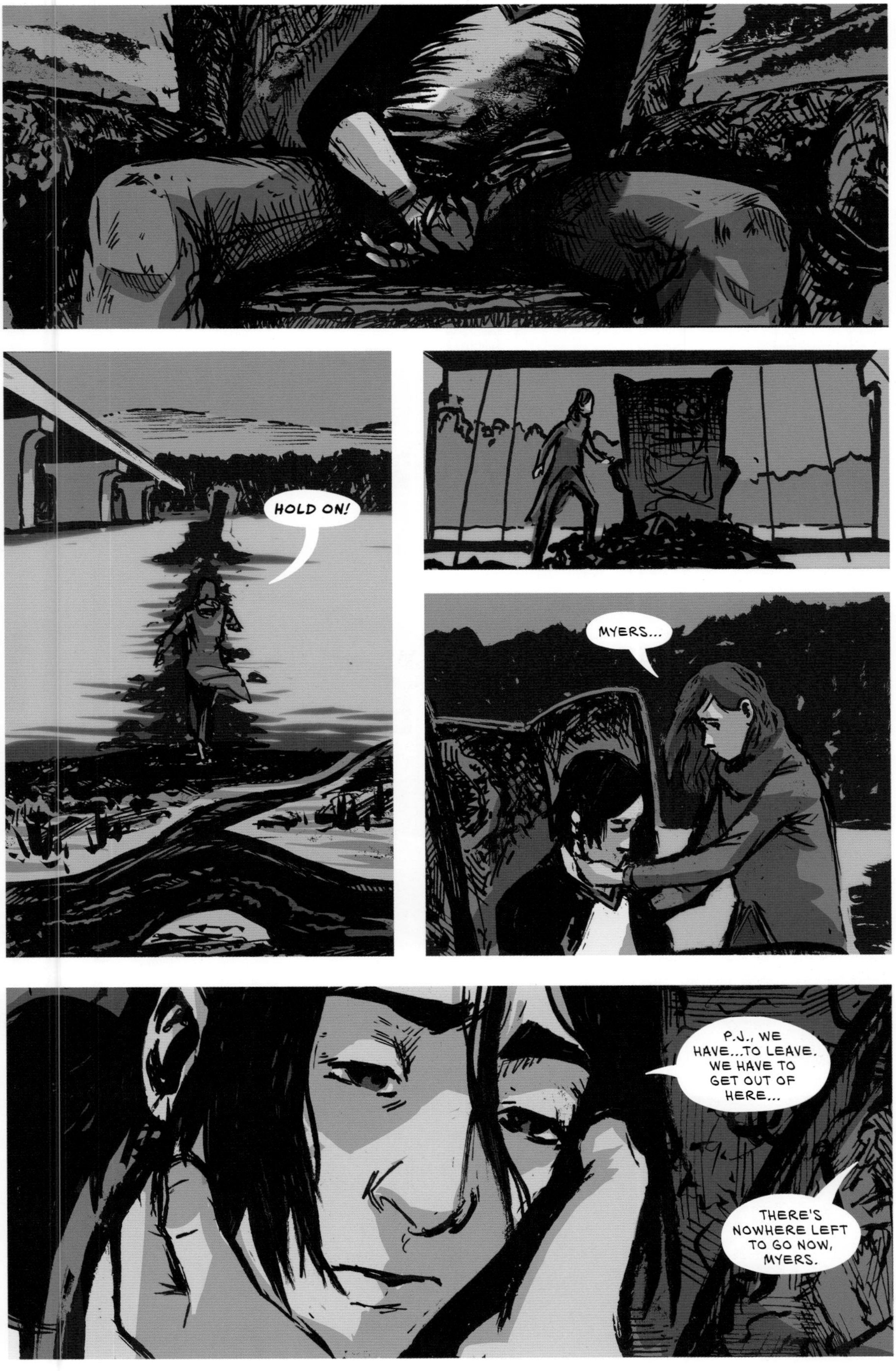
HOLD ON!
MYERS...
P.J., WE HAVE...TO LEAVE. WE HAVE TO GET OUT OF HERE...
THERE'S NOWHERE LEFT TO GO NOW, MYERS.

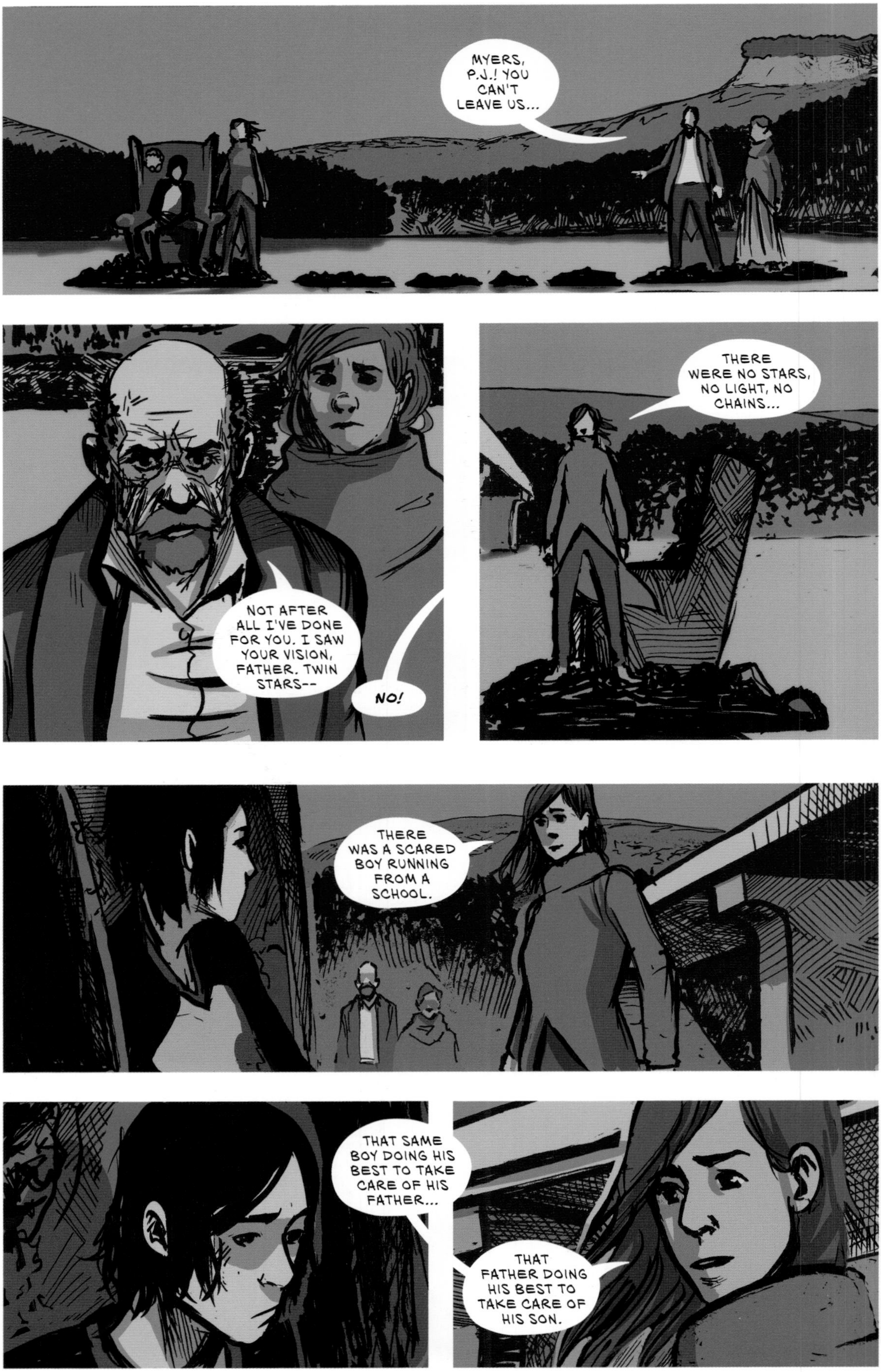
MYERS, P.J.! YOU CAN'T LEAVE US...
NOT AFTER ALL I'VE DONE FOR YOU. I SAW YOUR VISION, FATHER. TWIN STARS--
NO!
THERE WERE NO STARS, NO LIGHT, NO CHAINS...
THERE WAS A SCARED BOY RUNNING FROM A SCHOOL.
THAT SAME BOY DOING HIS BEST TO TAKE CARE OF HIS FATHER...
THAT FATHER DOING HIS BEST TO TAKE CARE OF HIS SON.

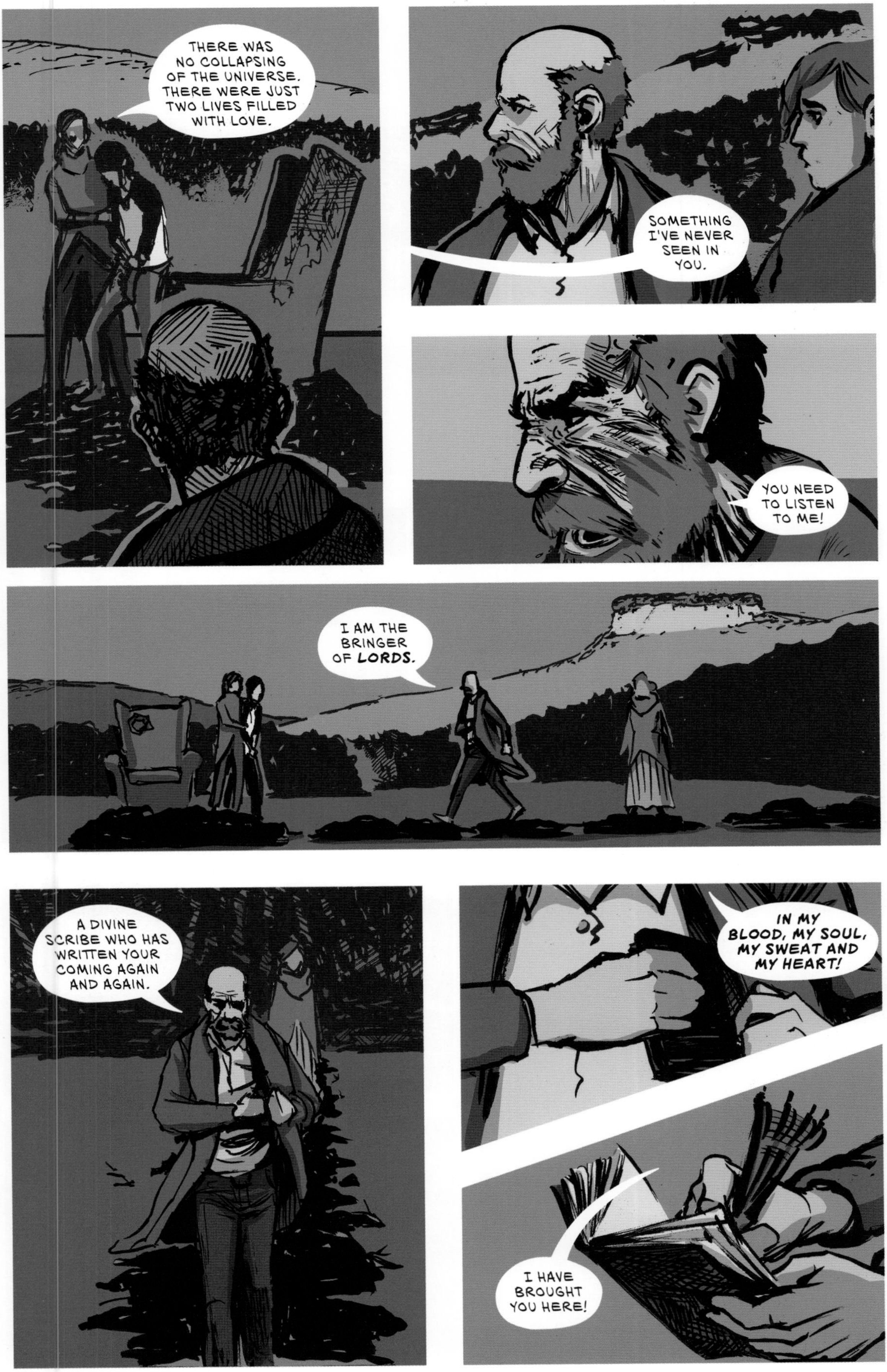
THERE WAS NO COLLAPSING OF THE UNIVERSE. THERE WERE JUST TWO LIVES FILLED WITH LOVE.
SOMETHING I'VE NEVER SEEN IN YOU.
YOU NEED TO LISTEN TO ME!
I AM THE BRINGER OF **LORDS.**
A DIVINE SCRIBE WHO HAS WRITTEN YOUR COMING AGAIN AND AGAIN.
IN MY BLOOD, MY SOUL, MY SWEAT AND MY HEART!
I HAVE BROUGHT YOU HERE!

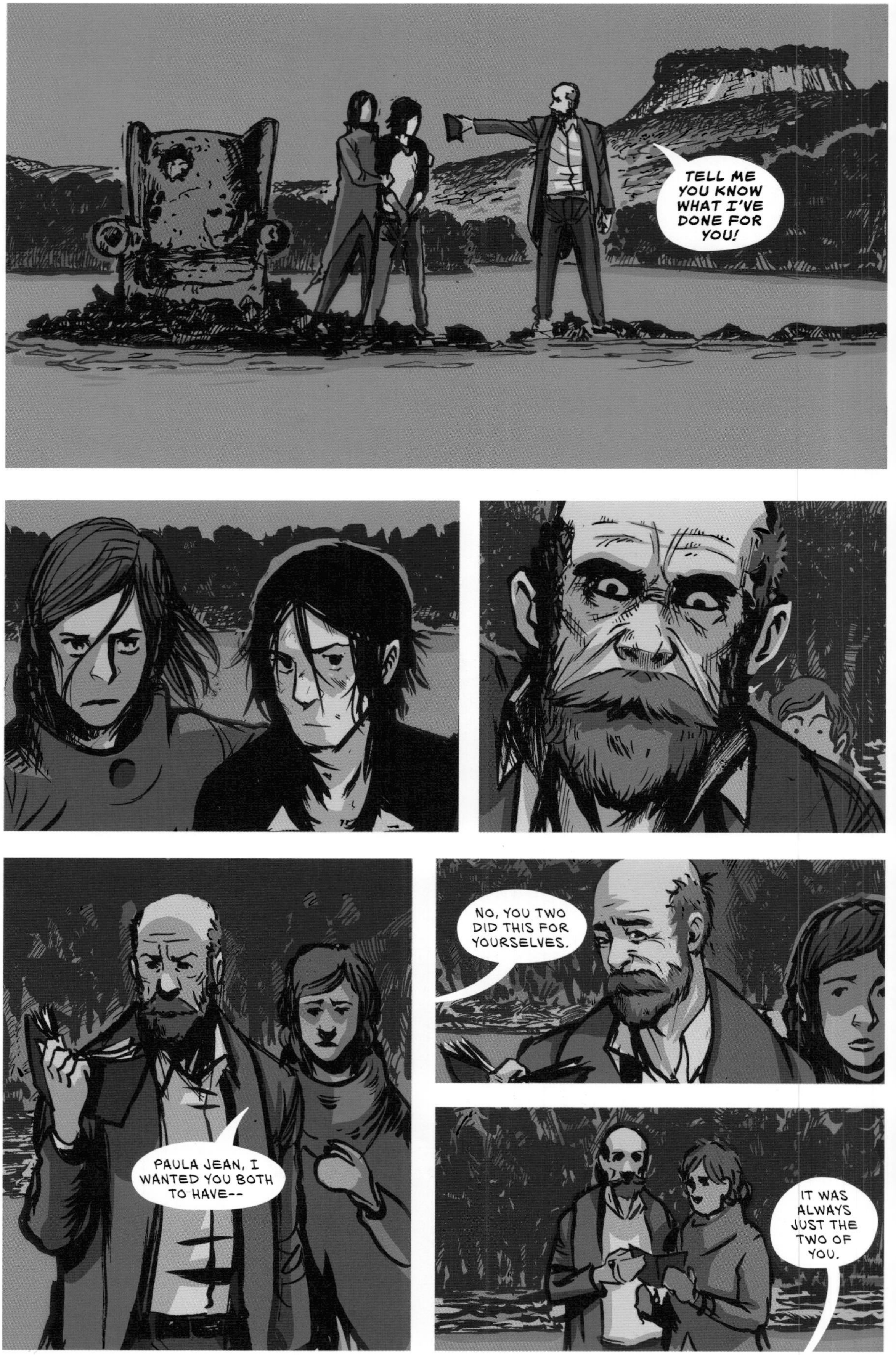
TELL ME YOU KNOW WHAT I'VE DONE FOR YOU!
PAULA JEAN, I WANTED YOU BOTH TO HAVE--
NO, YOU TWO DID THIS FOR YOURSELVES.
IT WAS ALWAYS JUST THE TWO OF YOU.

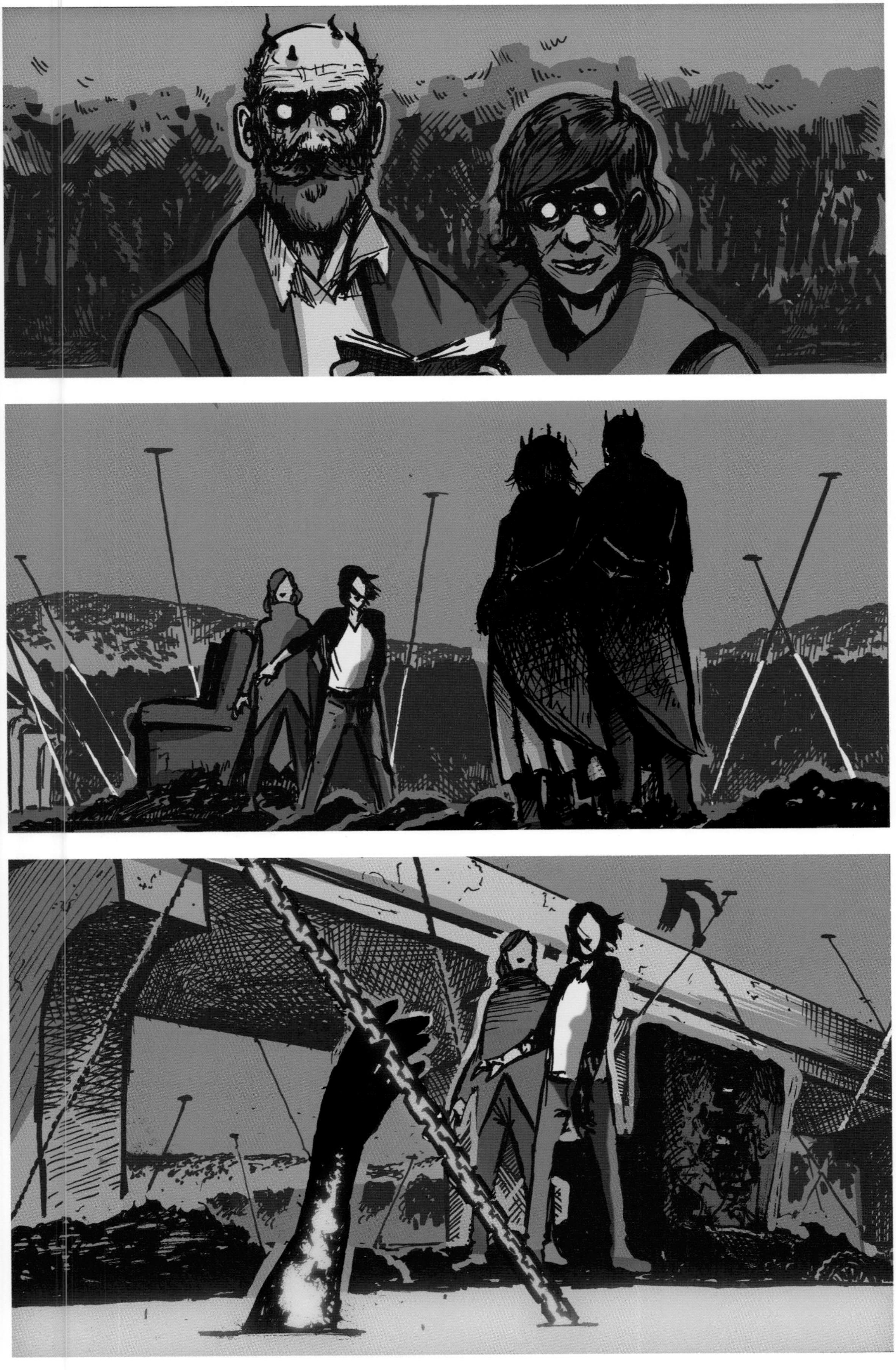

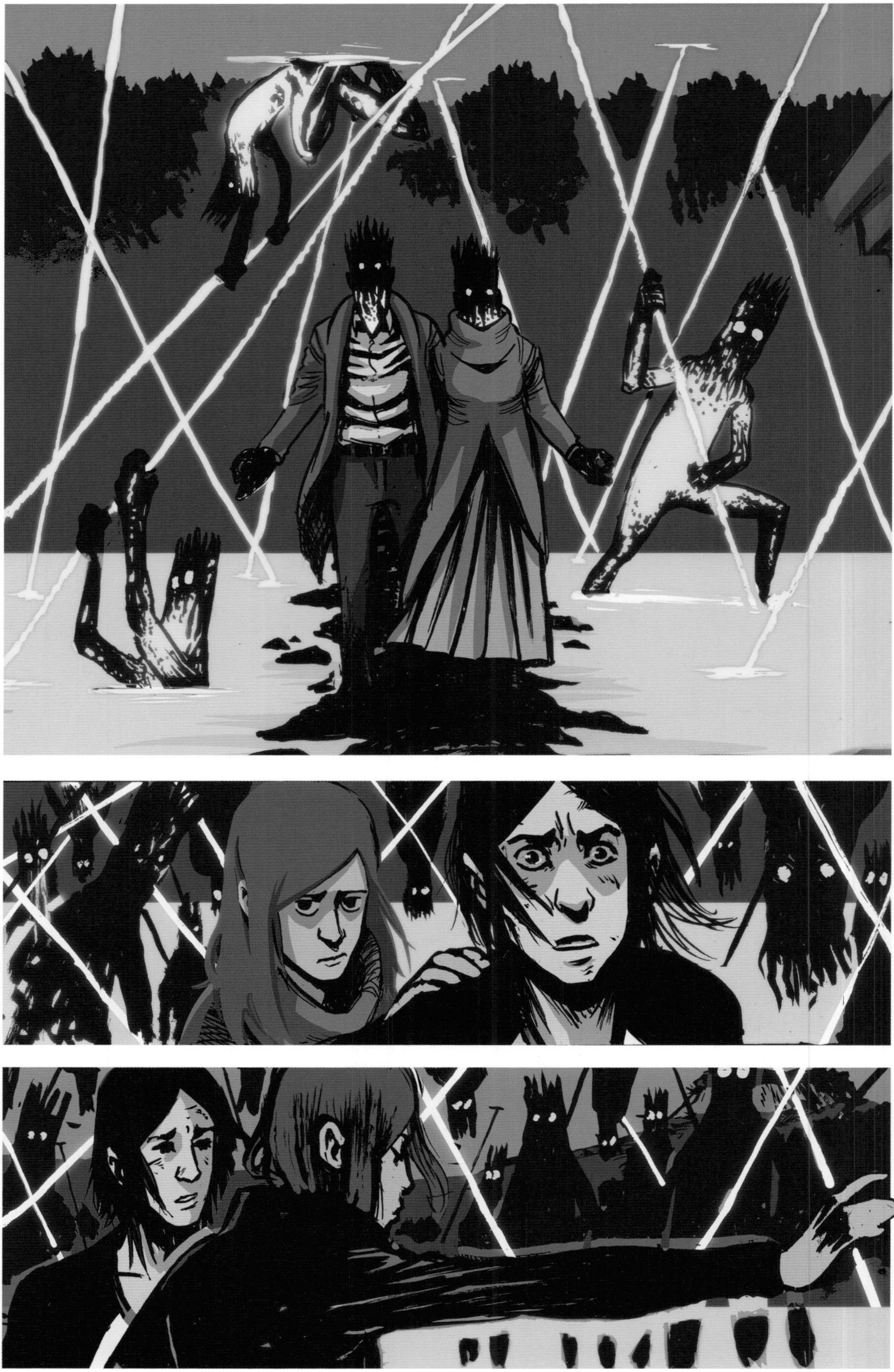

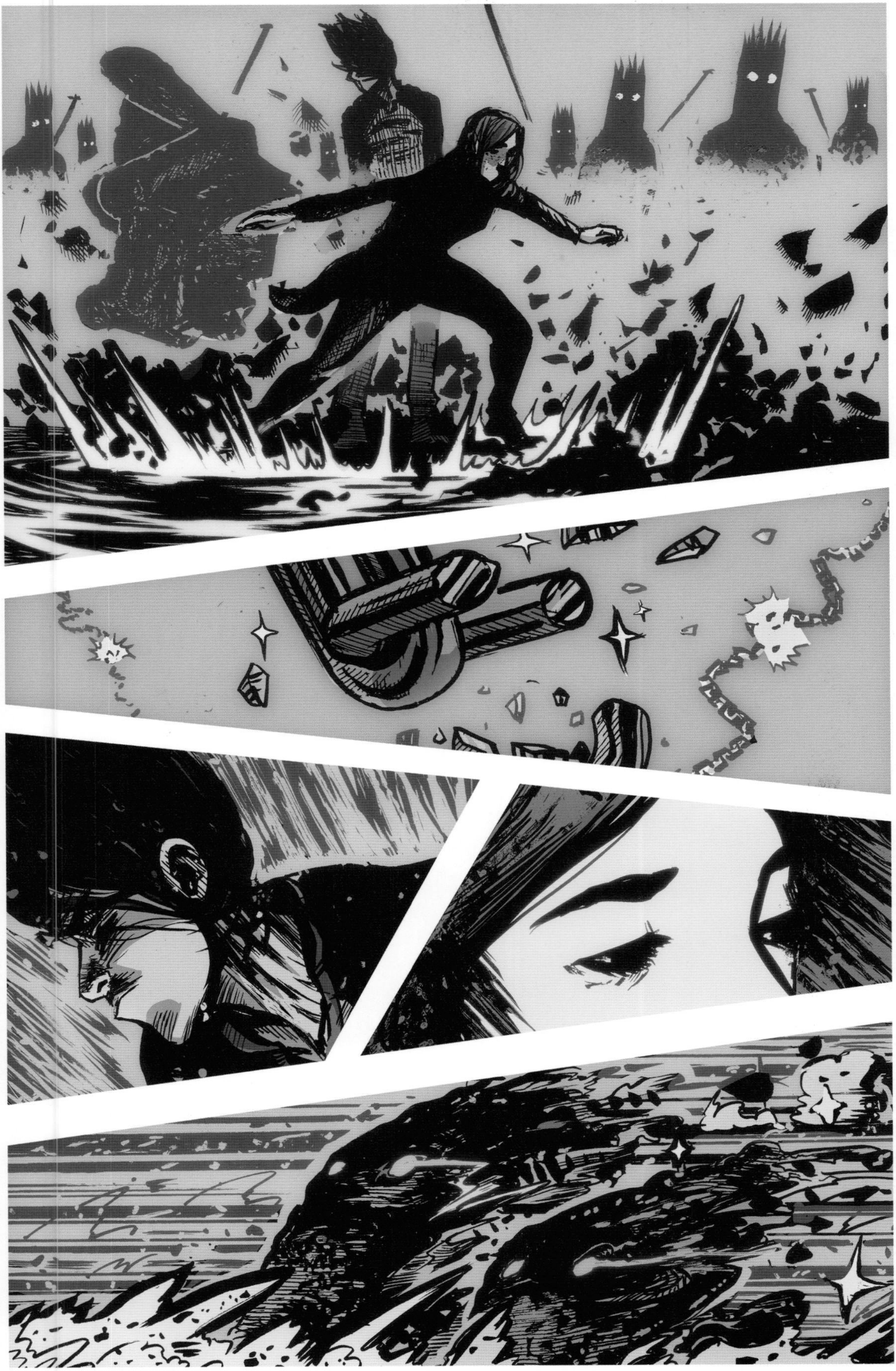

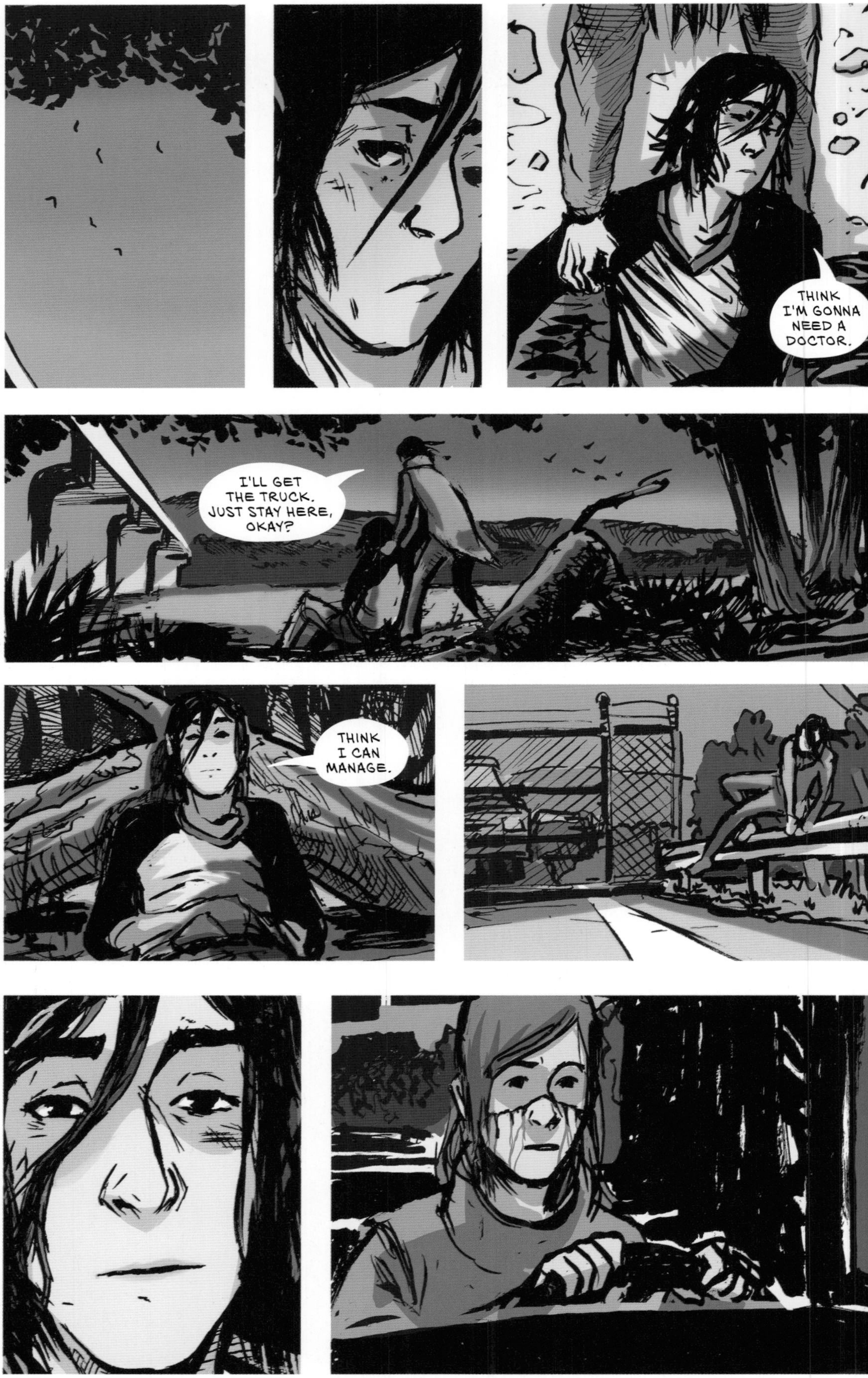
THINK I'M GONNA NEED A DOCTOR.
I'LL GET THE TRUCK. JUST STAY HERE, OKAY?
THINK I CAN MANAGE.

# CHAPTER THIRTEEN

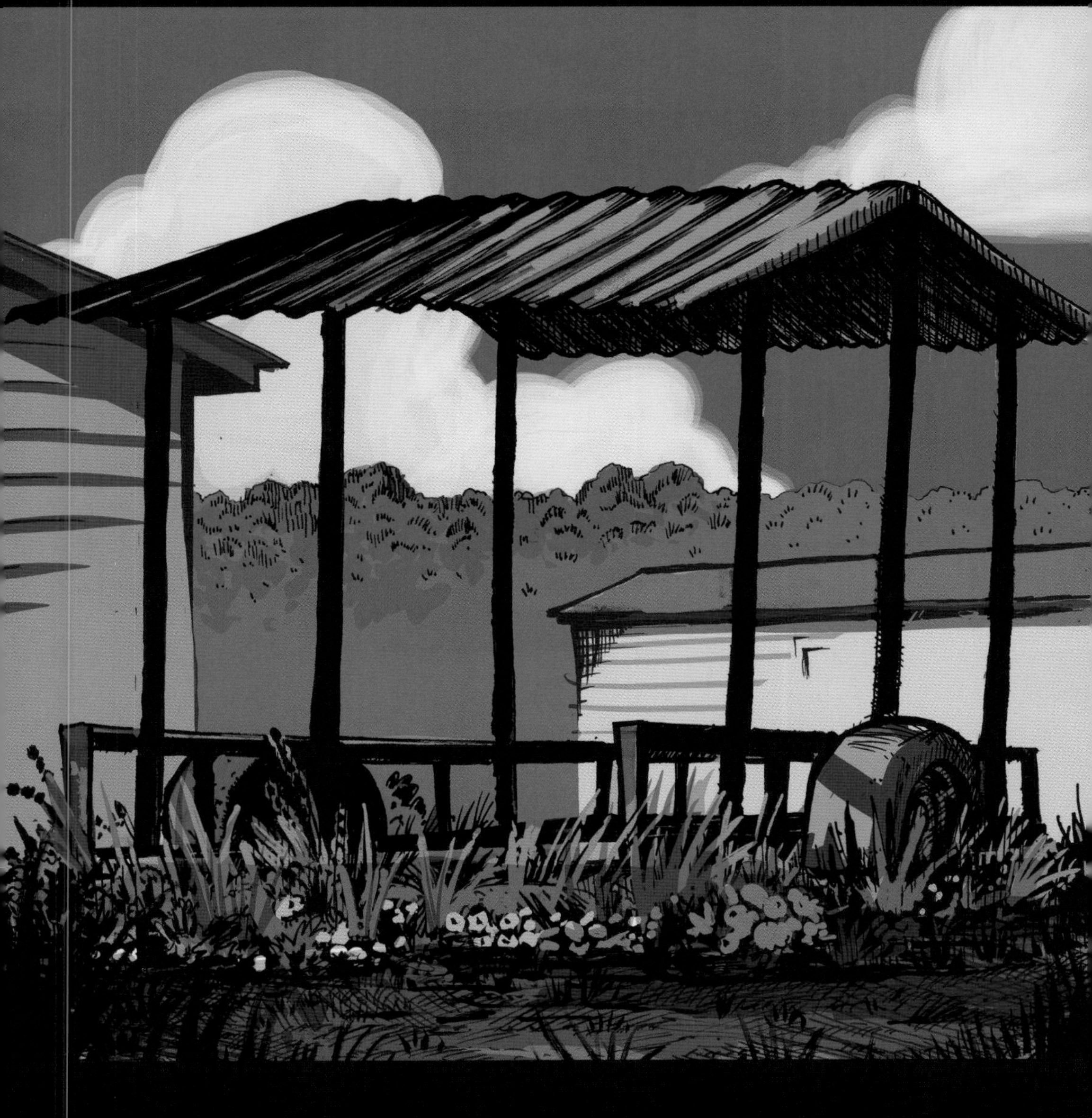

# DIFFERENT WAYS TO BURY OUR DEAD: PART TWO

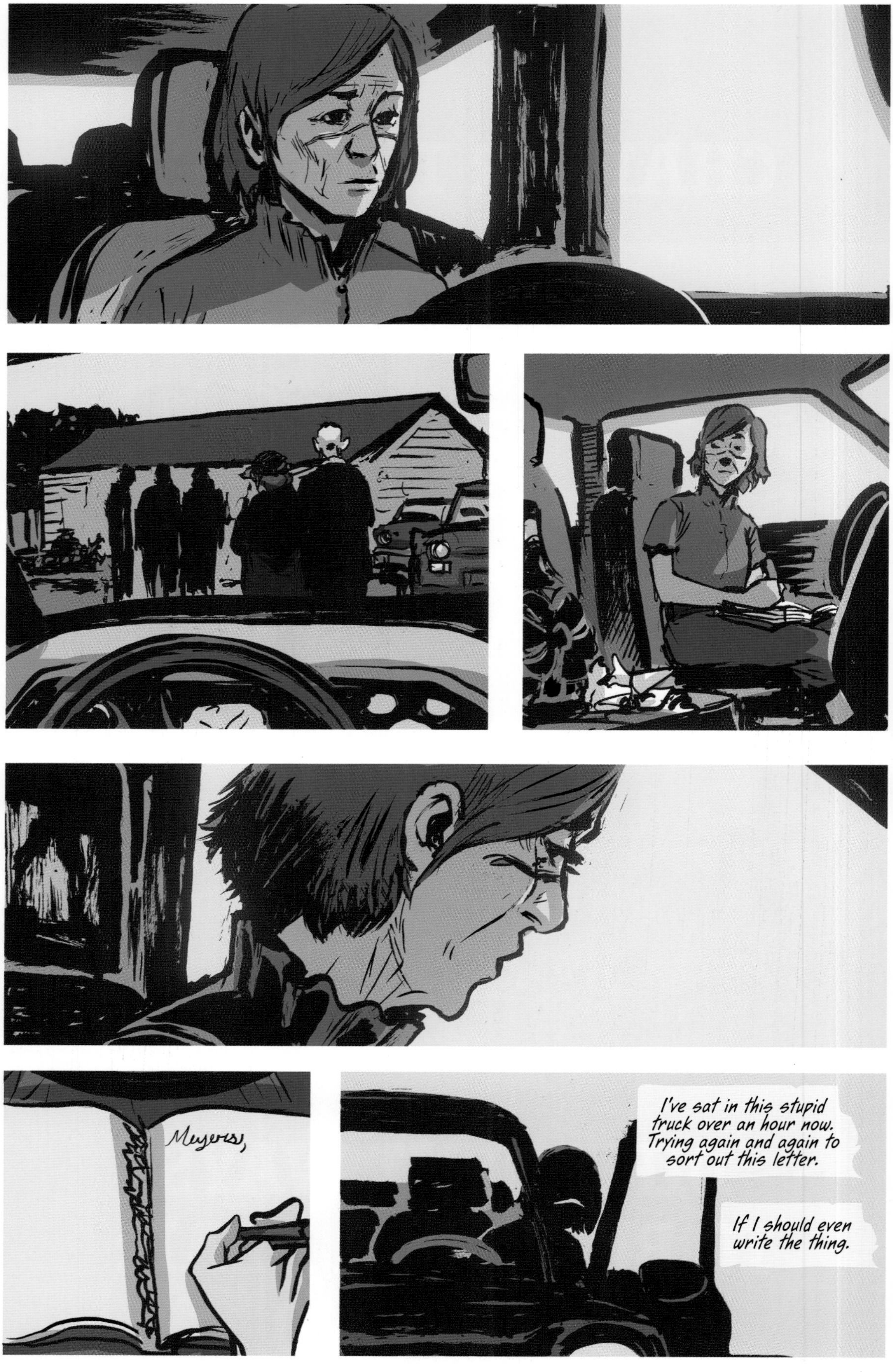
Meyers,
I've sat in this stupid truck over an hour now. Trying again and again to sort out this letter.
If I should even write the thing.

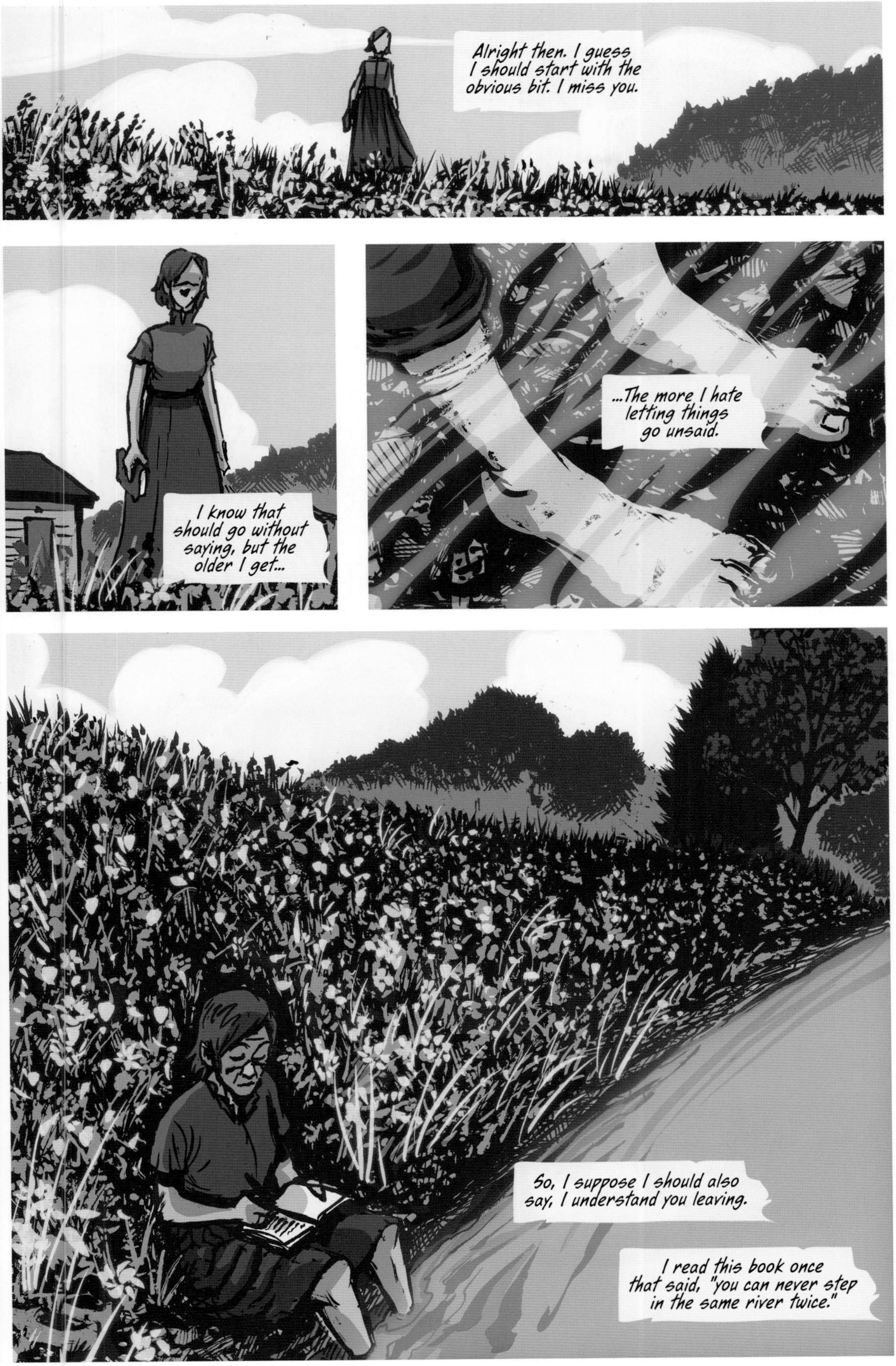
Alright then. I guess I should start with the obvious bit. I miss you.
I know that should go without saying, but the older I get...
...The more I hate letting things go unsaid.
So, I suppose I should also say, I understand you leaving.
I read this book once that said, "you can never step in the same river twice."

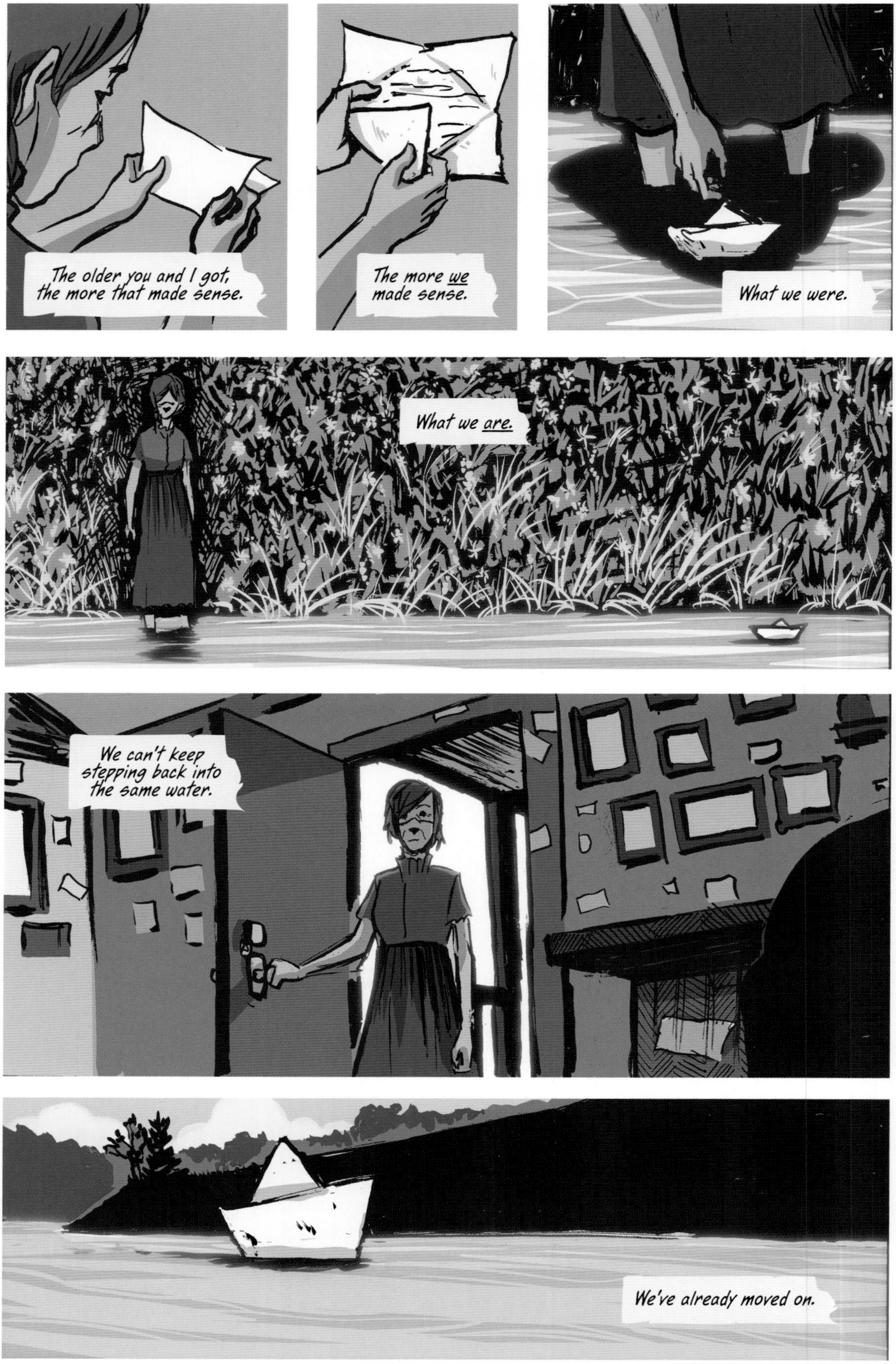

The older you and I got, the more that made sense.
The more we made sense.
What we were.
What we are.
We can't keep stepping back into the same water.
We've already moved on.

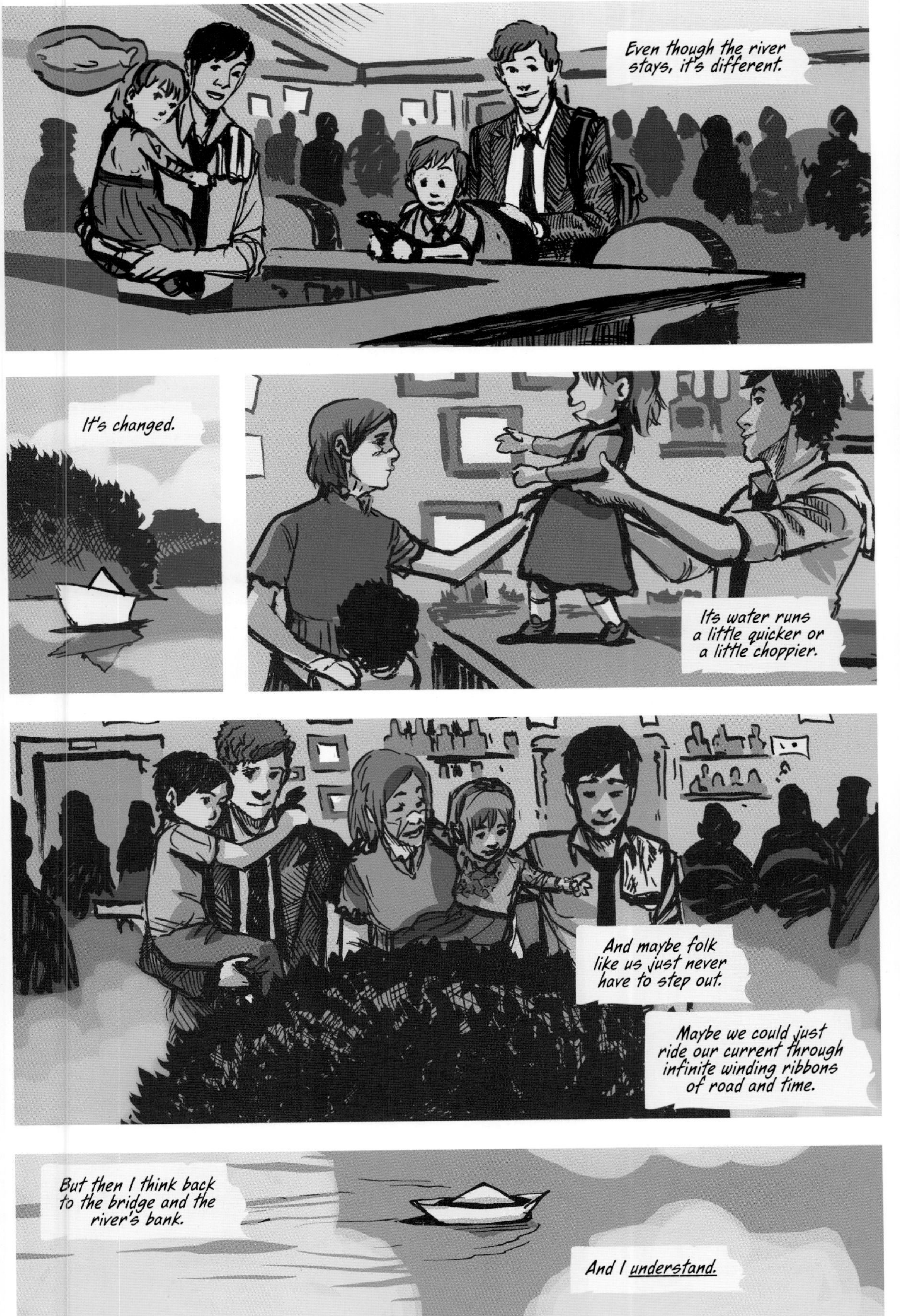
Even though the river stays, it's different.
It's changed.
Its water runs a little quicker or a little choppier.
And maybe folk like us just never have to step out.
Maybe we could just ride our current through infinite winding ribbons of road and time.
But then I think back to the bridge and the river's bank.
And I understand.

Nobody ever leaves the river.

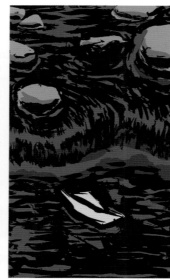

You watch it become more than what it was before.

You enjoy the water around your legs.

You feel the breath in your lungs.

You remember it's going to pass.

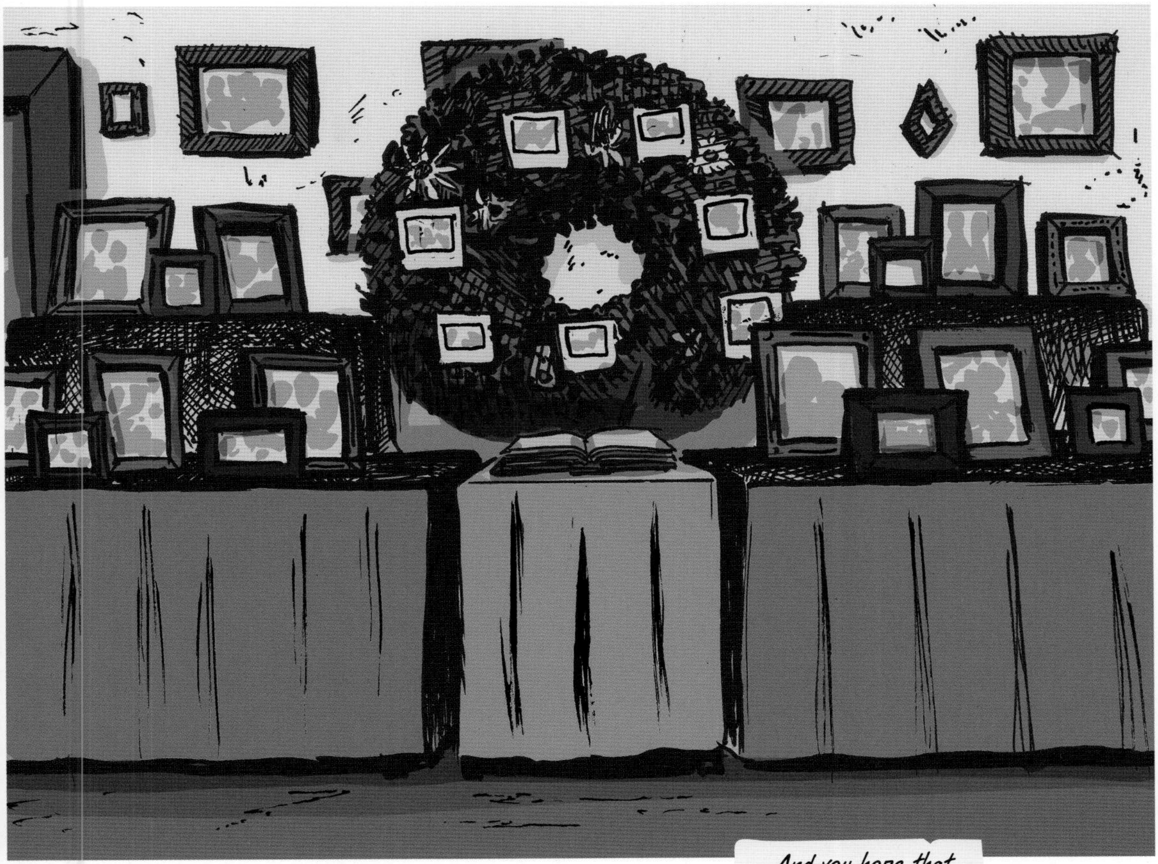

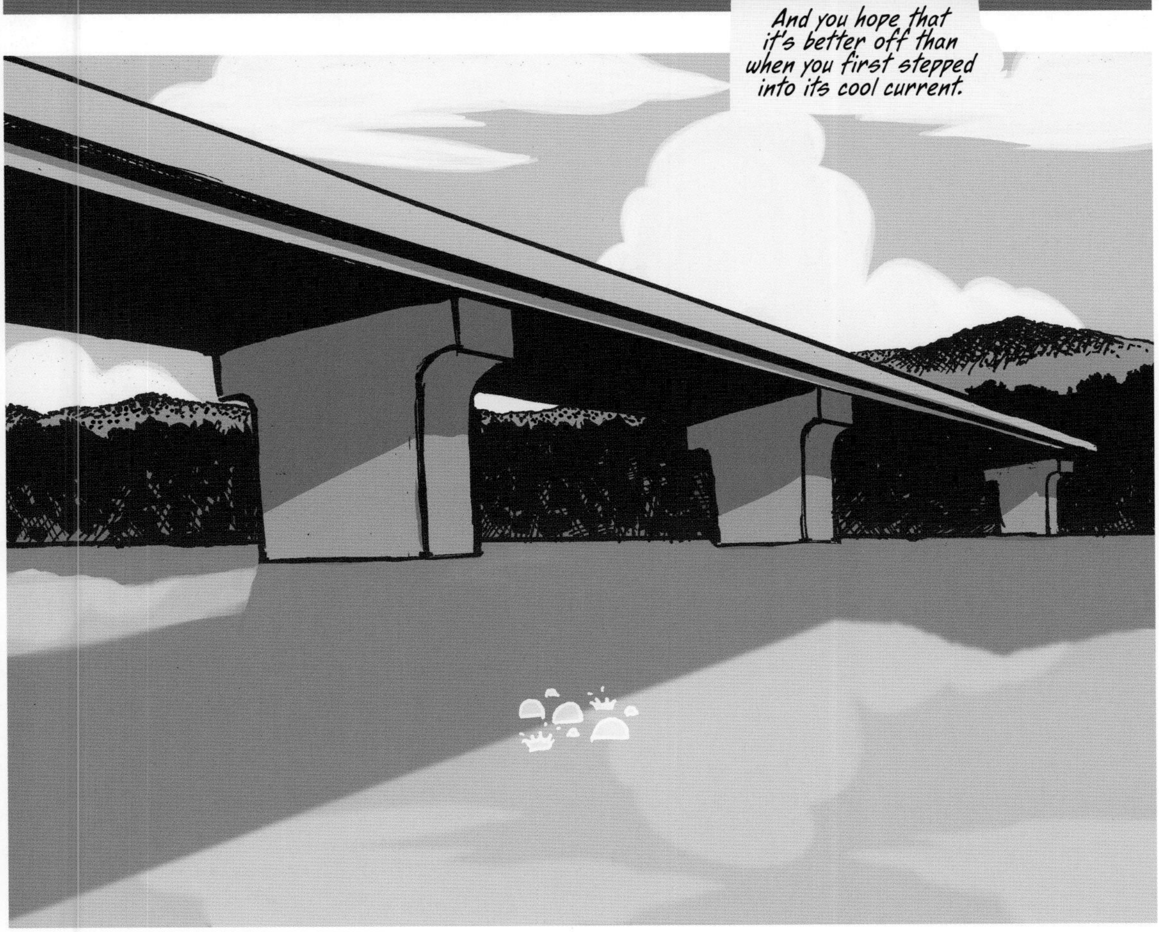
And you hope that it's better off than when you first stepped into its cool current.

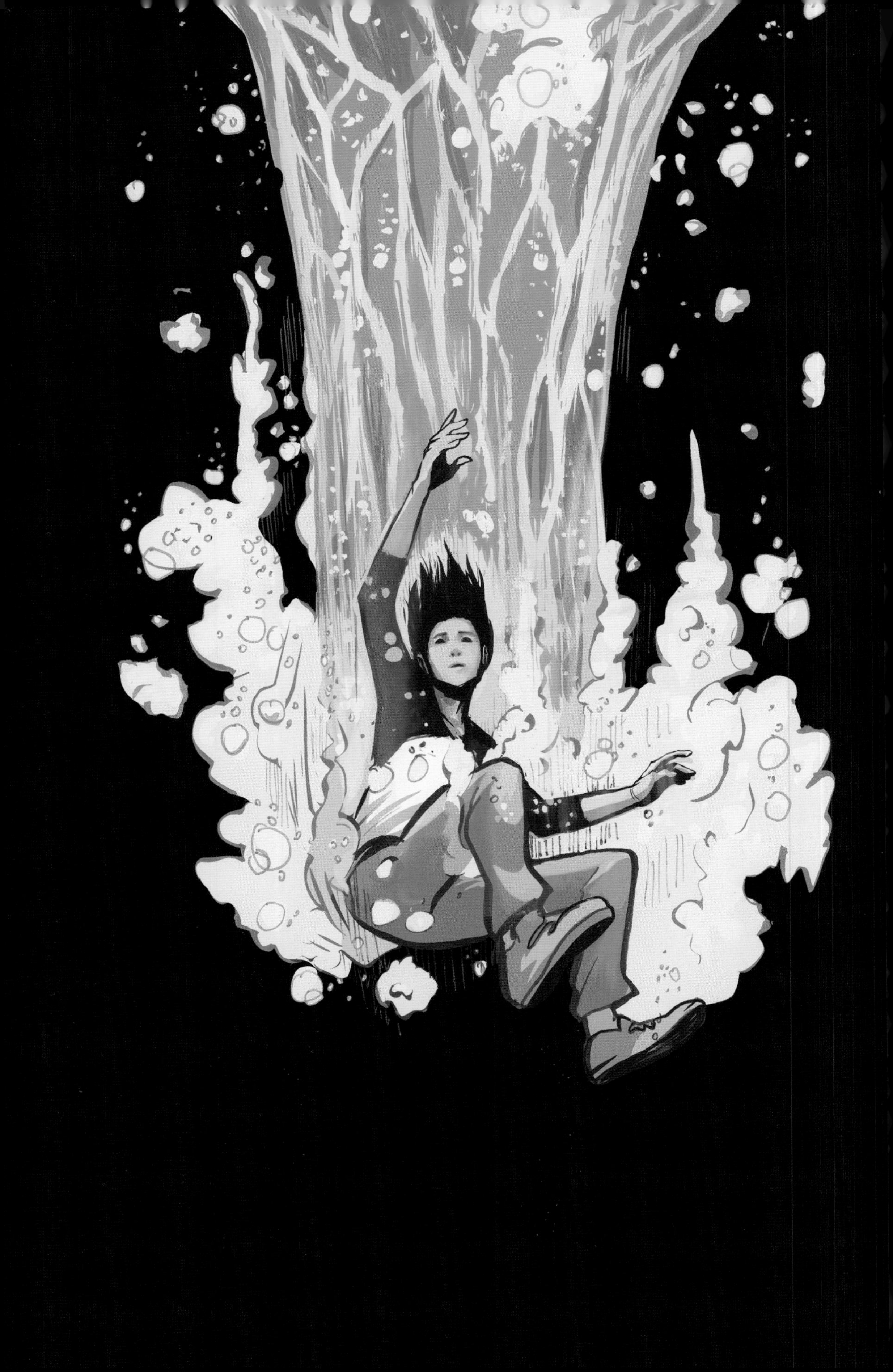

# AUTHOR'S NOTE

I am going to try and make this brief, for your sake and mine. As I write this, I am four days away from the one-year anniversary of my dad's death.

For the folks that don't know, making comics takes a while. I wrote this script as my dad's dementia was beginning to take hold. *(I want a more lyrical phrase to say than "seize his mind." I want to write this better because I so desperately want to not fuck this up. Maybe a line akin to "his dementia made his mind a loose kite, something that had been tethered to the ground tightly that was now loosed, chased by a weeping family." But "seize his mind" is more apt, aggressive and concise. Just like what happened.)* Then, between Matt drawing the book and my first pass at a lettering draft . . . well, three hundred and sixty-one days ago happened. Something aggressive and concise.

It changed some things Myers said. Because it changed me.

*(It changed some things Myers said because it reminded me.)*

Back in 2002, this whole damn place lost my friend Jeremy to suicide. When Jeremy's brother Joel came by our house, my old man told him: "Everyone's gonna handle this differently. But none of them get to tell you how to feel. That's yours."

Eighteen years on, I still think about that living room. Even knowing the room my dad was headed towards, to me he's still there on that couch, reassuring a young boy who lost his brother.

The world is hard and draining, and my old man's not around to help all of us anymore. If you or anyone you know or love needs help, please reach out.

National Suicide Prevention Hotline: 800.273.8255
The Trevor Project: 866.488.7386

And if you need information about Alzheimer's or Dementia, or want to donate, volunteer, or just need to talk to someone in a support group, please head to alz.org.

—**Adam Smith**

DISCOVER
# GROUNDBREAKING TITLES

FRANK "BIG BLACK" SMITH
BIG BLACK
STAND AT ATTICA
JARED REINMUTH
AMÉZIANE
Four days in 1971 changed the course of American history.

FROM NEW YORK TIMES BESTSELLING AUTHOR
LEV GROSSMAN
WITH LILAH STURGES AND PIUS BAK
THE MAGICIANS
NEW CLASS

FROM THE NEW YORK TIMES BESTSELLING AUTHOR OF BAD FEMINIST
ROXANE GAY
TRACY LYNNE OLIVER
THE SACRIFICE OF DARKNESS
WITH REBECCA KIRBY & JAMES FENNER

KURT VONNEGUT
with RYAN NORTH & ALBERT MONTEYS
SLAUGHTER
or the children's crusade
HOUSE-FIVE
a graphic novel adaptation

SABAA TAHIR
WITH NICOLE ANDELFINGER & SONIA LIAO
A THIEF AMONG THE TREES
AN EMBER IN THE ASHES GRAPHIC NOVEL

EMEI BURELL
WE SERVED THE PEOPLE
MY MOTHER'S STORIES

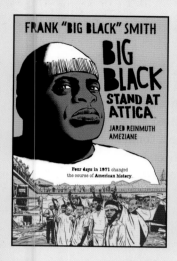

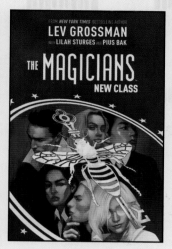

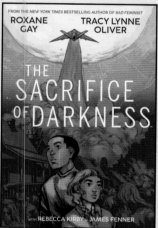

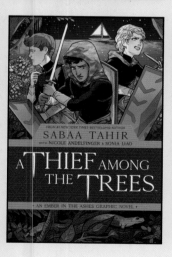

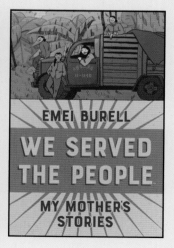

**Big Black: Stand at Attica**
*Frank "Big Black" Smith, Jared Reinmuth, Améziane*
ISBN: 978-1-68415-479-1 | $19.99 US

**The Magicians: New Class**
*Lev Grossman, Lilah Sturges, Pius Bak*
ISBN: 978-1-68415-565-1 | $19.99 US

**The Sacrifice of Darkness**
*Roxane Gay, Tracy Lynne Oliver, Rebecca Kirby*
ISBN: 978-1-68415-624-5 | $24.99 US

**Slaughterhouse-Five**
*Kurt Vonnegut, Ryan North, Albert Monteys*
ISBN: 978-1-68415-625-2 | $24.99 US

**A Thief Among the Trees: An Ember in the Ashes Graphic Novel**
*Sabaa Tahir, Nicole Andelfinger, Sonia Liao*
ISBN: 978-1-68415-524-8 | $19.99 US

**We Served the People: My Mother's Stories**
*Emei Burell*
ISBN: 978-1-68415-504-0 | $24.99 US

**Bear**
*Ben Queen, Joe Todd-Stanton*
ISBN: 978-1-68415-531-6 | $24.99 US

**Girl on Film**
*Cecil Castellucci, Vicky Leta, Melissa Duffy, V. Gagnon, Jon Berg*
ISBN: 978-1-68415-453-1 | $19.99 US

**Happiness Will Follow**
*Mike Hawthorne*
ISBN: 978-1-68415-545-3 | $24.99 US

**The Man Who Came Down the Attic Stairs**
*Celine Loup*
ISBN: 978-1-68415-352-7 | $14.99 US

**Waves**
*Ingrid Chabbert, Carole Maurel*
ISBN: 978-1-68415-346-6 | $14.99 US

ARCHAIA™

**AVAILABLE AT YOUR LOCAL COMICS SHOP AND BOOKSTORE**
To find a comics shop in your area, visit www.comicshoplocator.com
WWW.**BOOM-STUDIOS**.COM

**Adam Smith** is a comics and fiction writer working out of Kansas City. His work ranges from The Jim Henson Company and DC Comics to creator owned stories, some of which have been nominated for Eisner, Harvey, and Gem awards. He's elated to have co-created *At The End Of Your Tether* for Oni Comics and *LoveRunRiot* for Stela Comics. *The Down River People* is his second book with longtime friend Matt Fox. You can find him not saying much on Twitter at @ASmithWrites.

**Matthew Fox** grew up in rural Arkansas. About half his time was spent outside exploring, riding bikes, and playing make-believe. The other half was reading manga, watching anime, and playing video games. After school he met Adam Smith at a comic shop and they decided to make comics together. This is their second graphic novel. You can find him on Instagram at @matthewfoxcomics.